C000176432

Born in London, in July 192... middle-class Jewish backgrounc... She attended a small private school. After taking a degree in psychology at University College, London, and postgraduate training at the Maudsley Hospital, she worked as an Educational Psychologist in a Child Guidance Clinic. She married David Freeman, then a solicitor's articled clerk, in March 1950. They have three children: Michael, born in 1951; Jill, born 1953; and Peter, born 1955. Qualifying as a solicitor in 1970, Iris joined D. J. Freeman, the legal firm founded by her husband, where she specialised in employment law. She retired as a partner in 1986 but continues as a consultant. She and her husband live in London and in Oxfordshire. Her interests are her grandchildren, aged between nine and three, the theatre, reading and gardening.

'A thoroughly readable account'
Louis Blom-Cooper, *Guardian*

'Freeman's sympathy for Denning is evident . . . but her thoroughness means she details Denning's gaffes, notorious judgements, and the offended reactions to them'
Observer

'A great success . . . she has produced a book which is stylish and well crafted, fully researched and highly readable . . . This is a volume whose appeal will be very much to that middle England for whom Tom Denning was a hero for so many years . . . A quite remarkable story'
David Mellor, *Daily Telegraph*

'Perceptively and entertainingly written and can certainly be recommended to anyone with an interest in the law and its principal personalities in the changing social structure of our age'
Lord Hailsham, *Guardian*

LORD DENNING
A Life

Iris Freeman

ARROW

Published by Arrow Books in 1994

1 3 5 7 9 10 8 6 4 2

© Iris Freeman 1993

The right of Iris Freeman to be identified as the author
of this work has been asserted by her in accordance
with the Copyright, Designs and Patents Act, 1988

First published in the United Kingdom in 1993 by Hutchinson

Arrow Books Limited
Random House UK Ltd, 20 Vauxhall Bridge Road, London SW1V 2SA

Random House Australia (Pty) Limited
20 Alfred Street, Milsons Point, Sydney,
New South Wales 2061, Australia

Random House New Zealand Limited
18 Poland Road, Glenfield
Auckland 10, New Zealand

Random House South Africa (Pty) Limited
PO Box 337, Bergvlei, South Africa

Random House UK Limited Reg. No. 954009

A CIP catalogue record for this book
is available from the British Library

ISBN 0 09 949671 2

Printed and bound in Great Britain by
Cox & Wyman Ltd, Reading, Berkshire

FOR
DAVID

Contents

CONTENTS

Introduction

The hero of young lawyers in the early 1950s was Lord Justice Denning. I first heard the name when my husband, working for his final examinations, told me about this extraordinary judge, with his passion for justice. Thirty years later, when I, too, was a solicitor, we watched – as at a Greek tragedy – the decline of the ageing Master of the Rolls, and the drama of his retirement. I wondered what had driven him, what had made the man.

It is of more than passing interest to know what kind of men and women judge us, since their power to affect our lives is awesome. It is rewarding to view them against the social background and preoccupations of their age. Lord Denning's life practically spans the twentieth century. His cases cover most of the interests and activities of its second half. His recollections have helped me to make this book an account of the man and his time.

In many ways it was an advantage to meet and talk with the subject of my biography but there was one disadvantage. Lord Denning's legendary charm is as beguiling in his nineties as when he bowled over audiences all round the world: frequently I have needed to remind myself to hold fast to objectivity. One of the most endearing things was his patient correction of any factual error, without once seeking to change a word of criticism. Lord and Lady Denning were unstinting in their help and hospitality. They spoke candidly on distressing subjects. I am exceedingly grateful to them and saddened by Lady Denning's death in October 1992.

I was fortunate in meeting Sir Reginald Denning and Lord Cheshire shortly before their deaths: each gave me valuable insights into different periods of Lord Denning's life. To Dr Robert Denning, Mrs Pauline Simond, Lady Fox and Mr John Stuart my thanks for talking at length about their family life; thanks also to Mr David

Denning and Mrs Betty Beach for filling in some gaps.

I greatly appreciate the help of the following people and organisations:

Mr A. S. Adams; Mr O. Adler; Mrs J. Banner; Miss D. Belcher; Mr W. Boorman; Mr A. Bray; Lord Bridge of Harwich; Sir D. Buckley; Mr E. Caldwell; Mr L. Caplan QC; Mrs B. J. Carter; Mr P. Clark; Mr I. Cole; Mr J. S. Colyer QC; Mrs J. B. Cottis; Brig. A. B. Davies; Mr E. W. Denham; Lord Devlin; Lord Donaldson of Lymington; Miss R. Dunhill; Mrs J. Edgell; Miss C. Ellis QC; Lord Goodman; Mr R. Greiffenhagen; Mrs M. Gibb; Sir R. Gibson; His Honour B. Gillis QC; Mr C. Hall; Mr A. Hamilton QC; Lord Havers; Miss M. Hill; Mr R. W. Hodgin; Mr G. F. Holborn; Mr J. A. Hunter; Sir F. Lawton; Sir T. S. Legg; Mr A. Lincoln; Miss J Littlefield; Mr J. McDougle; Mr R. A. Newell; Mr P. Post; Mr A. L. Price QC; Mr R. D. Roper; Lord Roskill; Mr W. W. Russell; Lord Simon of Glaisdale; Sir T. Skyrme; Sir C. Slade; Mr M. J. Smith; Mrs F. Somerfield; Mr J. G. Starke; Miss S. Sussmann; Sir M. Williams; Lord Woolf.

The Warden and Fellows of All Souls College, Oxford; Birmingham University Faculty of Law; the Bodleian Library; University of Buckingham; Business Archives Council; Channel 4 TV; University of Glasgow Senate; Friends of the Hebrew University; Hampshire County Record Office; John Hanson School; the House of Lords Library; Iron Age Museum, Andover; Lincoln's Inn Library; Keeper of the Archives of Magdalen College, Oxford; Middle Temple Library; Ministry of Defence; Headmaster and Staff of Winchester College.

For permission to quote from books and articles and to reproduce photographs, my thanks to: Argent; Professor P. S. Atiyah; the British Broadcasting Company; Butterworth & Co Ltd.; Channel 4; the *Daily Mail*; the *Daily Mirror*; the *Guardian*; the *Hampshire Chronicle*; Mr and Mrs Neil Hickman; the *Independent*; the Masters of the Bench of the Hon. Society of the Middle Temple; The *Observer*; the Oxford University Press; the *Sunday Mirror*; Sweet & Maxwell; *The Times*; Lady Wilson.

Last, but by no means least, I want to thank my agent, the Hon. Toby Eady, my publisher, Tony Whittome, staff of D. J. Freeman, who gave me all the help and technical back-up that I needed, and

INTRODUCTION

particularly Mrs Suzanne Hyde-Plewis, who somehow managed to change a messy manuscript into a word-processed thing of beauty. The criticism of my son, Michael, was very helpful with the early chapters but without the advice, constructive analysis and encouragement of my husband, David, the book would not have been written at all.

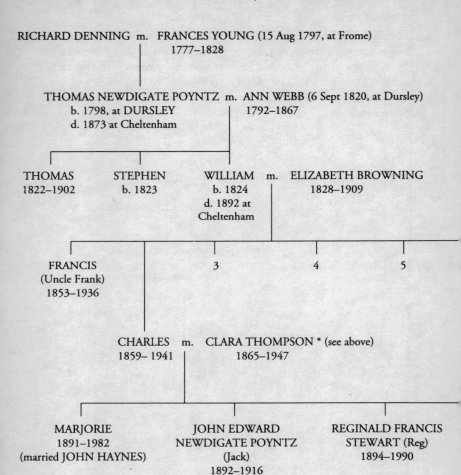

RICHARD DENNING m. FRANCES YOUNG (15 Aug 1797, at Frome)
1777–1828

THOMAS NEWDIGATE POYNTZ m. ANN WEBB (6 Sept 1820, at Dursley)
  b. 1798, at DURSLEY   1792–1867
  d. 1873 at Cheltenham

THOMAS   STEPHEN   WILLIAM m. ELIZABETH BROWNING
1822–1902   b. 1823   b. 1824   1828–1909
                                 d. 1892 at
                                 Cheltenham

FRANCIS   3   4   5
(Uncle Frank)
1853–1936

              CHARLES m. CLARA THOMPSON * (see above)
              1859– 1941   1865–1947

MARJORIE   JOHN EDWARD   REGINALD FRANCIS
1891–1982   NEWDIGATE POYNTZ   STEWART (Reg)
(married JOHN HAYNES)   (Jack)   1894–1990
                     1892–1916

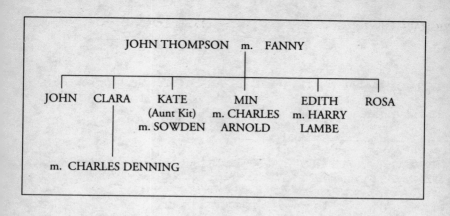

JOHN THOMPSON   m.   FANNY

JOHN   CLARA   KATE   MIN   EDITH   ROSA
           (Aunt Kit)   m. CHARLES   m. HARRY
           m. SOWDEN   ARNOLD   LAMBE

m. CHARLES DENNING

THOMAS NEWDIGATE POYNTZ   7
b. 1868

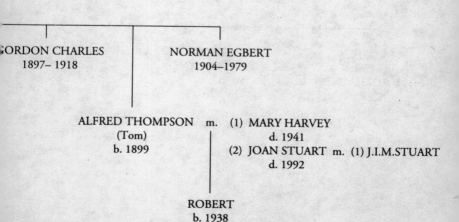

GORDON CHARLES   NORMAN EGBERT
1897– 1918   1904–1979

ALFRED THOMPSON   m.   (1) MARY HARVEY
(Tom)   d. 1941
b. 1899   (2) JOAN STUART m. (1) J.I.M.STUART
                      d. 1992

ROBERT
b. 1938

Part One

1899–1944

I

A Whitchurch Childhood

The temperature was unseasonably mild, though rain had fallen almost daily since Christmas. The Hampshire streams were overflowing and the dusty streets of Whitchurch had turned to mud. In a small, candle-lit bedroom above the draper's shop in Newbury Street, Clara Denning gave birth to her fifth child, two months before time. Her friend, Mrs Roe, hurried from her home across the road, wrapped the puny baby in a blanket, moistened his lips with brandy and said 'That's one we could have done without.'[1]

The child was born on 23 January 1899, as the Victorian age neared its end and the British Empire covered one-fifth of the land surface of the globe. A sense of pride united much of the world's most highly industrialised nation. A quarter of a century of social and administrative reform had widened the franchise, introduced universal elementary education and outlawed some of the worst abuses of labour. Children were no longer permitted to work full-time under the age of 13; women's hours were restricted – though not in shops, on farms, as out-workers or in domestic service, where so many were employed; and men's hours of work had fallen from about 60 to about 55 a week.

Much had been done to alleviate the condition of the poor, but not nearly enough: while the rich enjoyed the utmost luxury and leisure and much of the nation shared in the prosperity, there remained the city slums; overcrowded, vermin-infested tenements; sweated labour and the fear of unemployment; starving children in scanty, hand-me-down clothing and boots too large or too small for their stunted feet. The agricultural depression added to the misery. As many farmers were forced into bankruptcy and many thousands of farmhands were driven from the land, there was widespread migration from the countryside to overcrowded areas of towns.

Across the country the workhouse remained a place of last resort for those whose every hope was gone; it was the final humiliation for the destitute. The old, the orphaned, the infirm, the unemployed and the merely indolent were thrust together into institutions where, in theory, they worked for the meagre board and lodging provided under the Poor Laws. Casual wards were open to tramps, who walked from one workhouse to another. 'A man in tatters would stop at a cottage and hold out a tin mug. All he asked for was "hot water". To ask for more was a criminal offence. It was begging – contrary to the Vagrancy Act. The good-natured housewife took the mug – covertly put in tea and sugar – added a piece of her home-made cake.'[1]

The small town of Whitchurch had once been a thriving market-place, serving outlying farming communities, a staging post on the coach routes between London and Salisbury, Oxford and Winchester. Travellers from the capital to the West Country might take a meal or stay a night at The White Hart, which occupied a commanding position at the crossroads.

The coming of the railways had reduced Whitchurch to a backwater. The exodus of agricultural workers, at a time when the only available industrial work was at the papermill or in the whiting factory, had profoundly damaged the town's economy. With most of their remaining customers finding it hard to scrape a living, tradesmen struggled against falling sales and then faced difficulty in collecting the instalments, by which most people paid for goods.

Neither Charles Denning, nor Clara, his wife was originally from Whitchurch. Charles came to the town from Gloucestershire, probably in the late 1870s or early 1880s, as assistant to two elderly sisters, linen drapers of Market Place. In 1886, Clara, at the age of 21, 'handsome, with fine features'[1] and blue eyes, came from Lincoln to stay with family friends, the master and mistress of the Whitchurch workhouse. At a party in their home, she met Charles, who was then 27 and, by all accounts, charming. For the next two years they saw each other regularly.

On 17 October 1888, Charles and Clara were married at the Parish Church of St Mary Magdalene in Lincoln. They returned to Whitchurch and soon set up home and shop as one of several drapers of the town in an old house opposite The White Hart.

Nearly a century later, when Tom Denning, their fifth child was

Master of the Rolls, he described his father's family as 'poor as church mice'.[1] In 1899, though certainly not well-off, Charles and Clara would not have been considered poor; they would have been described as on the lower rungs of the middle class. They held adjoining freehold houses in Newbury Street, one, let to a chemist, bringing in a small income. There was ground enough behind the Denning home for a yard, a shed to house Charles's cart, a stable and a privy.

Charles came from a family in straitened circumstances, but one proud of having known better days. Handed down from father to son was the story of descent from 'the noble family of Poyntz', 'linked with another Norman family, Newdigate.'[1] Though his father had worked as a tailor and his grandfather as a card-maker, each had become an organist and music teacher and Charles grew up with a love of books and music. He sang in the church choir and sent poems to the *Andover Advertiser*, which published some of them. He was a dreamer with a gentle, happy disposition and was well regarded in the town.

Clara was the eldest daughter of John Thomas Thompson, 'a coal merchant in a good way of business.'[1] She had been a teacher in Lincoln (probably in a small private school), was a devout member of the Church of England, had a firm moral code, was devoted to her family and nursed an unconcealed ambition for her children.

There were six of them. Marjorie, the eldest, was born in January 1891, followed, in October 1892, by Jack. Reg (Reginald Francis Stewart) and Gordon Charles, arrived in June 1894 and May 1897 respectively. Clara's fifth and, Reg told the writer, favourite child was born in 1899, the year that Wessex commemorated the death – a thousand years earlier – of King Alfred. His fair-haired, blue-eyed, eight-year-old sister asked her parents to name the new baby for the old king. Charles and Clara agreed and gave him, in addition, Clara's maiden name, Thompson, which was always shortened to Tom. The family was completed in November 1904, when Clara was 39, by the birth of Norman Egbert Denning, sometimes known as Ned. In *The Family Story*, Tom Denning records that Grandfather Thompson 'provided for our mother by buying for her and father two old houses in Newbury Street', intending the Dennings to set up home and business in one and receive a small income from the other.

Numbers 5 and 7 Newbury Street were heavily-timbered houses with wattle and daub, that probably originated in the late sixteenth century. In 1863, the writer Charles Kingsley observed them from a window in The White Hart and described one of them thus:

> Opposite me, again, across a street, rather wider than this room, is a chemist shop, which is also a Post Office. The two storeys are rather lower than one of a London house, so that we will hope the folks inside are not tall. But there is a grand peaked roof, with dormers, in which, I suppose, servants are stuffed away.

It was not exactly the kind of house, he might have added, in which his Tom, the little sweep of *The Water Babies*, was made to climb the chimneys.

The Dennings occupied Number 5, two doors from the Town Hall. At the front was the shop, which was divided into two parts, for men's and ladies' wear. Through one of the two doors at the back was the kitchen–living room; on the first floor, reached by a narrow staircase through the second door, were three bedrooms and, above them, an attic, where, indeed, the servant slept. Beneath the house, not visible from the street, was a cellar. As was usual at the time, save in the grander houses, the house lacked indoor sanitation, water was drawn from a well outside the back door and gaslight was fitted only on the ground floor.

John Thompson had given his daughter and her husband a good start in life. He had not been so fortunate himself. He was the son of a sailor and had had to make his own way, starting life as a coal porter. Through hard work and, probably, exceptional intelligence, he built a substantial business. He was a strict moralist and a churchwarden. He lived with his wife, Fanny, a son and six daughters in a house in the Bail Gate at Lincoln. His bold, firm handwriting indicates his character; Fanny, who never learned to write, made her mark on documents with a cross.

A photograph of the wedding of Charles and Clara in 1888 was, as Denning records it, 'typical of the well-to-do Victorian family of the utmost respectability.'[1] The bride and groom are seated between their respective mothers. Their fathers and other members of the family are grouped about them, Clara's younger sisters and brother sitting at their feet. The gentlemen all wear morning suits, the older ladies are in tight-waisted, high-necked dark dresses with neat hats. The bride and younger ladies wear light dresses – are they all in white, or is that an illusion created by the old sepia photograph? – and elaborate hats. The two youngest bridesmaids have ravishingly pretty mob caps over their long ringlets, and carry garlands.

The Thompson family was close, loving and supportive. They played an important part in the lives of the Denning children. Letters kept them regularly in touch, visits were exchanged, birthdays were remembered and presents sent. The children saw less of their father's family: grandfather William Denning died in 1892, the year Jack was born, and his wife went to live in Milford Haven with the family of her youngest daughter. She died there, at the age of 80, in 1909. Instead of the warmth and real presence of the Thompson aunts and uncle, the Denning children heard from their father about his forebears. Charles Denning delighted his children with stories about the past and Tom inherited his gift for weaving fact and fancy into a vivid tapestry.

'The very name Denning,' he wrote in *The Family Story*, 'recalls the Danish invasion of the 9th century. DENNING means DANE-ING. "Ing" means "son of". So "Denning" is just "the son of the Dane" . . . The Danish pirates came in their long-boats. They landed in South Devon and pushed their way inland as far as Somerset . . . One of them took to himself a Saxon girl. They had a son. The neighbours called him Dane-ing . . .'

Then came the Normans, including the families of Poyntz and Newdigate. 'William the Conqueror gave the Poyntz family manors and lands. He made them tenants-in-chief of land in Gloucestershire under the feudal system.' The Newdigates linked with the Poyntz and a descendant, Sir Sydenham Poyntz 'became one of Cromwell's most famous generals.'

'It was about 1720,' Tom Denning continues, 'that Sir Sydenham's grand-daughter eloped with our great-grandfather's grandfather . . . There was a dance in the great house. The Newdigate-Poyntz daughter slipped out in her dance frock – with the lights shining into the night – and rode off with the Denning on his horse. Our great-grandfather – his name was Thomas Newdigate Poyntz Denning – told his children the story. It has come down in the family these nigh 300 years.'

The Newdigate Poyntz connection was important to Tom, as it had been to Charles. It satisfied their love of romance, of tradition, of English history; and it distanced them from a more work-a-day world. Tom noted that some branches of Poyntz Dennings 'did well'. There was the painter of miniatures, Stephen Denning, and the astronomer, William Denning of Bristol.

Although nothing was known of 'the Denning' with whom the Newdigate Poyntz heiress rode off on a horse, 'the union of the eloping couple,' Tom wrote, 'is evidenced by the eldest son of each generation ever since being baptised "Newdigate Poyntz Denning."' There is, in fact, a gap of 77 years between the elopement, 'about 1720', and the marriage of Tom Denning's great-great-grandparents, so that almost certainly there must have been another generation between.

Tom's great-grandfather, Thomas Newdigate Poyntz Denning, was the son of Richard Denning and Frances Young, who were married in Frome, Somerset on 15 August 1797. Soon after the birth of their baby, Richard and Frances moved to Dursley, in Gloucestershire, where he was baptised on 3 June 1798. Thomas Denning was only nine years old when his father died in 1807. He married Ann Webb, a laundress, in 1820. Their sons Thomas and Steven were born in Dursley in 1822 and 1823. Grandfather William was born a year later.

For a time the family lived in Cam and, when William married Elizabeth Browning on 13 April 1852, he set up home in Stinchcombe. His first son, Francis, was born before the family moved to Leckhampton, near Cheltenham, where William worked as a church organist and music teacher. Charles Denning was born at 4 Norwood Terrace, Leckhampton on 4 December 1859, as were three daughters and a third son, born in 1868 and baptised Thomas Newdigate Poyntz. When Charles married Clara, his brother Francis was one of the witnesses to sign the register.

A link is needed to establish the connection between Richard Denning and the Poyntz family. Yet tradition is no bad thing and Denning family trees – not just in Richard's line – show a recurrence of the Poyntz baptismal name, though not always in the eldest son. Jack, the first of Charles and Clara's sons was named John Edward Newdigate Poyntz. Years later, in a letter to Tom, his sister Marjorie wrote, 'I wonder if you know that *Thomas* N. P. Denning is the family name. Father wanted Thomas but mother wanted John Edward after her father and brother.' Perhaps the strongest evidence of an exceptional heritage – on both sides – is the achievement of those of Charles's and Clara's sons who survived the First World War: not only was Tom Denning Master of the Rolls, but Reg became a general and Norman an admiral and Director of Naval Intelligence.

In an age when infant mortality was high, Tom, Clara Denning's premature baby, just by surviving, gave a first sign of his fighting spirit. He remained delicate and at four developed pneumonia. Such remedies as were available in the chemist shop next door offered no certain cure; the illness often proved fatal. Tom was moved from the bedroom he shared with his brothers into his parents' room overlooking the yard. The steam kettle was kept boiling day and night to relieve his breathing; eventually, the congestion cleared and his temperature returned to normal.

The life of the household also returned to normal, although normal life, for Clara, was far from easy. She usually had a young maid to help her, since the farmhands of the outlying districts could barely support their families and twelve-year-old girls would start work as servants in local houses for little more than a roof over their heads and the food they ate. In Clara's case, the succession of girls were well treated and remained devoted to her into old age. Marjorie and the boys were also expected to help, taking turns at the household chores. Every drop of water needed for the house – water to drink, water to cook, water for washing, water to clean the house and wash the clothes – had to be pumped from the well outside the back door. Bath night was Friday, in front of the large kitchen range, in a small zinc bath, which had then to be emptied into the drain outside the back door.

The kitchen range itself caused a fair amount of work. Quite apart from it having to be stoked and then maintained at the right temperature, it had to be kept clean and bright. In his old age, in 1990, when Lord Denning was living at The Lawn, one of the finer Whitchurch houses, he received a letter from Mrs Grace Roberts, who had been a servant at The Lawn when Tom Denning was a boy. She wrote:

When I worked at The Lawn there was a very large black and steel range that I had to clean and polish every morning and get a 3 gallon kettle boiling by seven o'clock, most of the work had to be done on hands and knees, and with candles . . . I often used to see your lovely mother, she always had a lovely smile and a kind word to me when I met her . . . I worked for the Devenish family beer people when I was there, Hides had shops, Pengilly, Nashs, Bennetts the butchers, Nichols the lovely lardy cake baker . . . remember the milk was brought round by pony and trap all shiny and bright, the farmers had to take their milk in churns to top station . . .

Reg Weeks, Tom's contemporary and son of the local builder, gave his boyhood memories to the Whitchurch Historical Society in the early 1980s:

The great majority of houses had outside privies furnished with what were euphemistically known as 'sanitary pails'.

These were emptied periodically by a contractor (named Charlie Stagg) in a horse-drawn metal tumbril made for the job. The contents of the tumbril were in turn emptied and spread out in a field bordering Knole Lane . . . It was left to the elements to complete the job of dispersal . . .

The 'night cart' as it was then called, was usually in full operation by 10.30 pm and its presence was evident to anyone unlucky enough to be in its vicinity.

The Dennings' privy, or bog house, was some 75 feet across the yard, on ground that sloped gently upward from the house. 'It was hidden from sight by a corrugated iron fence. Flies swarmed there.'[1] Inside the shed was a deep pit, covered by a seat and, because of the incline, the nutrients would have drained towards the well and the house. Either long exposure to such conditions provided some kind of immunity from germs or the Dennings – even delicate Tom – had particularly robust constitutions. Except for the usual childish illnesses and a bout of scarlet fever, they remained in good health.

Next to the bog house was the stable that housed Sam, the big white cob, and Queenie, the little brown mare. Beside that was the cart shed. The boys were expected to bed the horses down with straw at night and clean out the dung in the morning. It was their job, too, to prepare the lamps, with their candles moving up on springs, and to help clean the cart in which their father carried goods to outlying villages.

The shop was open six days a week. Charles Denning served there every morning, with a girl assistant to help on the ladies' side. In spring, little girls came with their mothers to buy Easter bonnets 'made of straw and trimmed with flowers, daisies or buttercups – at 6½d each.'[1] Many of the cottagers were unable to get into town and relied on the visits of tradesmen to buy or order what they needed. In the afternoons, except for Wednesday, which was a half-day, Charles filled his cart with a variety of clothing, footwear and household goods, and set out on his journeys. When they were lucky, he took some of the children with him. Much was supplied 'on tick' – the customer was supposed to pay a few pence each week, when the tradesmen called. Charles knew only too well how poor his customers were and, whenever a harassed mother was unable to give him what she owed, he would never press for payment. He was well loved but hardly a man of business.

Charles rarely left Whitchurch, except to go on his journeys to the villages but when he was called for jury service in Winchester, he had no choice. 'He went every day for a week – at his own cost – which he could ill afford'[1] but even so, he found the time and the money to bring back for the children some chocolates covered with gold paper to look like sovereigns; they were a treat that Tom was to remember for many years.

By afternoon, most of the household chores were done. Alongside the square kitchen was a narrow room, scarcely more than a corridor; there the children sat, to eat their meals and do their homework, on a bench screwed to the wall. There, while Charles was on his journeys and the children were at school, Clara each afternoon brought the account books up to date and calculated how much the business was owed.

For the first five years of his life, Tom was Clara's baby. He was not spoiled – Clara gave all her children a strong sense of duty and a firm code of right and wrong – but he was petted. When he started school Clara was still troubled by his health and felt he needed special care. Each morning she fed him cod-liver oil, in an egg-cup of milk to take away the taste. 'When she wanted me to have a boiled egg, I exclaimed dramatically: "Although I do not like it, I will eat it." The others made fun of me for it – for years afterwards.'[1] He seems to have been regarded by all the family as someone special: throughout their lives his sister and brothers showed him great affection and reposed unusual confidence in him.

Tom, for his part, while he regarded his elder brothers, particularly Jack, with something akin to hero worship, was specially close to Gordon, with whom he did nearly everything. His early years have something of the quality of an idyll: devoted parents, a loving elder sister and brothers, much to see and do in a town where most of the tradesmen were his parents' friends and the pleasure of the books, pictures, songs and stories with which Charles Denning enriched his children's lives.

As Tom became familiar with the world outside his home, he found that Market Place was the centre of Whitchurch, the place where five roads met and there was always much to see. Looking out from his father's shop door, he saw The White Hart opposite, occupying the corner between Newbury Street and London Road. On the other side of London Road was the brewery of his father's friend, John Roe, where his brothers often played croquet on the lawn leading down to the River Test.

On his left, Tom would see Mr Todd, the chemist, in his front door, if he were not too busy with the jars and phials that lined the walls of his shop. To Tom's right, leaning against the draper's house, were the one-storey premises of Mr Hobbs, who 'carried on the business of saddlery combined with veterinary work. It was most interesting to watch the saddler at work repairing harness or making or re-stuffing horse collars and pads.'[2] Beyond that, the old Town Hall was on the corner of Newbury Street and Bell Street. Church Street, the next round Market Place, wound its way, in a south-westerly direction, to Andover; it passed some fine houses, including The Lawn, the Vicarage, All Hallows Church and Hurstborne Park, the seat of the Earl of Portsmouth, known to everyone locally as 'The Park'. Tom knew Church Street well. Every Sunday he accompanied his mother to church, where he loved to hear his father's deep bass voice in the choir. Sometimes he went with his brothers further along the road, to collect conkers or acorns in The Park.

Last of the five roads that met in the centre of Whitchurch was Winchester Street, along which Tom could see the river in many places and watch Llewellyn Lloyd, the miller, grinding corn for flour. 'At that time the river was to some extent used as a sewer and for many years there was an open drain running alongside Winchester Street, opposite the Methodist chapel, and this had an almost continuous stream of steaming black fluid running through it to the river.'[2] The water must none the less have been sweet. That stretch of the River Test provided some of the best trout fishing in southern England, and thick beds of watercress besides. The boys of Whitchurch bathed in it during the summer months.

Though it was only a small town, with a population about two thousand, Whitchurch could boast more than one brewery and a good assortment of inns, hostelries and public houses alongside its Anglican church and its chapels: Wesleyan, Methodist, Baptist, Primitive Methodist, Congregational and Particular Baptists. The Salvation Army, with their barracks in The Lynch, had a strong following in the town and, only a few years before Tom's birth, there had been a riot, in which John Roe, 'a big fat man, vigorously against the temperance movement',[1] had played no little part in breaking up the Army's Sunday band-playing in Market Place.

Education was also well catered for. Since 1881 elementary education had been compulsory; after 1891, it was provided free. The National School, a few minutes walk from Tom's home, took care that sons and daughters of the poorer townsmen and those from the surrounding villages would no longer need to sign their names with a cross. Reading, writing and arithmetic formed the basis of the curriculum. Scripture and history were also taught; moral certainty, a love of country and pride in Empire informed the minds of the generation who were to fight, and many to die, in the First World War.

Those who could afford to do so usually preferred to send their children to one of several small private schools in the town, the best of which was the Modern School, also known as the Whitchurch Grammar School, run by Mr and Mrs Charles Henry Geer. The Geers were friends of the Dennings and it was to the Modern School that Clara sent Marjorie, Jack and Reg. Tom would watch the elder children cross Newbury Street and disappear round the corner of The

White Hart. He knew that they would pass Roe's brewery and another pub, The Red House. Soon the road would divide: The Lynch would climb steeply on the left, while below there was the county police station and London Road would lead to the home of Mr and Mrs Geer, with its garden beside the river.

There were no more than 25 or 30 pupils in the school. Though they may not have known they were using the Latin 'beware', behind his back the children called Mr Geer 'Cave'.

He had never taken a degree but he wore a scholar's gown – torn and tatty – to show his learning. . . . His prime concern was to build character, and next to teach his pupils to write good English and to speak it. He always saw to their cricket, urging them in the game – as in life – to keep a straight bat. He played the organ, too, in church. His wife, lively and smiling, supported him. She taught music to the girls – and to a few of the boys.[1]

The *Andover Gazette* published regular accounts of events taking place in the Modern School: musical evenings at which the Geers themselves, their son and daughters and pupils from the school sang and played the piano. It was the kind of entertainment in which Charles Denning loved to take part.

At All Hallows Church, on Sunday mornings, Tom saw the carriage people of Whitchurch: those considered well above his family in the social scale. There were the Portals, who lived in a big house beyond Newbury Street, at the top of Bere Hill. Spencer Portal's family owned the papermill which made banknote paper for the Bank of England. Every Sunday morning he walked down to church in his frockcoat and top hat and read the lessons. Then there were the lesser gentry and the professional men and their families: Spencer Clarke, the solicitor (who was the Mayor for 50 years); Rustat Hemsted, the doctor; Carpenter Turner, the vicar; and the Devenishes.

Both Charles and Clara had grown up in homes where the Church of England played an important part, at a time when the evangelical movement placed great emphasis upon the scriptures. By the start of the twentieth century religious observance was becoming more relaxed and in some homes it was beginning to have a social rather than a morally compulsive foundation. In the Denning home belief in God's goodness was of fundamental importance and was to remain a mainspring of Tom's life.

The small world of Whitchurch was enlarged for Tom on those eagerly awaited occasions when Charles Denning took his fourth son on his journeys. They would set off along the narrow Whitchurch roads, where the still-narrower cobbled walkways were edged, in places, with posts to prevent the carts mounting the kerbs. Sparkle, their rough-haired terrier, ran beside the wheels. Soon the town was left behind and they wound through the country lanes to farmyards, hamlets and villages, as far as eight miles away. As they went Charles sang such Victorian favourites as 'There is a tavern in the town' and 'Little Brown Jug, how I love 'ee', recited Shakespeare, Byron, Scott, Wordsworth or wove tales of ancient heroes to enchant the heart of his small listener.

Tom Denning was only just a Victorian: a day before his second birthday the old Queen died and was succeeded by the son who had been heir to her throne for 60 years. In that Edwardian childhood the foundations of Tom's character were laid. The first five years of his life – the most formative – were spent in a loving and protective home, where he was taught firmly, but gently, the difference between right and wrong, the virtues of hard work and consideration for others, the pleasure to be obtained from the delayed gratification of desire. From the safety of his home, he looked out upon a world where, despite differences of class and of religious inclination, the inhabitants of Whitchurch shared a pride in their country and a common faith. The ideal of service was taught in school and given moral authority from the pulpit. Throughout his life the simple principles learned by Tom Denning in his parents' home, in church and at school were to remain his guiding light; he would apply them, with little modification, to the problems of a changing world.

2

Schooldays

In 1904 Charles Denning found difficulty in making ends meet and Grandfather Thompson helped his son-in-law with a loan of £100, a large sum of money when a pound of sugar cost twopence (less than 1p today). Even with help Charles and Clara could not escape what was, for them, a distressing and distasteful decision. The three eldest children were still at the Modern School, and Gordon and Tom had recently joined them there. Clara, who was pregnant again, expecting her sixth child in November, was ready to 'sacrifice anything'[3] for her children, but she was a realist, and knew it was impossible to find school fees for all the family. Together with Charles she came to a painful conclusion: Marjorie, Jack and Reg would finish their schooldays at the Geers', but Gordon and Tom must move to the National School.

The greatest difference between the schools was, perhaps, that Mr Geer 'wanted to make gentlemen'[3] of his pupils, while the aim of the elementary school was to produce literate, working men and women. Whatever its aim, the education at the National School was good enough for boys of ability to win free places at Andover Grammar School.

Though the 1902 Education Act had put education into the hands of county councils and the running costs of schools were now defrayed by the rates, the name of the National School had nothing to do with the State's recent involvement in education. For more than a century various religious groups had provided elementary education for the children of their poor. The Whitchurch school was built in 1847, when the vicars of Whitchurch and of St Mary Bourne, four miles away, raised £1000 from local gentry and tradesmen, leased a meadow for a shilling a year, and built a school midway between All Hallows Church and the railway. The National School of

Whitchurch, like many others, took its name from the National Society for the Education of the Poor according to the Principles of the Church of England.

The brick and flint school building, with the master's house beside it, was ten minutes' walk from Market Place. It was attended by children of Whitchurch traders and workmen, children from the workhouse and the sons and daughters of farm labourers, who might walk four miles each morning, carrying packets containing their midday meals. There were some 400 children in all. Lessons were given by the master, Mr Frederick Ball, his wife, who also taught the girls to knit and darn, and by an infants' mistress. The school day started with prayers and scripture; then the children were taught reading, writing, arithmetic and the history of the British Empire.

Tom could not remember when, exactly, he learned to read, though he knew he was very young. Soon he could lose himself in his father's books. Most prized was an edition of John Bunyan's *Pilgrim's Progress*. 'Published in 1824. Tattered with use. Well printed with etchings. We poured over the picture of Apollyon barring the way to Christian.'[1]

In old age, Reg recalled that Tom's great asset was his ability to 'eliminate everything that was going on; even though all the boys were racing about doing things, he could get on with his study and his books.' Though he was always happy to sit quietly reading, Tom was not a prig; he joined in playground games and tussles and, he would remember, on one occasion a ploughman's son hit his head against a flint wall, on another he shot a little girl with a pea-shooter. It must have added insult to injury for the girl, on complaining to Clara, to be told 'Boys will be boys.' Clara was not the woman to waste too much sympathy on playtime grievances. She was 'tremendously capable, brave and firm. If you were going along with her and you startled at something, she'd say "You'll be frightened of your own shadow next." ' Her 'courage was beyond any man's.'[3] Gently but very firmly she passed her own high standards to her children. 'Mother was so sweet to me once. I opened one of her drawers and took sixpence. She pointed out to me the error of taking other people's property, which sank in even to this day.' (The day was 22 February 1990 and General Denning was 95 years old.)

Clara was 'a simple worshipper of God', who 'brought us all up to be the same: to acknowledge where we got everything from.' After meals, the family thanked God for what they had received. On Sundays, they went to church, where Charles and the elder boys sang in the choir (the vicar did not think Tom good enough) and Mr Geer's 'stentorian voice'[3] boomed from the back.

Tom had left the Geers' school, but had not lost touch with them: the families were friends and Mrs Geer gave Tom piano lessons. After school, he practised on Marjorie's piano, which occupied a corner of the cramped room where the family took their meals, and even tried his hand at composing. In the summer he joined the boys tickling fish in the river at the end of the Geers' garden. 'To tickle a fish,' explained General Denning, 'you have to have straight banks . . . you lie down on the bank and put your hands under the water' (he demonstrated a slight cupping of the hands), 'and the fish came to lie there under the bank – and you caught a fish and threw it out.' It was Clara, of course, who did the gutting. 'Poor darling, she did everything.'[3]

Both Jack and Reg were good at games and taught 'the little ones' to play cricket in the back yard or on the recreation ground. Tom was keen but not much good. 'I think he was more bookish,' said Reg. 'My mother worked it up. She encouraged all of us and she was angry with us if we didn't achieve – in the nicest possible way. That is what urged some of us forward. She had a brilliant brain herself and noted a spark in Tom.' Not just in Tom, but in all their children, the mixture of Clara's practical, no-nonsense approach to life with Charles's romanticism and gentle courtesy produced a potent brew.

Amongst the highlights of a Whitchurch childhood were the annual Sunday-school treats, a summer picnic in The Park or a visit to nearby Beacon Hill, where once a beacon had burned to pass on the news of the sighting of the Armada. A cart, loaded with food and drink was pulled to a farm at the foot of the hill, and tea was served to the children in a barn. 'Strong tea – steeped with sugar,' Denning was to remember, 'it made me feel sick. Ever since I have always had my tea weak – very weak, with lots of hot water – and no sugar.'[1]

Empire Day, in Tom's schooldays, was celebrated with pomp and ceremony. On 22 February 1908, *The Times* reported Lord Rosebery's speech after the presentation of Union Jacks to 50 Edinburgh Board Schools:

What does that flag stand for? Of course it stands for the United Kingdom and the British Empire (cheers), but if the United Kingdom was like some kingdoms, and if the British Empire were like some empires, we should not take the trouble to give you the flag today.

It is because, as we think, it stands for justice, good government, liberty and christianity that we honour that flag (cheers). It is spread all over the world. The British Empire is a greater empire at this moment than has ever been dreamt of in the world before.

Similar sentiments were, no doubt, voiced by Mr Ball to the children assembled before the Union Jack in the Whitchurch National School. Then, with heartfelt pride, they would raise their voices in patriotic song before being given the rest of the day as a half-holiday.

There were many things to see and do when Tom was not in school. By modern standards, the streets of Whitchurch 'were a haven of silence, broken only by the occasional creak of horse-drawn carts proceeding usually at walking pace.'[2] In Market Place small boys found room to play marbles and conkers and girls to bowl their hoops. Then, in the first decade of the century motor cars began to appear in the town: crowds of children gathered to stare at the splendid vehicles, parked behind The White Hart, while their occupants took lunch on the way to the new racecourse at Newbury; or the children watched General Booth arrive by car to address the Salvation Army.

More exciting even than the car was the advent of the aeroplane. In 1909, the year Bleriot flew the Channel, a thrilling event for everyone, Whitchurch had its own aeronautic display: on Beacon Hill Geoffrey de Havilland practised flying, watched by a breathless group of youngsters. Back at home, they 'tried alike with paper and card'[1] to copy his machine – without success.

More cars were appearing in the narrow, untarred carriage ways round Whitchurch, showering pedestrians with dust as they passed. Complaints were heard everywhere, and there was general relief when plans were made to tar the roads. Since cars were still very expensive, horses and carts remained the principal means of transport in and around the town. For some time yet children would be able to gather at Harry Sampson's busy forge in Bell Yard, just behind the

Denning home, to enjoy the sight and sound of the hot iron thrust, sizzling, into cold water and to watch the farrier shoeing horses.

When Tom was eight or nine, he went, quite alone, to visit his grandparents in Lincoln and, despite his being very travel-sick, managed three changes of train to get there. In old age he would recall with pleasure riding on the coal cart to make deliveries beside one of his grandfather's drivers and visiting the fair with his cousin Gwen, the daughter of Clara's brother John. Only Aunt Rosa, who never married, still lived with her parents. Clara's next sister, Aunt Kit, lived in Finchley; Aunt Min, married to Charles Arnold, a bank manager, lived in Streatham; Aunt Edith and her husband, Harry Lambe, had emigrated to Canada.

By 1907, the two eldest children, Marjorie and Jack, had left home to start work. The financial burden on Charles Denning was lightened, but the family missed Marjorie's lively affection and Jack's leadership. Marjorie took a job as a shop assistant in Winchester and, later, in Oxford; 'attractive and gay', she 'made friends everywhere.' Jack was apprenticed to a draper, Handleys of Southsea. Like H. G. Wells's 14-year-old Kipps, he must have set out with some trepidation, a box and a portmanteau to live in accommodation provided by his new master. Wells tells how it could have been, even if Handleys did better for their youngsters than Mr Shalford did for Kipps:

What he put into Kipps was chiefly bread and margarine, infusions of chicory and tea-dust, colonial meat by contract at threepence a pound, potatoes by the sack and watered beer . . . [Kipps] was also allowed to share a bedroom with eight other young men, and to sleep in a bed which, except in very severe weather, could be made, with the help of his overcoat and private underlinen, not to mention newspapers, quite sufficiently warm for any reasonable soul . . . At half-past seven o'clock at night – except on late nights – a feverish activity of 'straightening-up' began, and when the last shutter was up outside, Kipps with the speed of an arrow leaving a bow, would start hanging wrappers over the fixtures and over the piles of wares upon the counters, preparatory to a scattering of wet sawdust and the sweeping out of the shop . . . Rarely much later than nine, a supper of bread and cheese and watered beer awaited him downstairs, and, that consumed, the rest of the day was

entirely at his disposal for reading, recreation, and the improvement of his mind . . . The front door was locked at half-past ten,
and the gas in the dormitory extinguished at eleven.

Shop hours were wearisome and exhausting – not until 1911 would
they be legally limited to 60 a week – and wages low, but each of the
Dennings embarked on a new life with the energy and enthusiasm
typical of the family. When Reg left school, he found work at
Gorringes, a fashionable store just behind Buckingham Palace, the
first of his family to work in London. Since train fares made large
holes in small pay packets, there were only occasional visits home.
They kept in touch by mail, which was cheap and astonishingly swift.
After they left Whitchurch all the children wrote to Charles and Clara
at least once a week. Charles wrote to each every Sunday and Clara
sent a letter in the week. All their lives the family would end letters to
one another, 'Ever your loving . . .' The phrase was more than a
formality. Their affectionate interest and pride in one another, their
generosity of response to another's need for help, calls to mind *The
Three Musketeers* and their slogan: 'All for one and one for all.' This
sense of the Denning family – 'a breed of mighty men', as Tom would
write, and Gordon's 'Dennings do not lose spirit, do they?' – is the
key to Tom Denning's personality.

Clara's ambitions for her boys were partly realised when they both
won free places at Andover Grammar School. The school was an
Elizabethan foundation, enlarged over the years by donations from
prosperous and public-spirited citizens of Andover. In 1570 (1569 by
the old calendar) John Hanson, a London merchant who had retired
to his native town, gave £200 to provide a salary of £15 a year for a
schoolmaster. A house was converted into a schoolroom by the
Bailiff and Approved Men, the town's elected council, and ten boys
were awarded free places. They were joined, when the school opened
in 1581, by a few fee-paying pupils. By 1810, an enlarged school was
also taking boarders and the newly appointed headmaster was
required 'To instruct Ten Boys in the Latin Language gratis in
fulfilment of the Foundation of the said school. Such boys to pay
annually two guineas for their other instruction in reading, writing
and arithmetic . . .'

The Grammar School was in its third building and Mr Robert

Owen Bishop had been headmaster for three years when Gordon and Tom started there together in 1909. Mr Bishop's aim was 'first and foremost to raise the standard of work, and this was enforced by rigid discipline, and a liberal use of the cane. Examination results were good, particularly in mathematics, to which a large share of the timetable was assigned.'[4]

Since Gordon was 20 months older than Tom, it might seem that Tom was exceptionally precocious to arrive at the Grammar School at the same time. In fact, the age of boys at that time elected to free places might vary between nine and twelve years. The two Denning boys were very close and their parents may have preferred to keep them together. Gordon always came to Tom's aid in any scrape at school. The two boys, with other Whitchurch children, made the journey to Andover by train. 'Each morning we set off. Mother had put up our sandwiches. We had them in our satchels with our exercise books. We walked up the steep hill. It was half-a-mile to the station. The station staff were all our friends. We went up into the signal box with the signalman. We went into the cab of the shunting engine. The driver used to boil his egg in water in his big shovel in the fire hole.' The first stop was at Hurstbourne, two miles away. The next was Andover Junction. 'We made our way round the road by the river – dawdling by the stream – through the churchyard – till we reached the school. Always late by a quarter of an hour. We had a good excuse. ' "The train was late." '

The classrooms had high ceilings, with tall windows set above the level at which boys, seated at their desks, might be tempted to look out. The plain, brown tiled walls, offered no distraction from work. Along the sides of the hall there were long seats on which successive generations of boys had carved their initials. In the middle was the stove, around which they ate their sandwiches, and, at the end, redolent of tradition, was the Charter-Board, the memorial to the school's founder, John Hanson.

If Mr Bishop turned a blind eye to the morning excuse that 'the train was late', in the afternoon he took his revenge: 'He tormented us. He did not give us enough time to catch the train home. Only seven or eight minutes to go a mile. We ran our little hearts out.'[1]

One afternoon, when Tom was about twelve, he received a nasty fright that had nothing to do with Mr Bishop. As the boys made their way home from Whitchurch station, Tom was confronted by a local farmer, Mr George Lee, seated on a large horse, brandishing his horsewhip. 'Were you the one who hit my boy?' demanded the threatening figure and Tom hastily assured him that he was not. Years later, when he was a young barrister, Denning would act in a case at Winchester County Court (*Grey* v. *Lee*) when two prominent Hampshire farmers were in dispute over an unsound pony bought at auction, and would remember when one of them, towering over him from the back of a horse, had given him an unpleasant afternoon.

Mr Bishop – nick-named 'The Walrus' – taught English and was also a first-class cricketer. He must have recognised Tom's ability and determination to succeed: he encouraged the boy's interest in learning and later steered his ambition in the direction of a university education. From the beginning Tom did well. He had a lively mind and an extraordinary memory. Just as his father was able to quote at length from the classics, so Denning would be able to lace his lectures and speeches with quotations from his favourite authors. 'All my prizes from the age of eleven were for English. I have them still, bound in handsome leather, with the school crest and the date AD 1569. The titles in succession are the Great Authors, Macaulay, Carlyle and Milton.'[1]

The year Tom was eleven, Edward VII died. Nine kings and an impressive array of princes took part in his splendid funeral procession. In the front row of mourners, beside the new King George V, was his cousin, the German Kaiser. Pride in their Empire and their flag, sorrow for their dead king and loyalty to their new, were felt by every schoolboy who heard of these events. 1910 was also the year Tom's first wife's family came to Whitchurch. The Reverend John Carpenter Turner – 'a very stern old man' – was succeeded at All Hallows by Frank Northam Harvey, a younger man with a family similar in age to the Dennings. Apart from church on Sundays, the Dennings saw little of the Harveys: at that time the families were on different social levels.

Much more momentous, from Tom's point of view, was Gordon's decision to leave school at the end of the 1913 summer term. At the top of his programme for the Athletic Sports on Wednesday 30 July, Gordon printed

23

THIS TIME NEXT WEEK, WHERE SHALL I BE?
OUT OF THE CLUTCHES OF R. O. B./ishop (Headmaster)

At 15, Gordon joined the General Steam Navigation Company and was posted as a cadet to the SS *Stork*, berthed just below Tower Bridge. When he was ashore he could meet Reg, working in Victoria. On 21 December 1913 Gordon wrote to thank Reg for 'the glorious time we had that Saturday night' and to send him two shillings as his part of the expenses – 'do not mention it to Jack as he sent it me.' He urged Reg: 'You will look after Elsie during her stay at home because you know last time she attracted all the country gallants.' Their cousin, Elsie Bevan, was the daughter of Charles's sister, Nell, 'a jolly old thing', whose husband, Ted Bevan, was a schoolmaster in Hornsey. Now that two of the Dennings were based in London, they were given a warm welcome at the Bevan home.

If, with Reg, Gordon was now one of the lads, with Tom he maintained a more intellectual stance. On a voyage to Genoa, he wrote '. . . I only wish you were able to make that run. You see, it is the same course as followed by Aeneas and Ulysses. We passed the *litora Circeae terrae* quite close, but heard none of the enchanting songs or the roaring of wild beasts described by Virgil, however the promontory is still called Cape Circea . . . At daylight we entered the straits of Messina and were once again "between Scylla and Charybdis." ' He congratulated Tom on winning the English prize and wished him a happy birthday. He did not expect to be home before the end of January, but 'I'll square up with you as regards presents when I get home.'

Gordon's letters give the picture of an easy-going, confident, likeable young man, delighted with life at sea. There were moments when he looked back nostalgically to schooldays: 'I hope Tom got on alright in the exam. Tell him I should like a copy of the papers (with answers to problems etc;) if he can spare the time.' It would have taken some time, in those days, to copy the papers in longhand. Tom was deeply immersed in his work, had taken to making pen and ink sketches, and was keen on cryptic writing. Fond as he was of his brothers, they had sometimes to chivvy him into dropping them a line.

A great scheme of army reform had been underway since 1907,

including the merger of the Yeomanry and the Volunteers into a new Territorial Army. By 1913 patriotic young men were flocking to join. In October 1913 Jack went home for his twenty-first birthday. On 2 November he wrote from Southsea to Reg, 'My dear old chap . . . Mum and Dad gave me a dressing case. Auntie Rosa 10/-' He had hoped to see Reg 'but apparently finances were low. If you are short I can easily let you have a quid . . . I sent Muriel [a Thompson cousin] a little autograph album for her birthday and had a reply yesterday. Who told [her] I had a girl. She is mistaken. I know one ripper I have designs on though . . . I am thinking of joining the Territorials, the Royal Garrison Artillery . . .'

Mutual help, for the Dennings, was natural and unselfconscious. Their father's financial difficulties bred in each of them a careful regard for money and, at the same time, they inherited his open-handedness and generosity towards others. In February 1914 Gordon wrote to his parents 'I was very pleased at being able to get home twice. I don't think I shall be able to do so again, it takes too much money. I shall be glad to get my rise so I can pay some of the money I owe you.' Then, on 3 May: 'I am getting 1/-a day now, so will be able to give 10/-a month . . . Hope you are all well and trade is good.'

One Sunday evening, in the summer of 1914, Tom wrote to Jack:

As Father did not write to Reg last week he is writing this week, and he has told me to write to you. You see I am obeying the command. Well, I hope you are well and prosperous.

Norman has got a new flannel suit with long trousers, 10 pockets, button-hole, a hole for [his] watch chain to pass through. They are the same colour as my old ones. He wore them today for the 1st time and after I had told him about pulling the trousers up when he sat down, in church he forgot to do so when he was kneeling but when he was sitting down, he kept gradually pulling them up till the 'permanent turn-ups' reached his knee. He also has a straw hat.

A week ago yesterday this (now) young gentleman fell into the river at Roe's; it appears he was endeavouring to get a ball out of the river with Madge bending over him (real style) when Madge slipped and put her hand on Norman and – great was the fall and splash thereof. He did not get the ball whilst he was in there. He looked like a scarecrow after a thunderstorm.

I have tried, but poorly, to show the difference in his appearance on the two instances of his daily life. They look like two prehistoric drawings on the walls of caves, don't they.

The two small pen and ink sketches are charming, (reproduced at the end of the book) one showing the young dandy in his new, long-trousered suit and straw boater, the other the bedraggled, short-trousered schoolboy. Tom reminds Jack he is waiting for a book. 'I suppose your great mind is occupied with affairs of state (eg gunnery), industrial problems (eg serving in shop) and "affaires de coeur" and this makes you overlook such a minor detail as breaking a promise (not a vow).'

On a more practical level, he continued:

I suppose Mother has told you of Reg's promotion (perhaps temporary) to 2nd sales in their department. His commission now amounts to about 13/-a week.

Mother is going to send your black waistcoat this week . . .

Hope you are well.

Ever your loving brother

Tom

How's cricket going on?

I scored 4 yesterday at school.

It may have been necessary to tell Tom to write, but his letters, when they arrived, must have given pleasure and some amusement.

In joining the Territorials, Jack had found an outlet for his physical and mental abilities and powers of leadership. On 14 June 1914 he wrote to 'My dearest Mother and Dad' that he was just back from camp and had a lovely time. He won the 100 yards, though he was the only one of 30 men to run in 'ordinary togs'. At Hanley's sports, he had won both the 100 yards and the 220 yards. 'I got a lovely trouser press. Of course having one I shall get it changed so I can have 30/- (which it cost) in something out of the shop.'

In December 1913 Tom had passed the University of Cambridge Examination for Senior Students and obtained 'the Second Class in

Honours' in 'Arithmetic, Religious Knowledge, English Language and Literature (including Composition), English History and Geography, Latin, French, Mathematics (Geometry, Algebra and Trigonometry), Heat, Sound and Light', with a distinction in mathematics. His last summer term of peacetime was a good one. The assassination in Sarajevo on 28 June of the Archduke Franz Ferdinand of Austria seemed unlikely to have much effect on the life of an English schoolboy. On the strength of his result in the Cambridge Local, the school awarded Tom the Hurford Scholarship, then worth £10.

In copperplate handwriting, the minutes of a meeting of the School Governors in 1914 state 'The Headmaster reported that H. W. Kitcatt had gained the Madgwick and A. T. Denning the Hurford Scholarship, being the two first boys in the Cambridge Local and that they were in all respects qualified to receive the prizes. The Clerk was directed to intimate this to the two parents.' (No doubt the two fathers!)

On a more mundane note, though perhaps of interest to the cricket enthusiast, the Headmaster also reported, 'that the old Lawn Mower on the Sports Field was worn out and that he had borrowed one for the last two months from C. Bennett, Ironmonger, who offered to sell it for £6.'

'How was it that the world was so unexpectedly plunged into terrible conflict?' asked Lloyd George in his *War Memoirs*. 'Who was responsible? Not even the astutest and most far-seeing statesman foresaw in the early summer of 1914 that autumn would find the nations of the world interlocked in the most terrible conflict that had ever been witnessed in the history of mankind; and if you came to the ordinary men and women who were engaged in their daily avocations in all countries there was not one of them who suspected the imminence of such a catastrophe . . .' As school broke up, Tom had no idea that during the holidays war would break out, devastating his family and leaving its lasting mark on his own thinking and attitudes.

The holiday started as Tom expected. He helped his father, read, cycled in the lanes around Whitchurch and walked in The Park. He played tennis at the home of the Earl's agent, Mr Tancock, a family friend. He played cricket with the local club in The Park, where the wickets were prepared by one of the Earl's gardeners, 'assisted by a pony clad in leather overshoes to avoid damage to the turf when pulling the mower.'[2] He made up, in energy and enthusiasm, for his lack of the sporting ability that distinguished his older brothers. As July ended there was talk of war between Germany and Russia, but little concern that Great Britain might be drawn into it. Most people prepared, in sweltering heat, to enjoy the August Bank Holiday weekend, sparing only passing thoughts for Germany, Russia and the problems of the Balkans.

The public mood began to change on Sunday 2 August, when it became known that Germany had declared war on France and demanded the right to march its army through Belgium. England abhorred a bully and opinion began to swing in favour of joining the war.

Bank Holiday Monday was a beautiful, cloudless day. In the afternoon the House of Commons was packed to hear Sir Edward Grey's statement on the crisis. 'Could this country stand by,' he asked, 'and witness the direst crime that ever stained the pages of history and thus become participants in the sin?' The overwhelming answer of Parliament and country was 'No!' That evening, it is said, as the lamp-lighter went along Whitehall, Grey stood watching at a window and remarked: 'The lamps are going out all over Europe; we shall not see them lit again in our lifetime.' In Whitchurch, Charles Denning, in as sombre a mood, took his quotation, presciently, from 'Lochiel's Warning' by Thomas Campbell: 'And coming events cast their shadow before.'[1]

Just after eight o'clock on the morning of 4 August, the Germans crossed the Belgian frontier. The British Government sent Berlin an ultimatum to end the invasion by midnight. Someone, somewhere, realised that midnight in Germany would be only eleven o'clock by Greenwich time. The hours ticked away without a reply and, as Big Ben struck eleven on the night of 4 August 1914, England was at war.

3

The First World War

Jack joined his Territorial Unit at Southsea, and Reg enlisted in the Queen's Westminster Rifles as soon as war broke out. Now Tom lost little time in replying to Jack's letters.

August 14th

Dear Jack,

Thanks extremely for your letter I received this morning. Rather a dry, ordinary opening for a letter of mine. The quotation I will write at my conclusion is from Horace III. It means 'It is sweet and honourable to die for one's country.' I am a rotter, Jack. I said to Mother that I would write to you properly tonight but my weak brain stupidly forgot and here I am, close on post-time, trying to rush through something like a letter for you. I must try to write you bi-weekly. Expect you will receive regular letters from me now if I remember.

Jack, in my diary I have made notes of the following quotations. I consider them good.

'I expect to pass through this world but once. Any goodness, therefore, that I can do or any kindness that I can show to any fellow creature, let me do it now. Let me not defer it or neglect it for I shall not pass this way again.'

'The immediately possible is hardly worth living for. It is the ideal that kindles enthusiasm and gives inspiration and vigour to all human effort.'

'In the world's broad field of battle
In the bivouac of life,
Be not like dumb driven cattle
Be a hero in the strife.'

Next time, perhaps tomorrow, I will continue these quotations and write one of my lately composed poems.

DULCE ET DECORUM EST PRO PATRIA MORI

A. Thompson Denning

To capture completely the spirit of the day it is only necessary to read Rupert Brooke's 'The Soldier' or Lawrence Binyon's 'For the Fallen'. The quotations from earlier writers chosen by the 15-year-old boy, idealistic, heroic, set down markers to the way he would lead his life. The older Dennings, in the mood of the time, enthusiastically accepted his use of Horace in this, and every subsequent letter he sent them; the words became something of a rallying call between the brothers: on 6 January 1915, Gordon ended a letter to Reg 'Tom's phrase: *Dulce et decorum est pro patria mori.*'

Years later, in 1980, when Lord Denning was writing *The Family Story*, he would include Reg's recent answer to a professor researching the attitudes of those who fought in the First World War:

> From the declaration of war in 1914 and until after I was wounded, it was with a proud and gay heart, because I considered myself privileged to be able to do something for the country in a time of dire need.

In the course of the war, the Dennings wrote to one another at least once a week, sometimes more; several hundred letters must have passed between them. The few surviving letters from Tom to Jack and Reg – all written before they went to France – may have been those that particularly touched or amused them, perhaps to the point where they sent the letters home for their parents to read.

Jack's letter of 1 September 1914 to Reg was more down-to-earth. After telling Reg that Marjorie had visited him at Southsea that weekend, and Gordon a week earlier, 'Are you being paid at all by Gorringes?' he asked, 'I am hoping to draw some off Handleys.' By that time Gordon had left England. On 28 August he had told his parents the *Stork* would shortly sail under sealed orders. 'Even our old steward, a German, but naturalised for 26 years, has not been allowed to come with us ... If we get through safely,' he continued, no doubt unintentionally chilling Charles and Clara, 'I shall have a jolly good holiday.'

There was not much for Charles's and Clara's comfort in those months. Trade was no better than usual and, above all, in the backs of their minds must always have been fear for the safety of their serving sons. Tom's confirmation, on 25 October, by the Bishop of Winchester gave them pleasure and satisfaction, but perhaps only the news that Norman had won a free place at the Grammar School made them forget, for a while, the trouble hanging over them. Norman, soon to be ten years old, joined Tom on the daily journey to Andover.

The Commander in Chief, Field Marshal Sir John French, had said that the war would be over by Christmas and most people believed it. Tom would have loved to join his brothers in the services, but saw little chance that he would be old enough to enlist before the Germans were defeated. A small gift from Reg gave him enormous pleasure. 'I was tremendously pleased with letter and button. It is in my drawer among my precious possessions. I don't wear it because I might lose it.' Then, always law-abiding and troubled that Reg should not, perhaps, have given him a regimental button, 'I hope you won't get into a row for sending it, if so, I will return it.'

The weather remained warm and Tom was able to bathe in the river and play cricket for Whitchurch against an army side. 'They had an officer, terribly fast bowler, most of the balls near your head. I missed first ball, played second, third ended the innings. The bowler took 6 for 13. He bowled Harvey clean so I have an excuse, but if I had played 3rd as I played 2nd I would not have been out. I wore white flannels, either yours or Jack's, I don't know which.' 'Harvey' was the vicar's son and a fine cricketer; he was to become Tom's brother-in-law, though Tom had, as yet, only 'glanced shyly'[1] at Mary Harvey at their confirmation.

Reg, writing on 16 October to wish 'My dearest old brother' a happy twenty-second birthday, sent Jack 'Congrats on doing so splendidly in the inter-regimental sports. I can tell you I am proud to have such a brother as you are ... Mother and Dad's wedding day tomorrow. Don't you think we are lucky to have the best Mother, Dad and Home in the world,' he added.

The best mother and dad were finding it difficult to cope with the writing of letters and the despatching of parcels to their sons. One Sunday evening before Christmas, Tom was deputed to write to Reg. 'Can't you get down for a weekend? Mother half-expected you this weekend. She says you can go to Aunt Nell's, why not come home. You come half-fare you know.' After delivering this lecture, Tom gave the Whitchurch news. 'We are going to have 1100 of the Royal Lancaster's (Kitchener's Army) billeted in Whitchurch. The Church Hall has already been requisitioned for military purposes. I suppose we shall have some.' His supposition, possibly wishful thinking, was not borne out by events. On a more personal note, he told Reg: 'Walters have reduced Marjorie's wages. I shall have to give her some of my £10.' The war was no longer expected to end before Christmas, but Tom hoped 'the war will soon be over, with honour to England . . . Anyway we are doing our best. Our family "a breed of mighty men" though I think I am the worst of the lot.' Years later, Denning echoed that sentiment in his Preface to *The Family Story*, when he wrote, 'we were five brothers. Two were lost in the First World War. They were the best of us.'

In later life, Denning was to become an immensely popular public figure. His personal charm, easy manner, simple mode of speech and genuine interest in people would win him friends around the world. He would be known for his consideration, his kindness and spontaneity. For many, he would stand as a symbol of England. He would enjoy comradeship and companionability. But the mainspring of his life would always be his family. The Denning family, that 'breed of mighty men', was the rock on which he built; more than his faith, more than his love of country, it was pride in family that sustained him and urged him – like his brothers – always on.

Tom had determined to go to university, and, encouraged by Mr Bishop, set his sights on Oxford or Cambridge; everything depended on his winning an award. Since Andover had a good reputation for mathematics and Tom had gained a distinction in the subject in the Cambridge Local, he decided to offer it for university entrance.

Gordon, too, was intent on exams. His ambition had always been to join the Royal Navy. On 31 December, to the family's great joy, he was transferred from the Merchant Navy to the Royal Naval Reserve – possibly a stepping-stone to the Royal Navy itself – and sent as a midshipman to the naval school, HMS *Excellent*, in Portsmouth. On 1 March 1915 he wrote home: 'I am glad to say I obtained a 1st class certificate, the only midshipman to get one. I obtained 704 marks out of a possible 800, which is considered a very good percentage.' Within two weeks the family heard of his appointment to one of the latest cruisers, HMS *Hampshire*, and shortly afterwards they learned that, on 8 April, Jack had also been commissioned, as a Special Reserve Officer. Reg, who always followed Jack's lead, thought of applying for a commission and, on 27 May, Jack wrote from Grimsby to Reg, who was with the Queen's Westminster Rifles in Saffron Walden: 'I am afraid I can't do anything for you just yet. I am sorry to disappoint you old boy but perhaps it will be only temporary, you may rely on me if there is half a chance.' Then Jack, who had always taken his position as the eldest brother seriously, felt a qualm: 'I am not so keen on your going to the front. I know you are safe here and as I shall be there within a week or two, it will be some consolation to know that, as I know you won't stick your nose in a wormhole as I shall if I get a chance. I am longing to see you old boy,' he went on, with a burst of slightly diffident affection, 'it may seem b—y ridiculous' (swearing was not allowed in the Denning home) 'for me to say that but you don't know what happy memories your ugly old mug brings back to me.'

Four days later, Jack wrote again, crisply 'I am answering at once to tell you not to *think* about applying any longer but apply at once.' The family intelligence network had clearly been at work, as Jack went on: 'Have you written to Auntie Nell. Elsie told me she hadn't heard from you. Try and drop her a line shortly.'

While Reg still hesitated, he received a letter from Tom:

I went to bed early last night and rose first this morning, having tidied up, went for a bike ride to the other side of Hurstbourne. It was a lovely morning and my haul was a bunch of laburnum (otherwise 'golden chains') from a tree by the wayside. Hardly anybody was about except some of the soldiers.

I started the above last Monday night, intending to send it but after I had finished doing the pony up for the night, I found it was 8.45 so I had to leave it. Being pressed by work on other weekdays, I had not time to finish it.

Reg had sent Tom one of the humorous postcards that were so popular at the time. 'It was good,' Tom told him, 'but did not produce so much laughter as the first one. Norman was disappointed because it was not for him . . . Just send him a p.c. next week instead of me.' Then the concerned elder brother gave way to the eager, younger one: 'How do you like it under canvas? How many are there in a tent? Are you comfortable there? Would you like a little delicacy from home now and again, to help the bully beef down?'

There followed a message from Clara: 'Mother has told me to tell you that if you don't try for a commission or get a stripe, she won't think you are very smart. (Read between the lines that she wants you to try to get a commission)'. The comment went well with General Denning's account of his mother's determination for her sons to succeed in whatever they undertook and Denning's own assessment of her as 'strong and determined, standing no nonsense.'

Now Tom handed on the news: 'Jack has sent a photo of a group of officers here. He has come out fairly well, but is trying to hide his teeth.' Marjorie, who had changed her job, 'is rather homesick at Bourne & Hollingsworth, she would like a letter from you to cheer her up and say something funny to make her laugh.' There followed some cricket news of 'the match between my side and the strongest team in the league. The result was that they won 174–18' (the '18' is written in very small figures beside a large '174'). Tom 'very nearly' bowled out their captain 'but as luck would have it, there wasn't enough varnish on the wickets.' Then, philosophically, 'well, all we can do is defeat them next time.'

'I suppose there's a finish to every letter,' said Tom, at the end of three pages, 'so here you are, DULCE ET DECORUM EST PRO PATRIA MORI. Be good.'

In April 1915 Reg was given home leave. He took the opportunity to indulge in the latest craze for photography but did not have time to develop his pictures before rejoining his battalion at Watford. On 25 April Tom sent him some of the photos. 'I have not developed those of Roe's dogs yet as Betts had no hypo . . . This morning I took a photo of Polly [their new mare] putting her head over the partition as if asking for hay, but I doubt whether it will be successful for as I was pulling the thing with the number on out, the plate part came up as well. I hadn't put that little thing across. The next time I take a photo,' Tom continued grimly, 'I won't make that mistake. It is a lesson.'

Gordon had sent home a photograph of his new ship, the *Hampshire* and Tom promised, 'if mother is agreeable', to enclose one. 'I took Polly for a run yesterday because three days standing in the stable must be monotonous . . . I took her round to be shoed on Thursday. When I went to bring her back, she was waiting and neighed when she saw me come in the door.' After some more chat about Polly and his own doings, Tom gave Reg gloomy news about the family finances: 'I reckoned up the year's takings for father. Owing to the war there was a perceptible decrease on last year's amount. Consequently there must be a corresponding decrease in the expenditure.' The 16-year-old accountant was not long depressed by bad news: 'I can harness and unharness pony completely now,' he continued, 'cropper and all.'

Shortly afterwards Tom wrote again, on a Sunday evening. This time, to amuse Reg – and himself – Tom started his letter in two kinds of cryptic writing; 'the first, you have seen similar ones before. It is like competitions in weeklys but it is all my own work. The second [reproduced at the end of the book] is in cipher . . . That photo of Polly did not come out . . . I am enclosing the three you took at Roe's. Emily [Roe] said it was not what she wanted as dogs were not big enough but I think she couldn't see them,' the fiercely loyal younger brother defended Reg's photography, 'owing to bad eye- sight.'

Reg turned 21, in June 1915. On 27 June, Jack wrote to him with great urgency from Grimsby: 'Tell your captain that you have a brother commissioned in the navy and one in the army . . . In all probability I shall come on leave next Saturday so let me know your O. C. Coy's name and I will write and ask him to give you leave. Also I will pay your fare if you cannot get a warrant. I must see you dear boy before I go to France.' But Jack, who had always been first in the brothers' activities, was not to be the first to go on active service; without being given embarkation leave, Reg's battalion was posted overseas. On 15 July Jack wrote again to Reg, now in France with the British Expeditionary Force: 'I saw the Earl when I was home on leave, he seemed to be very interested in you and thinks that it was a pity you did not take a commission . . . it was a rotten job . . . saying goodbye to everyone. I would much rather have gone as you did. Of course Mater would have been disappointed.'

Only a month later Jack, too, was in France and sent Reg 'a line to let you know I am over here . . . I am asst. adjutant and have got quite a good horse of my own . . . I have only received two letters since I arrived, isn't it annoying? One was from Pater and the other from Tom of all people.'

Tom was now 16, enthusiastically patriotic and 'dreadfully keen on going to Sandhurst in October'.[5] While he waited to be old enough to serve he immersed himself in his work, where he now had to contend with a new difficulty. All over the country, women were taking the place of enlisted schoolmasters; at Andover the replacement for the young mathematics master was unable to teach to the level required for university entrance and Tom was learning Differential Calculus, Dynamics and Statics from books. He was also reading widely in the English classics. Tales of battles, of heroic deeds and the triumph of good over evil particularly appealed to him; he loved Scott and Dickens but did not much like Thackeray; his favourite Shakespearean characters were Henry V and Julius Caesar, both men of action, and those he least liked were the 'lean and hungry' Cassius and introspective, melancholy Hamlet. Though he had read and enjoyed the adventures of Sherlock Holmes, Tom had not come across the work of Conrad or Arnold Bennett or other prominent writers of the day.

When he sat the examination for Hartley University College (later to become Southampton University) in the summer term, Tom came top in English and Mathematics. He was awarded a Hampshire County Council scholarship, shown in the minutes of the Higher Education Sub-Committee as payable from 12 October 1915, though there is no mention of its value. Mr Bishop advised him to stay on at school and try for Oxford or Cambridge. If either Tom or Mr Bishop gave any consideration to the profession that would follow, the most likely to have come to mind would have been teaching. Though Denning recounts the story of his telling his mother, at the age of ten, that he would be a barrister, he adds 'not knowing in the least what a barrister was'.[1] The idea does not appear to have seriously entered his mind during his schooldays.

Since Charles was in poor health, he sent Tom to Botley, near

Portsmouth, to buy a pony he had seen advertised, going cheap. (It cost between £5 and £6 and went lame soon afterwards!) Tom took over a part of his father's deliveries, trying to collect at least some of the money owing to him. All about him life was changing. Women who had never gone out to work were taking over the jobs of men called to the colours; grand houses were being turned into hospitals and nursing homes; there was a shortage of goods in the shops as the German blockade began to bite and British industry was turned over to war work. Goods were in short supply and prices began to rise. Duties were imposed on tea and tobacco; beer was reduced in strength and its price increased; the opening hours of pubs were curtailed by a government anxious about the effect of drunkenness on war work. The state was interfering in the lives of its citizens to a degree never previously experienced. In Whitchurch, the Portals' home on Bere Hill was in use as a military hospital; women, at the government's behest, knitted socks for soldiers and despatched parcels to 'the boys'; they visited the bereaved and sent letters of condolence, on black-bordered writing paper.

The first casualty in the Denning family was Clara's nephew Reg, son of her brother John and his wife Ethel. Gordon, recently transferred to the destroyer *Morris*, wrote home, in October 1915, 'I had a letter from Aunt Ethel; quite decent of her, she did not mention Reg Thompson being wiped out, that was rotten luck and I was awfully sorry to hear it.' Although the Thompsons in Lincoln, would have been devastated by the loss, Grandma and Aunt Rosa remembered to send Jack for his birthday a large cake with chocolate inside. Jack had a fondness for sweet things and the family would learn that his nickname in the mess was 'Candy Kid'.

Life in the trenches has been so vividly described that those who were not there can almost see and feel and hear the mud, the damp, the stench, the noise and the astonishing spirit of the men who lived in them. Reg, quoted in *The Family Story*, remembered '. . . at Ypres we were in the trenches for six weeks at a stretch – before we were relieved. The trenches were full of water. The only dry place was the fire step. We had to creep out at night and go back to collect our rations. We slept in our greatcoats. We used to wake up with the rats crawling over our faces and biting at the collars of our coats. We were covered with lice . . . On being relieved we went back to a rest camp and tried to get ourselves clean – in a big vat filled with hot water. Everyone accepted this without a murmur of complaint. It was part of the war we had to fight.'

When Jack heard that Reg's trenches were wet, he wrote: 'I am sending home by this mail for a pair of those light waterproof waders for you.' He kept careful note of his account with his parents for the various items he requested and, just before their wedding anniversary, sent them a cheque for £2 10s 'in payment of some of my debts . . . The little extra on the cheque is to buy some little thing as a memento of your wedding day . . .'

So far as he was able Jack kept up to date with family news. 'Thank Tom very much for his note,' he wrote on 12 December 1915, 'it was very like his moustache short and sweet. When does he go in for his exam?' Again, five days later, 'When does Tom have a shot at his exam?'

The examination, taken in December 1915, was at Sidney Sussex College, Cambridge. Tom was so painfully shy when he stayed the night that he could barely bring himself to ask where to find the bathroom and lavatory. He was not offered a place, but the experience may have helped when he went up to Oxford in March. 'Only one college offered me anything. It was Magdalen College, Oxford. They offered me an exhibition of £30 a year. It was not enough to live on. Father could not help. But I determined to accept it – and manage as best I could. Go without if need be. There were no grants in those days.'[1]

Denning's recollection, when he wrote The Family Story, was not correct. He did have his Hampshire Scholarship which, according to the minutes, dated 27 June 1916, of the Hampshire Education Sub-Committee (in Hampshire County Record Office), was increased to £50 per annum, when he obtained an exhibition at Magdalen. Nor was his Exhibition worth as little as £30 a year. The Tutorial Board proceedings of 11 March 1916 (in Magdalen College Archives) state that 'an Exhibition of £40 was offered to Mr Alfred Thompson Denning of Andover Grammar School.' Two pages later, is recorded that, on 29 March 1916, 'it was resolved that the Exhibition offered to Mr A. T. Denning be increased to £50 per annum.'

No explanation of the decision is given. Did Mr Bishop make

representations on Tom's behalf? Did the Tutorial Board learn that Tom would have little other means of support and appreciate that it would be impossible to manage on £90? The records do not say. At all events, Tom had jumped the first hurdle on his way to a university education.

Though he had been accepted by the college, he had still to matriculate as a member of Oxford University. To do so, he would have to pass another examination, called Responsions or Smalls, which would include Greek, a subject which was not taught at Andover. Once again without help, Tom set about a new discipline for the examination to be held in Trinity Term 1916. Provided he could pass, he would be able to go up in October, when he would be 17¾ to enjoy a precious nine months before he reached the age to join the army.

By the end of 1915 Jack, Reg and Gordon were all commissioned officers, a remarkable achievement for the sons of a small tradesman. The family were justifiably proud of them and would have understood Jack's dilemma, set out in his letter of 21 October 1915, when he was applying for a commission in the regular army: 'I did not know what to put Dad's "Position in Life" as, so my C.O. advised me to put down "Gentleman."'

1916 was the year that, more than any other, changed the lives of the Denning family. It began well. Jack had obtained his commission in the regular army and Marjorie became engaged to Sergeant-Major John Haynes, affectionately called 'Johnnie', who specialised in mechanical transport and was in charge of supply convoys passing through Whitchurch. In May (after having home leave), Jack wrote to Reg: 'I met the "Intended". He came and stopped one night in Whitchurch. It seems to be alright. I believe Marjorie wants to get married almost at once, much to pater and mater's delight.'

Jack's leave gave Tom what would prove to be his only opportunity, as a young man, to be with Jack. They played golf together, went to a tennis party and talked about Tom's future: should he become an engineer, either civilian or military? Jack 'did not want me to enter politics much; he did not think much of politicians.'[6]

Jack's distaste for politics and politicians was shared by his family. Denning 'supposed' that his father may have voted but never heard Charles speak of it. Tom himself showed little interest. It seems curious, therefore, that Jack should have thought to advise Tom against politics as a career. The explanation may lie with Arthur Mee. Arthur Mee was a journalist, a remarkable producer of educational books and magazines, the best known of which was *The Children's Encyclopaedia*, which he began to issue, in fortnightly parts, in 1908. In one of Mee's publications, Tom had read an article addressed 'To the Boy Who Would Be Prime Minister'. It had fired his imagination with the desire to make a name for himself. Many boys dream of success and their dreams remain castles in the air; some climb to positions of eminence but do little with their power; Tom wanted much more. He did not long for power for its own sake but in order to use it. His combination of practicality and romance would enable him, when the time came, not only to make a name but to make things *happen*. As for politics, he gave them little further thought: he never joined a party, rarely voted and would look in other directions to find solutions for what he saw as the ills of society.

In the spring of 1916 the German battle fleet had begun to patrol the North Sea. On 31 May Admiral Beatty, commanding the British battle cruisers, to which the *Morris* and three other destroyers were attached, encountered the German High Seas fleet. Denning, in *The Family Story*, described Gordon's part in the Battle of Jutland:

> In each ship itself, the orders were by word of mouth or through speaking tubes. In the *Morris* the speaking tubes failed. They were the means by which the Lieutenant-Commander could control the fire of his guns . . . No orders got through the speaking tubes to the guns. So each officer was left to himself. Gordon was in charge of the foremost 4-inch gun. A midshipman just 19 years of age. Quick as lightning, he grasped the situation. He leapt into action. The gun-crew followed his lead . . . Shells were falling all round. They were bursting close to the ship, scattering shrapnel all over . . . The enemy destroyers were so close that you could see the men in them. Gordon was sure that they hit one of the enemy vessels and maybe two . . .
>
> The *Morris*, together with the others, then formed a screen around Admiral Beatty's battle cruisers. Beatty lured the enemy on towards the great battleships of the Grand Fleet . . . Beatty's battle cruisers were joined by Admiral Hood with his battle

cruisers. Hood's flagship, the *Invincible*, led the fleet. In the *Invincible* was another young man from Whitchurch . . . Sub-Lieutenant Raymond Portal RN . . .

Shortly afterwards, Gordon was promoted, and appointed to the Royal Navy as a Sub-Lieutenant. On 6 June he wrote home: 'of course you know all about our scrap by now, the *Morris* played a prominent part . . . I have just written to Mrs Portal with the help of the Chief, telling her we were close to the *Invincible* when she went up and expressing my sympathy. I suppose it was up to me to do it . . . I am sorry for Portal, it was rather rotten for us to see those big ships going sky high, I had time to give him a thought but that was about all.'

On 15 September 1916, Gordon's promotion would be gazetted, 'for the cool and skilful way in which he, as officer of the quarters, while continuously under heavy fire, controlled the foremost 4-inch guns, the primary control having broken down.' As a souvenir, Gordon brought his parents a small piece of shell that had fallen near him in the battle. Charles had it mounted and, after his death, it passed to Tom, in whose library it still stands.

On 26 June, just before the expected big offensive on the Somme, Jack was hit in the head by shrapnel and sent back to the Casualty Clearing Station. Though his tin helmet saved him from worse injury, he was badly cut and could have been returned to base, or even to England; instead, he insisted on returning to the line. The main attack began on 1 July 1916 and the British sustained appalling losses. On that day 19,000 were killed and more than 35,000 were injured.

At this moment of national grief, Tom went up to Oxford to take Responsions and was given a room in Magdalen College. Nothing in his experience had prepared him for college life: he was moving into a new and more complex world, where he did not know the ropes and could not immediately fathom the roles of people whom he met. He so far mistook the position of Clement Webb, a Fellow of Magdalen, Classical Tutor and Secretary to the Tutorial Board, that on 8 July he sent a postcard home:

I hope to arrive by the 2.47 tomorrow, if not by the 4.34. The 'Moscow Expedition' [Napoleon's] today I thought quite alright but the unseen harder, yet I think I managed it fairly. I went to see Mr Webb, that secretary, last night. He was very inquisitive. The viva voce is in English tomorrow.

Tom was not kept long in suspense. By 12 July, Gordon was able to write from the *Morris*: 'I have just received Marjorie and Tom's letter, am so pleased he got through alright, I can't understand how he does it, if I had stayed at school for ever I am sure I could not, but I beat him in the Senior.'

The Battle of the Somme continued over the next three months, with unbelievable carnage on both sides. For every yard of land gained in the war of attrition being waged, the price was paid in lives and limbs. On 15 July Reg was gravely wounded and his battalion 'virtually wiped out'.[1] In *The Family Story* Lord Denning quoted his brother's account:

I was sleeping in a trench. (It had fallen in and buried me for a time.) At midnight an orderly arrived with the message, 'Get ready to move. We are to move forward to an appointed meeting place.' Enemy gas shells were falling all around. The Battalion Commander called the Company Commanders together . . . the enemy fire was intense . . . he said to us: 'Gentlemen, I do not know the objective, nor does the Brigadier, but we are to attack the enemy holding Pozieres' . . . He then gave orders which were the vaguest of the vague because he had received few from the Brigadier . . . I led my men to the attack. It was 7 o'clock in the morning. 'Come on, the Bedfords,' I shouted. We met a devastating fire. Many of my men fell . . . I saw some troops sheltering in disused trench, about 50 yards away. I dashed over to them, stood on the top of the trench and shouted to them, 'What are you doing? Who are you?' At that very moment I seem to remember a poleaxe blow on my head which felled me and toppled me into the trench.

The poleaxe was a bullet which passed through Reg's shoulder and into his head, from the neck to above the ear. He was left for dead and troops clambered over his body as they moved forward to the attack.

All day he passed in and out of consciousness until, late in the evening, someone realised he was alive and a corporal carried him back on his shoulders. At the Casualty Clearing Station an emergency operation was performed before Reg was sent back to England.

Still in the trenches, Jack was promoted to Acting Captain. On 20 August he wrote home: 'The more trenches I join the larger the rats seem to be, they are retrievers here not terriers.' He followed with interest the arrangements being made for Marjorie's marriage to take place in September. A period that should have given Clara particular pleasure was spoilt for her by the absence of Jack and Gordon. 'Personally I don't see,' Jack wrote on 2 September, 'why you should not have a jolly wedding, it would not worry me in the least, I'll bet if I'm home, fur will fly a bit.' A fortnight later Reg, back home in Whitchurch, wrote to Gordon: 'Things are in full swing for the wedding, presents rolling in etc; several people have been in to congratulate Dad on your performance.' In a PS Reg added that Clara would be sending Gordon's washing that night. One of the more fascinating aspects of the Denning correspondence is the revelation that from the time the children left home, Clara did the laundry that they regularly sent home.

The brief period when life at home may have had a semblance of normality for Charles and Clara was ended abruptly when it was found that, as a result of his wound, Reg had an aneurism of the occipital artery. He was taken into hospital at Tidworth, where a plate was put into his head which remained there for the rest of his life.

On 24 September Jack learned that his company would be involved in an attack to be launched, the next day, in the region of Guedecourt. 'He wrote in pencil a letter home and put it in his valise. It moves me to tears even now when I read it.'[1]

Sept. 24 16
10.30 a.m.

My own dearest Mother and Dad,
    This may or may not be my last letter to you, as we are for it I think tomorrow. I sincerely hope it will be successful. At all events I am determined to go in and win as I know you would have me do.

I know you may think this rather ridiculous especially if I come through alright.

But you may rest assured that should I get pipped I shall have done my duty, and always remember it is far better to die with honour than to live in shame.

This must be necessarily a short letter as we are moving shortly.

The main object is that to please me, do not worry if I get pipped.

I was awfully pleased to hear Gordon had been recommended and his promotion. Please congratulate him for me if I don't have the opportunity.

Well, darlings, best love to all I know, I am

Ever your loving boy,

Jack.

Denning sets out in full the description given in the War Diary of the action on 24 September and comments: 'There it is: the Regiment lost two Company Commanders (one of them Jack), 8 officers and 25% of other ranks. Nothing had been gained. The battalion had to withdraw. Had someone blundered?' The verdict of history is that, indeed, on the Somme someone had blundered. In the *Oxford English History* of 1914–1945, A. J. P. Taylor wrote: 'Kitchener's army found its graveyard on the Somme. Not only men perished. There perished also the zest and idealism with which nearly three million Englishmen had marched forth to war.'

Jack lay for three hours, with a piece of shrapnel through his stomach, before he was found and taken back to the Casualty Clearing Station. 'They got him there by 10 p.m. As he was taken in he said to a comrade next him, "I'm done for" . . . He was wandering all night, murmuring of home. He died in the morning of the 26th . . . They buried him in the war cemetery at Heilly-sur-Somme. They stamped out his name on a piece of tin and tacked it on to a rough wooden cross.'[1]

The telegram reached Whitchurch on 28 September when Gordon was home on leave. 'Mother opened it with trembling fingers. "Deeply regret to inform you that Capt. J. E. N. P. Denning Lincolnshire Regt. died of wounds Sept 26." Mother swooned to the floor.' Charles, with tears in his eyes, bent to pick Clara up. Tom never forgot the sight.

In *The Family Story* Tom recalls that he and Gordon went over to Tidworth together to tell Reg. 'He was ill in bed. We told him that Jack had been killed. He turned over. He sobbed and sobbed. Jack was his beloved brother – his hero.'

A visit to one dangerously ill brother, so soon after hearing of the death of another, must have been traumatic for the battle-seasoned 19-year-old Gordon and even more shocking for 17-year-old Tom. Tom clearly did not remember what was said. More likely, they went intending to tell Reg but held back when they saw how ill he was. On 7 October 1916 Gordon wrote to his parents: 'Hope mother found Reg alright at Tidworth today. Let me know when he is told of Jack.' On 9 October, after hearing that another operation had been performed on Reg, Gordon wrote to Tom: 'Poor old Reg: fancy having to cut him open again . . . I am rather glad it was the Colonel who told him about Jack as he could do it better than anyone else . . .' On 10 October Gordon wrote to Reg: 'It was hard to sit by your bed and cheer up and keep that awful news from you . . . buck up and get well, old Son! We want you more than ever now, you must be Jack as well now.' In Gordon's letters, throwaway remarks about a persistent 'cold' foreshadowed, had the family known, the further trouble that would soon afflict them.

'Well, my son,' asked Gordon on 9 October, 'are you all ready for Oxford . . .' Eager but apprehensive, a few days later, Tom went up to Magdalen, determined to make the most of the nine months left to him, before he would be 18½ and old enough to serve. 'Magdalen has been the college,' he would write, 'which has helped me to grow to what I am. It was founded by William of Waynflete over 500 years ago for just such as me – "a home for poor scholars." ' In 1916 Magdalen would not have recognised itself in that description; it had become, socially, one of the most prestigious of the Oxford colleges, the one at which the Prince of Wales was an undergraduate from 1912 to 1914.

The man who presided over Magdalen College was more than a figurehead. Sir Thomas Herbert Warren was a Balliol man, a fine classicist and good games player, who had been elected to a prize fellowship at Magdalen in 1877, the year after he had taken his degree, and was to remain there until his retirement in 1928. He played a great part in the development of the college, particularly after he was elected president, at the early age of 32. He had an unusual combination of scholarship, personal warmth and concern for his pupils and the political skills needed to promote the college. He increased the numbers of undergraduates and made every effort to improve the quality of both scholars and commoners. It was said that Warren was too concerned with the social standing of his under-graduates; his attitude to Tom, which was wholly disinterested and beneficent, disproves this.

4

Freshman and Subaltern

Oxford, in 1916, was a very different place from the large
industrial town it has become today. The countryside came
close to the east side of town, where the grounds of Magdalen College
are bounded by High Street and Longwall Street and a lovely stretch
of river. Around the central cloister of the college are many small
quads and buildings of all shapes and sizes. Tom's rooms were on the
first floor in Chaplain's Quad, 'right alongside the tower, whence
chimes vibrated and sounded into the rooms every quarter of an
hour.'[1] Tom, who had always shared a room with his brothers, now
slept alone; he who had pumped water from the well for his family to
use, now had a scout – a college manservant – who climbed the stone
staircase each morning with a big pail of cold water and poured it into
a round, low hip bath for Tom to use.

Oxford, that year, was empty – Tom was one of about twenty in
Magdalen – as most young men were in the services. The few
undergraduates were either medically unfit, Rhodes Scholars from
the United States or boys who were under age and awaiting their
call-up. While they waited, their military training and the process of
turning them into army officers was begun. Each morning after a
swift dip in the hip bath Tom 'got quickly into shorts – ran up the
High, along New College Lane, and into the Park – where we had to
parade. There we drilled and got the feel of military discipline.' The
young men lined up in alphabetical order: 'A for Armstrong
(afterwards Sir Thomas Armstrong, Principal of the Royal College of
Music); B for Bowra (afterwards Sir Maurice Bowra, great Oxford
wit); C (I forget); D for me.' Much of Tom's time was spent in
uniform and he was photographed in it outside Keble College, which
had been requisitioned as a barracks.

He might have to do a route march over Boar's Hill, learn bayonet

47

fighting, 'which I think is very interesting'[6] or go on night manoeuvres in Wytham Park but, between times, Tom worked hard for Mathematics Moderations, to be taken in June 1917, attending tutorials with A. L. Pedder, 'a dry old stick', who puffed away at his pipe, 'throwing spent matches over his shoulder into the fireplace.'

In The Park at Whitchurch, Portals and Harveys, home for the holidays, had played football and cricket with the local boys but had not invited them to their homes. Tom had little social experience of the men he was about to meet at Magdalen. Confident in his intellectual ability, serious yet humorous, self-deprecating and light of touch in relationships within his family and social circle, he was not sure whether he would be accepted by the public school men who made up, almost entirely, the university population.

Often freshmen asked one another, 'What school were you at?' Most men in my day were apt to name a famous public school. I turned the question on its side or prevaricated in one way or another. I felt ashamed at having been at grammar school. But I need not have worried. Everyone was very understanding.[1]

Despite reduced numbers and the restraints of war-time, to a marked extent Oxford life was as charmed as before. An American, at Magdalen from 1915 to 1919, described a typical Oxford man as 'well-read', though sport played an important part in his life; a reader of The Times; an 'unorthodox' Tory; given to a kind of slang that drops all but the first syllable of familiar words; using 'rugger' for Rugby, 'brekker' for breakfast and 'jaggers' for Jesus College. This 'typical' young man might belong to an artistic set, the severely intellectual set, the riding and racing set or the 'bloods', who drank champagne before breakfast![7] He might, as did J. Brett Longstaff, another American, visit the homes of the aristocracy, attend the theatre, dine out (still dressing for dinner), and even, if sufficiently privileged, go beagling with the Prince of Wales, who returned to Oxford for a day in 1915, specially for the occasion.[8]

Tom's life at Oxford was very different. Even if he had wanted to join such sets or participate in such activities, his finances would have prevented it. He was, as he described it, 'on very short commons'. The college Battels Ledger[9] records that, in the period from 30

September to 29 December, he spent a total of £32 3s 9d, which included £2 2s for college charges, 12s 6d for University dues and £8 8s for tuition. These fees were prescribed and there was no way in which Tom could economise on them. Where he could cut down he did. His room rent was £3 10s. Some men paid more than twice as much. Whereas most spent at least £1 on coal – and some spent more than £2 – Tom managed on 15s 10d and must often have been cold. Longstaff's book, written in 1965 but based on his contemporaneous letters home, makes several references to his friendship with Delmar Banner, who occupied rooms beneath his, next to the rooms reserved for the Prince of Wales's personal tutor (and costing £7 16s 8d). Banner, who was physically unfit for service, went up in 1914. He lived, according to Longstaff, in a 'beautiful' home at Bournemouth, overlooking the sea, and his family had two motor cars. He was 'really good to know – artistically stimulating.'[8] He was also, according to Denning, very good- looking. Despite the differences in their ages – Banner was in his final year when Tom was in his first – and backgrounds, the two men became good friends.

Tom gave much thought to his future. Fond as he was of his father, he turned for advice to his brothers. Where once he had talked to Jack about his career, now on 15 November 1916 he wrote to Reg a letter that betrays his immaturity and his youthful self-absorption:

I was awfully pleased to receive your letter this morning and to know you are again on service. I hope you will prove yourself again a good officer and second only to dear old Jack, whom I am sure no one could excel. He was born to be a soldier and had all the qualities to fit him for it, a splendid brain, a brilliant leader of men and great determination. Had he lived I feel confident England would never had produced a finer soldier.

Poor old Gord, I am sorry he is so bad, I hope it doesn't hinder his progress for he was getting on so well.

I feel very much now that I should like to go to Woolwich and have a regular commission. I think it would be putting my 'maths' to the best advantage. Dear old Jack talked it over with me on his last leave and I remember he said 'whatever you do, don't go into the poor old infantry; go into the artillery or engineers.' We couldn't quite decide whether I should be a civilian or a soldier. Jack did not seem averse to my taking a commission because we could see very much else really good and suited to me [Tom must have omitted the word 'not': 'we could *not* see']. Do you think I would make a good officer? Let me know what you think of the matter. Jack and I talked a good deal about it, even when we were going to the station to see him off . . . I could get into the navy now if I wished but am afraid I am not born to it as Gordon.

There remains engineering. But though I like it, I don't think it will satisfy my craving to be a leader of men and to travel, for I think I could manage men alright (that's just a little conceit so excuse it!) If I did do that I should of course join the Special Reserve. I must decide *now* what I shall do for I am at the parting of the ways. Against the army is the only point that I have a weak chin, which is really a great disadvantage for above all things a soldier must have great determination and will power and must be willing to take any risk in order to attain the desired end.

Thus there are left two openings – Engineering or the Army. Which? I am very ambitious, and I want to rise to the top and make a name. How shall I do it?

This is no doubt a lot of rot but they are my present thoughts. I must decide and that quickly . . .

At the end of the long letter, the reality of army service must have broken through: 'Don't go to France again if you can help it, I know Jack would not wish it, you have done your share,' then, a cry from the heart: 'I want to do mine, I am not doing enough just in the O.T.C.'

Tom had left Whitchurch at a time when his parents were still shattered by the blow of Jack's death, worried about Reg's serious condition and finding the greatest difficulty in keeping the business above water. The return of Jack's effects must have made more final the loss so far only manifested in a telegram.

'You know those two pipes Jack left behind?' Gordon wrote to Reg on 16 October. 'Well Dad has given me one and the other is for you. When I smoke mine I shall always think of 2 very fine soldiers, God bless them!' Gordon's 'cold' was causing more concern and, in November, tuberculosis, then a killer, was diagnosed and Gordon was transferred to the Royal Naval Hospital at Chatham. On the day that Tom was consulting Reg about his future, Gordon was telling his parents of his embarrassment at being given a blanket-bath by a young nurse. The Dennings were not accustomed to nudity. The following May, Tom would write home: 'Everyone here bathes without a costume – ladies of course are not allowed near the bathing place.'

While Tom was away in Oxford, his parents, at home, were bowed down with troubles. Clara had caught influenza. Financial difficulties loomed large. Apart from the usual problems with the business, Gordon would be expected to pay fees of two guineas a week when he was transferred to a sanatorium (though an application could be made to the Admiralty if these could not be afforded). Reg, who had taken over Jack's care for the family, offered to pay. 'Of course, my dear lad I would not allow you to pay my fee,' wrote Gordon on 23 November, 'you want your money for yourself.' Gordon was becoming weaker and his hopes of getting home for Christmas were dashed when he was sent to the King Edward VII Sanatorium at Midhurst. He had to console himself by going 'halves' with Reg in the purchase of a picture for their parents' Christmas present. Christmas 1916 could not have been a happy time for Charles and Clara, though they drew some comfort from having Tom home again.

The young man who returned to Whitchurch for Christmas had changed from the boy who went up to Oxford in October. 'I hear Tom is . . . transfixing all the girls in his O.T.C. uniform,' wrote Gordon on 13 December. But Clara was still a force to be reckoned with: 'I have been wearing "civies" today,' Tom told Reg, the same day, 'as mother doesn't want me to wear out my uniform.'

Tom was 6 foot 1½ inches tall and slimly built, with a fresh, still unshaven, oval face – of which the chin could hardly have been described, save by its owner, as weak – well-defined brows over brown eyes, straight nose and a full mouth, curved like a bow. Looking at the photograph taken in uniform it is not hard to believe he might transfix the girls, though at the time he was not interested in romance. If any girl appealed to him, it was Mary Harvey, whom he saw at the village dance in the Parish Hall; but he had not yet summoned up the courage to ask her to dance with him.

In January 1917, before he returned to Oxford, Tom went over to see Gordon in Midhurst. 'I was very pleased to see Tom yesterday,' Gordon wrote on 10 January, 'but it seems to me a lot of money for a short chat. I am sorry he missed his train, hope he arrived home alright.'

Sir Herbert Warren, like Mr Bishop before him, recognised the ability of the boy whose background and experience differed so much from those of the undergraduates who made up his usual intake. Tom's good humour and his combination of self-containment and eager interest in people about him may also have appealed to the man who had enough, perhaps, of the sophisticated and the world-weary. At all events, the 'President was very good to me. Owing to him my exhibition of £30 a year became a demyship of £80. (A demy is a scholar – a half-fellow.)'[1]

In March 1916 Tom had taken the Magdalen College examination for demyships. By 1917 the numbers of candidates had fallen still further because of the war and it seems that a group of colleges introduced a combined examination. Mr Pedder, Tom's tutor, was appointed the examiner for Magdalen and Tom must have been encouraged to take the examination in the hope of promotion to a demy. The College Tutorial Board proceedings for 10 March 1917 record his success. With the extra money, Tom could just about manage. He had never been inclined to self-indulgence and cut his expenses to the bone. Though scouts might be tipped liberally by wealthier undergraduates, 'they were very good: I don't think they expected much of me.' There was, just the same, little left over for clothes, fares and the small gifts Tom so much liked to give to members of his family.

Gordon's embarrassment at being given a blanket-bath was matched by Tom's, in chapel at Magdalen one Sunday. 'One of the demies is expected to read a lesson. I was taken unawares – in uniform – not with a surplice. I had not looked it up beforehand. I took the first reference that came in the Lectionary. It was *Genesis 39.7*. I read it out, getting more and more embarrassed as it told how Potiphar's wife made advances to Joseph.'

It was the first time, said Denning, that he had ever read any passage aloud, which alone might have caused him some uneasiness. The prescribed passage to be read aloud caused acute embarrassment to the adolescent boy brought up to believe in chastity and faithfulness in marriage. Tom's distress must have been plain for all to see. After the service, Clement Webb took him aside and 'consoled' him.

Tom was still thinking of applying to Woolwich, the army artillery school, when he sent home a form for Charles to sign, giving precise instructions. 'I will put the date in, he need not. Mind he signs in the right place. You notice,' he continues, 'some one has to be responsible for paying £35 and I don't suppose the pay will be sufficient to live on. Such being the case would you rather I didn't try too hard, as I would not stay in after the war. The entrance fee to the exam,' he added, since every pound was important, 'is £2.' Tom was devoted to both parents, but clearly recognised his mother's strength and his father's weakness of character – or, perhaps, that by comparison with Clara, her husband would always seem weak. Though it was Charles's signature that was required on the form the admonition 'mind he signs in the right place' was addressed to Clara.

Again Reg showed his determination to relieve his parents of financial worries. 'Tom says,' he wrote on 20 May, 'that on going to Woolwich an initial fee of £35 has to be paid. If he passes alright I am going to pay that for him.' As things turned out, Tom did not go to Woolwich or the artillery. In June 1917 a pitiably small number sat the seven papers of the Mathematics Moderations examination and Tom alone was placed in the First Class. There were five other successful candidates, including two women, who were, in those days, separately listed. '. . . undeserved,' Denning would write of his First Class, in *The Family Story*, 'the examiner must have made allowance.'

Britain's was no longer a volunteer army: conscription had been introduced in 1916. So far as Tom was concerned, it would have made no difference; as he wrote to Reg the previous November, he could scarcely wait to do his share. He was horrified to be told, after his medical examination, that he had a systolic murmur of the heart and was not fit to go to France. In later life, Denning would say that the doctor must have been tired of sending young men to the slaughter and was glad of an excuse to prevent one from going. At the time, he was very distressed and appealed, successfully, from the decision. 'I went to France,' he would write at the age of 80. 'My heart has never failed me.'

Denning enlisted at Basingstoke on 14 August 1917, as a Cadet in the Hampshire Regiment, and was attached to the Royal Engineers, Oxford University Officer Training Corps.[10] He was sent for training near Newark, where he was commissioned as a temporary second lieutenant on 17 November 1917. His daily rate of pay was 2s 6d – 17s 6d a week. Though he was old enough to serve, he would not be old enough to go to France until he reached his nineteenth birthday in January 1918. He was posted to barracks near Aldershot where, for the first time, he had his own horse. 'What I liked most was the horses. That war was fought with horses for transport. At any rate for our Field Company. We had them to pull the wagons for our pontoons and bridging equipment.'[1]

Whenever he was able, Tom got back to Whitchurch where his parents were under growing pressure. Neither was well. Trade was very poor. The shortage of food was becoming serious and Clara, who had always kept a good table, was finding difficulty in getting enough flour and potatoes. For a time Marjorie – whose husband was with his regiment – and her baby daughter, Betty, born in September 1917, stayed with her parents, a great boost to their morale, though they knew that, at any time, Marjorie might have to leave. Gordon had been transferred from the sanatorium at Midhurst to a hut in the garden of Bere Hill House, the Portals' home, which had been converted into a military hospital. The family spent as much time there as they could and Norman went to see Gordon every morning before going to school. It was only a brief respite for the young sailor; by the end of the year he had been transferred again, this time to a nursing home at Boscombe. His letters home still took a cheery line but the cheerfulness, now, was forced. The illness was taking its toll of his resources.

On 16 March, when Tom was on leave, he went to Boscombe with Clara and took Gordon for a drive along the front to Bournemouth. It was to be the last time he would see the brother with whom his early years had been so closely spent. Two days later Gordon wrote home: 'It will be nice for Tom to be at home once more as I expect he will soon be off.'

On 21 March the Germans began another offensive on the Somme and, within a few days, had advanced over 40 miles. Though reinforcements from England were increased, the Allies were still being forced to retreat. The Germans were only 40 miles from Paris, when on 12 April, Sir Douglas Haig, now Commander in Chief, delivered a personal message to the troops: 'Every position must be held to the last man: there must be no retirement. With our backs to the wall, and believing in the justice of our cause, each one of us must fight on to the end.' Yet more troops were sent from England and, at last, the time had come for Tom to do his share. Before he went, on 13 April, Denning drew up his first legal document, the 'privileged' will of a serving soldier, made without formalities, a class of testament on which he would deliver a masterly judgment after the Second World War.

In the event of my death I, Alfred Thompson Denning, bequeath the whole of my personal property and effects to my mother Clara Denning.

(Signed)
A. T. Denning
2/Lt RE

Whitchurch
Hants
13.4.18[6]

'We sailed from Southampton. We reached Rouen. Into the transit camp. We marched to the station. The band led us, playing the march *Colonel Bogey*; but left us at the yard gate. We clambered into the train with our equipment. A long slow ride till we heard the gunfire. Then I joined the Company with which I was to spend the remaining months of the war – the 151st Field Company of the Royal Engineers – attached to the 38th Welsh Division. I wore proudly the Red Dragon of Wales as an arm-flash.'[1]

By 27 April Gordon had heard from Tom. 'I had a cheery letter from Tom this morning;' he wrote to Reg, 'he had arrived at the Field Base, had a bath, found cheery companions and heard he had a good horse, so he seems happy.' When Tom wrote on 13 May, to send Gordon best wishes for his twenty-first birthday, there was a sense of anti-climax in his words: 'I am at present in hospital with German measles.'

The company was in the sector of the Somme opposite Albert, which was held by the Germans; night after night they dug in under shellfire. The River Ancre was flooded to a width of 200 to 300 yards and there were no bridges. The enemy held the other side in force. An entry in the *War Diary* for 15 August says baldly:

Lieut. Denning and 6 R E with light bridges got the infantry patrol across. The portable boat was quite useless. 25 men detailed for the purpose failed to get it along the main road.

'I remember those 25 men,' wrote Denning in *The Family Story*. 'They were an American contingent – newly arrived. They had been attached to our Division for instruction in the line. They dropped the portable boat every time they heard a shell coming. Our own men would have got it there.' It was rare for Denning to make acerbic remarks but the passage of years had dimmed neither the bitterness of the events nor his chauvinism.

From 21 to 24 August 1918 the infantry made the crossing of the Ancre. 'They had to wade at night through water up to their chests. We, the sappers, followed up making foot bridges across the river and the swamps – and repairing them – under continuous rifle fire. Then there was the task of getting the wheeled transport across – the guns and ammunition wagons.' Denning quotes from the *History of the 38th Welsh Division*: 'Meanwhile two battalions of the 115th Brigade had crossed the Ancre at Aveluy, over a bridge made by the 151st Field Company, RE, under the supervision of Lieuts. Denning and Butler.'

On 1 September Tom wrote home:

Dearest Mother and Dad,
Hope you are still well. We are at present having quite a good time, maintaining the bridge which we built. Today I had a day free so I rode over some distance to see Jack's grave. I found it and enclose the only two small flowers on it. That part of the country is very little hurt by shell fire or the war. The village itself is still very pretty. On the cross was

CAPTAIN M. P. DAWNING
1st LINCOLN REGT
26 SEPT 1916

I printed the name as well as I could on a board and stuck it in the ground. The grave maintenance people will very probably erect a new cross. It is a long way from here or I should get my men to make one. The cemetery has not of course been able to be kept in good condition lately, but the maintenance men will soon come along. I have written my name and the date I visited on the board there. Some other time – I can't say when – I hope to be able to get another cross, or a foot cross there.

I thought you would treasure these flowers, which were the only ones growing there.

It is all very peaceful there now.

Best love

Ever your loving boy

During the three months that Tom was in France, Gordon was sinking under his illness. His letters became more fretful, though he tried hard to remain cheerful. He derived comfort from a chat with the Roman Catholic Padre – 'What a wrong idea we were given as children concerning their faith –'[11] and from occasional visits from Constance Portal, a VAD who had nursed him at Bere Hill House, her home. 'I think Miss Portal's visit has done me a lot of good,' he wrote home on 15 April, 'she seems to know one's wants and feelings so perfectly.'

Since Gordon had been discharged from the navy and placed on the retired list, Clara had pressed the Admiralty for a pension for him, but Gordon himself was becoming slowly reconciled to the inevitable end of his illness. He derived much comfort from religion and was still concerned for his parents and interested in what the family were doing. On 7 May 1918 he told Reg that Marjorie who 'has been a great help and comfort' to their parents, 'is going to her hubby.' Then, he went on: 'I sometimes try to imagine the glory of "yonder", . . . and one lives more for our life "yonder", re-united again; and thinks less of this life, which is merely preparation to "yonder".' Above all else, Gordon wanted to go home to die.

On 16 May he wrote again to Reg:

It is a struggle, old Sportsman, but Dennings do not lose spirit, do they? . . .

I am longing for tomorrow when mother arrives. It is some time since I saw her and never in my life have I wanted her as I do now . . .

I feel proud to be an Englishman.

On 22 May, four days after his twenty-first birthday, Clara, on whose courage Gordon now depended, with a nurse collected Gordon and took him home in an ambulance. The room the boys had shared was now deserted and Gordon slept there alone. 'In the evening he asked Mother to read the *23rd Psalm*. As she read it, he kept pace with his hand on the bedclothes . . . He died the next morning.'[1]

Clara wrote to tell Tom and Reg, who was also back in France, and Tom replied, asking her to tell them of Gordon's last hours. She wrote 'in her firm bold hand' on 10 June 1918:

You would like to know what dear Gordon had to say to me at the last. He asked me to sit by him and hold his hand. Then he said: 'Give my love to the boys, Marjorie, Johnnie. Give my love to Miss Portal and Mrs Portal.' Then he said: 'Mother, I've got a little money for you and Dad. You have the model of the *Hampshire*. She was a fine ship. I had a nice time in her. My best shipmates went down in her.' After 'My love to Mrs Portal,' he said: 'Sweethearts – no, I have no sweehearts. This is my sweetheart, the only sweetheart I have,' and tapped my head . . . that was in the middle of the night . . . In the middle of the morning he pushed me a little way off and waved such a sweet goodbye. I cannot write it as I could tell you.[1]

So Gordon died six days after his twenty-first birthday, and left Tom his dressing-case, while Tom was in France on the River Ancre.

In *The Family Story* Denning recalls working under fire; on one occasion, 'we had to make a roadway across the marshes with logs and sleepers and anything we could lay our hands on. We had to erect

trestles and crossbeams and road-decks to get across the river itself.'
As they worked, shells were falling and enemy aircraft flew low
overhead to signal to the German gunners the position of the bridge
they were building. After a direct hit on the bridge, Denning and his
engineers had to start again, working two days and nights without
sleep. Later, Denning's company had to get pontoons over the Canal
du Nord, to replace bridges that had been destroyed. Again they
worked under shellfire, but this time were supposed to perform the
whole operation in gas masks (which they did not).

There were other crossings made too. 'I can still see the line of
infantry advancing under heavy fire – first one falling and then
another – with us following close behind them. I can still see the
battlefield strewn with hundreds of our best officers and men – lying
dead – shot as they went forward. I can still see the dead horses lying
in piles beside the roads; and dead Germans black in the face. Such is
war.'[1]

The Great War left its mark on all who lived through it. Tom
became disenchanted with commanders who, between 1914 and
1918, sent to their deaths three-quarters of a million men from the
United Kingdom alone; with bureaucrats who condemned disabled
survivors to plead for pensions that should, by right, have been
theirs. He remained idealistically patriotic. This combination of
contempt for officialdom and love of country would bear fruit in
Denning's time on the Bench. In his middle years – his most
splendidly innovative – he became known as the champion of the
underdog.

As things turned out, he was in no state to appreciate the end of
hostilities on 11 November 1918; he had fallen victim to the epidemic
of influenza that was raging across Europe; three days before the
Armistice he was taken by ambulance train to the base hospital at
Rouen. 'It was filled with sick men. So many that the nurses could not
cope with the need. One after another died in our ward. The
Armistice was at 11 a.m. on 11 November 1918. There was little
rejoicing in our ward. Too many were ill. There was relief. That was
all.'[1]

5

Oxford

In England, 17 November 1918 was designated Thanksgiving Sunday. Special prayers were said at services and, so the *Hampshire Chronicle* reported, 'the hymns were of a joyful character.' Before and after Evensong the church bells were rung. Four days later the Whitchurch Workhouse Treat took place and Mary Harvey attended with her mother. 'The inmates were given a tea of bread, butter, eggs and cake, being afterwards entertained by, amongst others, Mr Geer singing "Peg-away" and pupils of the Modern School playing the piano.'[12]

After the initial euphoria, the dancing in the streets, the crowding into the pubs when it was known that the war, at last, was over, the mood had sobered. Quietly, the country waited the return of its young men. In the House of Commons the Minister of Reconstruction made a detailed statement on plans for demobilisation. The order was to be governed by industrial requirements and broad social considerations. Drafts were to go first to concentration camps (the term had not then the ugly connotation it would later acquire) and after to a dispersal station at home. Each soldier was to receive a protection certificate, a railway warrant and a cash payment. Each would have 28 days leave on full pay. For a year after demobilisation, nearly all permanent civil service appointments were to be reserved for ex-servicemen.

Not long after the Armistice, Tom was discharged from hospital and sent to a convalescent home at Cap Martin, in the South of France. He was still weak but enjoyed a brief respite in the company of young officers from other allied armies. He arrived back in England early in February 1919 and was sent to a camp at Porton, not far from Salisbury, before being allowed home. His protection certificate, dated 5 February, stated that he would be gazetted out of service with the rank of Temporary 2nd Lieutenant on 6 February 1919 'unless he hears to the contrary from the War Office, on and after which date he will not be entitled to draw pay.' Despite the diagnosis of the medical examiner in 1917, Denning was discharged in the medical category A1. A gratuity of £35 provided a small nest-egg to help him on his way.

The only shadow on Tom's homecoming was the condition of his father. Even before Tom had left England, both he and Reg had known only too well how poor were the returns on the business. In May 1918, Reg had written to his parents offering to pay boarding fees for Norman and had advised: 'I still think you ought to get out of the business . . .' After Gordon's death, Charles had suffered a nervous breakdown and, when his sons learned he would be giving up business, Reg wrote: '. . . I think you have done the right thing and have been guided by God to do it . . . I think it would be very nice if we could have the old house made into a private home and then you could live there. I could let you have a £1 a week and then with your little coming in I think it would be sufficient . . .'

On his return to Whitchurch, Tom became painfully aware that, though Charles and Clara were still living in their old home, the property now belonged to the rival draper across the road. Tom described to the writer the sequence of events, as he had been told them: After Gordon's death his parents were devastated. When his father found 'he hadn't got enough cash coming in to pay the bills', he consulted the local solicitor and asked what he should do. He was told: 'Oh, I wouldn't see those London men for a hundred pounds.' He was advised to present his own petition in bankruptcy and, unwilling to burden his serving sons with this new grief, that is what, on 13 July 1918, he had done. 'A tremendous mistake,' recalled Denning, '. . . some of those travellers coming afterwards said to us, "Why on earth didn't you come to us?" But there it was. We were away and no one helped the poor old thing.' Charles was particularly distressed that it should have been Mr Nash, another draper, who purchased the two houses: 'in a way he felt he was letting down my mother . . . because these are those houses given them to start off with.' It must have fuelled Charles's feeling of failure that his parents-in-law had also to be involved; since 1904 the deeds of the property had been deposited with them as security for the loan made, at that time, to Charles and in 1918 they were required to join in the conveyance to the purchaser. Charles and Clara were able to live as tenants above the shop until, in 1922, Reg bought a house for them, close by All Hallows Church.

There must have been in Tom, to achieve so much as he has, a streak of iron determination. There was also a high degree of self-absorption. To a large extent the family were responsible for it: Clara had always regarded Tom as special. His elder brothers – though he regarded them as heroes – also marvelled at his ability and gave solemn consideration to his ambitions when he was barely more than a boy. Once Tom was set upon a certain goal, his affection for his family and his desire to help them, would not be seen – by him or by them – as an impediment to its fulfilment. It never occurred to any of them that Tom might possibly give up his university career to find a job. Rather it seemed that there was only one thing to do and Tom did it: four days after his discharge from the army he returned to Oxford. He did not neglect his parents' problems. He arranged to see a barrister in Lincoln's Inn – the events had for so long been suppressed that he could no longer remember the details – and was advised that it was too late to do anything about the bankruptcy. Whilst he was in London, Tom also went to the Ministry of Pensions to try to obtain some increase of the 'pittance' Charles and Clara were receiving. His first dealings with a ministry were not a great success but fuelled Denning's determination in later years to improve the lot of those unfortunate enough to depend on bureaucracy for a pension. The entire unhappy episode left Tom with a lasting determination that his finances would be placed on a sound footing.

Denning returned to Oxford on 10 February 1919, to lodgings in the High Street, just opposite Magdalen College. He spent the first afternoon in the Physics Laboratory, where he was told to tie a piece of cotton to a lead weight. 'It took me two hours before the demonstrator was satisfied. That decided me. Not Applied Mathematics for me. Only Pure Mathematics. That depends on reasoning, not on mechanical aptitude.' Tom was 'never anything of a mechanic. If the car breaks down – even if a wheel has to be changed – I am no good at it.'[1]

Regardless of preference, the Regulations for the 1920 Examination in the Honours School of Mathematics provided that half the

Examination would be in Pure and half in Applied Mathematics. Amongst the subjects to be studied were the Elements of the Algebra of Quantics, an *Introduction* to which was the most important published work of the Waynflete Professor of Pure Mathematics and Fellow of Magdalen, E. B. Elliott, 'a nice old thing', as Denning remembered him. In 1919, Elliott was in his sixty-eighth year, a retiring man, but known for his helpfulness. According to the *Dictionary of National Biography*, 'He cared deeply for the integrity of mathematics and had little patience with specious half-proofs or unsupported speculation.' The grounding Denning received in building, from point to point, a line of thought, would bear fruit in the lucidity of his legal decisions.

Tom's mathematics – other than the type needed for emergency bridge-building – were rusty. He went once a week to his tutor, A. L. Pedder, but, for the rest, he concentrated on his reading. The most important Oxford influence upon Denning, as he had been before Tom enlisted, was Clement Webb, an authority on the philosophy of the Christian religion. With his 'very nice wife', Mr Webb used to invite undergraduates to lunch at their attractively furnished house, directly over a waterfall, which, at one time, was the grist mill for the college. The visits were something of an ordeal for Tom, who remained 'so shy' that he feared he would not know what to say. He need not have worried; the Webbs were skilled at putting young visitors at their ease and drawing them out about their hopes for the future.

There were more men in Oxford than there had been in 1917. Tom found new acquaintances, including Edward Bridges, son of the Poet Laureate, who was to become Secretary of the Cabinet during the Second World War and head of the Civil Service. His friends came, as he did, from staunchly Church of England backgrounds. They expected the brave new world fit for heroes, that had been promised to them, to come firmly rooted in the past and built upon traditions they valued.

While Tom had been away, prices had risen and the change was reflected in the increase of, perhaps, £5 on the average quarterly battels. For the moment tuition fees remained £8 8s a quarter, but in the next term they would rise to £10 – not an inconsiderable amount from Tom's limited pocket. The Magdalen Battels Ledger lists his quarterly college bills for his time at Oxford:

4th quarter	1916	£32.. 3s. . 9d
1st "	1917	£32.. 2s. . 8d
2nd "	"	£32.. 5s. . 3d
1st "	1919	£23.. 5s. . 9d
2nd "	"	£44.. 12s. . 6d
3rd "	"	£0.. 18s. . 6d
4th "	"	£50..11s. . 7d
1st "	1920	£52..17s. ..11d
2nd "	"	£54..3s. . 4d
3rd "	"	£2..18s. . 9d

Tom's battels give only his college expenses. To set them in context there is, in the Magdalen Archives, a letter from a man who described himself (in 1986) as having been 'a necessarily economical under-graduate', but who spent in an equivalent period some 13 per cent more than Tom. In the period 1922–3, the man's battels for the autumn term totalled £58 4s 10d, for the Lent term £61 0s 8d and for the summer term £58 15s 8d. Seven years later, Warren's successor considered that an undergraduate could manage 'with care' on £260 a year[13] – and inflation could not have been responsible for this increase.

In 1919 Tom was not ardent for change. He never sought in politics a solution to the social problems that seemed to him most pressing: the rigid class distinctions and the position of women in society. Though he joined the Union, Tom did not feel at home there; he rarely attended and never spoke in a debate. He had neither the money nor the inclination to join in wining and dining, however modest. He would have been amused by a motion proposed at a meeting of the JCR on 26 October 1919 that the authorities be asked to allow lunches – an important part of college social life – to be served in rooms. Lunching in rooms played little part in Tom's life: only on one occasion, when the vicar of Whitchurch, his future father-in-law, visited Oxford, did he take advantage of the facility. Nor was he interested in any of the proliferating clubs and societies, literary and political, dramatic and musical. He was so intent upon getting his First that he put aside even the classics that he had enjoyed and confined his reading to his work. When he went home at the end of term, he was reasonably satisfied with his progress.

Tom was 20 years old and, despite his war experiences, still immature. He had never had a girlfriend. He had known Mary since 1910, when her family came to Whitchurch; he had glanced 'shyly' at her in church since both were confirmed in 1914; he had admired her from afar but never became acquainted with her until this first vacation after his discharge from the army.

Mary Harvey came of clerical stock on both sides. Her maternal grandfather, William Lewery Blackley, was an honorary canon of Winchester, described in the *Dictionary of National Biography* as a man 'whose Irish humour and eloquence made him an attractive platform speaker.' He was an accomplished linguist and capable parochial organiser; an advocate of temperance and the sponsor of a scheme for compulsory national insurance, as a means of eradicating 'pauperism'. Mary had been educated by a governess before being sent to Upper Chine School at Shanklin, on the Isle of Wight, then on to Reading University to study agriculture. She was a tomboy, fond of games and animals, with an outgoing personality. During the spring vacation, her acquaintance with Tom became a budding friendship.

On his side it was more than friendship. His early romantic interest in heroic subjects was now replaced by equally romantic, though at that time hidden, love of the lady. Mary, as he described her in *The Family Story*, was, at 19, 'not pretty. She was not fair. But she was good by nature and good to look at. The first glance showed her bright dark brown eyes sparkling with intelligence. Next her well-shaped mouth and chin, ready to break into the most welcoming of smiles at the least provocation. Her nose was fine and straight . . . Her complexion was clear . . . Overtopping all was her long black hair, falling a little over her wide open forehead. Never cut short. Always tied at the back of her head.' Tom was captivated by her.

He returned to Oxford for the summer term, 'one of the happiest of my life.' With examinations still a year away, warm weather, blue skies and Oxford at its most beautiful, those were halcyon days for Tom. Though his voice was not thought good enough for the choir at Whitchurch, on May morning, at break of day, robed in his white surplice, he, with the other demies, climbed the 200 steps to the top of the tower and sang. He had rooms in Cloisters. 'Each morning we used to run round "Adders" – our short name for Addison's Walk –

and plunge into our swimming pool [the river] in the nude. One morning a girl student came round the corner in a canoe. We had to stay in the water – shivering – whilst she went paddling by.'[1]

Most mornings he attended lectures or worked. In the afternoons he might take out a punt or canoe on the river, play tennis or, occasionally, cricket for Magdalen's second eleven. He could cycle in the countryside or sit in the sun and talk. He looked forward to the occasional parcel from Clara containing a cake.

The idyllic summer term was followed by a joyous vacation, during which Tom's friendship with Mary blossomed. He scarcely noticed that the country suffered, in that summer of 1919, as miners, police and then railwaymen went on strike; sugar and meat rations were reduced and there was concern about the delivery of milk and mail. Denning, in love, was alive with happiness. He played tennis with Mary at the Vicarage; he mowed the lawn for her; as summer turned to autumn he picked apples and helped her to store them. They rode their bicycles together in the still untarred and dusty lanes around Whitchurch; they took photographs and developed them in the Vicarage. When he tried to tell her how beautiful he thought her, she put him off. ' "You look at me through rose-coloured spectacles," she said. "Do not put me on a pedestal. I am not worth it." '[1] She enjoyed his friendship, but did not want to speak of love. He, a true romantic, could only think in terms of devotion.

Though the summer term of 1919 had been partly set aside for pleasure, the months leading up to the examination in 1920, when Tom would be awarded another First Class, were almost totally dedicated to work. Tom was to enjoy one happy, carefree day when, a week before the examination, Mary visited him in Oxford. It was in Eights Week, when Oxford takes to the river and girls in summer dresses line the towpath and clamber into punts or college barges to watch boyfriends and brothers row in 'the bumps'. That particular stretch of river not being wide enough for overtaking, the tradition evolved of one college's boat overhauling another's and bumping it in order to take its place in the league table, wildly cheered by the spectators, a scene described by Max Beerbohm in *Zuleika Dobson*, when the question on all lips was, 'Would Judas bump Magdalen?'

The shy, romantic young man looked forward eagerly to the day of Mary's visit from the moment when she promised to come. His pleasure at the sight of her was very slightly overcast for, though it was a glorious day, Mary and her friend 'were not wearing their pretty summer dresses. They came in coats and skirts. It had been raining before they left Reading. Such a disappointment for a lovesick swain!'[1] The disappointment was momentary: the glorious day was remembered long after Mary's death; it encouraged him in the days after Schools (the examinations), which, for many, are a giddy round of enjoyment, a last carefree fling before entering one's chosen profession. The trouble for Tom was that he had not chosen a profession. Strangely, for one whose eyes had been fixed on the stars, he decided that mathematics could lead only to teaching. He no longer thought of the army, nor of engineering. More in a spirit of resignation than of choice, he applied for a teaching post at Charterhouse School and one at Winchester College, which offered one.

Two curious circumstances surrounded Tom's decision. It seems that Tom could, if he wished, have remained in College for another year. The Tutorial Board Minutes for 20 July 1920 state:

> 3. Mr Denning was re-elected to his Demyship for one year: but on condition that he should not receive the emoluments for such time as he is not in residence . . .

Moreover, his appointment to Winchester was not, as first envisaged, to last more than one term. As a side note to the minutes is written:

> Mr Denning has been appointed to a Mastership at Winchester College for one term but was not assured of its continuance after Christmas: and if it were not continued, intended to return and study History with a view to the Civil Service Examination.

Did Tom, as he would afterwards write to Mary, believe that if she married him, she would be happy at Winchester? Or did the salary of £350 a year and his innocence of the world outside Whitchurch and Oxford combine to overcome his dreams of earth-shaking? Above all, what made Tom take the risk of accepting what could have proved only one term's employment? At all events in August 1920 the Headmaster of Winchester reported to the Warden and Fellows of the College:

After prolonged search in England and America, I have secured a young man of good ability, Mr A. T. Denning, who comes with an excellent Mathematical record . . . He also was a Lieutenant in the R.G.A., and saw one and a half year's active service. As Mr Broomfield is anxious to have a period of rest and a 'grace term' is long overdue to him, I arranged that Mr Denning should begin work in September . . .

It can never be easy for a shy, young man to walk into his first classroom as a teacher. How much more difficult for the graduate of a grammar school, at a time when the majority of Winchester masters had themselves attended public schools and many were from Winchester itself. Tom was wary of the boys and they were wary of him.

Tom was in Winchester when, the minutes of the Magdalen JCR meeting on Sunday 10 October report, votes of congratulations were passed unanimously to those who had distinguished themselves in the summer term: 'to Mr A. T. Denning on obtaining 1st Class in Mathematical Finals' and to all those who had rowed in the three events won by the College at Henley.

He taught mathematics at all levels of the school and 'Geology to the sixth form – reading it up the night before.'[1] It was said that the boys were not above ragging him when occasion arose; even his Hampshire burr would have been a source of amusement to youngsters used to the strangulated vowels and plum-in-the-mouth tones of the public schools of that day. Hilary Bell, who was a small boy at the time, remembered 'he had a very loud voice which could be heard all over Flint Court when he was teaching.'[14] (Had the boys but known it, this was a sign of nervousness: in his early days at the Bar, Denning's voice would rise at moments of stress.) He was, none the less, a good teacher. A boy who was 'up to him' for mathematics for one term only, R. Greiffenhagen, wrote to the author in 1990 when he was in his eighties, 'Hitherto the subject had been outside whatever gifts I had, but in that term he nearly corrected this situation and imbued me with a thirst for knowledge . . . [I] was looking forward eagerly to next term', but by the next term Denning had left Winchester. 'I have never had such a stimulating teacher', concluded Mr Greiffenhagen, 'if he could teach me, he could do anything: and he did.' It took Tom very little time to decide that, whether or not he was a good teacher, he must have more from life than to be a schoolmaster.

Some time during the summer vacation Tom had proposed to Mary and been refused. She told him 'there was another before me.'[1] She said her parents were against the match because the man was so much older than she. She did not tell Tom the name of that other nor does it seem, strangely, that Tom ever asked. Since Mary was not willing to marry him but did not discourage his friendship, Tom, in true romantic tradition, pressed his suit and waited for her to change her mind. He discussed his plans with her and sought her advice. She, for her part, though warning him that she was not in love with him, must have regarded him with more than ordinary friendship, since she kept the letters that he sent her from Winchester College. 'She told me tenderly – in words that she did not love me,' recalled Tom, in *The Family Story*. 'But in all other ways she did. She used to milk the cows each morning. She got up very early – before the household was awake. So did I. I would wait for her at our trysting place.'

To an extent, Mary must have felt constrained by social pressures. Tom's commission and those of his brothers had started his generation of the Denning family on their way across then rigid class barriers; Tom's years at Oxford were another step in that direction. Still Mary, as the vicar's daughter, was welcomed in circles where Tom would not have been invited. Those circles no longer included the numbers of bachelors to be found in pre-war days; there was a shortage of eligible young men. The First World War had bequeathed the world a generation of spinsters and maiden aunts and those women who found husbands came to consider themselves fortunate. Consciously or unconsciously, Mary had to come to terms with these problems – difficult to understand at a distance of 70 years – before she could admit love for Tom.

Although Tom did not take to schoolmastering, he was fond of the old city of Winchester and its Cathedral. He was made welcome at Minster House, immediately opposite the west end of the cathedral, the lovely eighteenth-century home of Tom Woodham, married to her mother's sister Norah, where Mary stayed when she was in Winchester. He cycled home for an afternoon 'quite often', though he did not always find Mary, who had gone to help on a farm at

Leominster. For her birthday, on 24 September, he gave her a copy of Ruskin's *Sesame and Lilies*. The young man who believed it wrong to confine young women of the upper classes to flower arrangement and charitable works and wrong to send girls, still children, from the lower classes out to service, found appealing Ruskin's view on the roles of men and women: 'You bring up your girls as if they were meant for sideboard ornaments, and then complain of their frivolity. Give them the same advantages that you give their brothers – appeal to the same grand instincts of virtue in them; teach *them*, also, that courage and truth are the pillars of their being.'

Sometime in his first term, Tom wandered into the Assizes at Winchester Castle and listened, from the public gallery, to the arguments in a civil case. 'I felt "That is what I should like to do. I would like to become a barrister as I told Mother long ago!" ' In *The Family Story* Denning states that he went back to Sir Herbert Warren in July 1921 and asked his advice. He must, in fact, have approached Warren some time earlier, because on 21 November 1920 he wrote to Mary from Chernocke House, Winchester:

> It being Sunday – a day on which I usually write letters – I now write to you. The President of Magdalen has written saying that my letter needs consideration but that they will do so in my interest. So that I must wait to hear from him. I have no doubt that he will advise me well.

Tom, who has clearly either discussed the matter with Mary or exchanged letters with her on the subject, adds: 'I am however almost decided that it will be better for me to stay here, for you say so.' In character, he looks to the bright side: 'I think that I shall like it. I thought at first that I should be unpopular on account of my severity but I hope to overcome that.' He had been invited to tea by a boy whose parents lived in Winchester. So, after all, he thought, he cannot have been too much disliked! Then, again, his youthful enthusiasm bursts out: 'I have now to set examination papers which will be printed. It will be strange but rather interesting to see my own work in print. What a child I am!'

Though he tried to put a brave face on his position, Tom remained restless, despondent and still very unsure of himself. On 26 November he wrote again:

. . . sometimes I feel that things are going all wrong, that I do not teach the boys in the right way, that I am too lenient but perhaps I may gradually get to do things better . . .

I feel restless again today. I feel that I don't want to settle down here doing the same thing day after day, a very mediocre schoolmaster with no ambition and no hope . . .

I have boundless ambition and today I want to cast myself free from here, go back to Oxford and once more throw myself with full force into that upward flight and either succeed or fall, before the tentacles here close round me and drag me down to the mediocrity and the monotony which is death . . .

'Perhaps,' he added, 'when I decided to come here I was playing for safety, well, not quite that, but that I felt if ever you came to me you would be happy.'

Before he went home for the holidays, Tom selected from a jeweller in Winchester two small brooches, intending Mary to choose one for Christmas. One, he reported in *The Family Story*, was 'a thin silver bar with a stone of amethyst.' As he was seeing her home from a party, they stepped into the church porch, and he showed her the brooches. "It is beautiful," she murmured, "but I cannot accept it." She ran off down the Vicarage path.'[1] Tom was greatly disappointed but Mary seems to have been more discomfited than the event warranted. She wrote, that night, from the Vicarage a letter that is inconsistent with Tom's recollection that she refused the brooch immediately:

1.15 am Thursday

Tom, dearest Lad,
It hurts me more than I can tell to write this, and to do what I feel I must do, that is to return those beautiful brooches.

I didn't realise what you were giving me. I had no right to accept anything at all and I *know* it would be wrong to accept such as these.

Oh, Lad, forgive me. You caught me on my weak side tonight in the porch. I should have been stronger. I should have helped you and not only tantalised you.

I shouldn't have told you that I would accept such a love token it was unfair to you and though I hate to have to tell you it was unfair to that one above all others whom I love. Oh Tom! forgive me, you always think so highly of me I know but *now* perhaps you will realise how wretchedly human and weak I am.

If you can anyhow understand what I mean take them with my love and believe I am not willingly giving up such priceless gifts aye, no. You said you were afraid your choice might be poor. Oh they are lovely. Oh! why mayn't I accept them. But I mayn't, Lad. I know I mayn't. My conscience and my heart tell me 'no'. I know you wouldn't have me do anything wrong deliberately.

I know, oh I know how you will be. I know what pain I am giving you but I can't do it Lad, I can't do it.

. . .

Forgive me Lad if you can. Have pity on one poor miserable being who is striving her utmost to do what is *right*.

Goodnight – nay, good morning. I had to write though. Forgive me.

Yours as always please
Mary[16]

The President of Magdalen must have appreciated the pent-up energy from which Tom was suffering and agreed to help Tom return to Oxford to read Jurisprudence. In *The Family Story* Denning reports Warren's saying, 'I thought teaching was not good enough for you. Do you want to come back again?' Tom wanted very much to go back again. The question was how it should be afforded. Warren must have told Tom that the fifth year's demyship, referred to in the Tutorial Board Order of 20 July 1920, could be re-activated.

There were also hopes that Warren would be able to influence the Trustees of a fund set up in memory of a former Lord Chancellor to award Tom an Eldon Scholarship, only available to a communicant member of the Church of England with a first-class degree. There could be no certainty until the Trustees' annual meeting, which would not take place until after the start of the next academic year. Warren was a persuasive and powerful sponsor. Once again, Tom decided to take a chance. He handed in his notice to Winchester College and prepared to enjoy the rest of his year there, happy that it would be the last.

When his parents heard the news, they were less than pleased. Charles was 'aghast' that Tom should so lightly throw away what seemed to him a secure position and a reasonable income. Charles's health was a little restored and, 'being anxious to do something towards the upkeep of the home, he started going long journeys on foot to try and solicit orders from some of his old customers.'[17]

Tom's friendship with Mary, if not, on her part, a romance, remained firm. When both were home, they spent much time together and Tom became as welcome a guest at the Vicarage as he was at Minster House. Mary's diary entries for Whitsun 1921 record Tom measuring out the tennis court with her on the 'beautiful, warm and sunny' Saturday, having supper at the Vicarage on Monday, and playing tennis there on Tuesday morning. They would of course, also have met at Church on Sunday, so routine an event Mary had no need to mention it.

At the end of the summer term, Tom left Winchester without regret. He bought *Anson on Contract*, his first law book, and began to study the subject that would never cease to interest and delight him. He took a holiday with Reg at Chamonix, in France, 'walking in the mountains, crossing the glaciers – coming down tired but happy to a good tea.'[1] That same summer Norman left school for the last time. A family conference was held to consider his future. Norman, like Gordon, wanted to join the Royal Navy but his eyesight was poor and the only branch for which he might be eligible was the Paymasters'. The Paymasters, as his brother put it, were in charge of all the stores and supplies for the victualling of the navy. 'They were secretaries to the Admiralty. They were the brains behind the administrative side.'[1] Norman took the examination and became a Paymaster cadet.

In October 1921, Tom returned to Oxford, this time to lodgings in the Iffley Road. The Tutorial Board, in October, confirmed that the academic year 1921–22 should be substituted as the fifth year for which Denning was to hold his demyship. His law tutor was Robert Segar, who, Denning would write, unkindly, if truthfully, 'had been an unsuccessful barrister on the Northern Circuit. He knew no law except on the Statute of Frauds – on which he once had a case. I learned nothing from him. I went to lectures of other dons and took notes.'[1]

The two pre-eminent lawyers in Oxford, at that time, were Sir Paul Gavrilovitch Vinogradoff and William Holdsworth. Vinogradoff had, even by Oxford standards, a towering personality and a remarkable intellect. He was born in 1854 near Moscow and was educated in the university there, before studying in Berlin and carrying out research in Italy and England on the feudal system. His most important work, *Villeinage in England*, was first published in Russian in 1887 and then, five years later, in English. As a professor of history in the University of Moscow, he became a highly influential teacher and was active in Russian educational reform and the movement for local self-government. When, at the turn of the century, the authorities repressed the students' freedom of expression, Vinogradoff resigned and came to England where, in 1903, he was elected to the Corpus Christi chair of jurisprudence at Oxford. He was considered the greatest authority of his time on the feudal laws and customs of England, a subject in which Tom was greatly interested.

William Holdsworth is best known for his monumental *History of English Law*. He was to become Vinerian Professor of English Law in 1922, be knighted in 1929 and, in 1943, would be appointed to the Order of Merit. His lectures on legal history frequently included studies of the lives and influence of great jurists, which fascinated Tom, who would often dwell on them in his own writing and lectures. In the years to come, Tom would be three times elected President of the Club named after Holdsworth by the Birmingham University Faculty of Law.

During that term, Sir Herbert Warren went up to London when the Trustees of the Eldon Scholarship were holding their annual meeting in the Lord Chancellor's room in the House of Lords. He persuaded them to award Tom a scholarship worth £100 a year for three years. On his return, Denning recalled in *The Family Story*, Warren sent him a note from High Table, saying: 'You are a marked man. Perhaps you will be a Lord of Appeal some day.' Under the terms of the Trust the award was payable for three years running from 4 June – which had been the birthday of Lord Eldon –'provided the Scholar keeps his terms regularly at one of the Inns of Court. If the Scholar be called to the Bar ... he thereby vacates his scholarship.' If, therefore, Tom was to derive much benefit from the award, he would have to 'keep his terms' at an Inn without delay.

The Inns of Court – Lincoln's Inn, Gray's Inn, Inner Temple and Middle Temple – have for centuries been responsible for legal education. Their governing bodies, the Benchers, have the exclusive right of admittance to practice as a barrister by a formal call to the Bar. During the Civil War, in the seventeenth century, the system of teaching broke down. Since there were no lecturers or readers to propose candidates for call to the Bar, the Benchers at first took the view that, having paid his fees, a student was entitled to be called. A century later it was decided to call students who had resided in an Inn for a stated number of terms. Eventually it was agreed that eating three dinners was equivalent to attending for one term. Though formal education was restored and an examination was introduced, the quaint custom of 'eating dinners' remained as part of the ritual of qualification.

Tom decided to join Lincoln's Inn for no particular reason other than its Under-Treasurer was Sir Reginald Rowe, a Magdalen man. He completed his application form for admission as a student on 17 October 1921, giving his father's profession as 'Businessman' and Sir Herbert Warren and Frank Northam Harvey as his two referees. On 14 October his future father-in-law wrote – revealingly – 'I have seen him daily for some years before he went to Oxford and during Vacation almost every day. Since he took his degree I have had abundant opportunities of knowing him intimately.'[18]

The Consolidated Regulations of the Inns of Court provided that a student at Oxford might keep terms by dining in the Hall of his Inn on any three days in each term. It was necessary to be present 'at the grace before dinner, during the whole of dinner, and until the concluding grace shall have been said.' Tom joined Lincoln's Inn on 4 November 1921, paying a fee of twelve guineas, entitling him 'so long as he shall be a student to attend all the lectures and classes of all the Readers and Assistant Readers', and entering into an Admission Bond 'in the penal sum of Fifty Pounds of good and lawful money of Great Britain' that he would pay 'all such sum and sums of money as shall grow due and payable for the Commons and diet of the said Alfred Thompson Denning.'[18] He went to London to eat the first of his dinners and stayed the night in Streatham, at Aunt Min's. Later he petitioned the Inn for a remission of six terms, which was granted, saving Tom some expense and interruption of his work at Oxford.

From the first, Tom was fascinated by the law. Not only did he study the textbooks and attend lectures – at the examination he was often able 'to repeat the notes word for word' – but he took a lively interest in the evolving law and in moots (mock trials). Denning, who had not once taken part in a debate at the Union, now enjoyed leading for one side in a moot organised by Robert Segar, against his friend, Pen Slade.

Although by and large he kept his nose to the grindstone, Tom became friendly with Jack Darlington, whose father was a vicar at Kennington and who would himself become Rector of Selborne and a Canon of Winchester. On 21 May 1922 Darlington wrote in his diary:

> Bluebell Sunday. One of the glorious days of summer. Bicycle out with Denning complete with camera and sandwiches. Had intended to go to church at Beckley but found a celebration proceeding there. A very thirsty day. Drank 3 bottles of lemonade and a glass of excellent cider. Eat our lunch afterwards. Snooze in a wonderful bluebell wood. Got back in time for St Clements Sunday School afterwards.[20]

Since a party at Magdalen, where he had taken 'one or two glasses' of port and found himself feeling dizzy, Tom had confined himself to lemonade. He was 'a little hesitant in case people thought I was odd but I stuck to my guns' and by the time he became a familiar figure at the Mansion House and the Inns of Court 'they always put out Malvern Water for me' and 'a little glass of port for the toast.'

At the viva voce in 1922, a young don, Geoffrey Cheshire, with whom Denning would become friendly in middle age, asked Tom about the new Law of Property Act, passed only on 29 June; since Tom kept abreast of current law he found no difficulty in discussing it. Years later, Cheshire showed Denning his marks: many alphas but one gamma, for jurisprudence. 'Jurisprudence was too abstract a subject for my liking,' Denning would write, 'all about ideologies, legal norms and basic norms, "ought" and "is", realism and behaviourism; and goodness knows what else. The jargon of the philosophers of law has always been beyond me. I like to get down to the practical problems which come up for decision. Contracts, torts, crime and the like.'[1] A strange remark from a judge who frequently propounded his own philosophy of law. Gamma for jurisprudence notwithstanding, when the results were posted, Denning had achieved the notable feat of his third First Class. In his letter of 15 November 1916 to Reg he had set out his ambition: 'I want to rise to the top and make a name.' His way to the top was now open.

6

Lincoln's Inn

Eating dinners in the lofty, panelled Hall of Lincoln's Inn, watched over by portraits of eminent lawyers of the past, was a pleasant reminder of the long-established traditions of the Bar. Its more prosaic aspects were at the forefront of Tom's attention when he came down at the end of Trinity term. It was usual for a student to sit the Bar Final Examination before starting pupillage, the practical part of training. It was also usual, in those days, for an aspiring barrister to have some means of support, however slim, not only whilst he studied for the examination and did his pupillage, but also during the first three to five years of practice when he might otherwise, it was generally agreed, have been expected to starve. Tom had nothing but his Eldon Scholarship. But there was a Prize Studentship, worth 100 guineas a year for three years, to be awarded to the top candidate in the examination. This would enable Tom, if he could win it, to avoid starvation. It was therefore vital for him to do well.

His second problem was pupillage. Though it was not then compulsory to be pupilled – which might cost anything between 50 and 100 guineas – it was very much to be advised. An introduction to a promising junior (only a junior can take pupils) in a good set of chambers was the golden key to a felicitous start at the Bar. Tom's difficulty would be to find such a junior. In the first place, the Bar was then very small by comparison with its present numbers; it was possible to be, at any rate, on nodding terms with all one's contemporaries. In the second place, the Bar was 'a very snobby, elitist profession',[21] whose members worked from chambers in the old Inns of Court and went for lunch there wearing top hats. The head of chambers was 'almost invariably a person of social standing',[22] often but not always a silk (King's Counsel or KC – a senior member of the Bar). Members of such chambers 'tended to work on the principle of friends and family first'[22] and Tom had no such connections.

During the war Reg had known Frank Boyd Merriman, a senior member of the Bar, who was later to be Solicitor-General and then President of the Probate, Divorce and Admiralty Division of the High Court. On being asked his advice, Merriman suggested Tom apply to Henry O'Hagan, 'a junior with a good commercial practice',[1] who agreed to take Tom for a fee of 50 guineas. Determined not to waste a moment in qualifying, Tom decided, regardless of the pressure on him to do well in the examination, to start his pupillage at once. In September 1922, he joined the small set of chambers at 4 Brick Court, Temple, at which address he would remain until he became a judge.

Tom's insatiable appetite for work, his remarkable, almost photographic, memory, his energy, enthusiasm and ability to devote his entire attention to whatever he had in hand, enabled him to survive the gruelling effort of the next months, helped, no doubt, by his lack of interest in the social round that would have distracted many a young man new to London life. Tom found lodgings in Beaufort Street, not far from Harrods in Knightsbridge, where, too, he would remain for some years, until his marriage. For whatever relaxation he allowed himself, which was not much, he looked to his visits to Whitchurch.

In October, Tom went back to Oxford for a couple of days to try for 'that most coveted of academic awards',[1] a fellowship at All Souls'. In the list of candidates offering law, Tom's biography was summarised in eight lines:

DENNING, ALFRED THOMPSON, B. A. Magdalen
　　　23 9 [his age]
First Class, Mathematical Mods, 1917.
First Class, Mathematical Greats, 1920.
Eldon Law Scholar, 1921.
2nd Lt., R. E., 131st Field Company, Oct. 1917
Served in France till Feb. 1919
Bar.

The omission, in print, of his First Class in Jurisprudence was made good in a handwritten amendment.

Amongst the other candidates were Cyril Harvey, with whom Denning would soon work on a new edition of *Smith's Leading Cases* and Cyril Radcliffe, who would create a remarkable practice at the Chancery Bar and be one of the rare men to be appointed from the Bar direct to the House of Lords.

Candidates dined in Hall with the Fellows and 'I remember,' Tom recalled at the age of 91, 'you had to talk to those old chaps. One was Lord Chelmsford (a Magdalen man, a First Class in Jurisprudence, who had captained the university cricket eleven in 1892, the year he was first elected a Fellow of All Souls'; and had been appointed Viceroy of India in 1916, at the early age of 47), 'I was terribly nervous.'[7] It is amusing to see that 'the old chap', Chelmsford, was then 54.

In addition to the papers in law, and a daunting philosophical essay on 'Criteria of Value', there was a General Paper. It was not the questions in the General Paper that were difficult, only the standard required in the answers. 'What are the tests of a good prose style?' was one question; 'Is the English character changing?' and 'What determines the "taxable capacity" of a nation?' were two of the others. Neither the candidates' papers nor the examiners' remarks survive the decision of any year: only the bare fact remains that Cyril Radcliffe – the outstanding legal figure of their day, according to Denning – was elected to the fellowship in law.

It was the first time that Tom had failed to achieve an academic goal that he had set himself. 'I could answer the legal questions all right,' he recalled in *The Family Story*, 'but we had to read Latin aloud. My pronunciation was mixed between the old and the new. That did not suit that stronghold of classicists. So I joined the distinguished company of "Failed All Souls"!' After nearly 60 years the failure still rankled. In his nineties, Denning recalled his tutor saying that the examiners thought he had a good memory but not much judgment. He entered his name for the examination the following year but remembered that he was too busy to take it.

Tom had already proved his intellectual ability with three First Class degrees but, almost certainly he was less prepared for an examination such as All Souls' than some of the candidates. His education, though good, had been narrow. His reading, in his schooldays, had been largely dictated by what was available: there was no public library in Whitchurch and the Grammar School's collection of books was limited. Even in 1944, when he became a judge, he did not know which King threw the Great Seal of England into the Thames. 'I know now,' he wrote in 1980, 'that it was James II, who thought it was the source of all lawful authority.'[23] Tom had read 'much of Shakespeare and many of our poets and novelists'[24] but, in the main, he had concentrated on his required work – hardly surprising when so much turned on his gaining an award to a university. In a small school with only five teachers, and some of those temporary, war-time replacements, he lacked the opportunity to test his mind in argument with others of like ability. Above all, he was young (and immature) when he went up to Oxford in 1916 and neither in that first year – much occupied with officer training – nor, perhaps more surprisingly, during his time in the army did Tom develop, intellectually or emotionally, from a boy into a man.

Tom's intellectual world had become dominated by 'numbers, letters and symbols',[24] the tools he needed for mathematics – and for bridge-building – rather than the 'words' that had once entranced and delighted him. Unlike some subalterns whose letters and memoirs refer to reading between spells of duty, Tom did not remember taking a book with him to France. Until he began to study the law he had almost given up the habit of reading for pleasure, though his regular attendance at church kept him in touch with some of the finest writing in the English language. Once started on the law, Tom had found the subject that, to the almost total exclusion of others, would always absorb his interest. In time (but that time had not come in 1922) he would be known, not only for his memory, but for the depth of his knowledge of law, his powers of analysis and his remarkable command of language. His learning would always remain tunnelled: his knowledge of other fields limited.

'As a pianist practises the piano,' Tom would write in *The Discipline of Law*, 'so the lawyer should practise the use of words . . . In chambers, if asked to advise, I took infinite pains in the writing of an opinion. I crossed out sentence after sentence. I wrote them again and again.' Painstakingly, diligently, Tom Denning started on his way to become Master of the Rolls.

Though Tom had raised money for the war memorial and collected the list of names, he was not in Whitchurch when the memorial was unveiled on 31 October 1922. Jack's name and Gordon's are inscribed there with 62 others. Apart from the two Portals killed in action, only the Dennings held commissioned rank. In 1963 Tom would return to live at Whitchurch and each year, on Memorial Sunday, he would slowly read out each of the 64 names and remember the men who were boys when he was a boy but had not grown old with him.

There was no silk in the set of chambers that Tom had joined, only Henry O'Hagan and Stephen Henn-Collins, each with 'a fine large room overlooking Brick Court. Each with his own complete library. The only other room was the small dark pupil room jutting over Middle Temple Lane. Two or three pupils there. And there was a tiny room – a cubby-hole – for the clerks. A senior clerk and a young lad working his way up. And a typist.'[1] O'Hagan did commercial work and some libel; Henn-Collins did work for the railway companies and copyright. The combination provided 'a good place to learn the trade.' Denning saw all the paper work of both but, strange as it seems today, did not attend conferences with solicitors, unless specifically invited. He did meet Bernard Shaw, who consulted Henn-Collins on copyright.

Though O'Hagan was Tom's pupil-master, it was Henn-Collins, the head of chambers, who would have the greater influence on Tom's development. The son of an Irishman, Sir Richard Henn-Collins, a former Master of the Rolls, Stephen was a 'very cultivated' man, a 'first rate carpenter', who spent his spare time making violins. He lived with his wife – 'a bit of a tartar' – in Beaufort Gardens, just behind Harrods; Tom would often walk home with him before having a meal alone in a restaurant near Sloane Square and then going on to the digs, a short distance away in Beaufort Street, probably to continue work on a case.

Like a number of large houses in the neighbourhood 145 Beaufort Street had been converted into lodgings. Tom occupied one of the cheaper rooms on the top floor. In the basement lived his landlady, Mrs Cross, 'a good old soul', who took care of the rooms and provided her lodgers with breakfast in the breakfast room, each at his chosen time. There were several permanent residents, both male and female; the only other lawyer, Anthony Moir, would become both Tom's personal solicitor – and Winston Churchill's – and his client.

When Tom went home at the end of 1922, it was for the first Christmas that the Dennings would enjoy in their new home. That year, Reg purchased The Hermitage, a small house, not far from the church, to become the family home. It is probably the oldest house in Whitchurch, dating from the fourteenth century; a pretty cruck house, with stout oak timbers rising, like the hull of a ship, upside down, to a gabled roof. With the move to The Hermitage, Charles could put aside some of the cares that had plagued him; his resumed journeys enabled him to contribute a little extra to the household expenses.

Another change in the Denning home, that year, had given Charles and Clara a new lease of life. In 1922, their son-in-law, Johnnie Haynes, now in the regular army, was transferred from Cork to Aldershot, bringing with him Marjorie and their three little girls: Betty, now four and a half, Peggy, just two, and baby Clare, who was born in Ireland in September 1921. As it had once been hard for Clara to manage, so now it was difficult for Marjorie, with children so close in age. Charles and Clara suggested that Betty stay with them in Newbury Street. What may have begun as a temporary expedient was so successful that Betty remained with her grandparents for some time, moving with them to The Hermitage, and returning to Aldershot for holidays. Like her mother, she started to attend the Geers' school, bringing an extra symmetry to her relations with her grandparents.

For Christmas, that year, Tom gave Mary *The Oxford Book of English Verse*. He saw as much of her as he was able in his brief time at home but, though still friendly, Mary had not changed her mind about marrying him. On his return to London he threw all his energies into his work at the Inn for his examination and in chambers for O'Hagan and Henn-Collins. When the results of the examination came out, Tom was the only candidate in the First Class. With the greatest satisfaction, he read the notice, signed by J. R. Atkin and T. E. Scrutton, awarding him the Prize Studentship, that assured at least his first three years at the Bar.

Sir J. R. Atkin and Sir T. E. Scrutton were, in 1923, two of the five

Lords Justices of the Court of Appeal. Atkin, like Denning a demy of Magdalen College, had been pupilled in the chambers of Scrutton, an acknowledged master of the common law. Like all pupils, Denning had done the rounds of the courts and formed his own views of the judges who sat in them. Atkin was 'intellectually clever' but Scrutton 'had common sense' and was 'more of a figure because of his personality.' A quarter of a century later, when Denning reached the Court of Appeal, his style would closely resemble Atkin's, as described by J. B. Butterworth in the *Dictionary of National Biography*:

> Gentle, firm, patient, learned in the law, dignified . . . For Atkin the law was dynamic and although he recognised the necessity for having settled legal rules, he was prepared whenever possible to develop legal principles to provide a remedy when proven injury had been suffered. His insistence upon the importance of principles together with a lucid style and the ability frequently to coin an apposite phrase made certain the recognition of his considerable influence upon the common law.

Denning, too, would have considerable influence upon the common law. He would also bring to his judicial work the common sense he admired in Scrutton.

Having passed the examination, Tom was entitled to be called to the Bar in the Hall of Lincoln's Inn, on the next call-night, 13 June 1923. The smooth, unchanging tenor of life in the Inns had undergone a mild tremor with the appearance, a couple of years back, of the first woman barrister. On Tom's call-night an Indian woman was among those admitted to the Bar and, after dinner, he recalled, each of them was required to make a little speech.

Through his time at school, at university and in pupillage, Tom had gained the sympathy and assistance of those who could help to bring his ambitions to fruition. Mr Bishop, Sir Herbert Warren, Clement Webb and Stephen Henn-Collins had all taken a warm interest in Tom's well-being. The Lincoln's Inn Black Book for 1920 to 1926 gives evidence of similar goodwill from those responsible for students at the Inn. An entry made on 7 May 1923 states:

Upon consideration of an application from Alfred Thompson Denning to read in the Chambers of H. O. Hagen Esq. (sic): of 4 Brick Court Temple E.C.4 The Committee resolved to advise the Council to grant Mr Denning fees for 6 months and to consider continuing another 6 months at the end of the first period. Which was adopted.

In June 1923, having completed his pupillage and been offered a seat in chambers – the same seat that he had occupied for the past six months – Tom was ready, after laying out another £12 on the purchase of his robes, to start his practice. With a mixture of optimism and apprehension he bought his first Fee Book. It was a slim book, some twelve by eight inches in size, with a hard black cover on which, in gold letters, were embossed the words FEE BOOK. Now all he had to do was wait. It was not until 28 December 1923 that he posted his first entry: Llewellyn v. Kay (Poor Person). Solicitors Devonshire Driford Brown & Co. 38 Old Jewry EC2.

A case brought under the Poor Persons Procedure – a kind of voluntary forerunner to Legal Aid – brought no fee: a person without means could submit his grievance to a Committee who would, if they considered it a proper case for litigation, allot a solicitor and barrister to represent him, without remuneration. While Tom waited for that first case, he devilled for the busy juniors in his own and other chambers. Which is to say, 'I used to look up cases, draft pleadings or opinions – all without payment . . . Like others, I did it in the hope that my work would be approved: that my name would be mentioned to the solicitors as a "good young man in these chambers." ' A young barrister, then as now, depended on a word from the clerk of his chambers to solicitors or their clerks. ' "Mr X is too busy. But we have a good young man available. He has already done a lot of work on these papers. Give him a try." '[1]

The work at 4 Brick Court was common law work and it was in that area that Denning would spend most of his time at the Bar. The common law – a peculiarly English form of law – had developed over the centuries from English customs that were in place before the Norman Conquest. After the Conquest, commissioners were sent about the country, entrusted with the power to try all cases of major crime. Their commissions were enlarged, in the course of the next two centuries, to enable them to try civil actions – disputes between subject and subject – as well as criminal matters. The law upon which the earliest judges based their decisions was usually the commonly accepted custom of the locality in the period before the Conquest. By the close of the thirteenth century, as well as sitting in Westminster, royal judges were making regular tours of the country, which was divided into 'circuits', administering, under the system known as 'assizes', a more uniform body of law, based on precedents derived from earlier judicial decisions. Until the beginning of the nineteenth century, legislation played scarcely any part in the development of private law: that was achieved, almost entirely, by the judges. As the courts dealt with cases of debt, of promises broken, of goods damaged in transit, of animals destroying a neighbouring farmer's crops, of personal attacks and other sources of friction between citizens, there evolved the English law of contract and of tort (which may be defined, loosely, as being civil wrongs, for example libel and negligence, as opposed to criminal wrongs). By the time Denning's practice started, statute had made some impact on these subjects but in England, unlike most European countries, there was no major codification; the common law remained the source of much legal bread and butter. Personal injury claims and small contractual matters – together with minor cases in the magistrates' courts – would be the work on which Tom hoped to cut his legal teeth.

While Tom was looking for ways of making his name known, his attention was caught by a case (*Scott* v. *Pattison*) that had been decided in the Divisional Court shortly before he qualified. A farm labourer had been engaged, by word of mouth, to work at a weekly wage for one year, commencing five days after the agreement was made. In those days, because of an old enactment, the Statute of Frauds, the agreement had to be in writing in order to be enforceable. When the labourer brought an action for wages which he alleged were due to him, the judges held that he could not sue under the agreement, since it was not in writing, but went on to decide that the man could sue on an implied contract to pay him according to his deserts (in legal phraseology: on a *quantum meruit*).

Bold, even in his second year at the Bar, Tom wrote an article on '*Quantum Meruit* and the Statute of Frauds', in which he took issue with the judges. After careful analysis of historic forms of action and earlier cases, Denning submitted that the Statute of Frauds did not apply in the circumstances of *Scott* v. *Pattison*, where the labourer had fulfilled his contract. The article was accepted by the prestigious *Law Quarterly Review* and published in the January 1925 issue.

It was rare for Tom to take time off during the week but, on Wednesday 24 October he hurried to Smithfield at lunch time: Mary had come to town for the Dairy Show. That weekend, in Whitchurch, he had supper with her and they made coconut ice. It was Christmas before he spent time with her again. It must have seemed to him then that she was slipping away. Mr Harvey had been appointed Rector of Fawley, in those days a pretty village near the sea, and was expecting to leave Whitchurch in the new year. On Sunday 30 December 1923 Tom went, with Reg, for the last time to tea at the Vicarage. He was not in Whitchurch when, on Sunday 20 January, Mr Harvey gave his farewell sermon. Nor did he see the Harveys start their move to Fawley, the following day. 'Gradually,' he wrote, in *The Family Story*, 'we ceased to write to one another.'

Tom had little time for a social life in the next couple of years, when he began to establish his practice. Nor did he go often to the theatre, apart from an occasional visit, in 'the gods', to the Old Vic, or have much intellectual stimulation other than the law. He enjoyed the occasional lunch or dinner in Hall, where the arrangements were reminiscent of an Oxford college or a gentleman's club. He liked dancing when occasion arose – in Cheyne Walk; at a country home in Cheshire; and on a visit to Jack Darlington's cottage in Somerset, when they drove an old horse barouche six miles to Ilminster, stayed the night in the house of another Magdalen man, and had the unaccustomed luxury of coal fires in the bedrooms!

He remained attached to Whitchurch and his family and shared the pride with which Clara wrote to him, on 2 September 1925:

My dearest Tom,
    I am wondering if you have seen *The Times* today, Reg is promoted Captain (August 12)
    . . . dad and I have been very happy about it all day. We are very delighted and truly thankful for the great achievements all our boys have attained.

I pray all the positions that bring authority & responsibility may
be used to the glory of God . . .

Clara had taken the lawn-mower to the cemetery on Monday, she
told Tom, to mow the lawn round Gordon's grave: '. . . it all looks so
very nice, just as the dear boy himself would like it.'

Tom still had his heart set upon marrying Mary. For her birthday
he sent her a letter of good wishes. Her reply came, coolly, from
Grantchester on 26 September 1925: 'I was so glad to hear of all your
doings again – you seem to have been working very hard, don't
overdo it old man! With many thanks for the good wishes – & with
my good wishes to you.' Mary's feelings for Tom remained
ambivalent. Two months later she sent a snapshot of herself to the
Castle at Winchester, where Tom was appearing in a case. Her letter,
a trifle less formal, must have encouraged him: for Christmas he sent
her a diary and told her he would probably be in Southampton in
January. 'Father and Mother hope,' Mary replied, 'that if you come to
Southampton on Jan 8th you will stay the night of the 8th here.'

The visit could not have been too strained. On 22 January 1926
Mary sent Tom, for his birthday, the 'promised enlargement' of her
photograph in guide uniform. Still she held back, though not quite
letting Tom go:

I am glad you enjoyed your brief stay here – and I am so glad to
know from your letter that you realised that I was quite
unchanged.

I was almost afraid when Father & Mother asked you that it
would convey a wrong impression to you but I am very glad that
you have been sensible enough to realise that I still wish to be your
'true companion'.

At the end of March, Tom knew that he would be in Southampton
again on 9 May. In response to his request for a bed for the night,
Mary wrote, on 1 April 1926, that they would have a full house. Nor
could she meet him, as he suggested, on 8 April. At this point the
correspondence between them seems to have died – 'Gradually we
ceased to write to one another' – and Mary's diaries, until 1928 make
no mention of Tom. It was not until 15 April 1928 that Mary re-

opened the correspondence, telling Tom that she and Mrs Harvey would be in London the next week. It would be 'nice', she thought, 'if we could have tea somewhere . . . and I wonder if we might go over the Temple.' Mary had, she told Tom, now got a car and had driven her father to Whitchurch on Thursday, where they 'saw your people.'

In the intervening years, Denning's practice had got off the ground. In his year of call, apart from his studentship, Tom received no income. He would have been surprised – though delighted – if it had been otherwise. The reputation he was starting to make as a devil was to stand him in good stead; from D. N. Pritt his work would even be the source of an occasional cheque.

Denis Norwell Pritt was, in 1924, a busy junior with a large and varied practice. Like many lawyers he was a politician, one who had moved from being a supporter of the Tories to the Liberal Party and thence to Labour. His natural sympathy was with the underdog. He was short-sighted, flat-footed and 'his face, in repose, bore an expression of warm-hearted benevolence.'[25] He showed his appreciation of Tom's assistance with unusual and much appreciated gifts of money.

The system of assizes and the division of the country into circuits were still in force. Tom joined the Western Circuit, which included Hampshire, his home territory, as well as Wiltshire, Dorset, Somerset, Devon and Cornwall. New members of the Circuit were expected to make a speech at the Grand Night at Winchester; and so in 1924 Denning made the first of the many after-dinner speeches he would give in that city. The possible embarrassment of recently admitted female members of the Bar attending Circuit dinners, was dealt with in different ways by different Circuits. On 2 June 1923 *The Law Journal* reported that the Oxford Circuit Bar Mess had taken a similar decision to that of the Central Criminal Court Bar Mess: to admit women barristers on the same terms as men. On the North-Eastern Circuit, 'where the dining arrangements are more equivalent to those of a men's club of considerable dimensions', the problem had been solved by the simple expedient of declaring that women would not be required to dine – though it must be said that they were not required either to pay a subscription.

One of Tom's first briefs came, on 8 April 1924, from Mary's uncle, Tom Woodham, who was Clerk of the Peace for the City of Winchester. Denning was briefed for the prosecution, a brief worth two guineas to Tom and 2s 6d to his clerk, which was promptly paid – no one knew better than Mr Woodham how much it was needed. Under the heading 'Sisters' Plight', the *Hampshire Chronicle*, on 12 April 1924, reported the pathetic story of two sisters, domestic servants aged 18 and 22, who pleaded not guilty to a joint indictment of incurring a debt of £2, and thus obtaining credit by fraud, and another debt of 16s 6d, also obtained by means of fraud.

> Mr Denning was for the prosecution and stated that accused went to a private hotel, kept by Mrs Tucker, and enquired terms. Mrs Tucker took them in on terms, from the Saturday to the Tuesday, on which morning they went out and did not return. . . . They left behind them an *attache* case, valued at 4s 6d. From Mrs Tucker's they appeared to have gone to a private hotel kept by Mrs Andrews. There they had some meals and an account was prepared for them, when the elder defendant said to her sister, 'Fetch the bag.' The younger defendant went out, ostensibly to get the money, but ran into the arms of a policeman who was making enquiries in the first case, and to him she admitted that they had no money at all. They were arrested, and when searched at the police station a half-penny was found on one of the defendants . . . the elder defendant . . . stated that she was a mental nurse. They had been staying in Reading, looking for work, and learning of a post at Hartley Wintney they walked there, but only to find it had been filled. The husband of the lady at Hartley Wintney, on learning that they had no food and nowhere to go, paid their fares to Basingstoke, where they took lodgings, hoping to get work at Basingstoke and pay for their lodgings. It was either doing that or going on the streets.

The jury found both defendants guilty, but the story had a happy ending.

> The Chairman said . . . as there was nothing else against them the Court were minded to deal with them leniently, they would both be bound over . . . It was understood that magistrates, members of

the jury, and others in Court, who felt sympathy . . . subscribed to the expenses necessary to take them back to Pontypridd, for which town they left the following day.

The bigamist Tom prosecuted at Assizes two months later was less deserving. Despite Denning's restrained prosecution and the defendant's plea in mitigation, the judge passed sentence of six months' hard labour.

On 14 May, a London brief, in Westminster County Court, from Theodore Goddard, paid another two guineas; but, to look, as Tom was wont to do, on the bright side, both travelling time and the fare were saved!

The breakthrough came when Stephen Henn-Collins mentioned Denning's name to the solicitors for the Southern Railway Company. 'I went all round the Southern Region . . . prosecuting persons who travelled with intent to avoid payment of fare.' The Southern Railway Company, in the person of Mr W. Bishop of their legal office, was Denning's most profitable client in 1924. A fee of 35 guineas was paid on 28 August 1924 for his appearance at an arbitration on ten claims.

The year 1924 had seen the appointment of the first Labour Prime Minister, Ramsay MacDonald, in January and the return of Stanley Baldwin and the Tories, after a massive election victory, in November. There had been strikes on the railways, in the docks and by workers engaged in the preparation of the Imperial Exhibition at Wembley. The King's opening speech at the Exhibition had been broadcast over the wireless, which was becoming a focal point in millions of homes. In the year when milk was reduced to 7d a quart, when the police advised cyclists to avoid roads where there was heavy motor traffic, Tom had little thought to spare for events outside the law. At the year's end, when he totted up his fees, he found he had made £94 10s, a very satisfactory start to his practice, even though the expenses cut down the income to £59. With another 100 guineas from his studentship, Tom could live without fear of starvation.

In his third year of practice, Denning's academic record opened to him another opportunity to make a name and, at the same time, some money. In 1837 John William Smith had published a useful guide to precedent – a collection of the leading cases of the time with his commentary upon them. In the succeeding years, *Smith's Leading Cases* had been brought up to date by various authors and was considered indispensable as a companion on circuit. Sir John Willes Chitty, the Senior Master, was preparing the thirteenth edition and asked Tom and a fellow barrister, Cyril Harvey, to help him. In April 1926 they signed a contract with Sweet & Maxwell to co-edit the edition for the sum of £600. There was an 18-month deadline. Each editor took responsibility for the notes to a particular leading case. 'It was an immense task – involving much research. But it taught me most of the law I ever knew. I was bold enough [even then!] to be drastic in some of my notes – rewriting them and suggesting new principles.'[1]

On occasion, Tom also supplemented his income by contributing to Butterworth's *English and Empire Digests*, which provided a comprehensive guide to the case law of England and to a body of cases from Scotland, Ireland and the Empire. He soon gave this up, as the work was arduous and the payment small.

There is, amongst the miscellaneous correspondence in the Denning Archive at Winchester, a letter written on 15 May 1926 by a judge with an indistinct signature. It suggests that, in the practical field as well as the academic, Denning was beginning to make an impact.

Dear Denning

I'm not even sure that I've got your name right but I want to tell you that (whether I decided the case of Murray against the Theatre Guild rightly or wrongly) you did your part admirably . . . I told Henn-Collins tonight . . . that you will assuredly do well.

In the next two or three years Denning was entrusted with more demanding work for the Railway Company. In 1930 he was instructed to prepare a manual giving guidance to the railway police and, on 8 January 1931, he would inform Mary, 'I have actually done a little Police Manual today and have taken special delight in a page telling the Railway Police to run in taxi-drivers who refuse a "fare"!' By that time he had obtained very considerable personal experience of travel by train; what bitter experience, one wonders, provoked such retaliation!

Meanwhile, Denning's list of instructing solicitors was growing, both in London and on the Western Circuit. Through O'Hagan, who acted for the Property Owners' Association, Tom was instructed by landlords seeking possession of dwellings; he was instructed in personal injury cases; in cases where a company relied upon printed exemption clauses; and in a variety of other common law matters. 'I had taken the Sale of Goods and Charterparties as special subjects in the Bar examination and knew *Chalmers and Scrutton* nearly by heart.'

His voice was heard (high-pitched when he was nervous, as the pupil at Winchester had observed) in County Courts all over London and its suburbs, at Brighton, at Woking, at Reading and at Ramsgate. He pleaded in Magistrates' Courts at Lewes and at London Sessions; he appeared at Exeter Assizes. He spent a considerable amount of time in trains and hanging around courts, waiting for his case to be called; all for fees averaging two guineas. By 22 October 1928 Denning's practice was so far established that, having entirely filled the Fee Book he had started nearly five years earlier, he was able to open a new book, this time in a shiny maroon cover. At the time the old black book was finished Tom had earned £663 over the five-year period.

The rise in pitch of Tom's voice, when he was nervous, may not have been its only distinctive note. Before the 1880s the educated classes spoke in their regional accents all their lives but by the end of the century 'standard English' was considered a sign of membership of the upper or professional middle classes. A rich Hampshire burr would have been in marked contrast to the tones more usually heard in the courts. Though Tom knew this very well, he recalled in old age that some stubborn streak within him – an attachment to his roots – kept him from adapting his mode of speech. Yet some who knew him before the Second World War, were unable to remember having thought at the time that his accent was unusual.

Remembering the boy who feared his Oxford contemporaries might regard him as inferior because of his grammar school education, it is easy to imagine that Tom may – perhaps unconsciously – have adapted his mode of speech ever so slightly.

Would he have wilfully added to his difficulties when he had to make his way at the Bar, by maintaining an accent not usually heard in the courts? It is possible. It is also possible that, like Reg, whose years in the mess left his Hampshire accent barely discernible, Tom's burr was modified, returning to its full glory when he grew in confidence and stature.

It had taken about two years for Denning to make his first appearance in the High Court (and that in a Poor Person's case), a very special landmark in a barrister's life. In 1959, in a lecture given at Oxford, he would recall:

> When I was called to the Bar it was believed by everyone that hospital authorities were not liable for the negligence of their professional staff in the course of their professional duties . . . It was brought sharply to my notice in my very first case in the High Court . . . A lady had gone to a dental hospital to have a tooth out. Whilst she was under the anaesthetic, the tooth broke and a piece went down her throat. She was told nothing about it. The operator who extracted it hoped that it would disappear through the stomach. But in fact it went down her wind-pipe and into her lung. She developed a cough, and not knowing the cause, it was not properly treated and she died. If she had been told of the piece of tooth, it could have been taken out of her lung and she might have lived. According to the law as we believed it to be, her representative could not sue the hospital. So we had to find out the name of the dentist who operated on her. How could we do this? If the hospital had refused to give us his name, I know of no way in which we could have compelled them to do it. As it happened, the hospital did, by letter, give us his name. So we sued him and succeeded. But it seemed to me that there was something wrong with the law if redress depended on the chance whether the hospital authorities were willing to give us the dentist's name or not.

Later in his career, in 1942, Denning would take a hospital case (*Gold v. Essex County Council*) to the Court of Appeal and obtain a decision that changed the law, making hospital authorities liable for the negligence of their professional staff.

There were three divisions of the High Court: the Chancery

Division, the King's Bench Division (KBD) and the Probate, Divorce and Admiralty Division (PDA), informally known as Wives, Wills and Wrecks. Cases involving such matters as trusts, wardship, company law, and tax were taken in Chancery. The work was generally regarded as being particularly prestigious. The King's Bench, the descendant of the old common law courts, for the most part heard cases relating to contract law and to tort. Straddling the courts was the highly regarded commercial work – shipping, banking and marine insurance involving vast sums – which was largely confined to a few chambers; Denning would get little of it. His first case in the High Court and the majority of his subsequent work there was in the King's Bench Division, though, as he tells us, he made 'an occasional appearance in Chancery too.'[1]

The judiciary, like the Bar, was very much smaller in 1925 than it is today. There were six Chancery judges, 16 KBD judges and only the President of the PDA plus one other. The Court of Appeal, which Denning would one day make his own, had five Lords Justices of Appeal, plus the Lord Chief Justice, the Master of the Rolls and the President of the PDA. The final appeal court, the House of Lords, had five Lords of Appeal in Ordinary, presided over by the Lord Chancellor of the day.

In 1926 the industrial unrest that had surfaced from time to time since the end of the war erupted. In March a Royal Commission proposed radical changes for the coal industry, including profit sharing and paid holidays for miners, but concluded that subsidies were placing an intolerable burden on the rest of industry and, since about 73 per cent of coal was produced at a loss, wage cuts were inevitable. The miners refused to accept the recommendations and on 1 May they were locked out. The Trades Union Congress called a general strike. A State of Emergency was declared and the country was divided into areas, with emergency arrangements run by Civil Commissioners. A message from the Prime Minister, Stanley Baldwin, was broadcast over the wireless, calling on the nation to 'keep steady'.

Tom was well aware of the social problems of the Twenties and Thirties and of the failure of Lloyd George's promise to make Britain a country fit for heroes. 'If that were the task set before the people,' he would write in *The Family Story*, 'it was never accomplished.' He would deplore 'the unemployment, the dole queues, the distress of the Thirties', but his role at the time was that of the passive by-stander. He supported neither the government nor the opposition. He condemned neither the employers nor the workers. Whatever the distress, 'for most of us life went on.' But in 1926, Tom's absorption in his personal career, with that of most of the middle class, was disturbed by the strike. What concerned him was the lawful governance of the country.

When the General Strike was called, he regarded the danger of violent disorder as a new threat to the country. Like thousands of others, undergraduates, professional men and office workers, he volunteered to keep services running. 'I served as a Special Constable (I have my truncheon and arm-band still). We were on patrol outside the Lots Road power station. The soldiers were inside safe and sound.'[1] Writing that at 80, Denning sounds like the patriotic, romantic adolescent who could scarcely wait to do his bit in the First World War. The call to arms to defend the country took precedence over 'the unemployment, the dole queues' and the distress.

It was only for a few days. The General Strike quickly fizzled out. The miners were left to fight alone, and Tom returned quickly to *Smith's Leading Cases* and the business of making a name.

7

Mary

In July 1927 Tom was best man when Reg, now a handsome, much sought-after captain of the Bedfordshire and Hertfordshire Regiment, married Eileen Currie, the daughter of Mr and Mrs Henry Currie of 17 Westbourne Terrace. Mr Currie was in shipping. In his fine London home, close to Hyde Park, at parties given in the elegant first-floor drawing room, Tom entered another social set. By the end of the 1920s Tom was 'seen as a coming young barrister' and the mothers of marriageable girls were always alert to add to their lists of eligible young men. 'I was invited to dances in the large London houses . . . Glittering with youth and beauty and wealth. I went for weekends to country houses. I met the finest in the land.' He met them, he dined and danced with them, but he took friendship no further. Though he was approaching 30, Tom had never had a girlfriend. '. . . I never lost my heart to any. I had already given it away – beyond recall.'[1]

When Tom received Mary's letter of 15 April 1928, proposing a visit to see the Temple, he responded promptly and enthusiastically. He suggested they might also dine and dance. On 17 April Mary replied that she would prefer a theatre so that 'Mother can come too . . . but don't you think as there are two of us that we had better meet you in time for the "show". We have not seen anything but "Marigold", but we rather fancy "The Stranger in the House".'

Tom took Mary and her mother to the 'show' on the Friday night and around the Temple the following day. Any hopes raised by her initiative were discouraged by Mary's bread-and-butter letter, written on Monday morning from the Mary Sumner House, where she and her mother were staying. Tom would be welcome at Fawley, Mary told him, when next he was in Southampton, 'for Assizes or whatever you come for! . . . but I shall completely understand if you

97

would rather refuse the invitation . . . I hope our meeting hasn't been all painful.'

On 12 July Mary wrote again. Her weekends were very occupied and she would shortly be off in the caravan for three weeks:

> You ask me to be candid about your coming here at all – and that puts me in a dreadful position. I hope you know me well enough to know that what I write I *mean* and therefore if I say anything that might hurt you, it will not be because I wish to hurt you – far from it – but it will only be what I feel.
>
>   Honestly, old man, you are the only person really to be consider[ed] – and it rests with you whether you think it wise or not. I *was* a bit troubled after meeting you in London to find that alas! things have remained in many ways unchanged for you and although I reverence your devotion and am surprised (and I would not be human and alas! I am *very* human if I was not *grateful*) this should be so after so many years and with no encouragement from me – For I think I have not given you encouragement. I know that in the memorable year 1919–20 I *was* unfair to you. I taxed you further than any woman ought to tax any man whom she has not *accepted* as a lover.

Tom had learned young the pleasure of delayed gratification and the need to work and wait for what he wanted. He was discouraged but not dissuaded. He managed only the barest contact with her in the next two years. In the autumns of 1928 and 1929, when Mary was taking part in pageants at the Albert Hall, he obtained little more than glimpses of her. For Christmas of both years he sent her his usual diary and a large box of chocolates, but received only a letter of greeting in 1928 and, in 1929, a card with a picture of two wire-haired terriers on it. On 27 December 1929 patience was rewarded, when Mary wrote: 'I have to go to a dance at Beaulieu on Saturday Jan 18th & I wonder if you could get away to come with me.' Tom could ask for nothing more. 'I stayed in the Rectory at Fawley. I told her that I loved her still.' She rejected him but, when he was gone, reconsidered her position. 'Tom Old Man,' she wrote on 20 January 1930:

I hope this letter will make you very happy, as happy as it makes me to write it.

Will you have me? I am almost ashamed to ask it of you, but since you went last night my life has been entirely revolutionised & I *want* you old man – & feel I must have you to make me happy.

She asked him to telephone and to come back to Fawley. She had told her parents, who were delighted.

Oh! Tom what a fool I have been not to love you years before. Come old darling as soon as you can. With all my heart and love and life's devotion I am

Your own Mary

The letter reached Tom in chambers and he replied almost at once.

My own darling Mary,

I have been simply dizzy with happiness ever since I got your letter this morning – it is so wonderful – I am simply longing to come as quickly as I can . . .

My darling you have made me so happy and I shall ever through my life try to make you very happy too.

Your own true sweetheart

Just as a knight, in one of Tom's romantic epics, must have rejoiced when, after serving years to win his lady's hand, he was at last allowed to wear her favour, so Tom looked forward to his prize. 'The very next Saturday she met me at Southampton station. We went to the jewellers together.' (Did she remember the little brooches she had rejected?) 'We chose her engagement ring – gold set with five small diamonds. She bought me a little gold pencil. She told me how to remember the day. It was St. Paul's Day, 25 January 1930.' Three days later, Mrs Harvey wrote to Tom from Fawley, with 'a tiny belated birthday gift.' 'I want you to feel,' she told him, 'that in giving our Mary into your care, we are really *happy* in the certainty of your loyalty and love.' Tom was 31 years old and was earning, by that time, £1000 a year.

Now began a brief period of happiness and fulfilment. Tom was in regular demand, both in London and on circuit, and was getting an interesting range of work. His long wait for Mary had been rewarded and he was able to enjoy with her, not only the homely pleasures of their earlier friendship, but the more extravagant entertainments of the London social set. They had tea at the Criterion, danced at the Berkeley and the Mayfair, went to the theatre and dined at the Hungaria.[26] They had their portraits taken by a fashionable photographer, though Tom was shocked at the cost.[6]

Both families were delighted with the match. Responding to a letter from Charles, Mr Harvey wrote: 'There is no one in the world that I would rather have for our child than your Boy. He has always had a warm place in my heart and I admire his character and above all his unexampled determination to succeed not only in his profession but in his winning the girl he has so long loved.'[27] From the Foreign and Political Department in Delhi, where he was working, Mary's brother Walter wrote: 'I'm delighted to think that you will be my brother-in-law, and that Mary has at last realised what wonderful things love and a lover are.'[27]

Reg and Norman welcomed Mary with similar warmth: 'I had a delightful letter from Reg this morning,' Mary told Tom on 31 January, 'he seems very glad about the engagement.' There was no reason to delay the marriage. Tom and Mary embarked enthusiastically on plans for an August wedding, during the Long Vacation. They wrote to each other every day and at weekends he went to Hampshire, dividing his time as best he could between Fawley and Whitchurch. On 22 January Mary had written to him 'I want *nothing ever* to come between you and your parents because of me – you, I know, are devoted to them and they have been good to you.'

The telephone was still a novelty. From time to time Tom indulged himself in an evening call to Mary – 'delicious,' she wrote, 'although absurdly extravagant' – but, by and large, they were content to write once – and sometimes twice – a day, telling each other the events of their daily lives. Mary asked Tom to tell her all about his work: 'Remember "Law" is a complete mystery to me. I shall want a lot of teaching.' In response, Tom detailed for her the ups and downs of 'our practice'.

He was, though he did not yet know it, embarking upon a life of frenetic activity, as he worked in London or travelled the southern counties, writing letters on the train, preparing cases into the night so that he might be free, on Saturday afternoon, to hurry to Fawley, then, on Sundays, to Whitchurch before returning to 145 Beaufort Street. '. . . things have driven me very late tonight,' he told Mary on 30 January, 'I have only just got back to my digs from the Temple and it [is] now 10.45 and the post is about to go – Henn-Collins and I have been working on a case which he has tomorrow which I may have to do for him – It is in the High Court – Sir Boyd Merriman (the late Solicitor-General) is leading and a good deal has to be looked up.'

The following day he reported: 'For the greater part of today I have been in the Special Jury Court – not actually of immediate profit to me because I was there for Henn-Collins – but I hope though the introduction to solicitors may bring profit later.' As his experience grew, so did his confidence. '. . . I dealt with a little matter this afternoon,' he wrote on 3 February, 'needing both tact and firmness and I feel sure that I handled it better than I could have done before – for I got my own way without suffering any tempers . . .'

He tried to pack into each day as much as was possible and worried frequently about getting new work. 'Since our practice has come to an end,' Mary teased after one such outburst, 'I suppose you will be able to get here on Friday evening . . .' On his way by train to Whitchurch, where he would stay the night before going on to do a case at Winchester, he wrote: 'I was offered four cases in all at various places, but can only do the Winchester one – it is unfortunate when they all come on one day – I am trying and hope to save two of them by adjourning them . . .' The next day he was able to tell Mary: 'I did the Winchester case myself . . . Then I got a man in chambers to "devil" a case for me at Whitechapel – which he won – I was pleased about that as it upheld an opinion I had given to the solicitors.'

St Valentine's Day prompted Tom to 'send thousands of kisses to my own true love . . . with a keen eye on Saturday when the kisses may be transformed into fact.' Mary, for her part, confided to Tom that she kissed her engagement ring – as a stand-in for him – each time she put it on or took it off. Though Tom scarcely had time to get his hair cut or visit a tailor, he pursued with characteristic energy the hunt for a flat. 'I made a tentative (and rather shy) enquiry about flats today,' he wrote to Mary on 28 January. 'I was rather stumped about the size.' Mary thought that '2 sitting rooms and 2 bedrooms is enough if the maid is a daily one, will our finances run to that?' she asked. Later they considered houses in Chelsea, where a number of barristers lived.

Henn-Collins had begun to worry about the hours Tom was working and to urge him to go a little easier, perhaps to take up a hobby. The plea fell on deaf ears. Though Tom enjoyed an occasional game of tennis or of golf, all his life the law would be his hobby as well as his work. 17 March 1930 was a red letter day for Tom, appearing in the House of Lords for the first time – and on the winning side. He was a little disappointed to find that his name was not mentioned in *The Times* report, on the next day. Mary, too, had started to worry that Tom was working too hard. 'If I work, my darling,' he wrote from The Hermitage on 23 March, 'it is for you – for I want so much to do all I can for you . . .' Doubtless, Tom believed what he wrote and Mary derived some solace from reading it. The words, just the same, revealed less than the entire truth. Tom was driven to work by something deep within him: the desire to do well had been instilled by his mother and fostered by the expectations of his family. Success was to be his gift to them as well as to himself.

The next morning, early, he wrote again, now completely practical:

I read in *The Times* today that Aubrey Laurence is dead, who is Chancellor of the Diocese of Winchester – that means that the position of Chancellor of the Diocese is vacant – which means that a member of the bar must be appointed to fill it – and the appointment is made by the Bishop. It is only a spare time job for a member of the bar, for many persons in big practices have held at the same time appointments as chancellors . . .

So it comes to this – would your father think it quite ridiculous for me to try to get the appointment . . .

I thought I would just mention it as I never believe in letting slip even the remotest opportunity – I expect it is one of the cases when one must be early in the field.

In 1916, when Tom wrote to Reg from Oxford about his ambitions and in 1920, when he wrote to Mary from Winchester, his aspirations were unfocused and diffuse. In the intervening years, Denning had discovered exactly where he wanted to go and, more important, had been learning the skills to get there.

'I, too, noticed the announcement of Laurence's death,' Mary replied, 'and of course I immediately wondered if my darling could do it – I knew he *could* but I know so little about such things that I dared not suggest it – however apparently you jumped into the minds of Father and Mother too – and now on receiving your letter Father has promised to write to the Bishop.'

The Chancellor is the judge of the Bishop's diocesan court, who must be a barrister of at least seven years' standing. Mr Harvey thought there was little chance of Tom's getting the Chancellorship and was proved right. Tom would have to wait a few more years before becoming, first, Chancellor of the Diocese of Southwark in 1937 and then, in 1942, Chancellor of the Diocese of London.

On Sunday 1 June 1930 Tom wrote to Mary from The Hermitage, after spending Saturday with her at Fawley:

> The Saturday we had longed for came up to and beyond expectations – for being with you was quite perfect . . . it already seems quite a short time to next weekend – and then we shall really be only 2 short months to our wedding day. I went to church this morning with mother and then a little walk by myself – and all the time I was dreaming of the perfect happiness of our honeymoon and our home . . .
>
> Mother was delighted with the Lilies of the Valley – and I noticed that they have been carefully placed by the table where I am writing – so they make me think specially of you . . .

Mary had been troubled by pains in her shoulder that had been diagnosed as rheumatism and Tom reassured her: 'My darling, I am not really worried about your rheumatism because I feel it will all go soon.'

Two days later, after discussing the wedding date with his senior clerk, Tom told Mary, 'he agrees that the 3 weeks at the end of August is the best time to be away so that we shall soon be able to make our final decision as to dates.' That day, 3 June, Mary went to bed with a temperature. On 5 June Tom despatched 'at short intervals today all sorts of telepathic messages to you to wish you soon to be quite well again.' He was convinced that the rheumatism would 'quite go when we are married.' After the Whitsun weekend, when, instead of the tennis they had planned, Tom could only sit in the garden with Mary or whisper to her through her bedroom door, Tom returned to London, still certain that she would soon be well.

On 11 June he wrote that Moir, 'the solicitor in these "digs" ', had been talking to him 'about marriage settlements and insurance policies and so on – and when we have decided what we will do in those directions I think it would be just as well to let his firm do it all for us – as they are a first-rate firm called Fladgate & Co. Moreover,' he added, with an eye on his practice, 'he does send me a certain amount of work so that we hope it will increase his loyalty . . .' Tom also talked the matter over with Henn-Collins, who 'seemed to think it would be wise for me to insure for a sum of £4000, for which the yearly premium would be about £100 – and then for us to have a marriage settlement of the £4000 policy.' Though Tom was still planning their future, Mary was feeling no better. On Friday 13 June she 'woke up feeling mouldy with temp 102.'[26] She was taken to a nursing home in Southampton and Mrs Harvey wrote to Tom: 'She has your photo looking at her from the mantelpiece in her room.'

Tom was at Exeter on 18 June, staying the night with Mary's cousin, Dr Blackley, when Mrs Harvey telephoned to tell Tom that the doctors had diagnosed tuberculosis. 'I fell to the floor in a faint – for the first time in my life. It was the shock. I knew what it meant. I remembered my brother Gordon. When I came to, the doctor and his wife were there. They helped me upstairs. I did not sleep much. But next morning I went down to the Castle and did my case.'[1]

Though Mrs Harvey had given Tom the bad news, Mary herself had written to him as soon as she knew the worst. . . . 'it hurts terribly to have to tell you that they have found TB in that one lung . . . The part that hurts most is that having kept you waiting all these years, I have hoped and longed to give you your heart's desire this summer . . .' In their letters both Tom and Mary acknowledged their pleasure in the physical side of love – their delight in 'kissing in the car' and in ordering the sheets and pillowcases 'for *our* bed'. Though Mary knew 'how much you want what I want . . .' their shared beliefs ensured their restraint.

'My dear old Tom, I am so very sorry my news bowled you over last night,' wrote Mrs Harvey, entirely literally, on the morning of 19 June. 'I am of course not telling Mary. Don't take it too hard, old man; the doctors are very confident of complete recovery.' As soon as he could, Tom remembered in *The Family Story*, he went to see Mary. 'I bought some grapes in Southampton and took them to her . . . With tears in her eyes she said: "I do not think I should hold you now." I pressed her hand. I kissed her brow. "We will go through it together!" She sobbed with gratitude. I kissed her brow again. I did not kiss her lips – for fear of infection – not from that time onwards.'

But before Tom could visit Mary, he had written to her, on 19 June:

My very own beloved sweetheart,
    It is just today that I have wanted to be actually at your side – just to hold you in my arms and comfort you – for, my beloved, this is indeed the time of all times when I want to be with you – for disappointments have come and hopes are delayed . . .
    My beloved, I grieve because I know it is so hard for you – so great a disappointment – but can we – let us – look beyond our immediate disappointments and look still into the future . . . for you will undoubtedly in the course of time be perfectly well again – and what joy we then shall have.

If Tom's life, in the past four months, had been hectic, balancing work with visits to Whitchurch and Fawley, it had been infinitely delightful for him. Now, with the wedding cancelled and Mary brought to Guy's Hospital, he was oppressed by fear for the outcome of the illness. 'I still marvel often at your wonderful love for me and your great steadfastness . . .' Mary wrote from Guy's on 26 June. By August she was able to go home to 'a hut in the garden. Set in the middle of the lovely lawn . . . I went every weekend and sat with her.'

For her birthday, that September, Tom had two brooches sent on approval to Mary by a jeweller and, this time, she was happy to choose one. 'Father and Mother Denning,' she told him, when she wrote to thank him on 24 September, had 'been to Camberley on Monday for little Jack's first birthday' [Jack, Reg's first son was named for the eldest brother killed in action]'– did you write to your little godson?' she reminded Tom.

It would be two years before Mary would be well enough to set a new wedding date. In that time, both personally and by letter, Tom instilled in Mary the courage to carry on. 'Reg has rather a good motto which he says to himself if times are difficult,' he wrote on 22 June 1930, '– and I say to myself too – Oliver Cromwell's "Trust in God and keep your powder dry." ' His charm eased their paths in many ways. At the hospital, the sister and nurses were happy to let him visit whenever he could find the time. Once, when he forgot to take Mary the envelopes for which she was waiting, he wrote to her triumphantly from the train: 'I have already persuaded the bookstall man to post you some envelopes and a ticket collector to post your letter to Miss Squires.' Another time Mary wrote: 'Mr Simmonds delivered my chocolates last night by 7.15 pm. They never deliver anything as a rule but I suppose Mrs Simmonds "fell for you".'

His practice was growing – though from time to time, when he lost a case, he still had qualms about his future. 'I sometimes have "panics" lest I should fail – but, oh, my darling, I feel that with you I can do so much – so that the "panics" fly away.' In August 1930, when their marriage should have taken place, he was working as a junior to D. N. Pritt KC on a case where 'two big American combines are at one another's throats and of course spare no expenses', and was expecting to 'have a hand' in a big action about the control of the West Indian fruit trade.[6]

One of the more attractive customs of the Bar was the giving of a red bag. All juniors carried their wigs and gowns in a blue bag unless and until they were given a red bag by a silk for whom they had done exceptionally good work on a case. On 23 October 1930 Tom wrote to Mary: 'I am pleased today because Pritt has given me a red bag – and written me a charming note with it which I will show you – the only sad thing is that now I shall not be using the blue bag on which you sewed my initials.'

Pritt, who, as a junior, had given Denning the only cheques he ever received for devilling, was a remarkable man. With great perspicacity, he wrote from 2 Pump Court, on 24 October 1930:

Dear Denning,

I would like to be able to boast in my old age, in the warm corner which is being reserved for me in a nice Berkshire workhouse, where I have 'acquired a settlement', that I did at any rate give a red bag to one of the most noted judges of the day; and the safest way to ensure that is, I think, to offer you one.

Will you honour me by accepting it?

Yours sincerely,
D. N. Pritt

Church on Sunday remained a very important part of Tom's life. At Fawley, Mr Harvey would sometimes give Tom and Mary Communion in her room. At Whitchurch, Tom – and any of the family who happened to be there – accompanied Clara to All Hallows. (Charles, who sang in the choir, would go alone.) It was therefore very uncomfortable for Tom to spend a Sunday in the home of people who did not attend church. On 7 December 1930 Tom wrote to Mary that he was troubled, after staying Saturday night at Guildford, that he could not attend church, 'as nobody here went.' The thought seems not to have occurred to him that he might have gone alone. Perhaps, as with his decision to drink lemonade, he was still troubled that people might think him a bit odd. Only much later would he begin to enjoy being thought 'a character'.

After a busy December, ever careful to divide his time between Mary and his family, Tom spent half of his Christmas break – the time he allowed himself could scarcely be called a vacation – at Fawley and half at Whitchurch. With Mary's Christmas letter to Tom was enclosed one from Mrs Harvey: '. . . you are a good son, Tom, and I love you for it . . .' As the Dennings looked back on 1930 it must have seemed eventful. The country was in the throes of a serious economic crisis. In September the pound had been devalued, unemployed workers had clashed with police and, finally, the unthinkable had happened, when naval ratings at Invergordon on the Cromarty Firth, had mutinied against proposed cuts in their pay. In October, the Labour Party had been routed in a General Election and virtually wiped out.

Trouble in the spring in India, where Marjorie and her army husband had been since 1927, prompted Charles, still missing his daughter, to write to Tom, on 27 April, that Marjorie and the children 'may have to come home.' Despite Charles's wishful thinking, it would be some time before, in 1945, Marjorie and Johnnie Haynes would go to live with her parents at The Hermitage; it would not be too long, though, before Betty, the first of Marjorie's four daughters, would come home to train as a teacher and once again make her base with her grandparents.

In the course of the year, Tom had seen a fair amount of both his brothers. His nights at The Hermitage often coincided with Norman's, when the two would walk to Micheldever station and catch a train back to London together. He had also spent time with Reg, visiting him at Camberley and taking the occasional meal at Reg's London club. When Reg was posted to India in February 1931, Tom 'dropped in to say goodbye to Reg and Eileen'[6] on 16 February, but then felt the urge to go to Waterloo, the following morning, to see them off by the 9.30 train.

Much of Tom's life in the early 1930s was dominated by bus and railway timetables. As he chased about, often catching a connection – or missing it – by the skin of his teeth, Mary began to press him to learn to drive. 'I find the obtaining of a driving licence is a bigger job than one thought,' wrote the reluctant Tom on 31 March 1931, 'it means going to County Hall and making a declaration of fitness – I shall try to find time but it is somewhat doubtful.' Tom had a remarkable facility for fitting into his busy schedule those things that he wanted to do and finding obstacles to prevent his doing the things he would rather not. It was not until 10 August that he obtained a licence; he even used it on rare occasions, but after nearly spilling the car into a ditch while attempting a turn in the 1940s, he declared that in no circumstances ever again would he get behind the wheel. Nor did he!

The next two years passed in much the same way as 1930, save that Denning was getting bigger – and better-paid – cases. His London connections were sufficiently well established that he no longer needed to take so much circuit work. The Hampshire solicitors, he wrote on 15 February 1931, 'apparently know now that my interests are in London – it is, of course, impossible to run both.' To some extent this eased his journeyings; still he was kept busy: meeting

Mary on her visits to London for treatment; arranging for her to stay with Aunt Min or a friend – Mrs Harvey was reluctant to permit Mary to stay at Beaufort Street – visiting her at Guy's during spells as an in-patient (Christmas 1932 was spent there); rushing to Fawley and to Whitchurch at weekends. Somehow, he managed to content all those on whom his own happiness depended, while maintaining a steely determination to build his practice at the Bar.

Among the many entries of two guineas in Denning's Fee Book, there were now a few satisfyingly substantial figures. A 50-guinea brief for the Attorney-General of Canada, with ten-guinea 'refreshers' (additional fees for each day after the first), sent to him by solicitors Charles Russell & Co., kept Denning in the Privy Council for five days in July 1931. *Regulation and Control of Aeronautics in Canada* was more than just a remunerative case: in it, Denning could feel himself at the very heart of affairs. With the growth of the aeronautics industry, a dispute had arisen between the Dominion and the Provinces of Canada as to which should have the right to issue certificates to pilots and to license and inspect aircraft and aerodromes. There were five silks in the case, including John Simon, a future Lord Chancellor. The decision in favour of the Dominion satisfied Denning's keen delight in winning and encouraged hopes that more work of this calibre would come his way. 'I am so pleased about the Dominion of Canada case,' Mary wrote on 8 July, 'I hope it will lead to more.' But by the end of the month she was begging him, for the sake of his health, not to work during the first fortnight of August.

Though nowadays the same accommodation would be thought spacious, in 1931 it seemed to the occupants of Henn-Collins's chambers that there were too many people in the set on the first floor. Denning heard that accommodation immediately below would become available but, worried about the outgoings, decided to make a reduced offer for it. On 26 January 1932, the Middle Temple Estates Office informed him that his 'application of the 21st inst., to be allotted the chambers at 4 Brick Court at an inclusive rent of £170 per an.' would receive consideration. 'I am afraid, however,' the letter continued, 'that there is very little chance of the Committee consenting to make any reduction in the rent of £200 per an.'[28]

The building where in March 1932 Denning would take on the

financial commitments of a head of chambers was on the corner of Brick Court and Middle Temple Lane. It was relatively modern, having been built in the 1880s. The gothic-style doorway – with Prince of Wales feathers carved on a shield above and to its left – gave on to a small hall, paved with flagstones. To left and right of it were sets of chambers and, immediately ahead, was the winding, narrow stone staircase.

The chambers in 4 Brick Court were somewhat curious: a sort of federation, of which two were doing patent work, with Rudolph Moritz KC at the head of one and K. S. Shelly, succeeded by Guy Aldous, at the head of the other. Opposite Moritz, on the first floor, Henn-Collins combined a very high-class common law practice with copyright, a practice to some extent inherited from his father. There was one head clerk for all the chambers: Tom Lloyd, who was quite a character in the Temple. 'He used to drink with solicitors' managing clerks and was good at getting the work in.' Lloyd's son became Tom's first clerk. Just as Tom could – and did – go upstairs to seek Henn-Collins's advice, so his clerk learned the ropes from his father.

Tom's set was on the ground floor, opposite Shelly. His own room, on the right as you entered the door, was, as he described those of Henn-Collins and O'Hagan, 'a fine large room overlooking Brick Court.' High-ceilinged, bright and airy, the room was lined with bookshelves containing Tom's newly acquired set of Law Reports, together with the other books he had collected over his years at the Bar. He worked on an upright desk. His briefs and instructions to advise, tied with pink tape, lay on side tables and in piles on the floor. The windows, that today look upon the car park, in those days, before the Second World War, looked across to Numbers 2 and 3 Brick Court, which then stood upon the site. Numbers 2 and 3 were in a very much older building, where once the writer Oliver Goldsmith had chambers. Though Tom had little time to stare at them out of his window, he did occasionally notice the milk being delivered by horse and cart.

When Tom had been asked, in February 1932, to supervise a new edition – the ninth – of *Bullen & Leake's Precedents*, or to give it its full title, *Precedents of Pleadings in Actions in the King's Bench Division of the High Court*, Henn-Collins warned him against the undertaking as he was already fully stretched. The fee of £250 had been too inviting. In the end, most of the work was to be done, with Tom's supervision, by Arthur Grattan Bellew, to whom Tom paid £180.

Arthur Grattan Bellew, an Irishman, was with Tom in chambers for a time, though he gave up practice, after the publication of *Bullen & Leake*, in 1935, to join the Egyptian Legal Service. With a break for military service during the Second World War, when he was taken prisoner by the Japanese, he passed the rest of his career in the Colonial Legal Service and was knighted in 1959.

Sharing the room next to Tom's with Grattan Bellew were Roy Wilson, 'a good person to talk things over with', and Jocelyn ('Jack') Simon. Wilson had 'a very good common law practice and might,' Tom thought, 'have become a High Court Judge.' Instead he became an authority on industrial matters and, as President of the Industrial Court, was knighted in 1962. For a time, in the late 1940s, Tom's family and Wilson's would be neighbours in Carlton Gardens.

Jack Simon was a member of chambers from 1935 to 1937, before moving to those of Seymour Karminski, which specialised in divorce. Simon would have a distinguished career, rising in politics to become Solicitor-General and in the law to become President of the Probate, Divorce and Admiralty Division, before being made a Lord of Appeal in 1971, taking the title Lord Simon of Glaisdale.

Since Denning's chambers were in Temple – and it was more convenient for him to lunch in Hall there than at Lincoln's Inn – on 10 May 1932 he became a member *ad eundem* of Middle Temple. He often shared a table with Theobald Mathew, whose humorous book, *Forensic Fables*, was popular among lawyers. In *The Family Story* Denning proudly claims that, in the fable of *The Double-First and the Old Hand*, he was the Double-First.

In the small room overlooking Middle Temple Lane, that corresponded to the room upstairs, where once Tom had done his pupillage, Denning now sat his pupils, each of whom paid 100 guineas for the pupillage. He did not, he told the writer, give much time to teaching them. Perhaps he felt that they must, as he had done, find their own ways of establishing a practice. Perhaps he did not have the time – or even the inclination – to exercise the somewhat paternal concern that Henn-Collins had shown for him. He must, none the less, have been considered a good master: on 1 July 1935 he would write to Mary that a retired judge had 'made enquiries in two very distinguished quarters for advice about a pupil and both said that Denning was the best person for him to come to.'

'By the time Tom had finished *Smith's Leading Cases* and *Bullen & Leake*,' recalled Lord Simon of Glaisdale, 'there was nothing he did not know about the common law and very little he did not know about the law generally. Yet his practice was nothing like the one he merited on his intellectual power and his knowledge of the law. He was curiously lacking in confidence. He always knew what the law was, but he didn't know what the result of a case should be. He used to canvass opinion round the chambers from one after another, even from myself: "Would you say that there was a good chance, or a fair chance, or a reasonable chance or some chance." But once he got on the Bench he seems never to have harboured a doubt.' Lord Denning, nearly 60 years later, found it difficult to accept that he canvassed opinion, but remembered being 'often hesitant about the outcome and nervous before the case started.'

Though Tom found some way to rally Mary's spirits when she felt low, he had his own moments of depression and began to feel that 'other people's weddings will keep presenting themselves.'[6] Acting as Jack Darlington's best man, at a time when Mary's doctors held out no hope of Mary's being fit enough to set a new wedding date in 1931, found him in uncharacteristically low spirits. A typical few days of juggled engagements in April 1932, when Mary was again in hospital, saw Tom spend a couple of hours with her on Saturday afternoon; go back to Guy's in the evening with eggs, jam and butter; lunch at the Curries in Westbourne Terrace on Sunday to see Eileen and his godson Jack, who were home from India; spend the afternoon with Mary; win a case in the House of Lords on Monday – and back again to Guy's. It was not until 26 August 1932 that Mary was able to enter in her diary: 'Dr Marshall says we may get married at Christmas.' Now, at last Tom and Mary could enjoy a partial replay of the months immediately following their engagement.

By September they had found a flat at 1 Brick Court – at a rent of £187 10s per annum, plus water rate – and started to order furniture. Once again, they planned to be married in a vacation: not the Long Vacation this time, but just after Christmas. On Saturday 24 December, 'a lovely day',[26] they collected their wedding presents from the Temple and caught the 4.26 train to Fawley. Tom spent his last Christmas as a single man at Whitchurch with his parents. On Boxing Day he was back in Fawley, to help Mary display their presents for visitors. Still there was a social divide, though Tom was now firmly established on the other side; at 2.45 on 27 December 'the Parish' came to see the presents, followed later by the local gentry, who stayed for tea.

On Wednesday, 28 December 1932, twelve years after he had first proposed to her, Tom Denning was married to Mary Harvey in her father's church, at Fawley. Mr Harvey did not give his daughter away: he officiated at the ceremony, with the Bishop of Southampton, who gave the address. Mary walked down the aisle on the arm of Barry, Major F. Barrington Harvey OBE the only one of her brothers who was not in India. The congregation filled the church as Mary came to stand beside Tom, barely reaching above the level of his chin. His best man, Arthur Grattan Bellew, stood on his other side. Apart from Charles and Clara, no other member of his family was able to attend Tom's crowning moment – they were all, at that time, stationed abroad.

Mary, the *Hampshire Advertiser* reported, wore 'a dress of parchment satin with a shoulder train of old Indian embroidery and a veil of old Lyons lace.' She carried a bouquet of arum lilies. Behind her walked her three little Blackley cousins, in 'ankle length frocks of emerald green rayon velvet and caps of latticed green velvet.' The children carried posies of Christmas roses and wore the crystal necklaces Tom had given them.

There was no reception. After the ceremony, Mary changed into a frock of brown silk and left, with Tom, to spend the first night of their marriage in Salisbury.

8

The Silken Gown

The day after their marriage, Tom and Mary travelled on to Torquay, arriving in the early evening at the Palace Hotel, where Mary wrote in her diary: 'We are amazingly happy.' Though on New Year's Eve there was a Fancy Dress Ball, they 'came to bed about 10.30' and were up early to greet the year that would, they expected, satisfy their prayers and hopes. After attending 8.00 am service at St Matthias's Church, they crossed the Downs to Babbacombe, setting the pattern for the remaining week of their honeymoon, which flew past, with walks in the mornings and dancing or watching 'pictures' in the evenings. On Saturday, 7 January 1933 they 'came home – great – the flat is really charming.'[26]

Though the flat was far from ready, their first visitors, Professor and Mrs Webb – who brought them 'a nice jug' for a wedding present – called the following afternoon and Mary 'gave them tea.' That evening Tom worked late but in great contentment, for he worked at last in the comfort of his own home. After the hectic years of delicately balancing the conflicting demands upon his time, it was a blessed relief to be settled in Brick Court, his home and his chambers a stone's throw from one another. He was no longer much involved in circuit work; most of his court appearances were within easy walking distance; he fell into the habit of bringing home papers and dealing with them, after dinner, in the flat.

Before dinner, if the weather was not too raw, he might stroll with Mary in the Temple Gardens. On Saturdays they visited his parents or hers, or walked in one of the parks. 'Still very cold,' Mary wrote in her diary on Saturday, 28 January, 'tho' a lovely day. Tom & I went to Regents Park in the afternoon – but skating has been stopped.' Then, a fortnight later, 'To Whitchurch – all well there – stayed the night.' On Sundays, when they were in London, they attended the

Temple Church or St Clement Dane's before Tom worked and Mary, sometimes, typed an Opinion for him. Occasionally she went to court to 'hear a little of his case.'[26]

On 6 February, Mary noted, Tom was in the House of Lords, 'so not home for lunch.' At the same time he was heavily involved in the preparation of a case to be heard before the Privy Council on 10 February.

The Fee Book still had a number of entries showing two guineas, but for some time there had been much more lucrative work. The brief for the plaintiff, in *Mann Taylor* v. *the Royal Bank of Canada*, where Tom was led again by D. N. Pritt, brought him a brief fee of 275 guineas, with 35-guinea refreshers. Even the guinea work led sometimes, agreeably, to better things: the firm of Soames Edwards & Co, regular supporters of Denning, paid him a guinea for a draft letter in the matter of *Beresford* v. *Royal Insurance*, which ended, in 1938, in the House of Lords.

Just as Tom's life had taken on a more even tenor, so a new peace and contentment had come to the older Dennings in Whitchurch. Despite the fact that Marjorie, Reg and Norman were so far from England – or perhaps because of it – The Hermitage had become a centre for all the Dennings. Clara and Charles were again at the heart of their family, sharing their happiness and the success that Clara so passionately wanted for them. In May Norman returned from a tour of duty in Singapore, where he had met and married Iris, the daughter of a master mariner, Captain R. J. Curtis. Tom and Mary spent the night of 6 May at The Hermitage, to meet the latest Mrs Denning.

Charles & Clara were also in better shape financially. After the death of his wife, Grandfather Thompson had gone to live in North Finchley with his daughter Kate Sowden (Aunt Kit), where he had died in 1930. By his will Clara inherited £600 of 5 per cent War Loan. She must already have had £300 from John Thompson as, on 14 April 1934, she made a note, possibly for Tom's benefit: 'I have £1,200 invested – £900 of it saved for me by my father – £300 left by my two boys Jack & Gordon.'[29] She started, but did not finish a direction for the division of these investments after her death, a task that she and Charles, like so many people contemplating their demise, would undertake on several occasions in the years remaining to them.

In a will made on 2 November 1933, using a printed form, Charles left Marjorie his marble clock and bequeathed to his three sons his most precious possessions, stipulating that Clara should keep them for her life. Reg would have 'the War Medals, football medals, plaque and Scroll of Honour of my son, the late Captain John Edward Newdigate Poyntz Denning, the dispatch from the Admiralty to my son, the late Sub-Lieutenant Charles Gordon Denning, for his services at Jutland, the name plate and picture of HMS *Morris*,' with other mementoes. To Tom, Charles left 'my secretary Book Case, the Plaque and Scroll of Honour of my son, the late Sub-Lieutenant Charles Gordon Denning,' and to Norman 'the brass Candlesticks given to me by the choir, "All Hallows", Whitchurch, the War Medals and dirk of my son the late Sub-Lieutenant Charles Gordon Denning.'

Some time later Charles sent Tom an undated letter, saying he had made 'a poor sort of a will' but had since sold the stock mentioned in it and re-invested 'in £200 2½% Consols in Mother's name – bless her.' Charles was 'rather exercised' in his mind about what might happen to The Hermitage. He hoped it would remain in the family, 'regard being had as to whether Marjorie or Norman might like to live in Whitchurch and rent the old place.'

With regard to The Hermitage, Charles prepared an undated note, curious in the light of Tom's writing in *The Family Story* that Reg purchased the house for their parents:

The cost of the Hermitage was £500, plus £25 paid Mr Waydelin for unexpired lease. Of this Reg found £265, Tom £160 and ourselves £100. Title deeds in Reg's name.

When occasion arises Reg to enter into full possession, reimbursing Tom to the extent of £210, namely the £160 he found and £50 of the £100 that was ours.

Alternatively, should Reg not want the Hermitage and wish it transferred to Tom, then Tom to pay Reg £315, comprising the £265 he invested and £50 of the £100 that was ours.

It seems unlikely that Charles would be mistaken about a matter of such moment to him but, when the author asked Denning specifically about his father's note, he still did not remember making any contribution. But then, it must be said that he had forgotten telling Reg in 1914 that he would share some of his precious Hurford Scholarship money with Marjorie;[6] nor at any time did he mention having given his parents help, if not earlier, then certainly before 1935, when, on 12 February, Mary wrote: 'I'm sorry about the reduction of your people's pension – I'm afraid it will pinch them rather but perhaps you will be able to help them a little more'.

Tom could not have made a contribution of £160 to the purchase price of The Hermitage in 1922, when he had no capital save what little may have been left of his gratuity and was embarking on his new career. He may have reimbursed Reg at a later date; alternatively, Reg, who was devoted to his brother and his parents, may have told Charles that Tom contributed. What does emerge is the mutual trust and sense of family property that lingered between the Dennings, much as it was in 1913 when Gordon sent Reg two shillings as his share of the expenses of their 'glorious' night out, adding 'do not mention it to Jack as he sent it me.'

The cosy, convenient arrangement, by which Tom could live and work in Brick Court, did not last long. The flat described in *The Family Story* – 'no heating except by coal – carried up to the bin outside the front door. No refrigerator. Only a safe on the north wall. No lift – but sixty stairs to climb' – was hardly the ideal home for a woman so recently recovered from tuberculosis. Nor, indeed, was the foggy London air the best for her to breathe. 'To live in London was a mistake,' Tom came to recognise.[1] 'It was before the use of smokeless fuel. It was before Central London became a smokeless zone. It was in the days when coal was the principal source of heat. Grime and soot came in by the windows and covered everything each day.'

By September, Mary's lungs had broken down again. A new treatment was tried, which had unpleasant side effects – 'Her lovely skin became covered with whitish scabs'[1] – but was unsuccessful. On 14 November, Mary was transferred to Brompton Hospital for an operation to collapse one lung. 'Pain beastly,' she wrote on 16 November. A second operation was performed on 11 December and, instead of spending, as he had planned, his first Christmas in his own home, Tom stayed at Aunt Min's on Christmas Eve and, on Christmas morning, he and Mary opened their presents together on her hospital bed.

She left hospital on 13 January 1934 and Tom took her to Mundesley Sanatorium, where she had stayed in 1930, when she first became ill. Mr Harvey had retired and moved to Number 7, Banister Gardens, Southampton. It was there, to her parents, that Mary went, when she left the sanatorium in March. Not until July was she able to go back, for just one week, to the flat in Brick Court.

As Denning's practice increased, he continued to push himself but, on 5 February 1934, he wrote to Mary: 'I have made up my mind at all events not to work too late in the evenings because it affects my work next day if I do.' Life was a little easier for him when the Long Vacation arrived. Mary spent August at her brother's home in Hove and Tom was able to be at the coast each evening, even though he went frequently to London by day. He allowed himself a few days' holiday, when Charles and Clara also took a week in Hove. As he had done when Mary was ill before their marriage Tom contrived to fit into each week of the weary months of 1934 – like pieces of the intricate jig-saw puzzles with which Mary whiled away the hours – time with Mary, time with his parents and time for his work.

Once it was clear that Mary could never live in London, the flat had to go. The Middle Temple Estate Office accepted the surrender of Tom's lease with effect from 17 November 1934 and Tom temporarily, he hoped, returned to a room at Mrs Cross's in Beaufort Street. When Mary was well enough, he decided, he would find a house in the country, from which he could travel up to town each day.

In 1934 Denning had his first contact with exemption clauses – clauses printed in a company's documents of contract, often in very small print, which are designed to exempt the company from as many grounds of liability on the contract as the ingenuity of its lawyers can devise. In his years in the Court of Appeal Denning would mount an attack on such clauses and find ingenious methods of circumventing them: in 1934, in *L'Estrange* v. *Graucob*, when he acted for the company, his only concern was 'to win it if I could.' Which, in the Court of Appeal, he did.

With Denning, the desire to win, the passion for success was bred-in-the-bone. As Clara had gently, but firmly, moulded the character of her children, so, with charm and persistence, Tom would pursue whatever was his aim of the moment. What gave an extra dimension to his personality was the humour with which he met defeat.

On 22 December 1934 Tom collected Mary from the Brompton Hospital, where she had been since November for yet another operation, and took her by train to her parents' home in Southampton; there she would remain until they found the house they were seeking in Sussex. It was a small house, called Fair Close, which they rented, halfway between Cuckfield and Haywards Heath, on Tylers Green. Each morning Tom walked the mile and a half to the station and caught a train for Waterloo. Each evening he went home again from the station by bus: 'It cost me one penny (old coinage).'[1] Just as Clara had employed the young daughters of local farmers, so Mary found Rose Dummer a 15-year-old girl from Wales to help in the house. 'She was our real friend,' Tom remembered in *The Family Story*.

They had not come entirely friendless to the area: even when Reg was in India, his wife was very often at their home in Haywards Heath with their children, Tom's godchild Jack, now five years old, and David, who was born in India in 1933. Through the church, Tom and Mary got to know other families in the area, as well as their neighbours. 'Everyone was very welcoming. We made many friends.'[1] Mary, as she had done in her father's parishes, became involved in committees and good causes and Tom found time to play an occasional, not very good, round of golf. This time, it seemed, Mary's recovery was assured. Only one thing was lacking to complete their happiness: children. A family man to his finger-tips, Tom longed for children but Mary had been advised for the time being against having a baby. As he had once felt that weddings kept presenting themselves, while his own had constantly to be postponed, so now he saw children all about him, while hoping for his own. At the homes around Cuckfield where Tom and Mary took tea or attended sherry parties children were often in evidence. Reg and Eileen's two small boys were frequent visitors to the house and, when Reg was on leave, Tom often joined his brother's family for Sunday walks.

Slowly over the next two years, Mary's health improved and so did Tom's practice. A brief fee of 235 guineas, in July 1936, was unusual, but there were a gratifying number of fees in the 50–100 guinea range –

sufficient to enable him to earn, in 1937, just over £3000. Though there were one or two men at the bar said to earn more than ten times as much, £3000 at the time was a good income. It enabled Tom to live very well.

From 1931, when Japanese troops entered Manchuria, it had been clear that the First World War would not prove 'the war to end all wars'. As early as 1934 the aggressive policies of Hitler's Germany convinced British Chiefs of Staff and some politicians that Britain must re-arm. In 1937, Paymaster Lieutenant-Commander Denning was instructed by the Admiralty to build up the Operational Intelligence Centre, where, in the event of war, the value of information received would be assessed. His new job, which would keep him in London, delighted all the Dennings. Norman and Iris took a house at Esher.

Mary was so far recovered that, in March 1937, she went on holiday to the South of France with her parents and Gladys Burlton, in whose home at Leominster she had once helped to look after the cows. Tom was still anxious about Mary. If she forgot, in any letter, to tell Tom that she felt well, he began to worry and she had to reassure him. In May, his name was put forward as Chancellor of the diocese of Southwark – an appointment he had sought unsuccessfully in the diocese of Winchester when he and Mary were first engaged. There was very little work involved, Tom recalled, though he used to advise the bishop occasionally. For every marriage licence issued the registrar was paid a fee, 'of which I got something. During the war, with so many marriages, I got quite substantial fees.' Tom's only other duty as Chancellor was to grant faculties for alterations to churches, such as erecting a new memorial.

The crowning moment of 1937 came when, at last, Dr Marshall said Mary might have a baby. In great content, as the year drew to an end, Mary wrote in her diary: 'Rose and I made the Christmas pudding and Christmas cake.' On Friday 24 December she noted that Tom was home for tea. They had a quiet Christmas Day, after going to church, and on Boxing Day Tom went to Whitchurch.

The year 1938 was 'the happiest of years' for them. For some months Tom had contemplated applying for silk, but held back, partly lest his practice might be adversely affected when he could no longer draft pleadings or go into court without a junior beside him. In

part, too, was the thought of refusal. 'In those days a junior was very
cautious before applying for silk. He had to notify all those on the
circuit senior to him. The word got round to solicitors. They would
cease to instruct him. If he were refused it was a bad mark against
him.'[1] In January 1938 Denning sent his letters to those senior to him
on the circuit. In reply he received a number of graceful acknow-
ledgements. 'I have no doubt of the result of your application,' wrote
one recipient of his letter, 'and wish you the best of luck.' Then
Denning wrote a short letter of application to Lord Maugham, the
Lord Chancellor, 'without giving any references' – in those days the
number of successful juniors 'was so small that anyone acquainted
with the profession knew them.'[1] From the House of Lords a letter,
dated 18 January 1938, informed Denning that the Lord Chancellor
would consider him, when making recommendations to the King.
'Tom has got "silk". Hurrah!' wrote Mary in her diary for Friday, 1
April. The following day, to celebrate, they went to see *Victoria
Regina* and 'much enjoyed it.'

'The list was published on All Fools' Day,' wrote one of the legal
journals, 'the significance of which could scarcely escape those who
had applied for silk unsuccessfully.' There were 15 new silks, on
whom the journal commented: 'Many common law juniors will have
especial cause to congratulate Mr A. T. Denning on his silken gown,
for he had one of the biggest of post war junior practices, and his
elevation will release this work for his competitors.'

Amongst the solicitors who had regularly instructed him, Denning
had built a reputation for hard work, intelligence and reliability. He
was unfailingly courteous to instructing solicitors and gave lay clients
confidence that he would fight hard for them. On 6 December 1937,
from the Solicitor's Office, at Waterloo Station, a member of the
railway's legal service replied to Tom's letter of good wishes on his
retirement: 'You have but little to thank me for, it is to your good self
my grateful thanks are really due.'[30]

After the publication of the list of silks, the congratulations poured
in.[30] A junior looked forward to being led by Tom. From 19–21
Moorgate, a solicitor wrote:

The scientific and thorough method (if I may humbly say so)
which I had the privilege to observe at many a conference with

you, made me long fear that you would one day be removed from the cut-and-thrust of ordinary day-to-day work – where your assistance will be badly missed.

From 2 Garden Court came:

Welcome to the First Class Carriage. You will find travelling much more comfortable and I hope more profitable.

Congratulations came from fellow barristers Neville Laski and Gilbert Beyfus, from Parliamentary Counsel Harold Chorley, Tom's ex-pupil John Monckton and Mrs Henn-Collins who, surprising as it seems today, still addressed Tom, formally, as 'Mr Denning'.

D. N. Pritt, by whom Tom had most enjoyed being led, wrote: 'A silk *and* a lawyer, – a rare and precious combination.' From Gerald Gardiner, a future Lord Chancellor, who had read jurisprudence at Magdalen at the same time as Tom, came the tribute: 'It will be a comfort to us fellows to have a leader who really understands pleading and interlocutory matters . . .'

At the silk ceremony, Tom recalled, 'David Jenkins and I were very much the junior ones. We had to go up to Maugham and were admitted. We had our photographs taken outside Westminster. Then we went back to the courts and we had to go around to each of the courts and the presiding judge would say "Mr Denning, His Majesty having been pleased to appoint you one of his counsel learned in the law, will you be pleased to take your place within the Bar, accordingly." Then you'd move in and you'd bow to the Court and the other barristers and the other barristers would move out of the seats and you'd sit down and the judge would say "Mr Denning, do you move?" You'd bow and say that you had no motion and go out.' That day, Friday 8 April, Mary recorded, 'A lovely day. Went to London to see Tom make his "bow". Great gathering of the Denning clans.'

Shortly before Denning took silk, he was in a case that lasted four days in the House of Lords. *Beresford* v. *Royal Insurance Company* was one of only two of his cases at the Bar (the other was *L'Estrange* v. *Graucob*) that Tom would include in *The Family Story*: ('I will not recount the various cases in which I was engaged. That is the bane of legal biographies.') The way in which Tom recounted a case was far from baneful and the cases he chose made good stories; when he wrote *The Family Story* he must have told each of them many times. He probably felt no need to look them up in the Law Reports, but launched straight in to the exciting part:

There was a Major Rowlandson once who insured his life for £80,000. The insurance was due to come to an end at three o'clock on a June afternoon. If he couldn't find the premium, it would lapse. If he died before three, all the money would come in. If he died after three, there would be no money at all. That afternoon at half-past two, he went to his solicitors in Chancery Lane. At a quarter-to-three, he came out and called a taxi. He said to the taxi-driver: 'Drive me to my flat in Albemarle Street'; and added: 'As you pass St. James's Palace clock, look at the time and note it.' The taxi driver went along Fleet Street and the Strand. He went along Pall Mall. As he passed St. James's Palace clock, there it was. Three minutes to three. Up St. James's Street. The taxi-driver heard a bang, stopped the taxi, got out. There in the cab was Major Rowlandson – dead! Two minutes to three – just in time!

The story told in the law report is not exactly the same, though it is in essence. It quite lacks the panache and is a great deal drier. In 1925 Major Rowlandson took out a number of policies on his life with the Royal Insurance Company. They totalled £50,000. Each policy contained a condition which provided, 'If the life ... assured ... shall die by his own hand, whether sane or insane, within one year from the commencement of the assurance, the policy shall be void as against any person claiming the amount assured.' In 1934 Rowlandson was insolvent: he had borrowed over £60,000 to finance an invention for hardening steel, which had proved a failure; in addition, he had raised £6,791 from the Royal on the security of the policies. A quarterly premium was overdue and the extension of time granted by the Company would expire at 3.00 pm on 3 August.

As he contemplated a way out of his difficulties, it must have seemed to the Major that, provided he did not die by his own hand within the first twelve months of the policies – and he was now well outside that limit – the Royal would pay up, even on a suicide. When the Company refused to do so, on the grounds that suicide was a crime, his niece's claim, as executrix, gave Tom a source of income from July 1935, when her solicitors asked Denning to draft a letter for a guinea, to March 1938, when his brief was marked 200 guineas in the House of Lords.

The story must be told in Denning's words:

We claimed against the Insurance Company for the money. They said No. It was a crime: and we couldn't get it although the contract said we could. We said that Major Rowlandson was *non compos mentis*. It was tried before Mr Justice Swift with a special jury. I was led by Sir William Jowitt. He put the case dramatically to the jury. 'Three minutes to three,' he said, 'two minutes to three.' The Judge, as I have said, was Mr Justice Swift. He went out to lunch. He always had a good lunch, did Mr Justice Swift! He liked one or two tots of whisky. In the afternoon he came back. In summing up to the jury, he said: 'Wasn't this the act of a gallant English gentleman, killing himself for the sake of his creditors?' The jury found him of sound mind. The Court of Appeal said that, as a result, we could not claim the money. We went to the House of Lords. Sir William Jowitt led me. He had to leave early and turned to me; and, referring to the suicide of Ophelia, said 'Give them all that.' I gave it to them. It didn't do any good. The House of Lords said that suicide, *felo de se*, was the most heinous crime known to our English law. A man rushing into the presence of his maker unasked. So we lost.

At the Bar, as on the stage, there have always been stars, men in such demand that their fees are the stuff of rumour. In an earlier generation than Denning's, many of these leaders among leaders were as much renowned for their oratory, their style and presence as for their legal skill: the names of Rufus Isaacs, Edward Carson, Marshall Hall and F. E. Smith were legendary. In a less dramatic mould, though with 'a reputation of being almost unbeatable when it came to digesting masses of complicated documents and evidence'[25] was Stafford Cripps. William Jowitt, Denning's leader in the Beresford case, combined the skills to manage 'the best class of commercial work, besides acquiring an all-round practice.'[25] In 1938 the names of Cripps, Jowitt and Hastings still appeared regularly in the *Law Reports*. Amongst others, Tom's contemporaries, already briefed in large numbers of reported cases were F. R. Evershed and Cyril Radcliffe. Though Tom no longer suffered from lack of confidence in the outcome of his cases, some of which involved difficult points of law or established them, in general his practice was more run-of-the-mill, even if, as reflections of human life, his cases were sometimes more interesting.

'At first I was short of silk's work,' he wrote,[1] though this seems not to have affected him financially, the higher fees paid to him counteracting the fall in instructions; his earnings in his first year at the inner bar, as in the previous year, were over £3000. It was unusual for Denning to have a little time on his hands. He took the opportunity to write another article for the *Law Quarterly Review*, returning to the subject of his first article – *Quantum Meruit*. A little extra time at home was also welcome, as Mary neared the date of her confinement. As often as he could, he went for 'long walks', sometimes taking Mary's dog, Meg. On 3 August 1938, at Nuffield House in Guy's Hospital, Mary gave birth to a boy. 'Caesarean section at 9.30,' she wrote in her diary.

'All went off admirably & we have a lovely little son. God bless him.' For a month after she went home, a maternity nurse helped accustom her to dealing with the new baby; then Mary and Rose Dummer took over his care.

Tom was in his fortieth year when his son was born. The most uxorious of husbands and devoted of family men, he was enchanted and deeply moved by the small bundle – more shawl than baby – that would carry the Denning name and the Denning genes into the next generation. He did not follow the family tradition and use the name of Newdigate Poytnz: the boy was baptised Robert Gordon. Mary's friend Gladys Burlton stood godmother; his godfathers were Mary's brother Walter and Arthur Cockin, the Bishop of Bath and Wells. At first, Meg, her dog, ignored Robert but later, Mary told Gladys in a letter, he was nearly always to be found sitting under the pram.[16]

As winter set in there was deep snow and it was bitterly cold. Tom attended the Judges' Dinner on 20 December, getting home at 1.20 am of the day that the pipes thawed, burst, and flooded the hall.

Nothing could spoil their happiness. Mary was busy wrapping parcels and writing cards. On Christmas Day she and Tom went to church at 11.00, staying to take Communion. After tea they lit a little Christmas tree 'for Robert'. On 29 December, in the early evening, Tom went to Whitchurch. Mary and Robert joined him there on New Year's Eve and, together they returned home at the close of what must have been for them the most perfect – because the most normal – year of their marriage.

For Tom personally, 1938 may have been 'the happiest of years' but, nationally and internationally, it was a sorry time. It became increasingly clear that Hitler was bent on aggression. Tom heard from his brothers the views of army and navy; he saw the many scientists and lawyers who had taken refuge in England from 'Hitler, who hated the Jews . . . Hitler, who established the nazi regime with its hated gestapo and police state.'[1] It was Hitler's threat to Czechoslovakia at the end of September, when Tom was much pre-occupied with his baby son, that brought the danger suddenly and forcefully home.

At the time there was little that Britain could have done militarily to help the Czechs, even if she had wanted to. Neville Chamberlain urged the Czechoslovak government to make whatever concessions were necessary to satisfy Hitler. The German dictator was not easily satisfied. In the middle of September, when the British people, as a whole, became aware that – as had happened in 1914 – the Germans were bullying a small nation, the country swung between indignation and nervousness. Though the Government was determined to settle the matter peacefully, preparations were also made for war and the fleet was mobilised.

This war, it was recognised, could not be kept out of Britain; the battle would surely be brought across the Channel and the civilian population would be in the front line. An air-raid siren was broadcast over the wireless, to familiarise people with the sound of its warning. Gas masks were distributed and schemes were prepared to evacuate children from London.

Though voices were raised against appeasement, there was general relief when Hitler agreed to a four-power conference – of Germany, Italy, Great Britain and France – in Munich on 29 September. The country learned over the wireless that a compromise had been reached; they watched on newsreels in the cinemas as Chamberlain emerged from his aeroplane on the last day of September, waving a piece of paper, signed by Hitler, which appeared to bear witness to 'the desire of our two peoples never to go to war with one another again.' Later newsreels showed Chamberlain, at a window of 10 Downing Street that night, telling a cheering crowd: 'This is the second time that there has come back from Germany to Downing Street peace with honour. I believe it is peace for our time.'

The peace Chamberlain brought home from Germany did not last his time. Less than a year later, on 1 September 1939, when they had already annexed the Sudetenland, German troops crossed the Polish frontier and German aeroplanes began to bomb Warsaw. In that year, Britain had advanced her preparations and people had become accustomed to the inevitability of another war with Germany. An ultimatum was delivered to the Germans, which expired, without a reply, at 11 am on 3 September 1939.

9

The Second World War

On that sunny, Sunday morning in September 1939, Tom and Mary were in church. Almost immediately after war had been declared the sirens sounded the air-raid warning. 'Robert was in his pram. Just one year old. We rushed home to see if he was safe. He was. The alert was a false alarm.' For a time the war made no real impact. The first few months were to be the period of 'phoney' war.

Tom volunteered for any kind of service and was asked to see Sir Alexander Maxwell, the Permanent Secretary to the Home Office. Shortly before Munich, in the greatest secrecy, the government had divided the country into twelve regions and had chosen a Regional Commissioner for each (two for London). Their duties were to co-ordinate the work of civil defence, health and food supplies and, if there were to be an invasion which cut off the regions from central government, to take over the entire regional administration. These arrangements had been made public during 1939 and now Denning was told that each Commissioner would have a legal adviser. He was invited to be the legal adviser for the North-East region, based in Leeds, and readily accepted.

His work in Leeds, as it turned out, was to be largely concerned with the need to detain potential 'fifth columnists'. Under Regulation 18B of the Defence Regulations made in 1939, the Home Secretary had the power to order the detention without trial of any person, if he had reasonable cause to believe that the person was 'of hostile origin or of hostile associations' and should be controlled. As Denning expressed it in 1949, when he gave the first series of Hamlyn Lectures, printed under the title *Freedom Under the Law*: 'If there are traitors in our midst, we cannot afford to wait until we catch them in the act of blowing up our bridges or giving our military secrets to the enemy . . . We must detain them on suspicion.'

In his lecture Denning illustrated the way this worked by the case of a Church of England clergyman who became known in his parish as 'the Nazi Parson'. Invited by the Nazis to visit Germany, at their expense, before the war, the man was shown only the best side of the system there and was very impressed by it. When there was imminent danger of invasion, the local people were sufficiently alarmed to inform the police, who passed on the information to officers of MI5, the body responsible for the investigation of 'fifth column' activities.

> The clergyman [said Denning] was taken before a lawyer, who questioned him closely, but he had no solicitor himself . . . The clergyman stated that he thought National-Socialism was excellent for Germany but that he did not think it would answer in this country: and he protested that he would not do anything to help the Germans . . . The question was, of course, whether his enthusiasm for National-Socialism was so great that he might, for instance, give refuge to a German parachutist who came by night to his vicarage – which was in a lonely village in the country. It was decided that, with the threat of invasion so near, no risks could be taken. So he was detained. This meant that he was kept a prisoner for some time, then in various detention camps, and it was nearly three years before he was released. Yet he had done nothing wrong.

Tom did not tell the audience at his lecture that he was, himself, the lawyer who had questioned the vicar closely. The incident must have made a considerable impact on him: more than 30 years later, in *The Family Story*, he returned to the subject. His style is less measured, more impressionistic, as he tells the story again.

> The military authorities used to receive – or collect – information about any person who was suspected: and lay it before me. I used to see the person and ask him questions – so as to judge for myself if the suspicion was justified. He could not be represented by lawyers. As an instance I would tell of a parson who was called the 'Nazi Parson' in a village in Yorkshire. He had often spent his holidays in Germany. The military authorities arrested him, and detained him . . . Although there was no case against him, no

proof at all, I detained him under '18B'. The Bishop of Ripon protested, but we took no notice.

As Denning tells the story this time, he seems both proud and a little defiant. In his years on the Bench, he had forged a reputation as the champion of the little man against the oppressive machinery of the state, save where he saw a danger to its security. Looking back on the case that seems, more than any other, to have impressed itself on his mind – perhaps because the man was a Church of England parson – Tom was willing even to exaggerate his own responsibility in the process, to say: 'I detained him under "18B".'

Yet even in 1941, the exercise of the Home Secretary's discretion to make an order '18B' did not pass unchallenged. D. N. Pritt took a case to the House of Lords, asking whether the Secretary of State had power to deprive a man of liberty 'on the mere allegation that there is reasonable cause to believe certain things about him said to be prejudicial to the interests of the realm.' Four Law Lords decided that he had. Lord Atkin, in a famous dissent, for which he is said to have been ostracised by the other judges, said:

> In this country, amid the clash of arms, the laws are not silent. They may be changed, but they speak the same language in war as in peace. It has always been one of the pillars of freedom, one of the principles of liberty for which on recent authority we are now fighting, that the judges are no respecters of persons and stand between the subject and any attempted encroachments on his liberty by the executive, alert to see that any coercive action is justified in law.

> *Liversedge* v. *Anderson*

It is difficult to understand how Denning in *The Family Story*, could describe these words, spoken in the context of that case, as being 'after my own heart'.

Between visits to Leeds, Denning was able to carry on his practice in London. The day after war broke out, there is an entry in his Fee Book of ten guineas to advise on claims for death duties and his instructions, in the next months, were much as they would have been in peace-time. Younger barristers, solicitors and clerks were appearing – or disappearing – in uniform. Everyone carried a gas mask. Arrangements were made for shelter in air-raids. But the work of the courts went on much as usual. With the object of preserving the practices of serving barristers, the Bar Council resolved that it should be a point of honour amongst those remaining to undertake work entrusted to them and, unless otherwise agreed, to share the fees with the man in the forces. To save expense to litigants – not to mention precious paper – directions were given to provide only one 'top'; carbon copies were permitted, where previously they would not have been accepted.

Momentous times did not put an end to frivolous litigation. In 1938, the *Daily Express* had published an article headed 'Why do people commit bigamy?' Harold Newstead, they reported, was a Camberwell man who liked having two wives at once. Unbeknown to them, there was in Camberwell an unmarried Harold Newstead, who sued them for libel, with Tom leading Roy Wilson. They won in both the court of first instance and the Court of Appeal. It was a Pyrrhic victory, he wrote in *What Next In The Law*; the jury awarded his client only a farthing damages and the Court of Appeal declined to interfere with the award.

Early in 1940 Tom and Mary found 'a lovely house' in Copyhold Lane, about a quarter of a mile from Tylers Green. In June Tom bought it outright – he would never buy on mortgage – for between £3000 and £4000. The house had been built for the Archdeacon of Lewes, who called it 'Monandale'. Tom did not like the name. He and Mary had loved the name of their rented house, which reminded them of the Fair Close where, once, fairs had been held in Whitchurch; they changed the name of their new home to 'Fair Close'. Food rationing had begun at the end of 1939 – butter, bacon, sugar and meat were all on coupons; with the help of their gardener, Mr Parker, who came from Haywards Heath, Tom and Mary started to keep chickens and bees and to grow vegetables on their two acres of land. Though travel had become difficult, Tom usually got home unless he had to spend a night in Leeds.

Throughout the country, at nine o'clock every evening, everyone listened to the BBC news, which was almost unremittingly grim. Neutral, as well as British merchant ships were attacked by German U-boats in the Channel. The Russians, with whom Hitler had signed a non-aggression pact, defeated Finland in March, after three months of fighting. In April the Germans occupied Denmark and Norway. It was a bitter blow for Britain to learn that neither the navy nor the army could help Norway withstand the power of the German airforce.

On the day in May when the Germans entered the Low Countries, anger at the failure of the Government erupted in Parliament. Against a background of mounting military disaster Chamberlain resigned with an MP's cry still ringing in the Parliamentary chamber: 'In the name of God, go!' Winston Churchill became Prime Minister. Over the wireless, people listened quietly as he told them: 'I have nothing to offer but blood, toil, tears and sweat,' but added, 'You ask, what is our aim? I can answer in one word: Victory – victory at all costs, victory in spite of all terror; victory however long and hard the road may be.'

By the end of May the Germans had advanced far into France. The British army was fighting a desperate rearguard action on the coast, in danger of being trapped between the Germans and the sea. The evacuation from Dunkirk began on 27 May. On the night of 3 June an armada of small private yachts and motor vessels slipped from their moorings and out of English harbours to join fishing smacks, cargo boats and the ships of the Fleet. The next day, the country learned that what would have been a terrible defeat had been turned – by the courage and determination of hundreds of civilians – into an epic of heroism. More than 338,000 men were brought back to Britain from the beaches of Dunkirk and the epic of the small boats lightened hearts and strengthened nerves to face the expected German on-slaught.

At that time Reg was appointed to the staff of XI Corps and became responsible for the administrative organisation and management of the defence of South-East England. On 13 August the German air force began a full-scale attack on the region. On 18 August Mary wrote to Gladys Burlton that little John Denning – Norman's son, who was much the same age as Robert – and his step-sister (Iris's daughter by a previous marriage) were visiting Fair Close 'and have settled down quite happily ... we are getting on well in spite of frequent air-raid warnings.' Whenever she heard gunfire, Mary took the children into 'a large under-the-stairs cupboard', even giving the little boys lunch there, when necessary. Tom had been in Leeds, she told Gladys, when a few bombs fell on Haywards Heath, without doing any damage. She added a piece of news of a kind that assumed increasing importance on the 'home front': her pullets were laying and 'we have had 1 egg for the last 4 days and today 2.'

The Long Vacation, which should have run from 1 August to 11 October that year, was cancelled. A rota was arranged to help those who had planned to do active war work during the vacation. In September, the Germans turned their attention to London and the Blitz began. Cuckfield was in 'Bomb Alley', the route followed by the German bombers from the coast. 'The enemy aircraft – carrying their bombs to drop on London – crossed over us each night. If they had not been able to use them all, they dropped them on us.'[1] The country was blacked out. At the start of the war street lighting had been forbidden, with such devastating results that occasional dimmed lights were again allowed in towns, though country lanes, without the beams of friendly light from cottages and houses, were frighteningly black on moonless nights. Vehicle headlights were painted black with only a small slit allowed to let through an almost totally useless glimpse of light. 'We were all "blacked out",' wrote Tom, in *The Family Story*. 'But troops billeted near us were careless. They used to leave the door open – so that their light shone out. The enemy dropped their bombs wherever they saw a light. So they dropped them near us. We used to take shelter under the stairs – not that it would do any good. One bomb dropped so close that our front door was forced open by the blast: but no other damage was done.'

The work of the courts went on, if not exactly as usual, then as close to normal as was possible in the circumstances. From time to time, sittings had to be held in the basement. Early in 1939 Denning had represented a company known as United Australia, in the Court of Appeal. The company had a secretary with authority to endorse cheques for the purpose of paying them into its bank account. He misused this authority to enable a cheque for £1900 to be paid into the account with Barclays Bank of MFG, a company of which he was a director. The sum was shown in United Australia's books as a loan to MFG: On 13 May 1935 United Australia obtained judgment in default of appearance against MFG for 'money lent' or 'money had and received'. MFG had the judgment set aside. In the course of the proceedings United Australia found out, for the first time, about the payment of its cheque into an account at Barclays. In October when MFG was wound up, there was still no order against it in favour of United Australia. Thereupon, United Australia sued Barclays for conversion. The Bank responded that by electing to go against MFG, United Australia had waived its right to sue them and Goddard, the judge of first instance, accepted this defence. The Court of Appeal upheld him. Denning thought the Court of Appeal 'were so wrong'[1] that he offered to conduct the appeal to the House of Lords without a fee. During 'those critical days in May and June – when our troops were being driven back to the beaches of Dunkirk – I was arguing in the Lords the important case of United Australia v. Barclays Bank. I appeared in robes. Geoffrey Streatfeild, KC appeared in uniform, being in the Army. The Law Lords [who, at the time, held their sittings in the King's Robing Room] gave their reasoned judgments just as carefully and just as effectively as if there had been no war.' It is scarcely necessary to add that Denning and United Australia won their appeal.

In the two years after Dunkirk, when there were grave fears of invasion, Tom travelled to Leeds many times. The train journeys were 'appalling'. Carriages were packed; people stood, sat or, if they could find the space, even lay in the corridors. Kitbags, suitcases, baskets, boxes were everywhere. When it was dark, a small blue light bulb – if it had not been removed by someone determined to sleep – threw an eerie light, not enough to read by; a journey that should have taken three hours could take 'seven or eight hours or more – owing to bombs, alerts and the like.'[1] Tom worried when he could not get back to Cuckfield because he had to stay overnight in Leeds or because there was an air-raid on London.

If 1938 had been the happiest of years, 1941 was 'the worst'.[1] At the end of 1940 Tom was rushed into hospital with meningitis. 'So ill that I would have died – except that a doctor from Brighton prescribed a new drug called M & B.'[1] On New Year's Day, Mary brought him home in an ambulance, but it was not until 11 January that he was allowed by the doctor to do any work.[26] Instructions from Fladgates, received on 26 January, must have been a source of satisfaction, as well as a fee of six guineas: the Prime Minister wanted to be advised on retaining the copyright of his speeches. (Tom did not meet

Winston Churchill; Anthony Moir was their intermediary.) It was the only light relief in that period. On Saturday 15 February he heard that Charles had been taken seriously ill and travelled to Whitchurch, never the most straightforward of journeys and particularly trying in war-time. Charles died, at the age of 81, the following Monday morning. By 6 pm Tom was back at Fair Close, returning to Whitchurch with Mary for the funeral on Wednesday, 19 February. 'Very cold but bright,' Mary wrote in her diary. Clara was 'splendid'. They reached home again about ten past seven that night. A week later Tom caught bronchitis, recovering just in time to go to London, on 3 March, for the Lord Chancellor's At Home.

Though Clara had been the driving force, her marriage to Charles had been a happy one, each supplying qualities that the other lacked. 'Trust and loyalty such as theirs,' Tom wrote in *The Family Story*, '– giving the children unshaken security – is what made us what we are.' After Charles's death, Clara wrote to her sons: 'I pray I may live to see my Marjorie come home . . . I feel so helpless and not much good to any of you only an expense, but I trust I will be able to leave something to help pay you back some of what you have done for me.' Clara's depression was understandable but, far from looking on her as 'not much good' to them, her sons regarded her with deep affection, admiration and gratitude. To cheer her, Tom and Mary invited her to spend a few days at Fair Close.

In 1941 Mary's health was still far from robust and with Tom so much away, she had come to depend on Rose's help. It was a blow to her when, on 7 March, Rose went for an interview for the Women's Royal Naval Service. Another young girl, Lily, came to help when Rose left. When he was home, Tom liked to work in the garden or play with Robert. He was quite at ease bathing his little son and helping with his physical care in a way that was not common among the professional classes at the time. On Saturday 5 April, Mary recorded that they took Robert with them when they went to pay for a new chicken house and see about another beehive; later Tom weather-proofed the chicken house and mowed the lawn. On Sundays Tom went early to church then stayed home to look after Robert or to work, while Mary was taken to the 11.00 service by Miss Greenfield, who lived opposite.

In May, Mary ran a temperature and was forced to stay a few days in bed. It was an ominous sign and Tom made every effort to relieve Mary, taking Robert for a haircut and to the station to see the trains.

While Mary was ill, on a brilliant, moonlit night, the German bombers dropped hundreds of high explosive bombs and 100,000 incendiaries on London, destroying parts of Westminster Abbey and the House of Commons. Tom was returning from Leeds. 'A few miles out of London a great red glare covered the sky. The train plodded on. Stopping every few yards. At last we reached King's Cross. There were the fires. There were bombs and explosions all the time. People were still carrying on. Even a few taxi-drivers. I found a taxi and asked the driver to take me to Victoria. He managed to get there – by going devious ways. But no trains moving at all.'[1] Tom spent the rest of the night in a shelter, listening to the bombs exploding all about him. At about midday a train left for Haywards Heath and he got home, so relieved to find Mary and Robert safe that he 'broke down and cried.'

By 19 May Mary was much recovered and Tom was in chambers when Reg looked in to say that he expected to be made a Brigadier. The opportunities to see his brothers were not as many as Tom would have liked; on 21 June, visiting Whitchurch with Mary and Robert, Tom was delighted to find Norman and his family also, unexpectedly, at The Hermitage.

Mary began to feel ill again a week later. She was confined to bed and the elderly woman who had once been her nanny moved into Fair Close to look after Robert. This time the doctor diagnosed gallstones and, on 1 September – a month after Robert's third birthday – Tom took Mary by car to the Brompton Hospital. At this moment, when he was worried about Mary and Robert, Tom heard from Clara, who cherished the hope that Marjorie would be able to live at The Hermitage and looked to Tom to bring it about. On 6 September she wrote: 'I think Johnnie should pay back to Reg and Tom the amount of money they put to buy it, Reg £250, Tom £150 and me £100 . . . I have no doubt you will be able to arrange that peacefully and satisfactorily.'

From the hospital Mary sent a number of letters for Robert. Two are undated and it seems probable that they were the earliest. 'Dearest little son,' she wrote in one of them, 'Mummy sends her best love and a big kiss. She is getting better and will soon be home with Robert and

Daddy again. Take great care of my Nan for me and be a very good boy and help her and Parker and Mrs Parker.' She ended with big kisses – xxx – for Robert and Big Hugs – ooo – for Daddy. She was kept abreast of all that was being done to occupy Robert and, in her letters, she tells Robert she is 'sorry you hurt your foot but I expect it's quite well again now'; she is glad he has found 'a nice little dog to play with' and wonders about its name; she hopes he 'had a nice time at Donald Hall's yesterday.' She sends him a 'a little bit of paper' with a recipe on it to give to Nanny and ask her 'if she would like to cook this for your dinner one day, or for Daddy's supper.'

Tom chose two of Mary's letters to reproduce in *The Family Story* because they 'tell so much of us.' From the first, written on 16 September 1941, Tom reproduced the paragraph:

> It seems a long time since I saw my Robert and I expect he is getting very big – you will have to ask Daddy to see how tall you are by the door in the sitting room, when Daddy is home next Sunday.

The second letter was written on Mary's forty-first birthday, 24 September 1941.

> My dearest little Son,
> Thank you ever so much for the nice birthday present you bought for me and which Daddy brought me. The tape measure is just what I wanted – to measure and see if I have knitted enough for your suit. And I love the nice card you chose, with the doggie on it.
> I am afraid I shall have to wait for my birthday party until I come home again and I hope that won't be long.
> I have nearly finished your green suit and then I will start the one with the nice wool you and Nannie bought the other day.
> I hope you are helping Nannie and Parker and Mrs Parker all you can.
> Please will you give Nan this letter inside yours.
>   XXXXXX for Robert
>   oooooo for Daddy
> Lots of love from Mummie

In his reproduction, Tom changed Mary's spelling 'Nannie' to

'Nanny', perhaps the more usual form of the word. On Saturday 18 October he took Mary home. She was sufficiently recovered to make jam but, by 8 November, she caught another cold. One evening, when Tom was working after Mary had gone upstairs, he heard her knock on the floor. 'I rushed up. She said "I've had a haemorrhage." She had coughed up blood. It was the beginning of the end.'

The last entry in Mary's diary was made on Monday 17 November 1941:

A lot of rain. Miss Hamilton [a neighbour] came at lunch time and brought a rabbit and some eggs. I had a strange haemorrhage about 8.30 pm. Dr Murray came and gave me an injection.

'The doctors did all they could,' Denning recorded in *The Family Story*, 'cylinders of oxygen were brought every day. Dr Geoffrey Marshall himself came down to see her. He said, "There is just a hope if we can get her to Brompton Hospital." The ambulance took a long time coming. At last it came. I went with her. I stayed all night. Early in the morning I was beside her. I held her hand. She spoke so low, that I could hardly hear. Just "Goodbye, my beloved." I kissed her goodbye. She passed peacefully away. Our romance was ended. 22 November 1941. Nearly 40 years ago now. But to me it is but as yesterday.'

Mary was buried in the churchyard at Cuckfield and, on Sundays after church, Denning took Robert to visit her grave and tend the flowers planted on it. 'Perhaps I shouldn't have done it,' Tom told the author, 'I remember now he always looked so sad.' Though Tom tried to keep the memory of Mary alive, Robert retains only one vague recollection of sitting or lying on his mother's bed and of someone carrying him away.[32]

Tom had little time to grieve as that 'worst of years' drew to its close. With the fear of invasion at its height, he made many visits to Leeds, as well as running his practice in London and doing some work on the Western Circuit. In that year of disasters his earnings fell below £3000 for the first time since 1936. His frequent visits to Leeds were partly responsible. The work was unpaid but Denning was allowed expenses of £500 a year. He thought he occasioned some surprise when he submitted a claim for only the exact sum he had spent.

The terrible year ended with the Japanese attack on the United States fleet in Pearl Harbour, bringing the Americans into the war. Soon, in England, the accents of American troops would be added to the unfamiliar sounds of Czech, Polish, Dutch, Norwegian and French forces, re-grouped in Britain and waiting for the opportunity to liberate their countries. In Fortress Britain, 1942 would be – though at the time it was hard to see it – a turning point in the war.

For some time, Tom's Aunt Rosa came to stay at Cuckfield. Later 'old Nanny' took charge and Tom spent all the time that he could with Robert. It was not ideal, but for the moment it was the best he could do. Friends and neighbours rallied to help and the family living opposite suggested an advertisement in *The Lady*. By chance, the woman who replied had been nanny to Lord Simon's grandchildren and came with very good references. She looked after Robert well and Tom took over whenever he was home.

He, too, was dreadfully lonely and turned, for comfort as always, to his family. He shared Reg's delight at being made a major general, with responsibility for administration of Southern Command. Denning's own career was also advancing. He added to his duties by accepting the appointment of Chancellor of the Diocese of London. Later in the year he would appear for the Archbishop of Canterbury, unsuccessfully seeking an order against the Bishop of Bath and Wells.

The good manners for which Denning would be admired on the Bench were already evident when he was in silk. In 1990 two lawyers who had been juniors to his juniors remembered the experience of working with Denning KC. Doris Belcher had been pupilled to Geoffrey Howard, who was led by Denning in a ten-day 'passing off' action in the Chancery Division. 'My pupil-master was at that time in great demand to attend on various summonses in the High Court, leaving me to "stand-in" as Junior Counsel. Our leader was as courteous towards me as if I were really there in that capacity, enquiring at the end of every interrogation, "Is there anything else I should have asked the witness?"'[14]

The editor of the *Australian Law Journal*, J. G. Starke, also wrote in 1990 of an occasion 50 years earlier when he appeared as second junior to Denning, with Harry Leon (later a County Court Judge and author, under the name of Henry Cecil, of a popular series of novels and short stories on legal themes). 'Leon was briefed in a case concerning guarantee law . . . After a long discussion in conference, the question emerged of the necessity for a leader. Harry Leon, who was a very shrewd judge of the capacity of KCs, had no hesitation in suggesting Mr Denning, which suggestion the solicitors at once accepted. In conference, Mr Denning was most pleasant and very respectful towards Harry Leon. He was also most patient and amenable with the solicitors, giving a clear and concrete answer in respect of every point raised. He showed complete mastery of the law, particularly in regard to authorities on the law as to guarantees. In court we were up against Pritt – a formidable antagonist, but Mr Denning coped with this, and conducted the case brilliantly.'[14]

Henry Cecil himself, in *Just Within the Law*, recalled being opposed to Denning, who was then a junior: 'I soon realised what a fine lawyer he was and . . . wondered what I was doing at the Bar when there were juniors whose knowledge and grasp of the law were so infinitely above mine.'

In his submissions to the courts, Denning revealed the innovative and fertile mind that would make his early years on the Bench so fascinating. In June 1942 he won a notable victory. *Gold* v. *Essex County Council* was a Poor Person's Case. Five-year-old Ruth Gold had been taken to hospital in June and July 1940 for treatment to the warts on her face. The treatments by Grenz-rays, ordered by a dermatologist, were clearly not having any effect, so the dermatologist ordered the dosage to be doubled. When Ruth attended for the next session, the radiographer did not properly cover her face and she was permanently disfigured.

The Judge, Tucker J, found that the radiographer was negligent, but thought himself bound by the authorities to decide that Essex County Council, who were responsible for the hospital, were not liable for the negligence of the competent and qualified radiographer. In the Court of Appeal, Denning argued that the radiographer was the council's servant and that the council was therefore responsible for his negligence. He differentiated the case from the one Tucker believed was binding on him and he brought evidence of Scottish, Canadian and New Zealand cases to show that the law in Ruth Gold's case should be more widely interpreted. Finally, he pointed out that the Court can refuse to follow an earlier decision of the Court on a point not argued before it. Lord Greene, the Master of the Rolls, accepted Tom's arguments and the other judges agreed. On a subject that was to become very much one of his own, Denning had succeeded in changing the law, to the great benefit of victims of medical negligence.

In July, he was instructed by the Attorney-General, Sir Donald Somervell, to defend a young sailor charged with murder. The case was heard in the Great Hall of the Castle at Winchester, where 22 years earlier Tom had watched the trial that persuaded him he would like to be a barrister. It was not Denning's usual field of work and made a great impression upon him. The sailor had strangled a girl on Southampton Common.

I went to see him the night before in the cells in Winchester. There he was, dirty and unkempt. I asked him what his defence was. He said the girl had slapped his face. He had put his hands round her throat, and she died. Was there any defence? Not much of a defence of provocation so as to reduce it from murder to manslaughter. But I thought I would put it to the jury.

It was, of course, then of the greatest importance to reduce the charge from murder to manslaughter, since there was a mandatory death sentence for murder.

I told the young man to clean himself up before the next day. There he was, when he was arraigned, as smart and nice a young sailor as ever you did see. The Judge was Mr Justice Charles, also of the Western Circuit. He ran dead against my client. I put him into the box and asked him: 'Did you have your ship torpedoed under you three times?' The Judge boomed out: 'Many a sailor has had his ship torpedoed under him and he doesn't go and strangle a woman!' Next, when I was going to put my defence of provocation to the jury, the Judge said he was not going to put it. There was not sufficient provocation here to reduce it to manslaughter. Was I, as Counsel, to put it? I did. It is the duty of Counsel to put every legitimate defence. I put the defence of provocation to the jury. The Judge did as he said he would. He told the jury that there was no defence of provocation here. That was virtually a direction to find him guilty of murder, because, if there was no provocation, it was clearly murder. Well, it was a Hampshire jury, and I am a Hampshire man!

No doubt Tom's Hampshire burr helped the sailor.

The jury found him guilty of 'manslaughter only'. The Judge turned to the jury and said: 'Get out of the box. You've been false to your oaths. You're not fit to be there.' As they left the box, they were heard to say 'The Judge was biased.' . . . But, to finish the case – the Judge, addressing the sailor, said that he had to accept the verdict: but he went on and sentenced him to thirteen years' imprisonment. I thought that was too long, seeing it was manslaughter only, as the jury had found. So I told the sailor he could appeal if he liked, but I had to warn him that in those days the Court of Criminal Appeal could increase the sentence if they so wished. Afterwards (I think I have lost it now), I received a little note which he wrote me from the prison in pencil. He thanked me. He said: 'In view of the possibility of an increase, I have decided not to appeal.' I am sure he has been restored to his friends and relations long since.[1]

This was not Denning's only experience of Mr Justice Charles. A young barrister, Guy Willett, was accused by the judge of inventing a defence to murder. Denning offered to lead him on appeal, when Willett was triumphantly vindicated. He gave Tom a gold pen, which Tom still sometimes used in his nineties.

In October 1942, the country at last had something to celebrate, with the victory over Rommel's troops at El Alamein in North Africa. It was marked in a way very dear to Tom's heart. A feature of Sunday in England had always been the ringing of church bells; in the war this had stopped, for the bells were to be used as a signal of invasion. Now, on Sunday 15 November, the church bells pealed out a celebration of victory: as Tom took Robert to church that day he hoped it was a sign of better times to come.

In December, Mr Justice Wrottesley was taken ill on circuit at Manchester. Lord Simon asked Denning to go as a Commissioner of Assize in his place. Denning knew that such an assignment was then in the nature of a trial run and that, if he did well, he might reasonably expect to be appointed a judge. He sat for three weeks in Manchester, where the leader of the circuit was George Lynskey, KC. 'It is often the practice of a Lord Chancellor to ask the leader of the circuit how a man gets on. George Lynskey told me afterwards that I had won "golden opinions".'[1] Both Lynskey and Denning were soon to be made judges.

For Christmas, Tom and Robert stayed quietly together at Fair Close, alone as they had been since Mary's death. At the beginning of March 1944 Denning was arguing a case in the House of Lords for the Prudential. During an adjournment on 6 March, Lord Simon offered him an appointment as a judge in the Probate, Divorce and Admiralty Division. It was not the work Denning would have chosen, but he accepted the appointment. As he wrote later, the only offer of appointment that he ever refused was the offer, when he was Master of the Rolls, to return to the House of Lords. By 3 April 1944, when judgment was given for Denning's client, the Prudential, Tom Denning was a High Court judge, at a salary of £5000 a year, and had been knighted at Buckingham Palace, taking the style Sir Alfred Thompson Denning.

PART TWO

1944–1962

IO

Joan

There were not enough judges in 1944 to deal with the volume of judicial work, particularly in divorce, where the demand was greatly increased by wartime separations. Ideally, men who practised in the divorce courts should have been made up but 'there were not really enough good divorce lawyers.'[33] By Tuesday 7 March – the day after Lord Simon had invited Denning to become a judge – three appointments were announced and the three new judges were sworn-in. All were to go to the Divorce Division, though only one, Harry Barnard, had practised there. Hubert Wallington had been admitted as a solicitor in the year Tom was born and had later gone to the Bar where he practised in the King's Bench Division. He was, Tom would write, 'an able common lawyer but a Roman Catholic quite unfitted for the Divorce Division. He allowed his beliefs to affect his decisions.'[23] Of Denning, *The Law Journal* of 11 March 1944 commented: 'He has been a very familiar figure in the Courts recently and has frequently appeared in the Chancery Division in complicated matters; his presentation of his cases has always been of assistance to the Court, and his early appointment to the Bench will be received with universal approval.'

At 45, Denning was then the youngest judge on the Bench. In part he may have owed his early promotion to the general shortage, after the slaughter of the First World War, of good men, at about the age of 50, who should have been coming to the fore, but this was not the whole story. 'Denning was a good candidate and would have been chosen' as a judge, even if there had been no immediate need for divorce judges. 'It was also thought he would be able to adapt for the time being to the work.'[33] *The Law Times* wrote: 'He has the reputation of being a brilliant lawyer and his elevation to the High Court Bench at this unusually early age would seem to presage a long and outstanding career of public usefulness.' How long, they were unlikely to have foreseen, even though, at the time, there was no judicial retirement age.

There is not much ceremony to the making of a judge. Resplendent in scarlet and ermine robes – hastily hired for the occasion from Ede & Ravenscroft – Denning was sworn-in before the Lord Chancellor, taking the oath of allegiance to the King and swearing to carry out justice and to do right 'to all manner of men, without favour or affection, fear or ill-will.' It was a proud and solemn moment, and a sad one. Where he had hoped Mary might have sat with Robert, there was only Robert, and Nanny.

Robert, with serious face under well-brushed hair, neatly dressed for the occasion in grey school coat and gloves, socks pulled up and highly polished shoes, watched with a sense of awe that increased as he passed the stone carvings and walked along the carpeted corridors of the House of Lords. Though he could not fully comprehend what was taking place, he was 'aware of the authority of the occasion.'[32] After the ceremony, Lord Simon showed Robert the Great Seal and asked whether he knew which King threw it into the Thames. 'Robert didn't of course.' (Nor, more interestingly, at the time did Tom.) Then, back at the courts, tightly holding hands, the little boy and the judge were photographed outside the judges' entrance.

The picture – which is the first in this book – captures the essence of Tom: his love of family and his devotion to the law. Gravely, the new Mr Justice Denning looks at the camera from beneath his long wig. He has assumed the symbols of the authority he will wield for so long and with such great pleasure; at the same time he has dedicated himself to service: the oath he has just sworn will be his guide for the next 38 years. The equally grave small boy, whose head reaches barely to his father's ermine cape – on which are pinned those other symbols of service, Tom's First World War medals – knows the other side of the judge: the gentle, loving father who last summer had taken Robert on holiday, travelling from Paddington in a blacked- out train, full of singing soldiers, to stay, just the two of them, at a little boarding-house at Criccieth, in North Wales.

After the ceremony, Denning took his seat straight away and Nanny took Robert home. The *Daily Mirror* of Wednesday 8 March, reported:

The unexpected appearance of the new judges at the Law Courts yesterday caused the biggest divorce stir of all time.

Within an hour of their being sworn-in before the Lord Chancellor, Justices Wallington, Barnard and Denning were sitting in court to try divorce suits which were taken from the lists of other judges.

Officials had to make a hasty last-minute rearrangement of the list to provide work for the new judges, and ushers and attendants were busy, collecting parties and their witnesses to direct them to the respective courts.

Tom's visit to Buckingham Palace on 15 March 1944 was even less ceremonious. He went alone. He knelt before the King, who tapped him on the shoulder with a sword. 'I wondered what to talk about and he did, too, I think. Then he talked about the position at Sandringham – that he didn't have any jurisdiction over his chapel at Sandringham.' That was all there was to it. Sir Alfred Denning – he thought he could scarcely be Sir Tom – went back to the Law Courts and got on with his work.

After the appointments were announced, Tom received more than three hundred letters of congratulations. The headmaster of Andover Grammar School, Mr C. L. Denyer, wrote: 'I often heard of your powers at school and at the 'varsity from my predecessor, Mr Bishop. He was intensely proud of you and often used to tell me what very high hopes he had of your future.'[35] Old school friends sent letters from Whitchurch; John Darlington from The Vicarage, North Greenfield; Mrs Cross from Beaufort Street; the President of Magdalen College from Oxford; and Harry Bull of the Hampshire Prisoners' Aid Society on prison paper from His Majesty's Prison at Winchester. There were welcomes from judges, congratulations from members of the Bar, from solicitors, from Tom's neighbours at Cuckfield and from complete strangers.

The Master of the Rolls, Lord Greene, hoped Tom would soon 'be freed from divorce and put to work more worthy of you.'[35] Henn–Collins's daughter remembered that, when Tom had first gone to Brick Court as a pupil, her father had forecast 'That young man will go far.' Eleanor Tancock, at whose home in Whitchurch Tom played tennis as a boy, told him the photograph that she liked best was the one with Robert. Mr Liggins, Charles Denning's old friend, thought that one day Tom would sit upon the Woolsack. (Nor was he alone in this notion.) Speaking as a selfish man,' wrote a lay client, 'I shall miss your kindly consideration and sound advice.' A member of the Bar told Tom: 'The appointment must be almost unique in the interest it has aroused in the members of the Chancery Bar who feel almost as if it had fallen to one of their own leaders.'[35]

They addressed him as 'Judge', 'Mr Denning', 'Sir Alfred', 'Mr Justice' and even as 'My Lord' and 'My Lord Justice'. Many told him that he should not think of replying, though there was never any point in telling Tom that: he always responded to the piles of letters that greeted each new appointment. As he became a well-known figure he was to receive an astonishing volume of correspondence from people he had perhaps seen only once or twice but who were confident he would remember them and would be interested to know of their doings. He had the common touch – a genuine interest in everyone he met. Usually he remembered everything they had told him; if he did not, his replies never betrayed him: he took great pains to respond in the spirit with which he was approached.

The letter from Mary's brother Barry gave expression to Tom's deepest feelings: 'I, like many others, can only feel how much more wonderful it would have been had you been able to see dear Mary's face when the announcements were made. Your Robert', the letter continued, 'is no doubt her mirror and will grow up in admiration of a great father who emerged from a great sorrow with fortitude.'[35]

Denning had never handled a divorce case while he was in practice. His belief that 'the only basis for a sound family life is a Christian marriage – the personal union of one man with one woman, to the exclusion of all others on either side, for better or for worse, so long as both shall live'[23] made him fundamentally averse to the notion of a broken home. In the next 18 months he was to receive a thorough education in the realities of unhappy married life. He disliked divorce work, finding it 'sordid in the extreme,'[23] and became convinced of the need to reform the law. If the break-up of a marriage was inevitable, the unpleasantness caused by the dissolution – particularly where children were concerned – must be minimised.

At the time divorce depended on proof of a matrimonial offence-adultery, cruelty or desrtion. 'Horrid details were the daily menu. In undefended divorce cases the chambermaid would give evidence that, when she took up the early morning tea, the couple were there in bed. "Was this the man?" asks Counsel, showing a photograph of the husband. "Yes, sir." "Was this the woman?" showing a photograph of the wife. "No, sir". In one contested case the husband said he had got infected with venereal disease from a lavatory seat. I did not believe him.'

Such details as Denning described in *The Due Process of Law* were distasteful to him but, strangely, he added: 'The sordidness was relieved when noble families were involved.' The common touch, for which Denning became loved and admired, went hand-in-hand with a degree of snobbery.

The work may not have been congenial but it gave Tom time to learn his trade. He had a remarkable ability, which would never desert him, to seize hold of the relevant facts of a case and to express them in an *ex tempore* judgment clearly and simply. In his first year he did not once reserve judgment. He was 'getting the feel of things' and was sometimes overruled, as in his judgment in *Churchman* v. *Churchman*, which dealt with connivance. As he gained confidence he 'started to put principles into writing'[23]. In *Smith* v. *Smith*, his first reserved judgment, he considered rights in the matrimonial home, a problem that would much occupy his mind when he reached the Court of Appeal.

Roy Wilson, once a member of Tom's chambers, told the delightful story that, on his return from army service (as a brigadier on the staff of GHQ India) he called on Henn-Collins, then a judge in the King's Bench Division. Henn-Collins took him round to see Tom. As they were waiting, Henn-Collins, with the familiarity of his years as head of chambers, skimmed through a reserved judgment waiting delivery. On Tom's return, he said: 'Extraordinary things you allow in your Court, Tom.' 'What do you mean?' Tom asked. 'Just look at this judgment,' teased Henn-Collins, ' "I am satisfied not only that the Respondent has committed adultery, but that she was actually committing adultery while she was denying it in the witness-box." '[36] One of the attractive facets of Tom's character was the grace with which he enjoyed a joke at his expense. Another characteristic was the will to learn from his mistakes.

A couple of months after *Smith*, Denning was faced, in *Emanuel* v. *Emanuel*, with 'the ever recurrent subject of presumptions and burdens.'[23] He gave judgment on 6 July 1945 and afterwards wrote a masterly article on the difficult subject, which was published in the October issue of the *Law Quarterly Review*. He proposed a new set of distinctions in both burdens and presumptions – to apply in all branches of the law – to help clarify the burden of proof in a case and the presumptions on which a person seeking to prove relevant facts may rely. The article was forerunner to many judgments in which he would set out guidelines to one or other aspect of law.

While Tom was chained to the divorce courts – which had, at least, the merit of keeping him in London with the expectation that he would get home at night – the fortunes of war were slowly turning. On 6 June 1944 – D-day – the long-awaited invasion of France began, with the landing of Allied troops in Normandy. Reg Denning had been keen to go with them. Promoted major general in 1943, he had much to do with the preparations for the landing and even offered to drop back to brigadier, if he might go with the troops. Within a few days he was transferred to Lord Mountbatten's headquarters in Ceylon as Deputy Administrative Officer under General Wheeler of the US Army. Shortly he was to become Principal Administrative Officer for the Allied forces in South-East Asia, working closely with the Chief of Staff, Lieutenant General Browning, to plan operations to recapture Malaya and Singapore.

A week after D-day Hitler unleashed his 'secret weapon', a pilotless, jet-propelled aircraft, which carried nearly a ton of high explosive and soon became known as the 'buzz-bomb' or 'doodle-bug'. As it flew, this new weapon made a curious buzzing sound and people learned to listen as it approached, praying that the engine would not cut out overhead – a sign that the bomb was about to fall. The first flying bomb, Tom would remember, destroyed a house on the other side of Cuckfield. 'Sometimes we would hear one coming – rush out and see it being chased by a Spitfire – watch it being shot down in smoke – and rendered harmless.'[1] In 'Bomb Alley', as well as in London, to which many of the original evacuees had returned, a new evacuation was planned.

'On one bright summer evening, in the clear sky we saw wave after wave of our aircraft – in regular formation – flying directly over us, going East. There must have been 20 or more aircraft in each wave. In all hundreds of them sparkling like silver arrows. They took at least half-an-hour to fly over us. We watched and watched.'[1] Only later did Tom learn that the planes were on their way to Arnhem, 'where so many young lives were lost',[1] in an operation to seize three bridges and gain control of the lower Rhine, which went disastrously wrong.

Blackout regulations were lifted and once again, in the train to Haywards Heath, as the evenings drew in, Tom could see to read his papers. He and Robert spent Christmas together at Whitchurch. In January, Tom returned to his old school – now playing wartime Box and Cox with another school at Andover – as the guest of honour at speech day. There were great differences from Mr Bishop's time. Girls, as well as boys, now attended the Grammar School and, instead of the leather-bound book prizes, stamped with the school crest, he presented envelopes containing, he had no doubt, 'something of value.'[37]

Night after night, in 1945, the sky was filled with the droning of aircraft, as it had been for the past five years, but now it was the sound of RAF and US Air Force bombers on their way to Germany. In April American and Russian troops met at Torgau, on the River Elbe, while the British, under Montgomery, pushed across the Elbe, further north, towards the Baltic. On 30 April, in his bunker headquarters beneath a devastated Berlin, Hitler committed suicide. As the Allies advanced across Europe, liberating the concentration camps, the British people learned the full enormity of atrocities committed by Nazi Germany.

On 7 May 1945 peace came to a battered Europe, when the Allied Supreme Commander, General Eisenhower, accepted the unconditional surrender of the Germans. That Sunday, 13 May, Tom took Robert to church as usual. In London great crowds were celebrating in the streets; at home in Fair Close Tom listened quietly as Winston Churchill broadcast to the nation. The war in Europe, said the Prime Minister, would end at midnight. There remained the Japanese to be subdued.

In May a general election was announced, the first since 1935. After a landslide victory for the Labour Party, Clement Attlee became Prime Minister and, on 2 August, William Jowitt, who had led Tom in a number of big cases at the Bar, was appointed Lord

Chancellor. The Labour Government was in office when the Japanese surrendered unconditionally on 14 August.

Though her courage was not diminished, the years between Charles's death and Marjorie's arrival at The Hermitage, were hard for Clara. On 13 May 1946 she wrote a codicil to the will she had made ten years earlier, which was more a cry of pain than a legal document:

> I feel Norman should have a share in The Hermitage. I have been given £8 a month from my three boys, I expect Norman has put £2 every month all these years. I thought Marjorie would have been here to help me before now. She has been very good to me and sent me a great deal. I have tried to help her with her children. I cannot see why they cannot come now. John is over age served all his time and the war is over. Everybody else I have heard or known about in India have come home.

By then Clara would not have much longer to wait. 'Peace came,' Tom wrote, 'in September 1945. There were all the celebrations. But I had no heart for them.'[1] Clara had been hoping that Tom would remarry and, slowly, his own thoughts were turning in that direction. He was a man still in the prime of life. Friendly, out-going and companionable, he liked people and wanted to be liked by them. Yet, apart from his family, he had not formed close associations. Hard-working and ambitious, he enjoyed the outward signs of his success, retaining a down-to-earth approach to his own problems and those over which he was required to adjudicate. For the time being he felt confined to work that was neither intellectually stimulating nor to his taste but he anticipated that he would – the sooner the better – be transferred to other fields. To function at his best, he knew, he must have a loving and secure background.

Tom's first marriage proved his enormous reserves of love, generosity of spirit, steadfastness and strength of character. Tom sustained Mary's courage at times when it might otherwise have failed her. Yet Tom was a more complex personality than he sometimes seemed. The son of the formidable Clara Denning remained in some ways emotionally immature. Despite Mary's warnings that she was only human, Tom needed to put her on a pedestal. As much as Mary came to depend upon Tom, so he required her advice and support for his own well-being. Though, in the event, he usually did – as he had always done – what he wanted to do, before doing it he needed to have her approval. Only from the secure home background that he so greatly valued did he feel safe to reach out to the many people with whom his life became interwoven. If he were to marry again, his wife would have to be the 'true companion' that he always wanted. She would also have to be a home-maker, not only for Tom but also for Robert. And indirectly, it was through Robert that Tom found her.

At Haywards Heath there was a boarding preparatory school, called Parkfield. In September 1945, Tom was invited by the headmaster to a party for parents and prospective parents. There he met Joan Stuart, the widowed mother of a boy who was moving on that term to Repton. 'Charming and captivating,' he described her. 'No hesitation on either side. Instinctively we were attracted one to the other. Instinctively we fell in love.'[1]

When the war ended Tom had not decided whether to stay in Fair Close or to leave Cuckfield and go back to Hampshire. Provisionally, he had put Robert down for the Pilgrims' School at Winchester. The meeting with Joan made everything straightforward: not only would he remain in the home where he felt so comfortable, but Robert would go to Parkfield.

Like Mary, Joan Stuart was born in 1900 and was a daughter of the church. She shared Tom's faith and his attitude to life, though her background and experience were more cosmopolitan than either Tom's or Mary's had been. Her father, J. V. Elliott Taylor, was the vicar of a church on Wandsworth Common and her mother was the daughter of an international banker, Walter Venables, whose wife was of Spanish and Italian extraction. Joan's paternal grandfather was the son of a coachmaker on the Isle of Wight, who made coaches for Queen Victoria. After marrying a deeply religious woman, Grandfather Taylor became, for a time, a vicar in a pleasant parish near Southampton, until both he and his wife came to believe it was their duty to establish a mission in the slums of Battersea. Joan's maternal grandparents lived in Putney, in great style, and travelled extensively, collecting pictures as they went. At the end of the Franco-Prussian war, Grandfather Venables had been one of the first men to re-enter

Paris to start the Bourse working again, accompanied by his wife, whose footwarmer concealed a gold bar.

After the First World War, Joan was sent to France to learn the language, before attending the Guildhall School to study Elocution and Voice Production. As her parents had, by then, moved to Haywards Heath, Joan stayed two nights a week with her widowed maternal grandmother, who had moved to Ashley Gardens.

Joan's elder sister Peggy married, at 20, an army clergyman stationed in Burma. In 1922 she came home ahead of her husband, with her two-year-old daughter, to prepare for the arrival of a second baby. Suddenly and unexpectedly her husband's leave was cancelled because an important clergyman was expected in Rangoon; Peggy decided to return to Burma and Joan went to help with the little girl on the long sea voyage. They reached Suez in reasonable comfort, 'then the weather became so hot, particularly in the Red Sea, that the vessel had to proceed backwards to get some air to the engine room to avoid the engineers fainting!'[38] Joan had only one thin tussore frock and knickers, which she wore every day – it was 'too hot for any such thing as stockings' – washing them out each night, ready for the following morning. Once into the Indian Ocean they hit a new hazard: the monsoon. Peggy passed the day lying down and Joan – though she was suffering from seasickness – spent it chasing her small niece about the deck or holding the child in her arms, when she napped, to prevent her from rolling off the couch.

They reached Rangoon in time for the birth and afterwards, before she sailed for home, Joan was given a taste of local British social life. Just as Tom would later decide, at their first meeting, to marry Joan, so in Rangoon, in 1922, her first husband 'made up his mind, virtually at first sight.'[39] She was at the Clubhouse when Jack Stuart, a tall, handsome Irishman, an army officer with a first-class degree in engineering, went in to get a golf club to kill a snake. Later he told a friend he intended to marry 'that young lady'.[39] He did not tell Joan but on his next home leave he came to visit her in Ashley Gardens. They were married in 1923. Her two daughters, Pauline and Hazel, were born in 1924 and 1928 and her son John in 1932.

In the early 1930s the family returned to England. They bought a house at Haywards Health and Jack joined Rendel, Palmer & Tritton, a firm of international consulting engineers. Among the projects for which he was responsible were the drainage of the Hula Valley in Palestine, building aerodromes during the war and preparing plans for oilfields in Iran. After returning from the Persian Gulf, Jack Stuart had a heart attack and died in 1942.

Joan's life was not easy after her husband's death. She had a large Victorian house, Brooklands, to look after, with a regular turnover of people billeted there; she was not left well-off and had three children to educate. Pauline, who was 17 when her father died, was to train as a teacher at the Central School of Speech and Drama. Hazel was at Roedean, and John at Parkfield. The scholarships won by Hazel and, later, by John for Repton, were a help, but money was tighter than it had been when their father was alive. Joan took a job as an editor on the *Church Times* and started to travel up to London three times a week. She was a capable manager, an intelligent and charming woman who always rose to a challenge, moving with an air of calm, quiet authority. She came from a background where belief in service was inbred and from a generation of women 'who felt lucky, after the slaughter of the 1914–18 War, to have husbands at all.'[40] Joan Stuart put her energies into the many jobs she had on hand and, though she was still good-looking, did not expect to marry again.

Pauline was about 21 when she accompanied her mother to the party at Parkfield. On the way home she told Joan that someone had tried to date her and her mother replied that someone had tried to date her too. 'She had met Sir Alfred Denning, who stampeded her into an engagement within three to four weeks.'[39] For Joan there were many attractions in the engagement. Tom was still good-looking, a charming, attentive and amusing companion, kind and considerate; he showed a ready interest in her family and a willingness to share her responsibilities; they had in common many beliefs and attitudes. She was troubled that her young son was assuming more responsibility than was good for him in his eagerness to help her and become the man of the house; she thought a resumption of a more normal family life would be good for him and also good for Robert.

Joan knew Mary through the Wives' Fellowship – and had seen Robert, who was the age that her own second son, Patrick, who had died in infancy, would have been. After Mary's death, she wondered whether to offer help with Robert but, not knowing Tom, she had hesitated to intrude. Now, with Tom urging her to marry him, she felt the match would be good for all of them. Everything that she knew about Tom suggested he would be a good husband. She was drawn to him. She believed that she could love him and give happiness to both of them and to their children.

Tom put it more romantically. 'Instinctively we fell in love,' he wrote in *The Family Story*, 'at first sight. Not in the headlong heedless way of youth. But in the deep sincere affection of maturity. We saw more and more of each other. We were like a couple of young lovers – meeting whenever there was the least opportunity.' By the time they became engaged, after the whirlwind courtship, they were, as Tom would write, 'full of love'.[6]

With the greatest tact, Joan started at once to take over from Nanny the responsibility for Robert. The 'rather forlorn little boy',[39] who had spent so much of his life in the care of nannies, adapted easily and happily to his new circumstances. Soon he was calling Joan's mother and godmother – who were also living at Brooklands – 'Granny' and 'Aunt Winnie'.

Pauline lived in London and worked as a drama organiser for the YWCA, where she wrote children's plays, based on fairy tales, with as many parts as possible for girls. Since Joan was frequently in London she kept her elder daughter easily in touch with her news. To tell Hazel was more of an undertaking. Roedean, at the time, was still evacuated to the Lake District and Joan went north to see her second daughter.

From the Royal Courts of Justice, on 19 October, Tom wrote to her, sending a message 'full of love' and telling her the Benchers would like to make their wedding in Lincoln's Inn. He hoped he might make himself worthy of her and added that, since she knew his faults, 'or some of them', she knew that he had 'a big task in hand'.[6]

From Keswick, on 20 October, Joan wrote: 'Hazel was on the platform to meet me though the train was ½ hour late & I think she was missing supper. I am very glad I came, Tom . . . Hazel seems very happy about everything.'[41] Joan had tried everywhere, she told Tom, to buy picture postcards of the scenery for Robert, but, like most other things at that time, they were difficult to find.

On 21 October, after receiving Tom's letter of 19 October, Joan wrote again. 'Your letter reached me last night & made me feel I wanted to fly straight back to you! I couldn't have believed it possible

to miss you so much.'⁴¹ Her letter crossed with his from Fair
Close, thinking of her and wondering what she was doing. He told
her of his 'happiness in our love' and his 'wretchedness at being
parted from you.'⁶ He brought her up to date with home news:
Granny – Joan's mother – and 'Aunt Winnie' had been to Fair Close
for tea. The local vicar hoped they would be married in Cuckfield.

At the same time as Tom's home life became happier, his career also
took a turn for the better. On 24 October 1945 Lord Jowitt, the new
Lord Chancellor, transferred him to the King's Bench Division and
he went at once on the Midland Circuit. He wrote from the Judge's
Lodgings at Leicester, on the first day, wishing Joan was with him.

I was met at the station by the under-sheriff and the stationmaster
both dressed up in their best top-hats and morning coats – then
driven here in the large car – welcomed by the butler and
housekeeper. Then news that the High Sheriff has sent me a bottle
of port, a brace of grouse and partridges and a pheasant, lovely
fruit and flowers – & wants me to dine with him on Saturday &
lunch on Sunday. I suppose I must have him back one day. Then I
had a sumptuous dinner all by myself – & after dinner I have been
working at my cases for tomorrow.

Three days later, on 27 October, Tom told Joan more about
circuit:

The High Sheriff of a county is appointed for 1 year only. In olden
days his office was of high importance – to see that all criminals
were brought to the King's judge – but now it is mainly
ceremonial. It is his duty to attend the Judge of Assize and see that
he is well provided for by the county . . . The High Sheriff here has
been very kind . . . He is going to provide a car to take me to
Lincoln (60 miles) on Thursday. He pays all my telephone calls –
including my private ones to you! . . . I have sat today in the Town
Hall . . . and the populace turned out to see me get in and out of
my car.

Then, aware that he would have found it hard to leave Robert the
entire week if Joan had not taken the child so closely under her

wing: 'It is a joy & comfort to know that you are keeping an eye on things at home . . . how much happier to be with you & Robert at home than surrounded by this pomp & responsibility here and separated from you.'

From the start their mutual trust and confidence was complete. Joan prepared herself to enter the esoteric world of law, to become a mother to Robert and to take from Tom's shoulders all the worries of home. For his part, he offered comfort, protection, support and advice in dealing with her children. He took the lease of a flat in Carlton Gardens, just off the Strand, and Pauline, who had been living with friends, was to move into it. As the circuit proceeded, he planned to visit Repton to meet John. He discussed money matters freely with Joan, evidently regarding her already as his partner in life even though they reluctantly accepted the need to wait until the vacation – and the school holidays – before they could marry. He sent her papers to put 'in the long drawer in big cupboard in the sitting room (very untidy) where I keep income tax papers etc;'[6] He even sent her unopened letters, in one of which she found eleven clothing coupons from an admirer – astonishing bounty in days of rationing! She wondered, briefly, whether she might keep them as 'they could be put to good use and to give them away is quite legal'[41] but 'experience with Jack' led her to believe 'that the sender of gifts invariably wanted something' and, she told Tom on 29 October, she had sent the coupons back with 'what I hope was a gracious refusal!'

Joan put herself on half-pay at the office in order to have time for other things. She wanted to get the flat ready for Pauline to move in by mid-November – a tiresome task in 1945, when so many necessities were unobtainable and permits were needed for even the smallest building or electrical work. She saw Robert practically every day, teaching him to play draughts and 'Battleships', and telling Tom on 26 October: 'I put him to bed, bath, reading and prayers quite successfully.' On 29 October she took him, with her mother and Nanny, on an outing by car, 'the only flaw being,' she wrote to Tom, 'that you were not there. Robert and I – and nannie – kept wishing you were.' On another day out a man in the teashop commented on a striking resemblance between Joan and Robert. 'I told him,' she wrote on 11 November, 'he was going to be my son, so it came to the same thing.'

From Robert, too, Tom had letters. 'Dear Daddy,' he wrote on 6 November, 'Thank you for your letters. I should have liked to have heard the fanfare of trumpets, perhaps you will let me go with you one day.' Then, on 28 November, 'Auntie Joan took me for a lovely drive to the Downs.' Tom must have been amused when he read: 'This is what the Enchanter has to say in our play – Partom Caughton Paradise Tempum Para Mara Dictum Domini. This is Latin I expect you know.'

At the beginning of November, Tom was in Lincoln – where Grandfather Thompson once had blown the Sheriff's trumpet when the Judge of Assize arrived. The present High Sheriff, he told Joan, was 'not so polished as the one in Leicestershire. I imagine he has made his own way in the world but he is doubtless a very good sort of person.' Tom was beginning to find it 'very difficult to fit these social things in with such a lot of work. I expect I shall have to make a speech at the Dinner the members of the Bar are giving this evening – & I am so bad at after dinner speeches.' Just the same, he found time to visit his cousin Gwen and revive old memories of his visit to his grandparents: family occasions, for Tom, were quite different from 'social things'.

For the rest of their lives Joan would make Tom's well-being her first concern and, already, she showed her protective attitude. 'It worried me,' she wrote, 'to hear your hoarse voice on the phone this evening . . . don't try & carry on if there is the least suspicion of its going to your chest . . .' Much as she valued his letters, she urged him to rest as much as possible, rather than to spend time writing to her. Though she looked forward to his meeting John, she told him not to make the journey to Repton if he felt too tired.

He went to Repton, of course, with chocolates and a cake, appreciating that John might resent Tom's marrying his mother and anxious to establish good relations. It was a foul day and to John's eyes, Tom 'duly came out of the fog in his official car'[40] to take him to tea. Tom may never have known how simply the balance swung in his favour. Amongst the jobs John did for his mother was to mow the lawn. He was very keen to have a motor mower, and asked whether Tom had one. 'He did,' John remembered. 'So it was all right.'[40]

As Joan coped with problems at home, planning their marriage with the least upheaval for their families, and wondering what John should call Tom, she was encouraged by his letters. She quickly understood Tom's way of romanticising his loved ones and feared it might lead to disappointment. 'You will be careful,' she wrote on 31 October, 'not to idolise me in your thoughts and love me as you *want* me and not as I *am*.' On 11 November she told him she liked a photograph of him in his wig but, 'I want a photograph without one sometime as I am really marrying *you* and not the judge!' The long separation after the month of courtship must have been trying:

> If you don't come back soon Tom I shall sink back into the complete business woman and be no use at all to you. It is much more stimulating than making puddings and beds, but perhaps I'll like that better when I've a husband to eat and sleep in them, a home without a husband and children is no home at all!

The circuit proceeded to Nottingham on 24 November, to Warwick and Derby and, on 5 December, to Birmingham. There was much work to be done and Tom was getting tired. 'It was one of my most instructive experiences,' he wrote in *The Family Story*, 'to be a Judge of Assize on an English Circuit.' He heard both civil and criminal cases at a time when many civil cases were still tried by jury and when flogging and capital punishment were still 'the order of the day.'[1]

> When a judge sits to try a case with a jury, he is himself on trial – before his fellow countrymen. It is on his behaviour that they will form their opinion of our system of justice. He must be robed in the scarlet of the Red Judge – so as to show that he represents the majesty of the law. He must be dignified – so as to earn the respect of all who appear before him. He must be alert – to follow all that goes on. He must be understanding – to show that he is aware of the temptations that beset everyone. He must be merciful – so as to show that he too has the quality which 'droppeth as the gentle rain from heaven upon the place beneath.'[1]

The question of red robes was tackled in a practical way by Mr Justice Cassels, who wrote: 'What are you doing about robes? They are very expensive now, & Lynskey had to pay an enormous sum.

Why not negotiate for James Tucker's? If you have to have a new set seriously consider hire-purchase and get relief on Income Tax.'[42]

As to the other attributes of a judge, Denning had impeccable judicial manners. Counsel, litigants and even prisoners at the bar bore witness to his patience, consideration and understanding, not to mention his alertness to matters they wished to put before him and others that they might have preferred him to overlook. Not only was Denning certain of the law, but he no longer seemed to have any doubt how it should be applied! Merciful, where mercy seemed to him to be justified, he had no qualms where he considered a severe penalty – even the death sentence – was justified:

> I remember a youngster of 18 coming behind an old woman of 80 and hitting her over the head and injuring her badly, and stealing her savings of £20 in money. I ordered him twenty-five strokes of the birch. Was I wrong? I remember also trying a case at Gloucester when an Army Officer, a Captain, was charged with murdering his wife.
>
> He was a small-arms instructor. His wife led him an awful life, nagging and going for him continually. One day, coming back from his course, she went at him so much that he picked up his revolver and shot her dead – pregnant as she was! Was he guilty of murder or manslaughter? Obviously of murder. Words are not sufficient provocation to reduce it to manslaughter. I so directed the jury. I don't know whether it was the tone of my voice or not, but I did tell them it was for them to come to their own decision. The jury found the officer guilty of manslaughter. I sentenced him to two years' imprisonment. All those in the gallery cheered.[1]

Joan was in court, in Gloucester, when Tom tried the small-arms instructor. The case made a great impression on her. When the jury retired, she could not bear to stay for the verdict and was relieved to hear that it was manslaughter. Had the verdict been murder, in those days the judge would have had no alternative but to pronounce the death sentence and, in macabre ceremony, was required to place a black cap on his head before he did so. Afterwards, the judge would write to the Home Secretary giving his views of the case and, if appropriate, passing on his own or the jury's recommendations to mercy. In the course of Denning's time as a trial judge, he passed sentence of death on some six or seven occasions. One, the trial of a Polish soldier, who had shot another Pole for stealing his girlfriend, was unusually difficult. The man spoke no English and tension was high as Denning pronounced the death sentence and the words were repeated in Polish. Then the accused began to speak rapidly and there was a pause while the court listened to the translation of his plea to be shot as a soldier, not hung. 'Looking less than his usual equable self, Denning promised that he would pass the request to the authorities.'[43]

From Parkfield, on 27 June 1948, Robert wrote to him:

Have you seen your name in the paper it say's: 'Two judges differed in the phrasing of the death sentence and the use of the black cap yesterday. *Mr Justice Denning* used the cap when he passed sentence at Pembrokeshire.' That is all I want to say because it will take up the whole letter. Thank you very much for the windmill it works very nicely.

At the end of November 1945 Joan was still juggling dates. The sensible thing, she wrote to Tom, would be to get married on Saturday 15 December. 'If you could get down Friday, we could marry Sat after lunch, & Pauline could come home Sat, stay the night and you & I could leave Haywards Heath about 6 p.m. and have a night in the flat & then you go back the next day.' This, she finished breathlessly, 'would leave the 9th weekend clear for Robert & by our leaving Sat evening 15th he would not miss you very much.'

Though there were still severe shortages, life on circuit was cushioned. 'I hope you won't be too grand for us all when you return!' Joan told Tom on 26 November. 'It will seem odd to come back to simplicity & domestic things.'

By December, Joan had taken Robert and Nanny to stay with her at Brooklands. She had also seen Pauline into the flat; met the family of Pauline's boyfriend, Derick Simond, a member of the BBC production staff; fitted Robert up as a 'holly berry elf' in a fancy dress costume that had last been worn by Hazel; and tried to get crackers in Brighton for the party she was giving for Robert's friends. She had failed to find construction toys for Robert on a visit to Gamages. She was 'a little worried over food for the wedding' as she could 'get nothing extra' but had told everyone '*light* refreshments.'

At Birmingham, on 4 December, Denning was faced with the case of a 35-year-old soldier, charged with wounding a man with intent to murder, wounding with intent to do grievous bodily harm and with unlawfully wounding. Evidence was given that the soldier returned home to find his wife on the settee with another man and, in a fight, wounded him with a knife. Directing the jury on provocation, the *Daily Mail* reported the following day, Mr Justice Denning said: 'If a man found his wife with another man in the act of adultery, or in circumstances which looked as if she were about to commit adultery, it might deprive any reasonable man of his self-control, and might deprive him of such self-control that he really could not have any specific intent to murder . . .' There was applause in the public gallery when the foreman gave the verdict of the jury: not guilty of any of the three charges. Reading this with a sense of shock, more than 40 years later, one must remember the sympathy felt, after the war, for soldiers returning to find broken homes.

It was customary for judges to have with them on Assize a young barrister who, as marshal, performed largely ceremonial duties. Michael Havers, a young naval officer on demobilisation leave, was at Leeds with Henn-Collins, Byrne and Denning. Thirty-six years later, as Attorney-General, in his valedictory speech on Tom's retirement, Havers recalled the three judges discussing cases over lunch. 'On these occasions Mr Justice Denning was likely to remark, for example, "I think the case of *McManus* v *Bowers* covers the problem." ' When Havers stood up to get the law report, Denning would add: 'I think you will find it in [1938] 1 King's Bench in the judgment of Lord Justice Slessor,' and, before Havers could open the book, 'I think it is in the paragraph which starts –' Denning's encyclopaedic knowledge of case law was to help many a young barrister at a loss for an appropriate reference; together with his superb command of language, it was the secret of *ex tempore* judgments that became classics in the law.

The plan to marry over the weekend of 15 December was not practical. When term ended, Tom, Hazel and John all came home. Tom made every possible effort, in accordance with their ages, to understand Joan's children and to persuade them to accept him. He was 'extremely tolerant'[40] and though there were moments when John, who had been the man about the house, was truculent, 'Tom was never ruffled.'[38] They were able to reach a happy accommodation since Tom, who was 'not mechanically or electrically gifted'[40] willingly left to John the jobs that he was accustomed to do. For Robert, 'it was wonderful having all these people doing things with you.'[32] Pauline played charades with him; John taught him to use tools, and gave him a salutary introduction to normal family life with a 'tongue lashing' for leaving John's 'very precious' plane in the garden, where it rusted.

By the time Tom Denning married Joan Stuart at Cuckfield Church on 27 December 1945 with a lunch at Fair Close to follow, their two families had begun to integrate. John called Tom 'Uncle Tom' and Pauline and Hazel used his name, but Robert without any hesitation called Joan 'Mummy'. Tom's difficult years were over: the second half of his life would be made smooth for him by a very remarkable woman.

After the marriage Joan sold Brooklands and the family lived in Fair Close, 'a warm, comforting home.'[40] The house was built in 1933. 'Good to look at and to live in,'[1] it had three large and two smaller bedrooms. Downstairs, one room was Tom's library, where he kept a complete set of Law Reports. When he was working in London, Tom walked each morning to the station at Haywards Heath – downhill almost all the way – to take the 7.55 or the 8.25 train to Victoria. Court rose at 4.15 and he hurried to catch the 4.45 home. In the evenings Joan met him with the car to run his bag, heavy with papers for the next day, back up the hill to Fair Close. In the train, when most of his fellow-passengers read their newspapers, Tom glanced at the pleadings in his next case and thought about his next judgment.

On all sides, as the family settled down, there were some adjustments to be made. Pauline visited often and sometimes stayed the weekend but she never lived at Fair Close. She was busy with plans for her marriage to Derick Simond. Apart from the move from Brooklands, Joan's mind was much exercised by the question of clothing coupons and – since rationing was practically back to wartime stringency – how she would obtain food for the reception she planned to give at Fair Close, after the wedding. Hazel, having won a place at Somerville College the previous autumn, was in her last term at school. She helped Joan with the move, came to Fair Close for the holidays and prepared to be a bridesmaid at her sister's wedding. On 24 April 1946, Tom gave Pauline away in Cuckfield Church, where he had so recently been the bridegroom.

Joan had felt some concern about John's reaction to the changes but, as things turned out, he enjoyed living in the country and Tom showed great tact, 'treating John as a young adult and not as a schoolboy.'[38] It was Robert whose life was most transformed by the marriage. He had been a lonely little boy, almost entirely reliant upon Nanny's company, except when he was at school, and very sensitive to any change in her mood. Tom was devoted to him but – because of Mary's illness – watched anxiously over his health. As Clara had once given Tom the hated cod-liver oil in an egg-cup of milk, so Robert was made to drink boiled milk.

Tom and Joan were grateful to Nanny for the care she had taken of Robert. For a time she stayed on at Fair Close to do the cooking but this did not work out and they agreed to part. They kept in touch for many years but, with Nanny's departure, Joan became, in all but fact, Robert's mother. The milk was no longer boiled. Under Joan's love and care Robert began to thrive, learning to climb trees and becoming healthily untidy.

11

King's Bench

Denning had taken James Cassels's advice and bought the robes that Lord Justice Tucker, advanced to the Court of Appeal on the day Denning was transferred to the King's Bench, no longer required. Before his promotion Tucker had been the nominated Judge for Pensions Appeals. This appointment, as well as Tucker's robes, fell upon Denning's shoulders. It was one that gave him the greatest satisfaction and 'perhaps the most rewarding series of cases' [1] in his career.

War pensions were granted under the terms of successive Royal Warrants. As Denning knew from the First World War and the difficulties over Gordon's pension, there had long been dissatisfaction with decisions of the Ministry of Pensions. It was primarily a question of the burden of proof – the subject on which, Denning had written in 1945 for the *Law Quarterly Review*, 'When the law puts on a party the burden of proving a certain fact in issue as a condition of giving him judgment, that burden never shifts and must be discharged or he will fail.' The burden had always been placed upon an applicant for a pension to prove that his disability or injury was due to war service. So widespread had been the discontent, as claimants failed to discharge the onus, that independent appeals tribunals were established. Each was composed of a legally qualified chairman, a doctor and a lay member, who all tended to adopt a rigid approach to the law; in the Second World War disappointed applicants looked elsewhere for help. By 1942 the business of the House of Commons was disrupted by the numbers of Members attempting to raise the cases of their constituents.

In an attempt to deflect the criticism, concessions on the burden of proof were made by the legislature, which also introduced appeals from tribunals to a nominated judge. Appeal could be made only with leave from the tribunal or the Pensions Judge, and only on a point of law, within a six-week time limit, which could be extended by the tribunal or the Judge. On past form, tribunals were not expected to be generous in exercising their discretion. So far as the burden of proof was concerned, both the Ministry and the tribunals continued to make decisions on the same principles as they had done before the new Act became law. The burden still rested on the claimant. Since the government were anxious that there should be finality to questions of entitlement, the Pensions Judge was endowed with unusual authority: there was to be no appeal from his decision. For Denning, the position might have been tailor-made.

On his first day, 11 January 1946, the first application was by a man named Phillips for leave to appeal after the tribunal had refused to extend the time for applying to them. Denning's grant of the application gave no indication of what was to come. Nor did his first reported case, on 14 January, an appeal by the Minister from a tribunal decision that a Mr Nugent was entitled to a pension, having become disabled whilst performing his duties as an auxiliary coast-guard. 'I am quite satisfied,' said Denning, allowing the Minister's appeal, 'on reading the whole of the Act . . . that what the Legislature had in mind with regard to those mariners and other sea-faring persons was injuries which they sustained, to put it generally, afloat . . . the right interpretation is that it does not apply to the case of injuries which are sustained in propinquity to the sea or harbour . . . It is not permissible for me to put any different interpretation on them in regard to coastguards out of sympathy.' (*Minister of Pensions v. Nugent*) There was no sign in this judgment that here was a judge who would shortly change the system.

A month later, on 26 February 1946, Denning gave his judgment in three cases, heard separately in January – *Starr, Nuttall* and *Bourne v. Minister of Pensions* – which was to change the burden of proof in pensions law. He set out the principles by which the Minister must be guided in deciding whether a claimant was entitled to a pension. In effect, Denning decided that if a man was fit for service when he joined the armed forces and unfit when he came out, he should not have to prove his disability was due to service: the Minister must prove that it was not. If the Minister could not discharge this burden, the man would be entitled to a pension.

The decision was duly acclaimed, if not by the Minister, then by Parliament, the press and the British Legion. Almost immediately people began to ask what was to be done about the large number of men and women who had been refused a pension before this new ruling had been in force, and might well have been granted one if its interpretation of the law had been applied. The Government declined to take any action.

There was an outcry. The *Sunday Pictorial* of 7 April 1946 reported another of Denning's cases and demanded action. Under the headline 'We Demand Justice for These Men!', they published a photograph of Denning ('This Judge Gives Them a New Hope for Pensions') and wrote:

One man, fighting a lone battle for himself against the law, has won a decision that may be the means of giving hundreds of ex-Servicemen pensions. It must do if justice is to be done.

. . . After serving three years in the Army [William Daniel Rowing] was discharged as medically unfit. He applied for a pension and was refused. He took his case to an Appeals Tribunal and was again refused.

. . . [H]e found it was possible to lodge a further appeal to the High Court within six weeks.

He did so, and a few days ago Mr Justice Denning not only gave Mr Rowing his pension, but set down a ruling that should give pensions to scores of others who lost their case at the Appeals Tribunals . . .

He pointed out that if a man is accepted for service and then discharged on medical grounds, that fact alone raises a presumption that his breakdown was due to his war service . . .

It means that since the Appeals Tribunals were set up two years ago, scores of cases may have been rejected on evidence no stronger than that brought in the case of Mr Rowing . . .

The country will demand a review of these cases as a result of Mr Justice Denning's decision. Only the Minister can right any wrongs that have occurred. It is too late for any of these old cases to go to the High Court.

The slogan of the day was 'Fit for Service. Fit for Pension.' The

British Legion chose 73 representative cases and sought Denning's leave to present them out of time. Denning set them down for hearing on 11 July. The *Sunday Pictorial* had estimated that scores of cases might be involved. Writing in 1988 in the *Denning Law Journal* of Buckingham University, Patrick Polden estimated that, as a result of the decision in *Starr*, 'as many as 27,000 tribunal decisions were probably vitiated by procedural defects.' The Minister feared that it might not be too late for the old cases if the nominated judge decided to allow appeals out of time. The Government sought a compromise with the British Legion: it was agreed that all the cases should be reviewed by the Ministry and that rejected claimants might appeal to a Special Review Tribunal, from which there should be no further appeal.

Then, as always, Denning liked to have his say. He wanted to pronounce in court on the subject of appeals being allowed out of time in circumstances where there was a change in the interpretation of the law. In 1947, in *James* v. *Minister of Pensions*, the opportunity arose. Mrs James's husband had died of Hodgkin's disease and, in September 1946, a tribunal decided that it was not attributable to war service. Two months later another tribunal decided that a Hodgkin's disease case *was* due to war service. The tribunal refused Mrs James leave to appeal out of time and she applied to the Pensions Judge. The Ministry knew this would be an important case. Sir Hartley Shawcross, the Attorney-General, appeared for the Minister, arguing that the question at issue was one of fact, not of law – and the Judge was not therefore empowered to hear it – and that Denning had no power to extend the time since he must follow certain decided cases governing leave to appeal out of time to the King's Bench. Denning rejected both arguments. He made clear his view that 'the circumstances of pension appeals differ . . . from ordinary litigation' and 'it is inevitable that, in a field where the law has had to be declared and developed so rapidly, there should be occasional errors.'

A striking case occurred the other day [he said]. The widow of a warrant officer named Finnerty who died of cancer of the lung, was refused a pension by the Minister and by the tribunal, who refused leave to appeal. I granted leave and when the appeal came on for hearing on 1 July 1947, the Minister conceded the claim because a careful study of the history showed that the man in the course of his service had been subjected to radium which might have had an influence on the onset or progress of the cancer.

In language that forecast battles he would fight in the future, Denning pronounced 'the doctrine of *stare decisis*' – the rule that precedent must be followed – 'does not apply in its full rigour to this branch of the law.'

After *James*, tribunals made a practice of granting leave out of time whenever an application was based on the effect of a later judgment. Shortly Denning tilted against another restriction that would often be a target for him. The agreement between the Government and the British Legion had made the decision of the Special Review Tribunal unappealable. Denning objected to any attempt to usurp the power of the courts. His opportunity to pronounce on the Special Review Tribunal arose in the case of *Gillibrand*. A tribunal had rejected Mrs Gillibrand's claim in September 1944. It was turned down again, on review by the Minister and, instead of going to the Special Review Tribunal, Mrs Gillibrand sought Denning's leave to appeal out of time. He agreed to remit her case to a tribunal, saying, 'from any decision of that Tribunal Mrs Gillibrand will have a right of recourse to this Court. She shall not be forced to go before a tribunal [the Special Review Tribunal] from which there is no appeal.' Ministry officials and Law Officers may have been indignant at this method of by-passing the agreed procedure, but could do nothing about it.

On 25 July 1947 Denning dismissed an appeal from the widow of a regular army officer, who had died of cancer while on war service. Denning's brilliant analysis of what constitutes proof, in *Miller* v. *Minister of Pensions*, went far beyond its immediate application.

In the pensions cases Denning showed many of the attitudes and used many of the stratagems that he would later employ to mete out justice in his very individual style. For nearly three years he wielded unprecedented – and never afterwards equalled – power to make decisions, as sole arbiter, from whom there could be no appeal. Not only service cases, but also cases of war injury to civilians came before him: cases of glaucoma, psychopathic personality, hysteria and cancers of various kinds; cases of diabetes mellitus, deafness, rheumatoid arthritis and all types of fractures; even the case of a mentally defective child, whose parents claimed her condition was due to her having been buried, at the age of five, with her mother under the rubble of their demolished home.

Despite his sympathy, Tom never bent the law to give claimants more than their entitlement. His achievement was to make the rules by which that entitlement must be assessed more favourable to the claimants and to ensure for them the right of appeal to his court. As he would always do when dealing with litigants in person, Denning so conducted hearings that even a loser felt certain that there had been a full, fair and considerate hearing of his case. That was not usual amongst judges of the time.

The pensions appeals were not the only work on which Denning was engaged at the time. In addition to hearing cases in the King's Bench, he went regularly on circuit and it was while he was away from London that he received a letter from Lord Jowitt inviting him to chair a committee to enquire into the administration of the divorce law. 'There are few subjects with which I, as Lord Chancellor, have had to deal since I took office,' Jowitt wrote on 30 May 1946, 'which have given me more concern than the tremendous increase in divorce, and my anxieties have not been decreased by the evident lack of agreement on fundamentals among those very well qualified to express an opinion on this subject.' Inviting Denning to chair the committee, Jowitt assured him: 'I do not do so lightly. The Cabinet Committee over which I presided were unanimous in thinking you would be the best possible Chairman that could be obtained for an enquiry of such importance and such difficulty, and I am happy to find that the Lord Chief Justice and the President agree with me in that conclusion. At the same time,' he added, 'the burden will be a heavy one,' and – for he knew Tom well, having worked with him at the Bar – 'I can conceive, one not altogether congenial to you.'

When the announcement was made in the House of Lords, the Lord Chancellor emphasised that the scope of the inquiry did not extend to the grounds on which decrees of divorce or nullity of marriage might be granted. The Committee's terms of reference were to examine divorce procedure and report 'what procedural reforms ought to be introduced in the general interest of litigants, with special reference to expediting the hearing of suits and reducing costs and to the Courts in which such suits ought to proceed; and in particular whether any (and if so, what) machinery should be available for the purpose of attempting a reconciliation between the parties, either before or after proceedings have been commenced.'

The increase in the number of divorce petitions consequent upon the war was still causing intolerable delay. There was general agreement that something must be done about it, and quickly. With his usual energy, Denning threw himself and the rest of his committee into the work. As Secretary, they were given 33-year-old Thomas Skyrme, a lawyer in the Lord Chancellor's department, who had been Lord Simon's secretary in 1944, at the time of Denning's appointment to the bench. Skyrme was to be knighted in 1974 and become President of the Commonwealth Magistrates' Association, Vice-President of the Magistrates' Association of England and Wales and Chairman of the Broadcasting Complaints Commission. Tom made a direct approach to Skyrme, telling him bluntly that he was new to this and Skyrme should tell him what to do.

'He was a good Chairman' with 'a quick grasp of what was needed and of salient facts. His incisive approach pushed the Committee's considerations along quickly.'[33] The Lord Chancellor was able to present to Parliament the Committee's first interim report by July 1946, only a month after their appointment. It was published by His Majesty's Stationery Office at a cost of one penny.

The Committee unanimously recommended, as a matter of urgency, that the period of six months between the decree nisi and the decree absolute should be reduced to six weeks. With its eye, as it was supposed to be, on a practical way to reduce delay, the Committee stated: 'Our recommendation has the advantage that it can be effected without an Act of Parliament. It can be done by a General Order of the High Court.' The complete abolition of the period before a decree could be made absolute, though it was in the Committee's sights, would require legislation and they preferred to defer consideration of it until a later stage.

The recommendation of the Committee was implemented at once. In November 1946 they presented a second interim report, recommending that divorce cases should no longer be tried only by High Court judges. They should be tried by County Court judges, sitting as Commissioners. 'The Commissioners should be accorded all the dignity of a High Court Judge. When sitting in Court they should wear the same robes as a judge of the Divorce Division and be addressed in the same may [*sic*] as a judge.' Other procedural reforms were also suggested. The recommendations in this report, too, were implemented at once.

Though Tom was engaged in the work of expediting divorce procedure, his views on marriage and divorce remained unchanged. In a lecture on the divorce laws at King's College, London, on Friday 31 January 1947, he said '. . . The institution of marriage is an essential feature of our present civilisation . . . I am convinced that men and women only achieve a fully satisfied life when happily married and bringing up their children, the man at his work to provide for them, the woman in the house to rear them, and each with sufficient leisure to develop their personalities and enjoy the family life.' Tom viewed marriage always in the context of his own faith: 'The law of England adopts the Christian principle that marriage is the personal union of one man with one woman, for better or for worse, exclusive of all others on either side, so long as both shall live. The principle must be kept continually in mind if we are to understand the divorce laws.'

The final report of the Committee was published in February 1947, less than eight months after its appointment. 'No Committee,' Denning would write in *The Due Process of Law*, 'ever worked so quickly or so well.' In its final report, after taking evidence from representatives of the organisations already offering marriage guidance, it recommended that there should be a Marriage Welfare Service to afford help and guidance both before and after marriage. 'We have throughout our enquiry had in mind the principle that the preservation of the marriage tie is of the highest importance in the interests of society.'

Lord Merriman, who in 1922 had recommended Tom to apply to O'Hagan and was now the President of the Probate, Divorce and Admiralty Division, had presented to the Committee 'a scheme which he was good enough to work out in considerable detail.' In the most diplomatic language, the Committee rejected it. Unfortunately they had neglected to take his views on some of their recommendations, in particular that there should be welfare officers attached to the Court, specially to help with the children. 'He never forgave me,' Tom wrote in *The Due Process of Law*. 'When I happened to go to his room afterwards on another matter, he said to me: "You are a blackguard. You ought to have put it to me." '

Whatever may have been the views of Lord Merriman, the recommendations in the report were implemented. The members of the Committee held a dinner to which the Lord Chancellor came and presented Tom with a leather-bound copy of the report, inscribed:

To Mr Justice Denning
With all my thanks
for the great work he has done.
23rd April 1947 Jowitt C.

The report had an excellent reception. Denning had a second taste of the public acclaim that had greeted his decisions in the pensions cases. A leader writer in The *Daily Telegraph & Morning Post*, on 6 February 1947, commented that the report's observations on reconciliation made a contribution to the study of human relationships. Steered by Denning, the Committee had produced a notable work of social reform. It led, two years later, to an invitation from the National Marriage Guidance Council for Denning to become their President.

Though he had given up his appointments as Chancellor of the Diocese of London and Southwark, Denning retained his interest in ecclesiastical law, a subject on which he had written an article in the *Law Quarterly Review* in 1944. While his Report on Matrimonial Procedure was fresh in the public mind, his advice was sought by a church leader on a proposal designed to overcome difficulties over remarriage in church after divorce. On 28 May 1947 Tom replied. There is nothing in the three-and-a-half-page letter to indicate the full title of the recipient, but Lord Denning told the author it was probably addressed to the Bishop of London.

'My dear Bishop,' Denning wrote, 'I have now thought more about the suggestion of establishing an ecclesiastical nullity procedure. I see many objections to it!' He proceeded to set out the objections, which ranged from the strictly legal to the purely practical. The cost of establishing courts and hearing applications would fall upon the applicants, Denning pointed out, so that only the rich would be able to avail themselves of the opportunity. 'That would give rise to a very undesirable distinction between rich and poor, tending to treat marriage in church after divorce as a social luxury not based on moral grounds.' To Denning's mind, 'by far the best plan is for the Church always to refuse to marry any person whose first partner is still living: to give its blessing in a special service to any innocent party who has obtained a divorce and is re-married by the law of the land: but to refuse the blessing of the Church to a guilty party.'

While Denning was engaged on work connected with the Committee on Matrimonial Procedure, he still sat regularly in the King's Bench Division. On 15 April 1946, he formed part of a strong five-judge Court of Criminal Appeal, headed by Lord Goddard, the Lord Chief Justice. The appellant, George Sims, had been tried on an indictment containing ten charges variously alleging sodomy or indecency (or both) against a number of different men and boys. The trial judge had refused Sims's application to be tried separately in respect of each individual man and boy and the jury had found Sims guilty of some, but not all of the charges. Appearing for Sims at the appeal Casswell KC argued: 'The effect of trying all the cases together was to make the jury say "This is a dirty old man." ' Goddard dismissed the appeal but, 'in view of its great importance,' said that the court would give reasons at a later date. On 13 May he read the written judgment, stating that it had been 'largely prepared by Denning J.' While still a comparatively junior judge, Tom had the opportunity to prepare – if not to deliver – an important judgment in criminal law.

On 18 July 1946 he gave judgment in a case with which his name would always be associated in legal circles, catapulting him into the eyes of the legal world and putting him at the centre of a legal controversy. *High Trees* (*Central London Property Trust Ltd* v. *High Trees House Ltd*, to give its full name) was a simple case of contract. It might, with a little ingenuity, have been decided in a way that would have satisfied Denning's sense of justice, without raising any eyebrows. Denning wanted more. Since the days of *Smith's Leading Cases* he had been attracted to the idea of an estoppel based on a promise given by one party to another. Now Tom saw his chance to develop a new principle.

By a lease under seal, made on 24 September 1939, Central London Property Trust had granted to its subsidiary, High Trees House, a 99-year lease of a block of flats, at a ground rent of £2,500 per annum.

The block of flats was new and was not fully let. Since many people were out of London because of the war, it became clear to the directors of both companies that it would not be possible for High Trees to pay the ground rent of £2,500. On 3 January 1940 Central London wrote to High Trees confirming an agreement between them that the ground rent should be reduced 'as from the commencement of the lease' to £1250. This was confirmed in a resolution passed by Central London on 2 April 1940. High Trees paid the reduced rent until 1945, by which time all the flats were let but the business of Central London was in the hands of a receiver.

On 21 September the receiver wrote to High Trees saying the rent must be paid in full and claiming £7916 arrears. To obtain a legal ruling, the receiver commenced proceedings in the High Court for a declaration as to the amount of rent payable. He claimed £625, which was the difference between the two figures for the quarters ending 29 September and 25 December 1945. High Trees relied for their defence upon the letter of 3 January 1940: they claimed that it constituted an agreement that the ground rent should be £1250 for the whole term of the lease. In the alternative, they pleaded that Central London were estopped from alleging that the rent exceeded £1250 and, as a further alternative, that Central London had waived their rights to claim any rent in excess of £1250 up to 24 September 1945, when High Trees received the receiver's letter. The case came before Denning.

During the nineteenth century, the Courts had laid down strict rules of law expressed in terms such as 'consideration' and 'estoppel'. Consideration was defined in *Jacob's Law Dictionary*, in the eighteenth century, as the 'quid pro quo of any contract, without which it will not be effectual or binding.' In the middle of the twentieth century, that definition was as good as it had ever been. Central London's letter of 3 January 1940 could not have formed a new contract since High Trees had given absolutely no quid for the quo that it received. The agreement, if it was intended by the parties to be one, lacked consideration. Though many lawyers thought some re-assessment of consideration was overdue, there was general agreement that the doctrine was so long-established that only legislation could alter it.

The use of estoppel was also hedged about with restrictions. Estoppel – an impediment or bar to a right of action arising from a man's own act – applied, according to the authorities, only to representations of fact, not to statements of intention. Denning saw his opportunity, in *High Trees*, to re-introduce the principle of estoppel based on promise, that he had noted in old authorities, which had been overlooked for many years.

The case was argued by Mr Robert Fortune for Central London and Mr Ronald Hopkins for High Trees. 'They argued it well,' commented Denning,[1] 'but they had not the reserves at their command as I had. I delivered judgment straight off the reel – with a tidying up for the Law Reports.'

If I were to consider this matter without regard to recent developments in the law, there is no doubt that had the plaintiffs claimed it, they would have been entitled to recover ground rent at the rate of £2,500 a year from the beginning of the term, since the lease under which it was payable was a lease under seal which, according to the old common law, could not be varied by an agreement by parol (whether in writing or not), but only by deed. Equity, however, stepped in and said that if there had been a variation of a deed by a simple contract (which in the case of a lease required to be in writing would have to be evidenced by writing), the courts may give effect to it ... That equitable doctrine, however, could hardly apply in the present case, because the variation here might be said to have been made without consideration. With regard to estoppel, the representation made in relation to reducing the rent, was not a representation of an existing fact. It was a representation, in effect, as to the future, namely that payment of the rent would not be enforced at the full rate but only at the reduced rate. Such a representation would not give rise to an estoppel because ... a representation as to the future must be embodied as a contract or be nothing.

So far, there had been no departure from mainstream law. Denning went on:

But what is the position in view of developments in the law in recent years? The law has not been standing still ... There has been a series of decisions over the last fifty years which, although they are said to be cases of estoppel, are not really such. They are cases in which a promise was made which was intended to create legal relations and which, to the knowledge of the person making the promise, was going to be acted on by the person to whom it was made, and which was in fact so acted on. In such cases the courts have said that the promise must be honoured . . .

As I have said they are not cases of estoppel in the strict sense. They are really promises – promises intended to be binding, intended to be acted on, and in fact acted on . . .

The courts have not gone so far as to give a cause of action in damages for the breach of such a promise, but they have refused to allow the party making it to act inconsistently with it.

On all the evidence, Denning continued, he was satisfied that the promise in High Trees was that the ground rent should be reduced as a temporary expedient while the block of flats was not let, owing to wartime conditions. By the early months of 1945 the flats were fully let and producing higher rentals than had originally been contemplated. Accordingly he decided that the full rate was payable for the quarters ending 25 September and 29 December 1945.

In practical terms, his decision produced a demonstrably just solution; a solution, moreover, that others might have reached by blurring the authorities. That was not Denning's way. He had little patience with the legal fictions employed by judges to do justice while apparently observing precedent. It was not the result of *High Trees* that created a stir: it was the fact that a comparatively junior judge had the courage to challenge the established doctrine of consideration and the creativity to invent – or rediscover – an estoppel based on promise, in order to modify the rigours of that doctrine.

'In my opinion,' he said, 'the time has now come for the validity of such a promise to be recognised.' Then he continued in words that he must have known would raise legal hackles: 'The logical consequence, no doubt, is that a promise to accept a smaller sum in discharge of a larger sum, if acted upon, is binding notwithstanding the absence of consideration: and if the fusion of law and equity leads to this result so much the better.'

Looking back, in 1978, in *The Family Story*, Denning wrote: 'There was no appeal. This was probably because the decision could be supported on other grounds. An appeal might have ruined everything.' But of course Denning had known there would be no appeal. This was 'friendly' litigation to establish the ground rent payable; neither side had any intention of appealing. As in the pensions cases, Tom had seized the opportunity to bring a fresh approach to old problems.

High Trees became the subject of learned articles in the legal magazines and comment and criticism in text-books; many eminent lawyers remain critical of the decision. Denning always enjoyed relying upon his own cases as precedent but, in 1951, in the Court of Appeal, he refused to extend the principle, even though the trial judge had considered it applied. 'Much as I am inclined to favour the principle stated in the *High Trees* case,' he said, in *Combe* v. *Combe*, 'it is important that it should not be stretched too far, lest it should be endangered. That principle does not create new causes of action where none existed before. It only prevents a party from insisting upon his strict legal rights, when it would be unjust to allow him to enforce them, having regard to the dealings which have taken place between the parties.'

In the front of 1947 King's Bench of the *Law Reports* in Lincoln's Inn Library are pasted two cards. One has a drawing of an unusual species of bird, described in the words, 'This Unique Genus living in the High places of the Forest, is known affectionately as the High Trees Penguin.' The other bears the message: 'Copy of a card presented to the Rt Hon. Lord Denning at a dinner of the British Institute of International and Comparative Law held at Lincoln's Inn, 8th October 1986 and inserted, at his suggestion, in 1947 KB where at p 130 is the report of *Central London Property Trust Ltd* v. *High Trees House Ltd*.' It would be interesting to know whether anywhere else in the world the judgment of so junior a judge is celebrated in this way.

From the start Denning's judgments were couched in simple language and he habitually referred to the parties by name, rather than in the impersonal terms of 'plaintiff' or 'defendant'. He frequently seized opportunities to draw attention to more general matters than, strictly, the case demanded. On 25 November 1946, hearing an appeal from a Master (one of the lower echelon of judges) in a landlord and tenant case, where the landlord had been given possession without there having been consideration of whether it was reasonable, he said:

> I desire to draw attention to the following points. In the case of houses within the Rent Restriction Acts the procedure in the county court is better suited to carry out the intentions of the legislature than the procedure in the High Court. In the county court the tenant receives a summons to appear at the court on a named day and on that day the judge inquires into the case to see whether the conditions of the Act are satisfied before he makes an order for possession. In the High Court the tenant receives a writ commanding him to 'enter an appearance'. If he fails to do so, as he may either because he does not understand what is meant by entering an appearance or because he thinks it sufficient to fill in a counter-notice ... or because he does not realise that he is protected by the Rent Restriction Acts, then judgment is entered against him automatically without any inquiry whether the conditions of the Acts are satisfied, and it may be a judgment which the court has no jurisdiction to give either in respect of possession or costs.
>
> (*Smith* v. *Poulter*)

This practical, common-sense approach to problems and the understanding of the difficulties faced by ordinary men and women in dealing with the legal system were hallmarks of his style of judgment. Though the legal principles to which he referred were necessarily outside a layman's knowledge, Tom found ways of expressing them which made them simpler. 'The question in point of law is where does the responsibility rest?' he opened, in the case of *Whitby* v. *Burt, Boulton & Hayward*, 'I will deal with the question first at common law and secondly under the Factories Act, 1937.' And, in a case reported in 1948: 'Messrs H. E. Green & Sons of Bristol are aggrieved by a compulsory purchase order which has been made by the Corporation of Bristol in respect of their land. They desire to question the validity of it on the ground that the compulsory purchase is not empowered by the Housing Act, 1936. On this question, I cannot consider the policy of the social legislation, but only the statutory powers. The sole question for me is whether or not the statutory powers enable the corporation to make this compulsory purchase; but I have to find the relevant facts in order to determine that question.'

Tom always enjoyed going on circuit and, whenever possible, Joan went with him. In the summer of 1946, the circuit took on something of the nature of a family expedition. Hazel was waiting to go up to Oxford and Robert should have been in his last term before starting at Parkfield – but he was taken out of school and the four of them set out in Joan's mother's old car, DGP 745, which they called Dog Pie.

It was the Western circuit, Tom's own and favourite circuit, visiting Salisbury, Dorchester, Wells, Exeter, Devizes and Bodmin. At each place they were tended by butler, housekeeper and cook but the attraction of the lodgings varied. In Salisbury, the house – the North Canonry – remained much as it had been when its wartime occupants, ATS officers, had left it. By contrast, at Wells they stayed in the home of an old Prebendary, with beautiful pictures and a library. Robert had reached the stage where he could read, but not well enough to enjoy a book without help. Hazel helped him and read to him from *Winnie-the-Pooh*.

Few wives, at that time, accompanied their husbands on circuit and Joan soon realised that, when the judges had left for court, the housekeepers preferred the family to go out. She usually found something for them to do while Tom was at work, though occasionally she went to hear him try a case. One of the most memorable moments of circuit life occurred at Haverford West, when a swarm of bees settled on the judges' car, as it waited outside the courts, and the judges were returned to lodgings in a police car, while the 'bee-man' took the swarm!

By the autumn of 1946, when Robert started at Parkfield, the two families had become one. Robert seemed so young to be a boarder and, without letting him see them, Tom and Joan often walked the half-hour to the school to watch him on the playing fields. About this time they were delighted to receive a letter from Rose Dummer, who had been Mary's maid when Robert was born, asking to come back to them. Rose was a good cook and, with the help of a daily, Joan found it easier to manage the other duties, including opening bazaars, which fall to the lot of a wife of a High Court Judge.

At that time Tom was usually home at weekends and, when the boys were home from school, they did things together. Both boys were good with their hands – which Tom was most certainly not – but he taught them to cut down trees, which he had learned as a sapper. As they became stronger and more skilled they evened out an incline to lengthen the grass tennis court by taking earth from one end to build up the other. They also 'extended the rather narrow terrace, steepening the slope to double its width'[40] and bringing home sandstone slabs that they had excavated from the golf course.

They played rummy or canasta and sometimes Tom read aloud to them from the *Pilgrim's Progress*. He much preferred the classics and seldom read a modern novel. He was not greatly interested in listening to music: his taste was 'low-brow', including Gilbert and Sullivan and other tuneful or stirring music. When there were guests, they might have tennis or croquet matches; often they walked across the fields to the village. Halfway there was a wooden stile with a wide seat. 'We used to sit on it and contemplate. The family named it the "contemplatious stile".' It was a very happy time for all of them. Tom rarely stayed late in London. 'I wanted to get home – to Joan and the family. Apart from my work, they were my great interest in life – where I found my happiness.'[1]

The winter of 1946–7 was a bad one, in every possible way. Serious fuel shortages added to the misery of freezing cold; blizzards and heavy snow made it difficult to travel either by road or by rail; electricity cuts and food shortages added to the frustration. At this unpropitious time Tom, with Joan, first visited the Welsh circuit. Delightful in summer, the Welsh circuit in that severe winter was miserable. At Brecon, to keep warm, Joan slept in a fur coat. At Carmarthen the snow was too deep for the official car and Tom walked to court in his gumboots. A sudden thaw at Lampeter brought water pouring through the dressing room ceiling, where Tom's wig was on a stand. In February Tom had 'flu and was forced to take a rest.

He was again on circuit in June 1947 when Clara wrote to him from The Hermitage.

My dearest Tom,
Very glad to have your letter. It is very nice for Joan & her children that you are able to take them about and give them a pleasant time.

Though Clara had wanted Tom to remarry and must have realised Tom's new-found happiness, she clearly hoped that Joan appreciated her own good fortune! Clara's health had never been the same since she fell down the steps to the cellar at The Hermitage, but her spirit was undaunted, her writing as bold and firm as it had always been.

I am sure it must be very delightful at Fair Close now. I hope you have a gardener who will be keeping the garden nice & growing you plenty of vegetables. John [Marjorie's husband] has just brought in a big bunch of young carrots from my garden, they are quite valuable now, also we have plenty of lettuce and spinach he has grown, he thinks he can dig some potatoes in a few days so is making good use of the ground which is really necessary these times but I did love my garden as dad and I had it.

Clara gave Tom the family news. Reg, who, in March, had been appointed Chief of Staff of the Eastern Command, 'says he is very busy, they are trying to get a house near his headquarters.' Tom probably knew this already, as the brothers kept in touch by telephone every week, even if they could not meet. Marjorie and John had been interested in two cottages, for sale at an original asking price of £500, but found 'they were sold a month ago for £450, the person who has bought them will sell them again for £600.' Although Clara now had her daughter living with her, she still longed to see her sons. 'I do look forward to seeing you. Reg says if they get to London they can come to see me more often . . . Very best love my dear son. I know Robert is longing to come home' – Robert wrote to Granny Denning and Granny Harvey from Parkfield – 'and be with you a little while. Granny sends him lots of kisses. Best love to Joan. I like to think you are in London you don't seem so far away.'

Hazel Stuart was in her third term at Somerville, when Tom went on the Oxford circuit in the summer of 1947. She was reading Modern Languages but wanted to change to Law. Looking back in 1990, she did not think her decision was due to any conscious influence on Tom's part; rather that she was influenced by his example. She found it easy to talk things over with him. At the time, no girl had ever read Law at Somerville and, while he was in Oxford, Tom invited the Principal of the college, Janet Vaughan, to tea. In his red robes, he thought he had impressed her: if anything impressed her, it was more likely to have been his persuasiveness and charm. At all events Hazel changed to Law in her second year and in 1949 took a First Class degree.

The years since his appointment to the Bench had been kind to Tom. He had his share of reversals in the Court of Appeal and some criticism from practitioners and academics over his judgment in *High Trees* but, on the whole he won golden opinions. He also tasted the heady fruit of popular acclaim – on which he would increasingly thrive – over his decisions in the pensions cases and his Report on Matrimonial Procedure. In the long vacation of 1947, however, he tried a case which led to the first serious criticism of his work as a judge.

At the Old Bailey – the Central Criminal Court – six men were charged with conspiring between 1940 and 1946 to contravene war-time Orders for the control and limitation of the manufacture and supply of toilet preparations. The charge related to a company, with which all the accused were concerned. Four of the men were brothers. Two brothers were directors of the company; one was an accountant whose firm audited the company's accounts; the evidence showed that the fourth – the eldest brother – had no involvement with the company other than to have lent his brothers money and to have taken a debenture over the company, which gave him a first charge on its assets. The trial aroused interest since the eldest brother, David Weitzman, was the Labour Member of Parliament for Stoke Newington and a barrister.

The trial was described by the *Daily Express* on 7 October 1947 as having been 'the politest trial ever at this court, it goes on and on – quietly, sedately, with no "scenes" between judge, counsel or witnesses . . . The public gallery is half-empty . . . During the whole fourteen days not more than six women have looked in at any hearing to listen . . .' Yet, from its start Gilbert Paull KC, David Weitzman's counsel, had protested at the 'disgraceful and scandalous manner in which the prosecution was being carried on.'

From Court No. 1, at the Old Bailey, on Monday 27 October 1947, the jurors sent this note:

> The members of the Jury wish to express to your Lordship their sincere appreciation of the kindness & consideration which you have shown during the whole length of the trial. We are uncertain as to the correct procedure in this matter, but we are anxious that you should be informed of our gratitude and our thanks.

In *The Family Story* Tom recalled six men were charged with 'black market offences . . . Five were convicted and one acquitted. The five appealed. Their convictions were quashed. But not on the ground of any fault in my summing-up. Only on the ground that the indictment was erroneous.' He never changed his view that the convictions were proper. 'The jury were a group of intelligent businessmen. They and I knew all about the case.'[1]

What happened in 1947 was that, after one of the longest criminal trials to that date, the jury acquitted one man and convicted five, including the four brothers. David Weitzman was fined £500 and sentenced to twelve months' imprisonment. He appealed and was granted bail by Lord Goddard, pending the hearing of the appeal, which came before the Court of Criminal Appeal on 9 March 1948. On 16 March the Lord Chief Justice said that 'they thought it right to deal at once with the case of Mr David Weitzman because it had been obvious all through the case against him depended on entirely different considerations . . . The Court desired to say that there was no case against Mr David Weitzman and there never had been . . . He was the eldest brother of a family of brothers and on the uncontradicted evidence it appeared he had been a very good brother . . . the fact that he lent them money did not show that he was participating in any unlawful business . . . The Court could not find in the whole of the mass of the evidence . . . any shred of the evidence which pointed to the guilt of Mr David Weitzman . . . the case against Mr David Weitzman should have been stopped at the close of the prosecution. The Judge had not put before the jury the main points to Mr David Weitzman's defence. In particular no reference was made to the evidence of . . . which was entirely favourable to Mr David Weitzman. There never was a case made out against him and it should have been withdrawn from the jury.' (*Times Law Report*)

On Wednesday 17 March 1948 the Speaker of the House of Commons read to the House a letter from Lord Goddard:

> I think it my duty to inform you that the conviction of Mr David Weitzman MP for conspiracy was today quashed by the Court of Criminal Appeal and his discharge ordered.
>
> I am glad to be able to say that the ground on which the court quashed the conviction was that there was no evidence at all of his participation in any conspiracy.

Subsequently, as Denning reported, the convictions of the other four men were also quashed, on technical grounds. Tom always maintained obstinately that the convictions should have stood. At the time he feared that the criticism over David Weitzman might endanger his chances of promotion. It did not. He was, as a rule, too good a judge. He was also compassionate and caring. So the question has to be asked why, in this particular case, he was blind to evidence that was favourable to one particular man.

Weitzman was not a stranger to Tom. He had been Tom's junior in the case of *Marquess of Salisbury* v. *Gilmore*, five years earlier. He had represented a party in the arbitration before Tom that was mentioned in one of the letters of congratulations Tom received when he became a judge. Weitzman's reputation at the Bar was above reproach. Like Denning, he was a soldier in the First World War. His generosity to his brothers would normally have appealed to Tom's own sense of familial responsibility.

Weitzman was a Jew. Did this affect Tom or were other considerations at work? It was, of course, the kind of case that would always outrage Tom. 'When supplies were restricted,' he said, in summing-up to the jury, 'people who had not any sense of national interest, if they were so minded as to circumvent restrictions and put on the market goods they should not, had an opportunity of enriching themselves at the expense of others.' He would have been outraged at the alleged involvement of a member of the Bar, from whom he always demanded the highest standards. Yet there was not, to quote the Lord Chief Justice, 'any shred of the evidence which pointed to the guilt of Mr David Weitzman.' Indeed, three years later Weitzman was made a QC and he continued to serve as a Member of Parliament for many years.

In the course of Tom's long career there would occur a very few cases where prejudice overcame his objectivity. *R.* v. *West* – the Weitzman case – was one of them. A year later, when he was sent to the Court of Appeal, letters from 'a very proud stepdaughter Hazel' and from Theobald Mathew, the Director of Public Prosecutions, recognised that 'a certain prosecution' had weighed heavily upon Tom. He was glad to have the worry well and truly behind him.

On 6 October Clara wrote to him: 'I suppose you still go to Church on Sundays . . . I am sorry your complicated case is taking so long. I pray God will give you wisdom to judge it rightly and that it will soon finish.' A week later, on 13 October, she wrote again. 'I suppose you are on with your long uninteresting case. It should not be too bad with six important sounding men been defrauding if they are proved guilty I expect they deserve severe punishment.' Clara, now 83, was 'feeling very poorly, besides the pain of my broken bone, the last few days have suffered such discomfort & internal pain, Johnnie got the doctor on Saturday.' She had barely six weeks to live. On 6 December 1947 the *Hampshire Chronicle* reported the death, on 29 November, of Clara Denning, the widow of Charles Denning, 'a man who by his geniality and kindness had endeared himself to many . . . Whitchurch people would like to take this opportunity of expressing their sorrow and regret at the passing of this grand old lady who by her devotion to her family and the Church passes on a noble example of Christian womanhood to those around her.'

It fell to Tom to sort out his mother's probate and the question of The Hermitage, which had troubled Clara for some time. His sister and brothers all reposed great confidence in him but he needed to use tact to satisfy each of them. Marjorie wanted to remain at The Hermitage, as her parents had wanted for her. On 17 June 1947 she had written to him: 'I know whatever you arrange will be right and fair. I am sure you are doing your best for me.' Some way had to be found of enabling Marjorie and Johnnie, who had made their home with Clara and looked after her in her old age, to stay in the house, while yet releasing the interests of her brothers in Clara's small estate.

On 9 March 1948 Marjorie wrote again, telling Tom her problems and adding, 'Am hoping you will understand and you know so well I have implicit faith in anything you do being right.' Three months later, on 7 June 1948, Reg wrote from his headquarters at Hounslow '. . . your scheme is in my opinion excellent and I know Norman is of the same opinion. In addition it is essentially in accordance with the wishes of Mother and Father . . .' Tom's scheme would enable Marjorie and Johnnie to go on living at The Hermitage.

It was some time since young John Denning, Norman's son, had been at Fair Close during the raids, but he still enjoyed visits to Cuckfield. On 27 June 1948, just before he left for America with Iris and his two younger children, Norman wrote to tell Tom that his son John was happy that they were going as he would be able to stay at Cuckfield when he was home from school.

In 1948 Reg was promoted Lieutenant General and became GOC Northern Ireland. He also bought the home at which he would spend the rest of his life – Delmonden Grange at Hawkhurst, in Kent. Clara Denning had lived long enough to know that her ambitions for her sons had been realised. She did not know quite how far her boys were to go. In the autumn of 1948, two judges of the Court of Appeal retired. Tom and Joan were again on the Western circuit, in Exeter, when Lord Jowitt offered Tom one of the vacancies. Together with Sir John Singleton, Sir Alfred Thompson Denning was appointed to the Court of Appeal on 14 October 1948. Tom was about to enter upon his most productive period.

12

Court of Appeal

Tom would miss going on circuit. He loved the pageantry that surrounds the Judge of Assize as much as he took pleasure from travelling about the country. It was important to have Joan with him. Though she was 'most discreet',[1] her presence added to his sense of comfort and well-being and gave him extra confidence and support. If the list collapsed and they had a free afternoon or at the weekend, he and Joan enjoyed 'the countryside of our lovely England.'[1] He liked the conversation over dinner with other judges and guests at the lodgings; he enjoyed the company of the young lawyers who took their turns as marshal to the judges.

When the letters of congratulation on his new appointment arrived there was one from Harry Fisher, son of the Archbishop of Canterbury, recalling the enjoyable fortnight spent as Tom's marshal. His family and friends, old and new, all expressed delight in Tom's appointment. In the bold handwriting that must have reminded Tom of their mother's, Marjorie wrote from The Hermitage: 'I do feel so proud of you,' adding a PS: 'Many people have asked why you are called Alfred. I always feel pleased that I chose that name for you.' Gerald Thursfield, Joan's brother-in-law (husband of her sister Peggy) wrote from Sunninghill Vicarage: 'There is great joy in doing God's Service. Yours is a very high call.' From Norman, working at the Naval War College, Newport, Rhode Island, with congratulations, came the offer to send food parcels for Joan 'if the dollar situation permits.'

Lord Simon, who, as Lord Chancellor in 1944, had appointed Tom to be a trial judge, wrote on 14 October 1948:

My dear Denning,
    I am delighted that my choice is so soon a winner. How absurdly

ill-informed the newspapers are – 'a divorce expert' no doubt, but what about the Common Law?

Yours v. sincerely
Simon

Henn-Collins, recently retired, wrote from Bucklesbury Common:

I think the job will suit your temperament and talents better than the rough & tumble of the KBD. But don't forget that you were once a judge of first instance, & give the poor blighters your sympathy. Cases so often change their make-up by the time they get to the C.A.

In 1948 there were, in addition to the Lord Chief Justice, Lord Goddard, the Master of the Rolls, Lord Greene and the President of the Probate, Divorce and Admiralty Division, Lord Merriman, eight Lords Justices of Appeal. The most senior by this time was James Tucker, whose robes Tom had worn for the past three years. Tom himself was the junior. He became a Privy Councillor and was now addressed as the Right Honourable Sir Alfred Thompson Denning. He also had the privilege of entering Buckingham Palace by the side door instead of the front.

Though officially Denning was appointed to the Court of Appeal on 14 October 1948 and was not sworn in until 28 October, he began to sit there earlier. On 12 October with Lord Justices Bucknill and Cohen, he heard an appeal which concerned the validity of the will made by a Royal Air Force pilot named Wingham who had died, during the war, as a result of injuries sustained in an aircraft accident. The decision in *Wingham* updated and clarified the law on privileged wills of servicemen. Tom had made such a will himself in 1918 and his judgment revealed how close this subject was to his heart. It also confirmed the signs already given that a powerful new legal mind was at work: creative thinking combined with a careful analysis of cases, all delivered in a vivid, lucid style, became the hallmark of Denning's judgments.

The validity of the will was at issue because the Wills Act of 1837 set out certain formal requirements for the making of a will. It must be in writing; it must be signed by the testator (or by some other person in his presence and by his direction); the signature must be made or acknowledged by the testator in the presence of two witnesses present at the same time; the witnesses must sign and attest the will in the presence of the testator and of each other. There was a saving for 'privileged testators', who could make wills without any formalities. Privileged testators were defined as a 'soldier being in actual military service'; a 'mariner or seaman being at sea'; and a 'member of naval or marine forces in actual military service.'

Roy Wingham had joined the Royal Air Force in February 1942. That October he was sent to Canada for training and, the following March, he wrote out and signed a document that he described as a will. On 11 August 1943 Wingham, who had become a pilot instructor, died in the Royal Air Force Hospital at Moosejaw, in Saskatchewan, from injuries received as a result of an aircraft accident. The question to be decided by the courts was whether the document of March 1943, which had not been attested, created a valid will. The judge at first instance decided that it did not: Wingham, he held, was not in 'actual military service'. Unanimously, the Court of Appeal reversed him.

The words 'in actual military service' had always caused difficulty in interpretation. It had been thought a soldier was in actual military service if, under Roman Law, he would have been privileged as a legionary *in expeditione*. The first judgment in *Wingham* was read on 3 November 1948 by Bucknill. Answering the question of when a man may properly be described as being on active military service, he said: 'In my opinion, the tests are (a) was the testator 'on military service'?; (b) was such service 'active'? In my opinion, the adjective 'active' in this connection confines military service to such service as is directly concerned with operations in a war which is or has been in progress or is imminent.' Cohen delivered a concurring judgment.

Then Denning, newly appointed to the Court of Appeal, read his judgment. After referring to the first case in which the scope of privileged wills came under review and the test, subsequently adopted, of whether the soldier would have been regarded as being *in expeditione*, Denning continued:

Sitting in this Court, I am free to say that this test should no longer be applied. The words of our statutes are plain English: 'in actual military service.' I find them easier to understand and to apply than the Latin: 'in expeditione.' If I were to inquire into the Roman Law, I could, perhaps, after some research say how Roman Law would have dealt with its soldiers on Hadrian's Wall or in the camp at Chester, but I cannot say how it would have dealt with an airman in Saskatchewan who is only a day's flying from the enemy. Nor can anyone else. This supposed throw-back to Roman Law has confused this branch of the law too long. It is time to get back to the statute.

It is easy to see Denning's judgment, a mixture of common sense and preference for English solutions to English problems, appealing to those whose activities are regulated by the courts as much as, in this instance, it did to those who regulate them.

Rid of this Roman test, the court has to decide what is a proper test. It must be both simple and certain . . . The plain meaning of the statute is that any soldier, sailor or airman is entitled to the privilege if he is actually serving with the armed forces in connection with military operations which are, or have been, taking place, or are believed to be imminent.

Always ready for the broad-brush approach, Tom went on to list, though it was not strictly necessary for the case in hand, those who would be included and those who would not.

It does not, of course, include officers on half pay or men on the reserve, or the Territorials, when not called up for service. They are not actually serving. Nor does it include members of the forces serving in this country, or on routine garrison duty overseas, in time of peace, when military operations are not imminent. They are actually serving, but are not in actual 'military' service, because no military operations are afoot. It does, however, include all our men serving – or called up for service – in the wars, and women too, for that matter. It includes not only those actively engaged with the enemy but all who are training to fight him. It also includes those members of the Forces who, under stress of war, both work at their jobs and man the defences, such as the Home Guard. It includes not only the fighting men, but also those who

serve in the Forces, doctors, nurses, chaplains, [Women's Royal
Naval Service, Auxiliary Transport Service], and so forth. It
includes them all, whether they are in the field or in barracks, in
billets or sleeping at home. It includes them although they may be
captured by the enemy or interned by neutrals . . . Doubtful cases
may arise in peace-time when a soldier is in, or is about to be sent
to, a disturbed area or an isolated post . . . As to these cases, all I
can say is that in case of doubt, the serving soldier should be given
the benefit of the privilege.

This is more than a judgment: it is in the nature of a paean, a song of
thanksgiving for those who served in the war so recently ended and a
promise to those who might serve in the future. It has a Churchillian
ring, a popular appeal. In it there are echoes of the war-time song,
'Bless 'em all. Bless 'em all. The long and the short and the tall.'
Above all, it is a masterly exposition of the law in full accordance with
the needs of the time.

The war and its aftermath had been a time of great social change,
and there was a danger that the gap, so often seen, between justice and
the law, in some areas would become too wide without sympathetic
updating either by statute or the judges. The parliamentary programme had been full. Apart from nationalisation, there had been
introduced insurance to provide for unemployment, sickness,
industrial injury, old age and various contingencies; national
assistance to guarantee a minimum weekly level of income; and the
national health service which, from July 1948, would provide free
medical care for all, regardless of the ability to pay.

The great reforming Education Act of 1944 had been the brain-
child of a Conservative member of the war-time coalition, R. A.
Butler. It was none the less approved by the new Government, who
set about the training of teachers and the building programme needed
to implement it and, in 1947, raised the school-leaving age to 15.
Under Lord Jowitt's guidance, in 1947, the revolutionary Town and
Country Planning Act was piloted through the Lords, as well as a
much-needed Companies Act. With such a legislative burden, it was
unlikely that parliament would find time to attend to various
recognised deficiencies in existing law. The question was whether,
bound as they were by precedent, the judges could do it.

The rule on *stare decisis* was laid down before Tom was born: a decision of the House of Lords on a question of law was decisive and bound the House in subsequent cases; it was also binding on all lower courts. An erroneous decision could be changed only by Act of Parliament. In 1944, in *Young* v. *Bristol Aeroplane Co.*, the Court of Appeal, too, imposed upon itself the compulsion to follow its own earlier decisions, unless a case could be brought within three exceptions. Tom was not alone in chafing at the rule. By 1949 matters had reached the stage where, at times, the Court of Appeal would give judgment and express the wish to be over-ruled by the Lords.

Most judges, Denning wrote in *The Discipline of Law*, become restless under precedent 'when they are compelled to do what is unjust or unfair.' They may seek ways of getting round it, but will not depart from precedent altogether. Denning was that rare judge, bold enough and sufficiently clear-thinking, learned in the law and appreciative of the needs of his time, who could advance a principle without falling foul of precedent. Trouble would come when he no longer took care to work with the grain of the law.

'Not many of the Judges – even in the Court of Appeal – have any conscious philosophy of the law,' he wrote in *The Family Story*, 'but subconsciously each develops his own philosophy.' Denning's philosophy was summed up in the words 'Let justice be done.' It led him into difficulties. An ingenious turn of the law, required to do justice in a particular case, might, in some future matter, lead to a path down which he did not wish to stray. Worse, to follow it could lead to a different injustice. Denning would back-track or add another small twist in order to achieve the result that seemed fair. At this stage in his career every twist and every turn was carefully supported by a reasoned analysis of cases on which he depended. He always paid lip-service to precedent. Even so, amongst some academics and some practising lawyers there was occasional uneasiness – as well as much wonder – at some of his observations.

It seemed to Denning that the interpretation of statute according to the established rules also, at times, led to injustice. Six months after his promotion to the Court of Appeal, he seized an opportunity to voice his views. Sitting with the Master of the Rolls, Lord Greene, and Lord Justice Asquith, he heard an appeal from Bloomsbury County Court on 2 and 3 May; judgment was reserved until 1 June.

The case concerned a tenancy agreement subject to rent control. Both Asquith and Denning prepared judgments and showed them to Greene, who endorsed their reasoning and their conclusions in his own judgment. Tom said:

> It is as well to bear steadily in mind the facts of this case. The flat was let from 1935 to 1939 at 175L. [pounds] a year. The landlords were under no obligation to provide hot water, but they did in fact do so. The flat was empty from 1939 to 1943. Then it was let at 250L. a year, but with the significant difference that the landlords bound themselves to provide hot water. The cost of fuel and labour had, of course, greatly increased between 1939 and 1943; and, whilst in 1939 it was no doubt economically possible for the landlord to provide hot water free for his tenants, it may well have been economically impossible for them to do so in 1943 unless there was some increase in the rent. At any rate the tenant then agreed to pay 250L. a year for the flat. Now the tenant says that the increase from 175L. to 250L. was invalid ... It is difficult to suppose that the legislature intended not only to peg rents at the 1939 level, but also to enable a tenant to get additional benefits without extra payment.
>
> (*Seaford Court Estates Ltd* v. *Asher*)

This recognition of social realities and the ability to put facts succinctly were characteristic of Tom's work. Equally typical was his ability to analyse the problem.

> If I thought that the legislature foresaw the situation and neverthe-less intended that result, I would, of course, give effect to it. But the question is whether it did so.

The relevant sections of the Rent Acts did, said Denning, peg the rent at the 1939 level but authorised the landlord to increase it in certain cases. 'The question is whether this is one of the cases in which an increase is authorised.'

After consideration of the meaning of the crucial word 'burden' in a sub-section, Denning continued:

> The question for decision in this case is whether we are at liberty to

extend the ordinary meaning of 'burden' so as to include a contingent burden of the kind I have described. Now this court has already held that this sub-section is to be liberally construed so as to give effect to the governing principles embodied in the legislation . . . and I think we should do the same. Whenever a statute comes up for consideration it must be remembered that it is not within human powers to foresee the manifold set of facts which may arise, and, even if it were, it is not possible to provide for them in terms free from all ambiguity. The English language is not an instrument of mathematical precision. Our literature would be much the poorer if it were. This is where the draughtsmen of Acts of Parliament have often been unfairly criticised. A judge, believing himself to be fettered by the supposed rule that he must look to the language and nothing else, laments that the draughtsmen have not provided for this or that, or have been guilty of some other ambiguity. It would certainly save the judges trouble if Acts of Parliament were drafted with divine prescience and perfect clarity. In the absence of it, when a defect appears a judge cannot simply fold his hands and blame the draughtsmen. He must set to work on the constructive task of finding the intention of Parliament, and he must do this not only from the language of the statute, but also from a consideration of the social conditions which gave rise to it, and of the mischief which it was passed to remedy, and then he must supplement the written word so as to give 'force and life' to the intention of the legislature . . . Put into homely metaphor it is this: A judge should ask himself the question: If the makers of the Act had themselves come across this ruck in the texture of it, how would they have straightened it out? He must then do as they would have done. A judge must not alter the material of which it is woven, but he can and should iron out the creases.

Unanimously, the Court of Appeal decided that the landlord was entitled to increase the rent and they referred the case back to the county court for consideration of the level of increase.

In the *Law Quarterly Review* of January 1950, R. E. Megarry wrote that *Seaford Court Estates Ltd* v. *Asher* 'is a case which will often be referred to both by those who are interested in the Rent Acts and by those who are not; for, in addition to putting a liberal and practical interpretation upon a difficult sub-section in the Acts, the case gave Denning LJ the opportunity of uttering words on statutory interpretation which are likely to achieve a wide currency outside the sphere of the Rent Acts, much though their presence is needed there.'

Tom's recognition of social realities and his ability to find an answer to problems that would be generally recognised as fair were at the heart of his work. More often than not he arrived at the same decision as his colleagues while placing special emphasis on the social background to a case. In *Wingham* and *Seaford Court Estates*, within a short time of his promotion to the Court of Appeal, he delivered judgments which won general admiration – though it must be said that when *Seaford Court Estates* reached the House of Lords, where the decision was upheld, Lord MacDermott commented: 'I cannot but think that the principles applicable to the interpretation of statutes as enunciated by Denning LJ . . . are stated rather widely.'

In 1949, Tom was invited by the Hamlyn Trust to give a series of lectures, in the autumn, at the Senate House of London University. The Trust had come into existence as the result of a bequest in the will of an elderly lady with a taste for the law. As the terms of Miss Hamlyn's will were vague, the Trustees obtained the Court's approval of a scheme for 'the furtherance by lectures . . . among the Common People of the United Kingdom . . . of the knowledge of the Comparative Jurisprudence and the Ethnology of the Chief European Countries . . . to the intent that the Common People of the United Kingdom may realise the privileges which in law and custom they enjoy in comparison with other European Peoples and realising and appreciating such privileges may recognise the responsibilities and obligations attaching to them.'

It was a project close to Tom's heart and he readily accepted the invitation to be the first Hamlyn lecturer. During the long vacation, he prepared four lectures. He worried about what to call them and, as always when anything troubled him, he talked it over with Joan. Tom often found that he went to bed with a problem and woke to find it solved. So it was this time. One morning he told Joan he had his title: Freedom under the Law – 'it is a telling phrase. I make so bold as to claim to be "the first and true inventor of it".'[1]

In his Hamlyn lectures, which were later printed, and have been reprinted many times, Denning gave eloquent testimony to his belief in the great English heritage of freedom; at the same time, he served notice, on all who chose to hear, of the crusade on which he was embarked – to lead the judges in the reform of procedures for preventing the abuse of power. The first lecture was delivered in October. 'I hope you have not come expecting a scholarly discourse replete with copious references,' Tom began. 'If you have, I fear you will be disappointed: for, I have come as the Hamlyn Trust bids me, to speak, as it were, to the common people of England and to further amongst them the knowledge of the laws, so that they may realise their privileges and likewise their responsibilities . . .' The people of England, he said, have 'succeeded' to the greatest heritage of all – freedom under the law; but rights are no use unless you can enforce them, and 'it is in their enforcement that English law has shown its peculiar genius.'[31]

Interspersing legal history with legal anecdote, Denning talked about the mechanisms on which English freedom depended. In first place he counted the writ of *habeas corpus*, which entitles a prisoner to challenge unlawful detention. One of his favourite stories made its first recorded appearance:

So in 1771, when the coloured slave James Sommersett was held in irons on board a ship lying in the Thames and bound for Jamaica, Lord Mansfield declared his detention to be unlawful. 'The air of England is too pure for any slave to breathe,' he said, 'Let the black go free,' and the slave went free.

And, giving a modern instance, when a magistrate refused to order the extradition to the United States of a communist, who had been taken forcibly from a Polish ship in Cowes Roads, Denning added: 'The law of England knows no colour bar, whether it be the colour of a man's skin or of his politics.'

In the second lecture, Tom turned to freedom of mind, conscience and religion, comparing it with the position in totalitarian states. After dealing with the position of Jews in England, he said: 'So also with all other races, it is a cardinal principle of our law, that they shall not suffer any disability or prejudice by reason of their race and shall have equal freedom under the law with ourselves.' At a time when the population of England remained largely homogeneous, and he could not have envisaged the immigration to come, he said:

> It is perhaps easier for us to proclaim racial freedom than it is for other countries such as the United States and South Africa which are faced with a problem with which we have never had to deal. Nevertheless, concerned here as I am with the common law, it is clear beyond peradventure that the common law of England has always regarded a man's race or colour as just as irrelevant in ascertaining his rights and duties as the colour of his hair.

Denning spoke about the English courts and the jury system, contrasting them with the French mode of trial. 'In making these comparisons, we no doubt think our system is better but we ought always to remember that it is the system which suits the temperament of our people. It would not necessarily be the best for other people.' Four years later, addressing French judges in Paris, he said: 'At the outset I would warn you that the way we arrange things in England about the judges would probably not be at all suitable in France.'[44]

The third and fourth lectures concerned justice between man and the state; and the powers of the executive. Denning noted the significance of the social revolution of his time:

> One hundred years ago the responsibility of the State was very narrowly interpreted. It only provided the bare necessities of the community as a whole, such as defence against aggression, the maintenance of order, and the provision of workhouses for the destitute. When a man grew old and unable to work he had to be kept by his children or go to the workhouse. If he fell sick and could not pay for medical treatment, he had to rely on charity. If he was injured at his work and perhaps disabled for life by some slip or miscalculation on his own part, or by the fault of his mate, he got no compensation from his employer, although it was in the employer's service and on his work that he was injured. The law, I regret to say, did little more than provide a defence for 'rights of property' and 'freedom of contract'. It did not recognise any right to freedom from want. All was left to the charitable instincts of the few.

The social revolution of today has changed all that . . . The principle that runs through all the recent legislation is that the State is responsible for seeing that all the supplies and services which are necessary for individual well-being are available to all.

Denning considered the various tribunals established to monitor and enforce the new rights and duties and compared them with the French administrative courts. The most important principle, he concluded, was the independence of the tribunals from the executive, which 'is reduced to vanishing point where, as sometimes happens, an appeal from the tribunal is only to the Minister and not the courts.' Denning was stepping into an arena where, in future, he would become involved in some notable battles.

So drastic a departure from all our traditions could only be justified if the ordinary courts had not kept pace with current thought: and were apt to retard, rather than advance, the social reforms which the new age has introduced. That, indeed, has been suggested. One Minister of the Crown, in an unwise moment, when he refused an appeal to the courts, gave as his reason that he feared 'judicial sabotage' of his plans . . .

In these days no reproach can be levied at the judges that they have not kept pace with the times. The judges of England have no politics and always carry out the intention of Parliament . . .

This view was far from universally agreed: social reformers frequently voiced the opinion that judges were conservative and backward thinking. Reviewing the position, at the end of his last lecture, Denning concluded that the principles were not yet settled, by which the new powers of the executive were to be controlled. English procedure for securing personal freedom was efficient, but the procedure for preventing the abuse of power was not. New and up-to-date machinery must replace the old. 'This is not a task for Parliament . . . The courts must do this. Of all the tasks that lie ahead, this is the greatest. Properly exercised the new powers of the executive lead to the Welfare State: but abused they lead to the totalitarian state . . . Let us prove equal to the challenge.' On behalf of the judges, whether they wished it or not, Denning had thrown down the gauntlet.

It is not surprising that Lord Jowitt wrote a letter rebuking Tom. 'But he was induced to do it,' Denning wrote in *Landmarks in the Law*, 'because one of the government departments did not like what I had said.' The Hamlyn lectures foreshadowed the judgments which would, in the next decades, bring under the scrutiny of the courts all those who were seen to abuse or misuse powers vested in them. The lectures also made Denning a much-sought-after speaker at universities, law societies and professional gatherings of many kinds.

In 1949 Tom was invited to become President of the National Marriage Guidance Council. Throughout his life, he would accept appointments only to those organisations in which he was genuinely interested and to which he believed he could contribute more than just his name. The Marriage Guidance Council was such an organisation and Tom remained its president until 1983, chairing its Annual General Meeting, attending its conferences and sorting out various difficulties for it. In this, as in all his other activities, he liked to have Joan's active support. Though he occupied the high moral ground, he took a matter-of-fact approach in respect to sex. In January 1949, he was reported in the *Daily Mirror* to have said that there was still a vast amount of ignorance: 'In the case of my own boy, I always tell him for better or for worse. I try to do it naturally and he isn't the slightest bit shocked by it . . . ignorance is one of the most fruitful causes of sexual maladjustment.'

Denning played his part in the gradual liberalisation of divorce despite his personal belief in the sanctity of marriage. He had little doubt that the place of a wife and mother was in the home, looking after the children. He was equally convinced that marriage must be a partnership. Hearing an appeal in a case of desertion (*Dunn* v. *Dunn*), in October 1948, he said: 'The decision where the home should be is one which affects both the parties and their children. It is their duty to decide it by agreement, by give and take, and not by the imposition of the will of one over the other.' When the Court of Appeal held unanimously that desertion could take place even though the couple were living under one roof, it was Denning who pointed to the difficulties caused by the housing shortage, which often forced 'the innocent party to a matrimonial dispute' to remain under the same roof as 'the guilty party, because he or she has nowhere else to go or has not the means to go elsewhere.' (*Hopes* v. *Hopes*)

For Tom, the breakdown of marriage endangered the foundation of society. As he became aware of the added threat posed by the housing shortage to families that now needed, not one, but two homes, he was deeply concerned. His interest was first aroused in November 1947, when he was sitting, as a judge of the King's Bench Division, to hear 'minor business' in chambers. One case concerned the possession of a house, bought 15 years earlier, where the owner had lived with his wife and invalid son. During the war he left his wife, bought another house and lived in it with another woman. As he wanted his wife to divorce him, he offered to give her the house if she would do so, and when she refused he took proceedings to obtain possession of the house. The case came before a Master of the King's Bench. Since the husband owned the house and the wife had no title to it, the Master made an order for possession. On appeal, the case came before Denning. 'I could see that here was an injustice. It cried aloud for a remedy.'[23] Determined to give it one and to see that his judgment would be reported – which, in chambers, it would not – Denning adjourned the case to the open court. He said:

> It is contended for the husband that, as he is the owner of the house, I must make the order for which he asks. On behalf of the wife it is argued that I have a discretion in the matter. In my opinion, at common law the husband has no right to turn the wife out of the house. It was the house which he provided as the matrimonial home. She has behaved quite properly. She has done nothing wrong.
>
> (H v. H)

The husband, on the other hand, Tom thought, had behaved badly. Denning would always strive to find authority to decide a case on the merits as he saw them. This time he turned to section 17 of the Married Women's Property Act 1882, which authorised the judge in the case of a dispute between husband and wife over the ownership or possession of property, to make such order with respect to the property in dispute 'as he thinks fit.' Since Tom thought it would be unjust to turn the wife and invalid son out of their home, he declined to do so.

H v. H was a straightforward dispute between husband and wife.

Three years later, sitting in the Court of Appeal with Somervell and Romer, Denning had to consider the position when it was not the husband, but the husband's trustee in bankruptcy who wanted to evict the deserted wife. Before Mr McWhirter left his wife, he told her she might have his freehold house and furniture and, on the understanding that she would remain in the home, she obtained a maintenance order of £4 10s a week. When her husband became bankrupt, his trustee in bankruptcy wanted possession of the house in order to sell it and, as Mrs McWhirter refused to leave, brought an action for possession. Mrs McWhirter appealed from the order of the county court judge that she must vacate the house.

The Court of Appeal unanimously reversed that decision. For Somervell and Romer the case turned on the special position of a trustee in bankruptcy – he could be in no better position to evict the wife than her husband could. Denning accepted this but went further:

> The first question on the facts is whether the wife has any right of her own to stay in the house. Under the old common law as it existed until 70 years ago she had no rights at all apart from those of her husband. She was treated by the law more like a piece of his furniture than anything else . . . He could bundle his furniture out into the street, and so he could his wife . . . Even if the husband did not turn her out, nevertheless when he ceased for any reason to be entitled to the house she would have to leave it: for she had no right of her own to stay there . . .
>
> All that has changed now. A wife is no longer her husband's chattel. She is beginning to be regarded by the law as a partner in all affairs which are their common concern. Thus the husband can no longer turn her out of the matrimonial home. She has as much right as he to stay there even though the house does stand in his name.

Referring, as he liked to do, to his own case, *H* v. *H*, and to others, Denning said: 'It is now settled law that a deserted wife has a right, as against her husband, to stay in the matrimonial home unless and until an order is made against her under section 17.' He continued:

> the right of a deserted wife to stay in the matrimonial home

proceeds out of an irrevocable authority which the husband is presumed in law to have conferred on her . . . This authority flows from the status of marriage, coupled with the fact of separation owing to the husband's misconduct.

(*Bendall* v. *McWhirter*)

Denning described the wife's right as an 'equity', which would hold good against any successor to the husband's title, unless he neither knew, nor should have known of the wife's situation.

The deserted wife's equity was one of Denning's boldest creations and provoked a storm of criticism. What, asked the property lawyers, was to happen if the husband sold the house? What if he mortgaged it and was unable or unwilling to pay the mortgage instalments? And, if he became bankrupt, was a wife to be in a better position if he had deserted her than if he was still living with her in the matrimonial home? It was thought that it would become unsafe to buy a house or to accept it as security for a loan without first making embarrassing inquiries into the owner's domestic circumstances. Legislation, not litigation, it was said, was the only way to effect such a drastic reform; justice for a deserted wife should not be bought at the expense of the husband's creditors or of a purchaser without knowledge of the wife's circumstances.

Whatever its shortcomings, for some 13 years Denning's view was followed by judges of first instance and by the Court of Appeal, though not without reservations. It was not until 1965 that a case relating to the issue reached the House of Lords. (As Denning wrote in *The Family Story*, it is in the Court of Appeal that a judge has the chief opportunity to influence the law: very few cases go to the Lords.) Given the opportunity, in *National Provincial Bank* v. *Ainsworth*, the Lords ruled that the wife had no right entitling her to remain in the former matrimonial home, when the bank – to whom the husband had mortgaged his property – sought possession. Unanimously they decreed that a deserted wife had no equity to occupy the matrimonial home. 'It blew the deserted wife's equity to smithereens.'[23]

Denning's defeat – for so he regarded it – was the catalyst for statutory intervention. As, once, the government had been forced by publicity over a Denning decision to make concessions on pensions cases so, in 1965, it was moved by public opinion to introduce legislation. The Matrimonial Homes Act, which became law two years later, gave wives (and husbands), whether deserted or not, the right to register a charge or caution, which would be discovered when a purchaser or mortgagee made the usual searches, against the property owned by their spouses. Not for the only time, Tom's defeat became a victory; but not a complete victory – the charge did not defeat the claim of a spouse's trustee in bankruptcy.

In the cases for which Denning devised the deserted wife's equity, the wife had neither a title to the property nor a claim to any interest in it. Gradually he developed a response to another area of injustice, where the property stood in the name of one spouse, yet the other, by contributions to the family finances, had directly or indirectly facilitated its purchase.

In 1952 it was clear that he was already thinking in terms of 'family assets' (*Rimmer* v. *Rimmer*), though he did not use the term until 1955.

> In the case of the family assets, if I may so describe them, such as the matrimonial home and furniture, when both husband and wife contribute to the cost and the property is intended to be a continuing provision for them during their joint lives, the court leans towards the view that the property belongs to them jointly in equal shares.
>
> (*Cobb* v. *Cobb*)

In Denning's hands the principle, as he put it, 'was capable of great expansion'[23] and was enlarged to take in cases where the contribution of one spouse was not money, but work enhancing the value of the house. It was not until 1970, in *Pettit* v. *Pettit*, that the Lords were able to review the cases of the last 20 years. As in 1965 they 'blew the deserted wife's equity to smithereens',[23] so in 1970 they scuppered both Tom's use of section 17 of the 1882 Act and his idea of 'family assets'. To the relief of property lawyers the Lords made it clear that ordinary rules were to apply when determining the ownership of a matrimonial home.

13

Candler, Christianity and the Cheshire Homes

Tom's work on the family home served the valuable purpose of concentrating the minds of government ministers on social legislation, but, as judicial law-making, it was not among his more successful projects. In the field of negligence his judgments were of an entirely different order: they were seminal to the development of the law. In particular, Denning's dissenting judgment in the case of *Candler* v. *Crane, Christmas & Co.* was regarded by lawyers, almost without exception, as a brilliant advancement of the law of negligent misstatement.

The law of negligence is relatively modern; it developed piecemeal and liability depended, amongst other things, on whether a duty of care was owed to a person in particular circumstances. No remedy had ever been given for a negligent misstatement. In December 1950, with Cohen and Asquith, Denning heard the appeal of a Mr Candler, who had lost his £2000 investment in a small private company, made in reliance upon the company's accounts. He brought an action against Crane, Christmas & Co., the company's accountants and auditors, claiming that he was induced to invest the money because of erroneous accounts they had put before him. The judge found the accounts were 'defective and deficient', presenting a false position of the company, but dimissed Candler's claim because the accountants owed him no duty of care. After a five-day hearing of the appeal, judgment was reserved. On 26 January 1951 Denning read the first judgment:

> If the matter were free from authority I should have said that [the defendants] clearly did owe a duty of care to him. They were

professional accountants who prepared and put before him these accounts, knowing that he was going to be guided by them in making an investment in the company.

The first submission put forward by counsel for the defendants, Denning said, was that apart from a contractual duty or a fiduciary relationship, no action had ever been allowed for negligent statements. He continued:

> This argument about the novelty of the action does not appeal to me in the least. It has been put forward in all the great cases which have been milestones of progress in our law, and it has always, or nearly always been rejected . . . On the one side there were the timorous souls who were fearful of allowing a new cause of action. On the other side were the bold spirits who were ready to allow it if justice so required.

Asquith and Cohen – as Denning knew they were going to do – found for the accountants. Cohen quoted from the judgment, in a case on similar facts, of Benjamin Cardozo, the distinguished American Chief Justice, who influenced the trend of the New York Court of Appeal towards the modernisation of legal principles. Another of Cardozo's judgments had previously found favour with the House of Lords and his views would, Denning knew, carry much weight. The American judge warned that the liability upon professional men would become extensive if the duty of care was extended to an 'indeterminate class of persons who, presently, might deal with [a company] in reliance upon the audit.'[45]

'Faced with this apparently strong adverse authority,' said Professor A. L. Goodhart, editor of the *Law Quarterly Review*, 'it undoubtedly took judicial courage for Denning to reach a contrary conclusion.' By careful analysis, he overcame the hurdle of cases which, in the opinion of most lawyers, laid down that there could not be liability for a negligent misstatement. He then considered whether, as a matter of public policy, the duty of care that was owed by professional men to their clients should be further extended. Cardozo had decided it should not and most lawyers shared his reluctance. In general, Denning agreed; but this was not a case where reliance was placed on professional work in circumstances un-expected by the accountants. Crane Christmas had known exactly why Mr Candler wanted their accounts. They had behaved badly and should, Tom thought, pay for it.

Denning was careful to restrict the extension of the duty of care: in the case of accountants, it was owed 'to any third person to whom they themselves show the accounts, or to whom they know their employer is going to show the accounts, so as to induce him to invest money or take some other action on them. But I do not think the duty can be extended still further so as to include strangers of whom they have heard nothing and to whom their employer without their knowledge may choose to show their accounts.'

In the *Law Quarterly Review* of April 1951, Goodhart wrote: 'There can be little doubt that *Candler* v. *Crane, Christmas* . . . will give rise to more debate than any other case in recent years.' Considering the case in the October issue, Warren A. Seavey of Harvard Law School commented: 'It is the brilliant dissent by Denning LJ which makes the case memorable.'

Denning's judgment was born as much from moral, as from intellectual seeds. One of the great dissenting judgments of the common law, it was vindicated triumphantly in the House of Lords, not for the benefit of Mr Candler, whose case never reached their court, but in 1963, in the case of *Hedley Byrne*. For about 20 years, after that, the courts adopted a liberal approach to claims of negligence and Denning played a leading part in the evolution of the law. In the course of time, Cardozo's fears threatened to become the reality, as ever more extensive claims were made against professional people which, if allowed, would have left them with liability 'in an indeterminate amount for an indeterminate period of time to an indeterminate class.' In 1990, in the *Caparo* case, the Lords undertook a review of the law.

As the Law Lords analysed the leading cases and read Denning's judgment in *Crane Christmas*, Lord Roskill told the author, he said: 'You can see what Denning's gifts were. Not a word was out of place. The reasoning was perfect.' Lord Bridge of Harwich, in the first speech, quoted extensively from Denning and said: 'It seems to me that this masterly analysis, if I may say so with respect, requires little, if any, amplification or modification in the light of later authority and is particularly apt to point the way to the right conclusion in the present appeal.'

The value of Denning's dissent had been to open up the liability for damage caused by the negligent words of professional people, as it had already been liberalised with regard to negligence causing physical injury to persons or to property. The care with which Tom had restricted the scope of his extension gave the Lords, as they began to close the door, authority to do so. It was a remarkable achievement for Denning in 1951; nor, in that year, was it his only contribution to the law of negligence. In the few days before reserved judgment was given in *Crane Christmas*, Tom sat, with Somervell and Singleton, to hear an appeal on medical negligence.

The case of *Cassidy* v. *Minister of Health* reached the Appeal Court in January 1951. After an operation to alleviate a contraction of two fingers, Mr Cassidy was left with a hand that was bent stiff and, to all intents, useless. The trial judge found that Cassidy had not proved negligence against any of the hospital staff. The Court of Appeal decided that the facts spoke for themselves: there *must* have been negligence in the treatment of Cassidy at the hospital. The next question to be considered was whether the Minister, who was responsible for the hospital, was liable. At that time, the question of liability, if any, was thought to depend on the nature of the contract under which the staff were working. If they were employed under service contracts – that is to say they were *employees* of the ministry – the Minister was liable; if they were employed under contracts for service – and were self-employed – the Minister was not. One old test used to distinguish between the two was the degree of control that could be exercised over their work. A doctor, said the Minister, was not an employee because he could not be told how to do his work.

Denning would have none of it. 'What possible difference in law,' he asked, 'can there be between hospital authorities who accept a patient for treatment and railway or shipping authorities who accept a passenger for carriage?' Each was liable for the negligence of its employees. He dismissed the old cases holding that hospitals were not liable for the negligence of doctors or nurses as 'due to a desire to relieve the charitable hospitals from liabilities which they could not afford.' The other members of the court did not go as far as

Denning, but found other ways of distinguishing old cases, so that the law could be made to fit the changed needs of the time.

Anxious as he was to right a wrong, Tom was always keenly aware that the law of negligence must no more be pushed to extremes in medical actions, than in professional misstatements. 'We must not condemn *as negligence*,' he said in *Roe* v. *Minister of Health*, 'that which is only a misadventure.' As a rule, Denning's approach might be described as moderation in all things.

Tom's success with the Hamlyn lectures had 'put him on the map as a speaker.'[46] Early in 1950 he was asked to talk at University College, Dublin, and went across to Ireland for a weekend. In May, he spoke to the Marriage Guidance Council, at Rustington. In June, he addressed the Annual Dinner of the Holdsworth Club at Birmingham University. From then on he was always in demand. Though Tom often repeated themes, or used the same quotations and stories to illustrate his points, each speech was carefully worked and reworked until he was satisfied that it was as good as he could make it. He addressed the Association of Municipal Corporations' Conference at Southport and, going against the trend of the time, told them he thought that local government should be based on the community unit. Perhaps remembering that his father and other Whitchurch men had manned the fire engine of his youth, Tom regretted the loss of local fire services and hospitals. Though large-scale organisations might be more efficient, Tom feared they could disregard the spirit of man and lead to a totalitarian state.

In May 1950, petrol rationing ended and Joan started to drive Tom about the country to his many engagements. He felt happier when she was with him and was disappointed if an event was 'men only' and Joan could not attend. On one occasion he found himself the speaker at a dinner to which Joan had not been invited – though other ladies were there – and ticked off the chairman in no uncertain fashion.

In September 1950, through pressure of work, Tom refused an invitation from the Archbishop of Canterbury to chair a Commission to examine the work of the Ecclesiastical Courts. He was always reluctant to refuse any request for help from the Church. His faith was so much a part of his life that he had little need to speak about it.

All the family knew the pleasure and comfort he took from attendance at church, but rarely, if ever, heard him discuss religion at home. His 15-minute broadcast on the BBC Home Service, on 14 September 1943, probably said everything he wanted to say on the subject:

> My belief in God is due in part to my upbringing – to what I have been taught – and in part to what I have found out in going through life . . . My experience as a lawyer has verified what I was taught about God. Many people think that religion and law have nothing in common . . . People who think that have got a wrong idea both of law and of religion. The aim of the law is to see that truth is observed and that justice is done between man and man . . . But what is truth and what is justice? On those two cardinal questions religion and law meet. The spirit of truth and justice is not something you can see. It is not temporal but eternal. How does man know what is truth or justice? It is not the product of his intellect, but of his spirit . . .
>
> How, then, is the right spirit created in man? . . . Religion, or rather the Christian religion, is concerned with the creation of a spirit out of which right acts will naturally flow . . . The law has been moulded for centuries by Judges who have been brought up in the Christian faith. The precepts of religion, consciously or unconsciously, have been their guide in the administration of justice.

More especially, it was the precepts of the Church of England that were Tom's guide. He had no need to speak about them within the family: he took for granted that they would follow the direction of the church into which they had been confirmed.

Tom had been, for many years, a member of the Lawyers' Christian Fellowship, an interdenominational society of Christians founded, in 1852, as the Lawyers' Prayer Union. In 1950 he became President and delivered, two years later, the centennial address, which is still distributed to new members. 'In primitive societies,' he started, 'the influence of religion on law was obvious, but it is not so obvious in modern societies.' He regretted the severance. 'Although religion, law and morals can be separated, they are nevertheless still very much dependent on one another.' In his address, Tom ranged over many of the legal problems that had become his particular concern.

After giving examples where strict adherence to the letter of the law killed its spirit, he said, 'our conception of justice is only the Christian teaching of love.' How, he asked, is a judge to know what is justice? In answer, he quoted from Lord Atkin's speech in *Donoghue* v. *Stevenson*: 'The rule that you are to love your neighbour becomes in law you must not injure your neighbour.' Later he said:

> It is, I suggest to you, a most significant thing that a great judge should draw his principles of law, or rather his principles of justice, from the Christian commandment of love. I do not know where else he is to find them. Some people speak of natural justice as though it was a thing well recognisable by anyone, whatever his training and upbringing. But I am quite sure that our conception of it is due entirely to our habits of thought through many generations. The common law of England has been moulded for centuries by judges who have been brought up in the Christian faith. The precepts of religion, consciously or unconsciously, have been their guide in the administration of justice.
>
> . . . In any discussion of punishment it is important to recognise, as Christianity does, that society itself is responsible for the conditions which make men criminals. . . . The child, who has lost his sense of security, feels that he must fight for his interests in a hostile world. He becomes anti-social and finally criminal. The broken home from which he comes is only too often a reflection on society itself, a society which has failed to maintain its standards of morality . . . When we try to reform the criminal, we are only treating the symptoms of the disease.
>
> We are not tackling the cause of it . . : Nevertheless, though society itself is largely responsible, neither religion nor the law excuses the criminal himself. Christianity has always stressed the responsibility of each individual for his own wrong-doing.

Finally, after considering other aspects of law and morality, Tom returned to the subject which always concerned him, to family life and the institution of marriage. 'The Christian Church,' he said, 'has always maintained that marriage is a life-long union, for better or worse, so long as both shall live . . . The well-being of the whole community requires that children should, so far as possible, be brought up by their own parents as members of one family, with all the give and take that family life demands, and also with the security that it affords. The institution of marriage is the legal foundation of this family life. The principle of indissolubility was the binding force which cemented it.' The abandonment of that principle, Tom believed, had 'a grave effect on the family unity and on the national character. It is almost impossible for the State to retrace its steps so as to make the divorce law more difficult. The only real remedy is the growth of a strong public opinion condemning divorce, and, I would add, condemning infidelity. It should not be regarded, as it now is, as the private concern of the parties with which no one else has anything to do. It is the concern of everyone who has the welfare of the country at heart.'

Interested as he was in matters connected with the Church, Tom always tried to find time for organisations with a religious or moral purpose. In 1947 the King and Queen had established an educational trust, based on Christian principles, at Cumberland Lodge, in Windsor Great Park, where students from the Inns of Court could spend weekends with Benchers and barristers. Three years later Sir Walter Moberley, the principal of Cumberland Lodge, asked Denning to become Chairman of the Trustees. This was an organisation bound to attract Tom: combining as it did a Christian approach to education and a close association with young people from many nations and from all walks of life.

Tom accepted Moberley's invitation and put his usual energy to work at fund-raising and dealing with all Cumberland Lodge's administrative affairs, right down to its staff problems. He and Joan attended weekends at Cumberland Lodge, mixing easily with the students. Their warmth and evident interest in every person they met sent students away with fond memories of the Dennings. Many told stories of meeting Tom, long afterwards, and being amazed and delighted that he could remember them and pick up a conversation where it had been left.

By the time Tom's path had crossed again with that of the young don who had examined him in the 1922 viva voce, Tom was a High Court judge and Geoffrey Cheshire, an eminent jurist, was the

Vinerian Professor of English Law at Oxford. Over the next few years, the professor and his wife, became the 'greatest friends'[1] of Tom and Joan; and it was to Tom that Geoffrey turned, in 1951, for help with his son Leonard's plan to establish homes for terminally ill patients.

Leonard Cheshire studied law at Oxford in the 1930s and learned to fly in the University Air Squadron. He joined the RAF just before war broke out and was an outstanding leader of bomber command, much decorated and receiving the highest award for gallantry, the Victoria Cross. After demobilisation, in 1946 he wrote an article in the *Sunday Graphic*, suggesting the establishment of co-operative settlements for ex-servicemen and women, where the strong would support the weak, the rich the poor, the skilled the unskilled, until all could stand alone. Rather to his surprise, the scheme was received with enthusiasm and a fund was raised. Cheshire took over a ramshackle house near Market Harborough and his first community started there in June 1946, moving later to Le Court, near Liss in Hampshire.

A change in direction occurred in 1948, when an early member of the community was terminally ill with cancer. Nothing more could be done for him medically; the hospital needed his bed and Leonard was unable to find any place where the dying man could receive the attention he needed. Cheshire decided to look after him in the community. He soon became aware that there was a desperate need for non-profit-making homes for helpless invalids and began to build up a Home for the Disabled at Le Court. By August 1948 it became known as the Cheshire Home.

Geoffrey and Primrose Cheshire were 'dead against' the project:[47] they thought their son was wasting his education. Once they saw that he meant to keep it going, the professor resigned his chair, sold up at Oxford and bought two little cottages on the Le Court Estate, where he and Primrose settled in the summer of 1949. Geoffrey was soon deeply involved in his son's project.

In the summer of 1950, Le Court became a registered charity, administered by a local committee, admitting only the chronic sick. A second home, St Teresa's, founded the following year in Cornwall, had a similarly chance inception. It, too, was managed locally and was independent of Le Court, save for Leonard's involvement in both. It became clear that Leonard had found a gap in the services provided by the welfare state and that his vision and inspiration could attract help and support, including finance, in many quarters. Geoffrey advised that the committee needed strengthening and that a Trust should be established. He invited Tom to Laundry Cottage, his home on the Le Court estate, to meet Leonard, who was 'slightly overawed' by Lord Justice Denning 'and conscious that a lot depended on whether or not he would take it on. He made a big impression on me because his questions were so astute. At the same time he had a feeling for disabled people. He had the human side as well as the intellectual side.'[47]

Tom did agree to 'take it on'. He remembered Gordon. The concept of aid for the weak combined with self-help was one with which he could fully identify. A first meeting of five chosen trustees was planned for Sunday 30 March 1952, at Laundry Cottage. On the day, deep snow was on the ground and two of the five were unable to reach Le Court. Tom was never to be prevented by the weather from getting where he wanted to go. He duly arrived at Geoffrey's home and the work began of giving Leonard Cheshire's creation form and order. Leonard, who had become a Roman Catholic, had considered whether part of his work should be devoted to a special Roman Catholic Trust, but concluded that his homes should remain undenominational. Tom certainly preferred it that way: some years later, when Leonard suggested the appointment of a Catholic trustee, Tom replied that trustees are appointed for what they are, not for their religion. 'But,' Leonard recalled, 'he would have been quite happy for them all to be Church of England – the religion of the state.'[47]

Between them, Tom and Geoffrey drew up the Trust Deed. Then Geoffrey, who had been asked by Leonard to be chairman, told his son: 'Your first chairman should be Denning.'[47]

With Joan, Tom threw himself wholeheartedly into the expanding work of the new Trust. They 'visited the Homes and talked to the residents.' They 'looked for new Homes and got them. Leonard Cheshire was the inspired leader in everything. Geoffrey and I trailed behind.'[1]

Something more than the value of Tom's name as a Lord Justice of the Court of Appeal may have prompted Geoffrey Cheshire to propose that Denning, rather than himself, should chair the Trust. There were times when Leonard's vision out-ran the prudence of the other trustees and it would have been hard for his father to oppose him. Denning's sympathetic understanding, his easy command of facts and figures, as well as his greater detachment, made him the ideal person to temper Leonard's enthusiasm. 'Over the years,' Leonard remembered, 'they turned down things which I thought mistaken; equally they saved me from a lot of mistakes.'

A small office was found for the Trust in a Mayfair mews (where now the Hilton Hotel stands) and Margot Mason (later Margot Gibb) became the secretary. Once a month, on a Saturday, Tom travelled up to London for meetings; occasionally Margot went, on Trust business, to Tom's room in the Law Courts or, at weekends, to his home in Cuckfield. Tom, she remembered, gave a lot of time to the Trust. 'He kept things bubbling. He bent himself to try to follow Leonard's train of thought and it was not very easy for him. He and Geoffrey Cheshire were wonderful.'

Margot was a tennis player of county standard and there was, at Fair Close, a tennis court. During a break in discussions, Tom would invite Margot to a game. 'He gave me a fishing net of a tennis racket. He had a tennis court which was terribly bumpy. And he was absolutely determined that he was going to beat me ... He didn't have any idea of stroke play. He just had tremendous will-power that he must get the ball back over the net. He used to wear me down with his determination.'[48] Though he had little natural aptitude for sport, in games, as in everything else, Tom liked to win.

By 1955 there were five Cheshire homes in England and Leonard wanted to expand to India. Tom was appalled; quite apart from the financial problems, he believed that the very real need for more homes in England was the first call upon the Trust. While Leonard established the first overseas home in Bombay, Tom and Joan devoted their energies to raising the money and founding a home at Dulwich. Tom gave many informal talks to schools and clubs, telling them about the work of the Trust and encouraging fund-raising.

In India, Leonard met Wilfred Russell, who became a trustee in 1956, and was deeply impressed by Tom's grasp of affairs as well as by his 'simplicity and modesty ... There were problems enough in those days and he always seemed able to get to the root of each one.'[14]

It was Tom's idea to arrange 'an incredibly successful lunch' at the head office of the National and Westminster Bank, after which an overdraft was arranged which changed the whole course of the Trust. 'It was the fact that a distinguished judge was prepared to back the strange adventures of a young, much-decorated bomber pilot . . . which made so many people sit up and take notice and make donations to the Trust.'[14] Though Tom was primarily inclined to devote his immense energy and ability to the service of English people, once the work of the Trust was expanded overseas, he entered with a will into the new challenge. Whenever he and Joan went abroad, they made sure to visit any Cheshire home within journeying distance. Their visits were as welcome in the Commonwealth as they were in Dulwich. Tom gave up the chairmanship of the Trust only when he became Master of the Rolls.

The question had to be settled of where Robert was to go to school when he left Parkfield. John Stuart was at Repton. David Denning was at Winchester and Tom had taught there many years before. It had an excellent academic reputation; Tom had happy memories of the city though not of his time as a schoolmaster. It was not too far for Tom and Joan to visit Robert. All things considered, they decided that Robert should go to Winchester when he was 13. Joan drove Tom and Robert to Chernocke House, where the housemaster, Mr Emmett, welcomed them to the new boys' tea. In his pocket diary, Tom noted all Robert's leave-days: he would allow only the most exceptional circumstances to interfere with the pleasure he took from spending those days with his son. 'So far it's not too bad,' Robert wrote home on 20 January 1952, before listing the esoteric matters that he must learn in order to be tested by the prefects. From Chernocke House, where in 1920 Tom had longed to be set free from the life of a schoolmaster, in October 1952 his son sent him a newspaper cutting about Tom's broadcast talk, on the Third Programme, demanding new principles of justice. 'I have never heard a more important broadcast,' wrote Collie Knox in the *Daily Mail*, 'than that given by Lord Justice Denning pleading for a new equity. It should have had a peak spot . . . The brave words of this progressive judge should be published, so civically pregnant are they. So they put him on the Third.'

Tom was peculiarly ingenious at finding ways to reach the decision that seemed to him to be just. He was also, more than most judges, apt to disregard the inconvenience that would attend uncertainty in the law. Always he kept his eye on social changes and the necessity for the law to respond to them. He made clear that he believed the response must be judge-led. Some of the Law Lords were so incensed that they expressed their condemnation in strong language rather than their usual diplomatic words.

Towards the end of 1950 Denning dissented from Cohen and Somervell in a case depending on the construction of a statute (*Magor and St Mellons* v. *Newport Corporation*). Referring to what he had said in *Seaford Court Estates*, Denning repeated: 'We do not sit here to pull the language of Parliament and of Ministers to pieces and make nonsense of it. That is an easy thing to do, and it is a thing to which lawyers are too often prone. We sit here to find out the intention of Parliament and of Ministers and carry it out, and we do this better by filling in the gaps and making sense of the enactment than by opening it up to destructive analysis.' The case reached the House of Lords in July 1951 and they took time for consideration before dismissing the appeal (with Lord Radcliffe dissenting). The case would not have warranted inclusion in the Law Reports, as their editor commented, if it had not been for the Lords' observations on the construction of statute. Lord Simonds commented: 'It appears to me to be a naked usurpation of the legislative function under the thin disguise of interpretation. And it is the less justifiable when it is guesswork with what material the legislature would, if it had discovered the gap, have filled it in . . .'

Gavin Simonds had a successful career at the Chancery Bar before being appointed to the Chancery Bench, from which he was promoted direct to the Lords in 1944. 'Simonds's notion of justice . . . did not extend to the overthrow of long-established principles of law by judicial decision; he preferred . . . that the law should, so far as possible, be certain of ascertainment, and that radical changes were a matter for parliament, not for the judiciary.'[25] He was, Denning wrote in *The Discipline of Law*, 'a dominating intellect but cast in a most conservative mould.' In the 1950 election the Labour Party's majority had been reduced to five, compelling the Government to go to the country again the following year and in October 1951 Winston Churchill became prime minister for the second time, about five

weeks before his seventy-seventh birthday. To mild surprise, he
appointed Simonds Lord Chancellor. At the time, Tom was a little
hurt by Simonds's rebuke and most lawyers were surprised by its
vehemence. There had been other occasions when Simonds criticised
Denning's approach to the law and Simonds's antagonism was
becoming the object of comment. Outside the law, Tom found
Simonds pleasant enough and, in later days, Simonds and his wife
would visit Tom's home for the fishing.

Shortly before that blistering attack on Denning, another criticism
had been delivered, by Viscount Simon, who was very critical of
Denning's judgment 'but wrote me a letter to soften the blow.'[24] In
the early summer of 1950, Denning heard an appeal in the case of a
dispute between film distributors and film exhibitors. Denning's
judgment gave the facts:

> On July 25, 1941, the distributors agreed to supply news reels of
> British Movietone News to the exhibitors for showing at the
> Pavilion Theatre, Aylesbury, at ten guineas a week for a minimum
> period of twenty-six weeks, the agreement being thereafter
> terminable by one month's notice . . . [In] March, 1943, the Board
> of Trade decided to control the supply of cinematograph film . . .
> The legal machinery by which this was done was the Cinema-
> tograph Film (Control) Order, 1943 . . .

In 1943 news reels – whoever was making them – contained nothing
but war news. All cinemas showed them and arrangements were
made between distributors and exhibitors to ensure supply. The new
agreements in the case stipulated that the principal agreement (of
1941) would remain in force during the continuance of the 1943
Order. The Order was a war-time measure and might have been
expected to come to an end when the war was over, but the economic
crisis that followed the war prompted new legislation, under which
the Order was continued. By 1948, in post-war conditions, the
exhibitors, London and District Cinemas, no longer found the news
reels supplied by British Movietone News acceptable. They gave
notice under the terms of the principal agreement. The distributors
claimed that the notice provisions were suspended whilst the Order
remained in force, and Slade accepted this argument. Whether or not

the cinema chose to show the news reels, he decided, they must pay ten guineas a week for their rental until the expiry of the Order.

Denning was always ready to make statements on the principles governing cases. Delivering the single judgment of the Court, he said that courts should not always follow the literal meaning of the words in a contract but should consider the background against which the contract was made and changed circumstances, not in the contemplation of the parties, in order to 'do therein what is just and reasonable.'

'This does not mean,' he added, 'that the courts no longer insist on the binding force of contracts deliberately made. It only means that they will not allow the words in which they happen to be phrased to become tyrannical masters. The court qualifies the literal meaning of the words so as to bring them into accord with the contemplated scope of the contract.'

The *Law Quarterly Review* commented at the time: 'The importance of the case lies in the clear statement in Denning's judgment of the principles which guide the courts in those cases which may be termed frustration of purpose, for they have not been previously analysed with such care', and Professor P. S. Atiyah, wrote in 1984: 'Looking back on the judgment, 30 years later, it is really difficult to see why so much objection was taken to it.'[49] But, in 1951, the Lords were appalled and took the opportunity of making plain their disapproval. 'With all respect to the learning and acumen of the learned Lord Justice,' said Viscount Simon, 'I do not agree that there has been a recent change as the result of which the courts now exercise a wider power in this regard than they previously used . . . When the authorities referred to by Denning LJ as justifying the proposition . . . are examined it will be found that they do not support any such notion.'

In a few short months Denning had challenged the accepted principles of statutory interpretation and the literal construction of contract. More conservative lawyers feared he was going too far, too fast. They disliked his habit of arriving at a decision on the merits of a case and then examining the law to see whether anything prevented him from achieving the desired conclusion. Tom himself was supremely confident that his was the way forward. His unfailing charm, good humour and courtesy concealed a streak of arrogance.

He would have preferred not to be criticised but he could react philosophically since he always knew he was right.

In 1978, when Denning wrote his first book, *The Discipline of Law*, he chose to open with what he called the most important subject in the daily practice of law: the construction of documents. On the one hand, he told his readers, there were 'the strict constructionists' and, on the other, 'the intention seekers'. Those who knew *Seaforth Court Estates* and *British Movietone News* had no doubt on which hand Denning stood. That 'Misuse of ministerial powers' was the subject of the second part of the book, indicates another of Denning's priorities. His concern at the misuse and abuse of power of any kind was emphasised in his Hamlyn lectures. His determination to contain it was the driving force behind much of his judicial work.

At the time, statutory tribunals proliferated and the courts had no control over them, provided they kept within their jurisdiction. A tribunal might go wrong in fact, it might go wrong in law – the only way its decision could be challenged was to show that it had gone outside its jurisdiction, never an easy task. In December 1951, the case of Thomas Shaw and the Northumberland Compensation Appeal Tribunal reached the Court of Appeal. Shaw had lost his employment as clerk to a hospital board when the National Health Service came in. Dissatisfied with the compensation offered to him, he referred the matter to the Compensation Appeal Tribunal, who were required to assess the proper amount in accordance with complex regulations. The Tribunal made an error of law. Shaw applied to the Divisional Court for an order of *certiorari* (one of the old prerogative writs by which the Court of King's Bench controlled the action of inferior courts and made sure that they did not exceed their jurisdiction) to remove the decision into the King's Bench Division, where it could be quashed. Though the Tribunal admitted its error, it disputed that it had exceeded its authority and denied that Shaw was entitled to an order of *certiorari*. Lord Goddard, in the Divisional Court granted the order and the Tribunal appealed. Denning had no doubt that the courts had power to correct the error. He said:

> There is a formidable argument against any intervention on the part of the King's Bench at all. The statutory tribunals, like this

one here, are often made the judges both of fact and law, with no
appeal to the High Court. If, then, the King's Bench should
interfere when a tribunal makes a mistake of law, the King's Bench
may well be said to be exceeding its own jurisdiction. It would be
usurping to itself an appellate jurisdiction which has not been given
to it.

Then Tom answered his own argument:

... the court of King's Bench has an inherent jurisdiction to
control all inferior tribunals, not in an appellate capacity, but in a
supervisory capacity. This control extends not only to seeing that
inferior tribunals keep within their jurisdiction, but also to seeing
that they observe the law.
(*R. v. Northumberland Compensation Appeal Tribunal ex parte
Shaw*)

In a comprehensive and compelling historical survey Denning
showed that *certiorari* had not been confined to cases of excess of
jurisdiction. As the Tribunal did not appeal, the decision became
authoritative. It opened the way to judicial review of tribunals and a
variety of other quasi-judicial bodies.

If the machinery to control the abuse of power was to be updated,
the courts had need of tools with fewer limitations than *certiorari*.
The next advance was made in March 1953, when dockers claimed a
declaration that they had been unlawfully suspended. The Dock
Labour Board responded that *certiorari* was the only means by which
the court could interfere with a statutory tribunal. In *Barnard* v.
National Dock Labour Board Denning made it clear that he saw no
reason why the court should not intervene by declaration or
injunction to prevent a tribunal from disregarding the law. The
Northumberland case and *Barnard*'s case set in train the advance to
the modern system of judicial review.

14

The Road to Justice

Much as he disliked the concentration in executive hands of excessive power, so Tom distrusted its unfettered use by unions or trade associations. He saw the unfortunate effects of the closed shop on people who fell foul of their union. In 1951, in the case of *Abbott* v. *Sullivan*, the Court of Appeal was told that Mr Abbott, a corn porter, had gone to work while six of his gang stayed away. The Trade Union committee fined him ten shillings and ordered him to pay the day's wages to the other six men. In the street outside, Abbott punched Sullivan, the convenor, on the nose; Sullivan called the committee back and struck Abbott's name off the register of corn porters, which meant that Abbott could no longer be employed in the London docks. Abbott brought an action for damages against the union, the committee and the convenor but the Court found against him; Denning dissented and, knowing that the man's livelihood depended upon his name being on the register, said:

> These bodies . . . which exercise a monopoly in an important sphere of human activity, with the power of depriving a man of his livelihood, must act in accordance with the elementary rules of justice. They must not condemn a man without giving him an opportunity to be heard in his own defence: and any agreement or practice to the contrary would be invalid.

Though the courts were beginning to command some control over the exercise of power by domestic tribunals, they had not yet awarded damages to a member against his trade union. When Mr Bonsor was expelled by the secretary of the Musician's Union, which operated a closed shop, he could no longer work as a musician. For four years he was reduced to such work as chipping rust from a pier at Brighton and claimed damages from the union. The court unanimously held that his expulsion was invalid but the majority believed they could not award damages. Denning thought that they could:

> This exclusion has lasted for four years, and his loss of earnings must be very considerable, to say nothing of the worry and trouble to which he has been put. And the exclusion was unlawful. It was done by the secretary of the Brighton branch, who had no right to do it . . . We have already held that this exclusion was a breach of contract. Yet it is said that we cannot award the plaintiff damages for the injury done to him. If this be so, then it is a grievous thing; for I know of no other case where the law allows a party to break a contract with impunity. A man's right to work is just as important to him, indeed more important, than his right of property . . .
>
> (*Bonsor* v. *Musician's Union*)

In putting the case for damages, as in bringing the over-mighty under control, Denning was persuasive. When the case reached the Lords two years later, they upheld his dissenting judgment and awarded damages to Bonsor. 'It was too late to do him any good,' Tom wrote in *The Discipline of Law*, 'he had died during the time it took for the case to get to the Lords.'

For Tom, 1952 was a year of achievement and, despite the tension between him and Lord Simonds, his career was evidently destined to reach greater heights. His elder brother – five years his senior – was at the end of his career. Reg, who had joined the army as a gunner in 1914, retired in 1952 as a lieutenant general, after commanding the forces in Northern Ireland. Inactivity never suited a Denning: Reg became Chairman of the Soldiers, Sailors and Air Force Association (SSAFA) and both he and Eileen devoted their next years to its work.

Early in 1953, Tom was elected President of Birkbeck College, London University. On 18 March he delivered the 12th Haldane Memorial Lecture there, returning to the subject of the rule of law in the welfare state; and on 28 April Tom and Joan, together with the Vice Chancellor of London University, the Chairman of Convocation and the Master of the College, received the Queen Mother, who officially declared open the college's new building.

In 1953, five of Denning's lectures and addresses were published under the title, *The Changing Law*. Like its predecessor, *Freedom Under the Law*, the book was an immediate success and *The Times* called it 'an important book'. More conservative judges looked askance at Denning's readiness to talk publicly about justice and the law. Though the brilliance of some of his judgments was recognised (and in June 1953 he became Chairman of the Society of Comparative Legislation and International Law) there were lawyers who felt that Lord Justice Denning shared some of the characteristics of an unexploded bomb. This had little effect on Tom's popularity. By 1953 he was the hero of most law students. It was even said that, when stumped for an answer to an examination question, it would be safe to write 'Denning LJ, in a dissenting judgment, said . . .' Amongst lawyers, Tom was also much admired.

Alongside his work in the Courts, and his increasing involvement in educational and welfare organisations, Tom's busy speaking schedule continued in the evenings and at weekends. On 27 February 1953 he delivered his presidential address on 'The Need For A New Equity' to the Bentham Club – graduates and members of the law faculty of University College, London. In May he gave the Earl Grey Memorial Lecture at the University of Durham, addressed French judges in Paris and, at King's College, Newcastle-upon-Tyne, spoke on another favourite theme: the influence of religion on law. It is seldom that, outside his judgments, a judge has set out so extensively his philosophy of law and life.

In 1954 the Nuffield Foundation invited Tom to visit the six universities of South Africa. This was further afield than he was accustomed to travel and he would not go without Joan. Since the visit was to take place in the long vacation, when John would be between school and National Service, it was decided that the boys should go with their parents. They sailed on 29 July on the *Athlone Castle*. Six days later was Robert's sixteenth birthday and Tom gave him a watch. During the voyage Tom prepared his lectures and Joan typed them for him. The question 'What is justice?' was never far beneath the surface of Tom's judicial work. Now he determined 'to show, as well as I could, what is the right way to arrive at justice.'[50] Though he worked at his lectures, life on board ship also gave Tom a new kind of holiday. Swimming before breakfast, deck tennis and

parties delighted all the family. Robert won first prize as a grandfather clock at the fancy dress dance in Cabin Class, while Tom and
Joan attended their ball, dressed as the moon and a star.

When they landed, on 12 August 1954, they went by train direct to
Johannesburg. It was exciting new country to all of them and they
watched, fascinated, as they passed seemingly endless areas of veldt
that faded gradually into night. During their week in Johannesburg
Tom attracted unprecedentedly large audiences for a lawyer. 'His
lectures and informal talks made a deep impression upon his audience
who could not fail to recognise his profound scholarship and
sincerity, his penetrating insight into the problems of humanity, his
objectivity and enlightened approach to the interpretation of the
principles underlying law and human justice.'[51] The family was met
with great warmth and responded with the friendly informality that
would always win them hearts. A weekend in a game reserve was
arranged for them, and a visit to a gold mine. The presence of the boys
must have underlined for their hosts that Sir Alfred Denning was not
only an eminent English judge but a family man, as interested in their
lives as in their legal problems.

Robert had to be back in England for the next school term. So at
Durban – the next stop – he and John joined a coach tour that was to
take them, by the Garden Route, to Cape Town, in time to join the
Carnarvon Castle, sailing on 3 September. Despite difficulties on the
way, when floods held up the coach, they had five days to spend in
Cape Town and, when they saw Table Mountain on the first day, did
not hurry to climb it. The second day it was wreathed in mist, and the
third and fourth; only on the last day did it appear again, too late to
climb before the boat sailed.

On the voyage home, in great good spirits, the two boys wrote
alternate paragraphs of joint letters to their parents. Meantime Tom
lectured at Pretoria, Bloemfontein and Grahamstown. Everywhere,
he and Joan were made welcome and responded with their own brand
of unaffected charm. At Howard's College, on 9 September, Tom
stressed the roles of judiciary and press in safeguarding freedom. A
leader in the *Eastern Province Herald*, on 16 September, commented:
'There has in recent years been an intensive campaign . . . to persuade
the people of South Africa to accept docilely the proposition that
Parliament should be able to do anything it pleases . . . A powerful

corrective to the erroneous and undemocratic view of the nature and functions of parliamentary government was supplied by Lord Justice Denning.'

Tom and Joan stayed nearly a week in Cape Town, at the home of Dr Davie, the Principal of the University. They were luckier than John and Robert: the air was clear and they were taken for a picnic on Table Mountain. For Tom, the tour had been hard work. Even in his off-duty moments he was usually surrounded by an admiring audience and, when he had an audience, he never failed to sparkle for them. On 12 October, when the Dennings were back in England, Professor W. R. Hahlo of Witwatersrand wrote: 'His personal charm and urbanity, his genuine interest in our problems, his open-mindedness and his readiness to listen to different points of view, made him friends wherever he went among English and Afrikaaner speakers alike.' The Dennings could not help but be conscious of apartheid. In a predominantly black country all their hosts were white. On later tours, when he would have the opportunity to address African audiences, Tom would weave the same magic and win the same applause.

With the new Humber motor car that had (after some difficulty, because of the export drive) replaced Dog Pie, driving was less of a hazard and Joan was happy to go anywhere. Each summer the family explored a different part of Britain. One year they rented a house at Helford for a month; three times they took the car across to Ireland; on one occasion they followed Dr Johnson's tour of Scotland and, at one stop, John caught the biggest fish of the season, a 2-lb sea trout, with a worm. One Christmas vacation, when Robert was 11 years old, they tried a skiing holiday at Lenzerheide, in Switzerland. It was not an immense success. On the first day, Hazel injured a leg and though Tom enjoyed the toboggan he thought himself too old to venture upon skis. He and Joan took a Whitsun holiday in Montreux, travelling to Switzerland by train. They stayed a week in the Hotel Laurier and nearly missed the train home because they were in a boat on Lake Geneva.

King George VI died on 6 February 1952 and his daughter was proclaimed Queen Elizabeth II. As a Privy Councillor, Tom received, on 7 February, a telegram summoning him to attend the Accession Council. At St James's Palace, he was amongst the first to sign his name. Winston Churchill was present, as the recently returned Prime Minister.

The invitations to the Coronation were inscribed on thick cream board. In dark blue print, surmounted by the Royal Crest, the Earl Marshal invited the Right Honourable Sir Alfred Denning and Lady Denning to be present at the Abbey Church of Westminster on 2 June 1953. Their tickets told them to enter by No. 8 door (Poets' Corner). Detailed instructions were given for acceptable forms of dress: Velvet Court Dress (New Style); Velvet Court Dress (Old Style); Cloth Court Dress or Alternative Dress.

Handsome in her full-length gown, with long white gloves and a tiara on her head, Joan took her seat beside Tom several hours before the coronation processions were due. Delight was subdued by fatigue before the historic ceremony began. To celebrate the occasion, the Bar Theatrical Club held some readings, in which Tom took part.

That month the annual meeting of the National Association of Parish Councils was held in Blackpool. Tom, as President, invited Edward Bridges to make a speech. Bridges, described by Churchill in *Their Finest Hours* as 'a man of exceptional force, ability and personal charm', accepted though, as head of the Civil Service, it was unusual for him to speak in public. He and Tom had met at Magdalen in 1919 and, over the years, had seen each other from time to time, but were not on intimate terms. In Blackpool they renewed their acquaintance and their wives became friends. It was not the best of times for Joan. A day or two before the meeting, she had been badly stung by the bees and was still swollen and uncomfortable. Characteristically, she made light of her own troubles and helped to make the gathering a success. After a congenial weekend, on 14 June 1952 Bridges wrote to Tom:

Dear Denning,
[or don't we know each other well enough for xtian names! I think we do!]
    I want to write to thank you and your wife for all that you both did to make our time at Blackpool so enjoyable. I don't know how you managed, with all your other ploys, to find so much time to arrange things so that *we* had nothing to worry about . . .

It was characteristic of both Tom and Joan that, whatever their personal problems, they would still devote themselves to the comfort and enjoyment of their guests.

In July 1954 rationing finally came to an end. Joan felt a sense of great relief that she would no longer have to watch Tom carving the joint, and hope that it would go round. Three months later – making less impact on the country – Simonds was replaced as Lord Chancellor by the Attorney-General, David Maxwell-Fyfe, who became Viscount Kilmuir. Like Simonds, Kilmuir believed that a judge should keep out of the public eye except in the performance of his judicial duties. It may, or may not have been Tom's high profile that, in part, provoked Kilmuir's observations on the subject, known as the Kilmuir Rules. In general, Tom agreed with the Rules for others, if not for himself, but the great demands made upon him to take presidencies and chairmanships, to write articles and to give lectures and speeches made it inevitable that his views would reach a very much wider audience than the one usually found in a court of law.

At the time when Denning was a judge of assize a verdict of murder carried a mandatory death sentence. On several occasions Denning put on the traditional black cap and pronounced the words: 'You shall be hanged by the neck until you are dead and may the Lord have mercy on your soul.' Asked how he had felt at such a moment, Tom replied that for 'murder most foul' death was the appropriate penalty; if some mistake were made by the trial judge and jury, there was always the possibility of appeal and, where there was a case for mercy, the Home Secretary had the power to commute the sentence. Though Tom referred to the Home Secretary's powers, in this, as in all things legal, he placed his faith primarily in the good sense of judge and jury.

In the early Fifties there was growing opposition to capital punishment and a Royal Commission was appointed to investigate the case for abolition. At the time Denning was against abolition though he believed that the death sentence should be passed only in cases which really deserved it and where it was likely to be carried out. 'The punishment inflicted for grave crimes,' he told the Commission in 1953, 'should adequately reflect the revulsion felt by the great majority of citizens for them.' He was satisfied that a judge

and jury would appreciate whether there were any special circumstances suggesting a recommendation for mercy and questioned the
Home Office practice of instituting an inquiry into the medical
condition of a person sentenced to death.

The trial and subsequent hanging of Ruth Ellis in 1955 for the
murder of her lover brought the issue into sharp focus. Public
opinion was turning against hanging, and the majority in parliament
swung behind the electorate.

Tom had a combination of obstinacy and grace: on the one hand,
he might hold, in the face of all argument, to a view which he was
convinced was right; on the other, if he came to believe that he had
been wrong, he would happily turn about and admit his new view
with good humour and charm. In the course of the debate on capital
punishment he began to modify his views. Writing in 1984, he said:

> After the debate in Parliament I altered my view. I asked the
> rhetorical question: Is it right for us, as a society, to do a thing –
> hang a man – which none of us individually would be prepared to
> do or even to witness? The answer is 'No, not in a civilised
> society.'[52]

Tom used every opportunity to make known his views on aspects of
the contemporary scene. At a time of growing industrial lawlessness
he commended schoolmasters at Hurstpierpoint College on their
own sense of responsibility to the community: 'When you look at the
men in the docks and on the railways, you find no sense of duty or
service to the community at all.' Commenting on legal aid in *The
Observer* of Sunday 24 July 1955, he wrote: 'It was a standing
reproach that there should be one law for the rich and another for the
poor, simply because the rich could afford to go to law and the poor
could not.' He also noted with satisfaction that legal aid was a help for
lawyers who were now being paid for the kind of work that had been
done, when he was at the Bar, as Poor Person cases.

In the summer vacation of 1955 Tom was to address the American
and Canadian Bar Meetings. With Joan and Robert, he sailed on the
Empress of Canada, looking forward to the voyage and to the
journey across Canada, from Quebec to Vancouver, planned for the
family by the Canadian Law Society. On the Canadian Pacific

Railway, the Dennings were given the Inspection Coach, with a private suite of carriages, an observation platform at the rear of the lounge and a personal cook-steward. They passed lakes like inland seas, timber forests, the vast wheat-growing areas, where only an occasional farm broke the long, flat landscape. As they approached Calgary, farms became more frequent, cattle and horses appeared and, in the distance, the foothills of the Rocky Mountains. They stayed a few nights at Banff, in the heart of the Rockies, and were taken to see the beauty spots, then on again, by rail, to Vancouver. It was a blissful ten days, a complete holiday before the speeches that were the purpose of the journey.

Tom was a 'passionate family man right across the board'[32] and it was always a pleasure for him to visit, correspond with – or help –any single member. He took this opportunity to visit Marjorie's daughter Peggy, married to Alan McGill, a surgeon on Vancouver Island, and spend a few days with her, before continuing to Seattle, by ship, and then, by train to Philadelphia where, in intense, damp heat the American Bar Meeting took place. At the inaugural meeting, the ladies wilted in smart dresses, with hats and gloves, as they waited for the arrival of President Eisenhower. By the second day, the numbers had – as, at conventions, they frequently do – dwindled; and it was on the second day that Tom was to make his speech. He had put a great deal of work into it and was disappointed to find a half-empty hall and an inattentive audience. Very soon the remaining delegates began to sit up and take notice. At the end of an hour they gave him a standing ovation. The word got around and, in the following four days, whenever Tom spoke, it was to a substantial and appreciative audience.

From Philadelphia, the Dennings returned to Ottawa for the Canadian Bar Meeting, where they were received with great warmth and Joan, to her delight, was given her first orchid. Both Tom and Joan found the long receptions tiring and solved the problem of being non-drinkers by taking Canada Dry Ginger, which had the colour of whisky. Again Tom had great success with his speeches and established a long-enduring association with Canadian lawyers. He was presented with the honorary degree of Doctor of Laws from the University of Ottawa and was made a life member of the Canadian Bar Association.

On his return to England, he arranged for the publication of the speeches he had given in South Africa, the United States and Canada in a book entitled *The Road to Justice*. 'The nearest we can get to defining justice,' he said, 'is to say that it is what right-minded members of the community – those who have the right spirit within them – believe to be fair.' Two years later, in January 1957, the Lord Chancellor, addressing the Mansfield Law Club, of which Tom was President, at the City of London University, commended these two series of lectures. Concerned, as was Tom, that the law must adapt to meet constantly changing social problems, Lord Kilmuir endorsed Denning's views on disputes between citizens and the state. After the disapproval of Lord Simonds this evidence of his successor's approval must have been welcome to Tom.

Denning's nine years as a Lord Justice of Appeal were among the most contented and productive of his life. At home, he was at ease. His life with Joan perfectly represented the Christian marriage that was his ideal. He enjoyed the extended family she had brought him. He regarded Pauline, Hazel and John with warmth and affection; he took pride and pleasure in their successes and was always ready with advice, encouragement and a word in a useful ear. His deepest love was reserved for Robert, his only son.

At Winchester boys had to decide quite early whether to do arts or science. Tom would have liked his son to follow him into the law but respected Robert's right to make his own choice. A little to Tom's regret, Robert chose science. The very real affection and easy relationship between them is revealed in Robert's letters: 'mummy and daddy' become 'mum and dad', when Robert remembers, in 1956, but 'if daddy is in his short pants,' he wrote in May, 'summer must be here.' In June he heard that Joan had bumped the car – 'lucky it wasn't me' he commented. There was no exciting lecture tour planned for the long vacation of 1956. The family took the car across to Ireland and toured.

Oxford entrance and two years' National Service were looming. On 2 October 1956 Robert wrote to ask Reg how to get his call-up quickly so that he might be released in time to go up to Oxford in October 1958. Reg was delighted to help. 'All for one and one for all' remained the watchword for Tom and his brothers; five months later, when Robert passed his War Office Selection Board, Reg wrote to

Tom: 'I don't imagine Robert will want much help, but if he does this fellow will help him.' Meantime, Tom and Joan were planning a dance for Robert at Fair Close and, in November, Robert wrote to them: 'I hope you know all these people you are asking. You seem to go on asking an endless number. We don't really want more than 80. It will be overcrowded. Don't get rash about asking people.' The temptation to Tom to 'get rash' must have been irresistible as he and Joan planned to give his son the dance that Tom himself never had.

It is never easy for two mature people to enter into a second marriage and it was not without much effort on Joan's part that Tom enjoyed the comfort and security that meant so much to him. She had been much alone, when her first husband was abroad, and was inclined to make small decisions on her own but when she saw this was hurtful to him, she readily adapted her way to his. His work, his speaking engagements, his committees demanded much of Joan's time. Gradually, willingly, she gave up her separate interests – the Wives' Fellowship, Moral Welfare, the Cuckfield Church Almshouses, the Girl Guides and the East Sussex Housing Association – to drive Tom about the country and to accompany him to many of his meetings. Tom's career was as important to her as it was to him.

Tom was always interested to hear what Joan had done while he was at work, but she found – as many lawyers' wives have done – that she could not simply give him a broad outline of a story; he wanted precise information about anything that caught his fancy. Occasionally, without even noticing it, he would fall into the kind of cross-examination more usually heard in the courtroom and Joan would remind him that she was not in the dock. She became a grandmother on 9 June 1951, when Pauline's first daughter, Katherine, was born. Tom was her godfather (and, as such, he insisted, years later, on proposing her health at her wedding). When her sister Miranda was born, on 12 April 1954, Katherine stayed at Fair Close. Tom was charming with children and enjoyed the additions to his family. Yet, as Joan's grandchildren grew up, they never called him 'Grandpa', he was always 'Uncle Tom'.

Tom enjoyed success; other people's as much as his own. He was proud and delighted when Hazel took a First Class degree and followed it by coming second in the Bar Final Examination. He arranged a pupillage for her in chambers where, at the end of six months, she was given a seat. When Hazel first went to London, she stayed in the flat at Carlton Gardens and took over the lease when Pauline and Derick moved to their own home at Richmond. When she introduced her future husband to the Dennings, Tom 'acted like a father: he saw bad points and good points.'[53] He liked the young Chancery barrister, but Michael was a Catholic and Tom's upbringing and belief made it hard for him to contemplate Hazel marrying anywhere but in the Church of England. As usual with Tom, matters were resolved in a manner satisfactory to him. It was down the aisle of Cuckfield Church that Tom walked, with Hazel on his arm, on Saturday 5 June 1954, for her marriage to Michael Fox, which was followed by a tea party in a marquee on the lawn of Fair Close. Like her sister, Hazel started married life in the flat at Carlton Gardens. Michael Fox scored well with John and Robert: he gave them 'a lovely present which I'm sure John and I didn't deserve.'[54]

When John Stuart completed his National Service he went up to Oxford, to read physics at Magdalen College, then joined the fibres division of ICI in Harrogate. Most weekends he drove home to Cuckfield in a little Ford Popular car – the success story of budget motor manufacturing in the Fifties. Unless Tom and Joan were away, the house was usually filled with guests, the young people mingling with the visitors from all Tom's spheres of activity. Playing with distinguished guests John concluded that 'there is nothing like croquet to bring out the worst in people.'

There are two kinds of people attracted to the Bar: those who are happiest in the rough and tumble of the adversarial system and those who most excel in the handing down of judgment. Denning was of the latter kind. In the Court of Appeal, from 1948 to 1957, he made great contributions to the law. In some cases he advanced a principle, either making new law or – as in *Crane Christmas* – laying foundations on which law would be made in the House of Lords. Though, in others, he was only enunciating an established principle, he did so with such clarity that his words became the standard exposition.

One of the problems in the 1950s was the meaning of the phrase 'the landlord intends', since the landlord's intention to demolish or reconstruct premises, or to occupy them himself, usually precluded a tenant from obtaining a new tenancy at the expiry of his lease. The decision was more difficult when the landlord was a limited company: how, the courts had to decide, can a limited company form an intention? For this question Denning had a simple answer:

> A company may in many ways be likened to a human body. It has a brain and nerve centre which controls what it does. It also has hands which hold the tools and act in accordance with directions from the centre. Some of the people in the company are mere servants and agents who are nothing more than hands to do the work and cannot be said to represent the mind or will. Others are directors and managers who represent the directing mind and will of the company, and control what it does. The state of mind of these managers is the state of mind of the company and is treated by the law as such.
>
> (H. L. Bolton (Engineering) v. T. J. Graham)

In 1954, official recognition of the clarity with which Denning pronounced a principle was accorded by the inclusion of an extract from his judgment in *Ladd* v. *Marshall* in the Annual Practice volume. The test to be observed in all future cases before new evidence could be adduced in an appeal was set out in Denning's words.

Misuse of power by the executive and by unions was not the only source of danger covered in Tom's lectures. He also told how, in the nineteenth century, 'anyone who had a bargaining lever was able to exploit it for his own benefit. It was all done under the name of "freedom of contract". However harsh were the terms of any contract, the judges enforced it . . . it mattered not to the judges of that day that one party had the power to dictate the terms of a contract and the other had no alternative to submit . . . You would find innocent parties bound by harsh terms of which they knew nothing until their powerful opponent produced them, so to speak, "out of the blue".'

In the 1930s Denning had gone happily about the country winning case after case 'most unrighteously'[1] for a vending-machine company, after persuading the Court of Appeal that exemption terms in a printed contract were binding. Now that he was a member of that Court, he turned his attention to the protection of the small man or woman from what he called the unfair use of bargaining power. In *Karsales* v. *Wallis* – the case of the motor car that did not go – Denning embarked, in 1956, on a crusade against printed exemption clauses that would bring him into conflict with the Lords before, finally, stimulating legislation for consumer protection.

Most of the time Denning's decisions were in agreement with his colleagues; he was, he said, reluctant to dissent. When he did, 'it was for my own peace of mind. So long as I did what I thought was just, I was content. I could sleep at night.'[1] Some of his dissenting views, in the end, became the law, either because of a decision in the Lords or by legislation. Whether or not he dissented, he often arrived at his decision by routes different from those taken by his colleagues. There were times when his observations (not all of them strictly necessary for the case in hand) became authoritative; at others his remarks were received with misgivings, criticism, or even with censure.

In 1951, Simonds quoted from Denning's judgment in *Howell* v. *Falmouth Boat Construction*:

> When government officers, in their dealing with a subject, take on themselves to assume authority in a matter with which he is concerned, the subject is entitled to rely on their having the authority which they assume. He does not know and cannot be expected to know the limits of their authority, and he ought not to suffer if they exceed it. That was the principle which I applied in *Robertson* v. *Minister of Pensions* and it is applicable in this case also.

'My Lords, I know of no such principle in our law,' said Simonds and, in what must be the ultimate legal snub, 'nor was any authority for it cited.'

If the widely known tension between Denning and Simonds was one aspect of Tom's time in the Court of Appeal, the admiration of students and young lawyers of the Fifties was another. Everyone had a Denning story and all those who could told it in an approximation of his rich Hampshire burr. Not only in England but in countries abroad, Denning was the only judge known to many outside the law. Within the law, he was not only highly regarded, but well liked. Even those most critical of his unorthodoxy and those who complained of his populism, succumbed, outside the courts, to his charm.

Though he was seen as the champion of the little man, though he promoted the need for 'new rules of law, to control the new order and to reflect the new outlook', Denning was deeply conservative. One of the few higher judiciary to cross the class barrier, he had been for many years a member of the establishment and his innate disposition was, in any case, to cherish tradition. Tom understood the need for change, but valued a great deal of the old order. Above all he was devoted to England and to the Established Church. An apparent danger to the latter pained him but danger to his country and to social order were enough to make him put aside objects which, in other circumstances, took first place in his thinking.

Strangely for so ambitious a man, Tom frequently put forward the view that 'once a man becomes a Judge, he has nothing to gain from further promotion and does not seek it.' So he told the French judges in Paris in 1953, and so he wrote in *The Road to Justice*: 'The judges of the Supreme Court are all paid the same, no matter whether they sit to try cases at first instance or whether they sit in the Court of Appeal . . . we think that the decisions of a judge should not be influenced by the hope of promotion . . .' True it may be that 'some judges when invited to go to the Court of Appeal, refuse the invitation',[50] but Denning was not that kind of judge. His eye was set unwaveringly on the heights. When, in 1957, he was invited to become a Law Lord, he accepted only after he had established that a seat in the Lords would not necessarily preclude him from becoming either Lord Chief Justice or Master of the Rolls. 'I feared that, if I accepted the Lords, it would lessen my chances. I went along the corridor and talked it over with Hubert Parker – then a Lord Justice like me. I decided to accept.'[1]

15

The House of Lords

On 5 April 1957 Harold Macmillan's secretary wrote to Tom: 'At the Prime Minister's request I write to let you know that the Queen has been pleased to approve that you be appointed a Lord of Appeal in Ordinary. Garter King of Arms has been instructed to communicate with you with a view to settling your title.' Four days later Tom was told by letter that the Lord Chancellor wished him to continue to sit in the Court of Appeal until the end of term and that the appointment would take effect on 18 April. As things turned out, it was on 24 April that Denning was created a Lord of Appeal in Ordinary.

Some three hundred letters of congratulation were addressed to Tom on this occasion. The National Association of Parish Councils saluted their president; the Citizens Advice Bureaux thought the appointment 'magnificent'; a County Court judge thought it 'a loss to the Court of Appeal and a gain to the House of Lords'; the Law Society of University College, London, told Tom that students 'always express the interest and excitement they gain from your judgments', and the Oxford University Law Society were delighted at the promotion of the judge whom they regarded as the most progressive on the Bench.

From the Secretary of the Law Society, from judges, barristers and solicitors, from law societies of universities in England and abroad, from the National Marriage Guidance Council, Birkbeck College, the Bishop of Chichester, friends and relations, letters arrived by every post. Tom's Oxford friend, John Darlington, wrote from Selborne Vicarage:

I still have a photograph of you outside a country inn near Oxford, holding in your hand a glass which, in fact, contained, I believe, nothing more compromising than lemonade.

And I still have memories of you on the drive to Shepherd's Dance at Ilminster.

Tom's solicitor, Anthony Moir, also reminiscing, remarked, perhaps a little wistfully: 'The 145 Beaufort Street days, when we used to breakfast together seem a very long time ago.'

Mavis Hill, a law reporter, wrote: 'I am so conscious of the gap you will leave in the Court of Appeal that I cannot forbear to add my regret that it will now be impossible for you to be in two places at once.' Sir John Beaumont, a member of the Judicial Committee of the Privy Council, warned: 'You will have, I suspect, some tussles with Gavin [Simonds] behind the scenes.'

Though Tom was entering distinguished and often critical company, he had no qualms. All his life he had managed to adapt to every new situation he met, without changing fundamentally from the boy born and bred in Whitchurch. He had lived happily in Cuckfield for the last 20 years, but it was to Whitchurch he turned for his title when Garter King of Arms, in the person of Sir George Bellew, got in touch with him.

Arms are granted by Letters Patent from the Kings of Arms – senior officers of the College of Arms – under authority delegated to them by the Queen. Tom loved tradition and pageantry; he entered with enthusiasm into consideration of his coat of arms. At length, it was decided that his motto should be 'Fiat Justitia' – Let justice be done – and that the upholders of his shield should be two earlier judges, Lord Coke, 'the great Chief Justice in the time of the first Elizabeth', and Lord Mansfield, Lord Chief Justice in the second half of the eighteenth century.

There were, in 1957, eight Lords of Appeal in Ordinary: Simonds, Morton of Henryton, Reid, Radcliffe, Tucker, Cohen, Keith of Avenholm and Somervell of Harrow. Retired law lords and previous Lords Chancellor sometimes made up the numbers of a (usually) five-man final appeal court. There was little of the splendour of courts lower in the hierarchy. No longer, as when Tom was at the Bar, were cases heard in the Chamber of the Lords, where 'the lawyers and all their books had to huddle together in a little cubby-hole, a little box'; in 1957, sitting in a committee room of the House, or, for Privy Council cases, at Number 11 Downing Street, Tom worked – for the first time since his call to the Bar – without robes or a wig, wearing only a plain dark suit. In addition to appeals from the Court of Appeal and Court of Criminal Appeal he heard appeals to the Judicial Committee of the Privy Council from courts in all parts of the British Commonwealth.

On Wednesday 15 May, when Baron Denning of Whitchurch in the County of Southampton was introduced to the House of Lords, there was all the colour and pageantry that he could desire. In the Robing Room Tom tried on the parliamentary robes, specially brought for the occasion by the robe-makers, Ede & Ravenscroft; at a rehearsal he learned what he had to do; at luncheon – provided by his sponsors, James Tucker and Raymond Evershed – Tom, for the first time, tasted quails' eggs; finally, in the Great Chamber of the Lords, carpeted and upholstered in red, he was introduced to the House in a ceremony dating from 1621. From a seat at the back, Joan watched the proceedings.

In single file, the procession entered the House, led by the Gentleman Usher of the Black Rod and Garter King of Arms, wearing his tabard, his silver-gilt sceptre of office in his right hand and the new peer's patent of creation, on a vellum scroll, in his left. Then came Lord Evershed, followed by the new Lord Denning and Lord Tucker, each in his parliamentary robes, his cocked hat in his left hand. In Tom's right hand he carried his Writ of Summons. On reaching the Bar of the House, each member of the procession bowed towards the place where the Queen would have sat, had she been present on the occasion; then the procession passed along the side of the House where the Lords Temporal sit, repeating their bows at the Table and at the Judges' Woolsacks. Before the Woolsack, Tom knelt and presented his Writ to the Lord Chancellor while Garter King of Arms presented his Patent. Back at the Table, the clerk read the Patent:

ELIZABETH THE SECOND by the Grace of God of the United Kingdom of Great Britain and Northern Ireland and of our other Realms and Territories Queen, Head of the Commonwealth, Defender of the Faith: To all whom these present shall come, greeting. Whereas our right trusty and well beloved Counsellor Geoffrey Baron Oaksey, Companion of Our Distinguished

The newly sworn-in Mr Justice Denning
with his five-year-old son Robert

Marriage of Tom's parents Charles Denning and Clara Thompson, 17 October 1888

Far left: He was not spoiled but he was petted. Tom Denning, aged about four

Left: Tom (left) was especially close to his brother Gordon

Below: Charles and Clara set up home and shop in Newbury Street, Whitchurch in the early 1890s

Above: Captain Jack Denning

Right: 2/Lt. A.T. Denning, Royal Engineers, 1917

Below: Midshipman Gordon Denning, 1916. He served on HMS *Morris* in the front line of destroyers at the Battle of Jutland

Right: Roy Wilson, who was in Tom's chambers

Far right: Tom in the 1930s

Stephen Henn-Collins K.C.

Marriage of Tom Denning and Mary Harvey, 28 December 1932.
Arthur Grattan Bellew (left) best man

The new silk, 1938.
(Photo by W.H.House)

Below: Tom and Mary with
Robert, 1939

Charles and Clara Denning

Above: The marriage of Sir Alfred Denning and Mrs Joan Stuart, 27 December 1945. Robert is holding Tom's hand; Jack Denning, Reg's son, is behind Robert; Eileen Denning is between Jack and Tom

Above: The marriage of Robert and Elizabeth, 30 December 1967

Lord Denning and his grandsons, 'a special place in Tom's heart'. August 1978

Wherever he spoke the Master of the Rolls drew admiring audiences and Tom made friends. India, January 1964. *(Hampshire Record Office)*

Below Left: The Master of the Rolls in procession on Legal Sunday, at Winchester Cathedral with Lord Ashburton on his right. (copyright *Hampshire Chronicle*)

Below: The Lords Justices in the Master's room, 1982. Front row, left to right: Cumming-Bruce; Waller; Stephenson; Master of the Rolls; Lawton; Ormrod; Eveleigh. Back row, left to right: Kerr; Dunn; O'Connor; Ackner; Donaldson; Griffiths; May; Watkins; Slade; Oliver; Templeman; Fox. (Photo by Argent)

The strongest
evidence of an
exceptional heritage
– Lord Denning
(left), Admiral
Denning (centre)
and General
Denning

Tom and Joan in
their garden beside
the River Test

Service Order, upon whom has been conferred the Territorial Decoration has resigned his Office of a Lord of Appeal in Ordinary and the same is now vacant: now know ye that We, of our especial grace, have in pursuance of the Appellate Jurisdiction Act 1876, as amended by subsequent enactments, nominated and appointed, and by these presents do nominate and appoint, Our right trusty and well-beloved Counsellor Sir Alfred Thompson Denning, Knight, to be a Lord of Appeal in Ordinary by the style of Baron Denning of Whitchurch in Our county of Southampton, to hold the said office so long as he shall well behave himself therein . . .

There followed the reading of the Writ of Summons: '. . . We, strictly enjoining, command you upon the faith and allegiance by which you are bound to Us, that . . . you be personally present at our aforesaid Parliament . . .' Then Tom took the Oath:

I, Alfred Thompson, Baron Denning of Whitchurch in the County of Southampton, do swear by Almighty God that I will be faithful and bear true Allegiance to Her Majesty Queen Elizabeth, Her Heirs and Successors, according to Law. So help me God.

Afterwards Tom took off his splendid robes (some peers buy them, but he did not) and took his place on the cross benches. He waited a few minutes before he left the House.

They sent full details of the occasion to Robert, who was by then an officer cadet at Eaton Hall, Chester. 'Daddy's introduction,' he wrote on 20 May, 'seems to have been quite an affair. I'm sorry to have missed it but it wouldn't have been worth my while to come down. You all seem to have enjoyed yourselves at any rate.' As Tom had guarded Robert's leave days at Winchester, so he tried to keep free the day on which Robert would pass out of the Officers' Training School. There was an anxious moment when the expected date was changed to 25 July and Robert wrote that he was receiving 'many conflicting letters about whether you will be able to come or not.' In the end, everything turned out right and, on a short leave before being posted to Libya with the Green Jackets, Robert joined 'a big family gathering'[32] on the Helford River, that included Hazel and her first baby, Matthew, just three months old, and John Denning, Norman's son, who drove down on his motorcycle. After nearly tipping the family into the water, Tom left rowing to its younger members.

Tom found the pace of his new work leisurely. Since the Lords never sat judicially more than four days a week, he had Fridays, Saturdays and Sundays to devote himself to his many outside interests. He and Joan played a little golf; he did odd jobs around the garden; but by and large he used the extra time for meetings of his various committees, for visits to the institutions in which he took an interest and for speaking engagements. He opened the new Cheshire Home at Spalding in Lincolnshire; he addressed the conference of the National Association of Justices' Clerks' Assistants on the role of a judge; he spoke in September, at the Law Society's Conference at Harrogate. He accepted an invitation to become Chairman of the Quarter Sessions for East Sussex, sitting about five days in the long vacation and two or three in other vacations. 'It enabled me to keep in touch with the criminal law – to sum up to juries – and to sentence prisoners. But best of all – to sit with the magistrates of the county – to have the benefit of their advice – to lunch with them at the lodgings – to get to know them.'[1] Almost always in these activities, Joan was his companion and his driver. Work may expand to fill the time available for its completion, as the political economist C. Northcote Parkinson wrote in *Parkinson's Law*, but Tom had the gift of making elastic the time which he could fill with work.

Tom did not, as Geoffrey Cheshire always hoped he would, write a book on the law. His published work, whether collections of his speeches or, later, specially commissioned books, was addressed to a general public – if one that was interested in law – rather than to scholars; only his occasional articles for the *Law Quarterly Review* indicate what might have been.

A question mark hung over Denning's future in a House of Lords dominated by Chancery lawyers. Though Simonds was no longer Lord Chancellor he still played an important part and, as John Beaumont had predicted, Denning was soon engaged in a tussle with Simonds. In July, Simonds presided over a court comprising Lords Reid, Cohen, Somervell of Harrow and Denning, to hear an important case in international law, *Rahimtoola* v. *Nizam of*

Hyderabad. In September 1948, when Indian troops were invading Hyderabad, more than £1 million was in the account of the Nizam and his government in an English bank. Without authority from the Nizam, one of the men entitled to operate the account transferred the fund into the name of the High Commissioner for Pakistan, who accepted the money on the instructions of his government. When the bank received conflicting instructions from the Nizam and from Pakistan, it refused to admit either claim until the court decided the rights of the parties. The question that reached the Lords was whether Pakistan could claim sovereign immunity from action in the court. Tom considered the precedents were out of date. 'During the long vacation – on the Helford River – I spent much time on the case. I came to the conclusion that, when sovereign states engaged in commercial transactions, they should not be entitled to claim immunity.'[24] In this, his first case in the House (he had sat previously only in Privy Council appeals) Denning dissented; his judgment referred to questions and authorities not mentioned by counsel. Simonds rebuked him and the other lords agreed. In *Rahimtoola*, Denning was, as often, ahead of his time. Twenty years later, his view was given statutory effect, in the State Immunity Act 1978 – but, before that, a differently constituted House of Lords had approved Denning's view that states engaging in commerce could not claim immunity in respect of their transactions.

In May 1958 Denning dissented again over an important constitutional question but, this time, Simonds, supported by Goddard, Reid, Radcliffe and Somervell, refused even to permit Denning's memorandum of dissent to be noted in their judgment. The single speech was delivered by Simonds and appeared to be unanimous. The facts were not in dispute.

On 8 February 1957, George Strauss, MP wrote a letter, on House of Commons paper, to the Paymaster-General, Reginald Maudling, complaining that the London Electricity Board were disposing of scrap metal at too low a price. Maudling passed the letter to the Board, who said the complaints were unfounded and asked Strauss to withdraw them. He withdrew any imputation of dishonesty but maintained that the Board's conduct amounted to obstinacy and folly. On 4 March 1957 the Board's solicitor wrote to Strauss. 'Your letter is wholly unsatisfactory and we are instituting proceedings which we expect to serve upon you during the course of next week.'

Since the Bill of Rights says that 'the freedom of speech, and debates or proceedings in Parliament, ought not to be impeached or questioned in any court or place out of Parliament', Strauss complained that the solicitor's letter was a breach of parliamentary privilege and that the Board and its solicitors were punishable by the House of Commons. Though the Commons' Committee of Privileges decided that correspondence between an MP and a Minister was a 'proceeding in Parliament', the House itself, by a narrow majority decided that it was not. The Attorney-General, Sir Reginald Manningham-Buller, secured the agreement of the Committee and of the House to refer to the Judicial Committee of the Privy Council this question: whether the House would be acting contrary to the Parliamentary Privilege Act 1770 if it treated the issue of a writ against a Member of Parliament in respect of a speech or proceeding in Parliament as a breach of its privileges.

Seven law lords, headed by Lord Simonds, sat to consider the matter. 'I found myself in a minority of one,' Denning wrote in *The Family Story*. Six of them 'avoided any direct ruling. They held that the House of Commons could treat the issue of a writ against a Member of Parliament – in respect of a speech or proceedings in Parliament – as a breach of its privileges. I thought otherwise. I prepared a memorandum of dissent. I held that every Englishman had a right to seek redress in the Courts of Law without interference by the House of Commons . . .' Denning 'took great pains' with his memorandum and asked that it should be published as a dissenting opinion, or that the report of the Privy Council should state that there was one dissentient. The other six would not agree and the published law report – re the *Parliamentary Privilege Act 1770* – gives an impression of unanimity. In 1985 Denning supplied his papers to G. F. Lock, a member of the Study of Parliament Group, for an article on 'Parliamentary Privilege and the Courts: the Avoidance of Conflict in Public Law'. Lock published Denning's memorandum as an appendix to his article and it could at last be seen that, after considering the effect of the Bill of Rights and the 1770 Act, Denning concluded:

In short, the Bill of Rights is directed to the courts of law. It directs them not to question proceedings in Parliament. The Parliamentary Privilege Act 1770 is directed to the two Houses of Parliament. It directs them not to seek to impeach or delay actions in the courts. If each of these two – Parliament and the courts – obeys these mandates, there will be no conflict. The right of every Englishman to seek redress in the courts of law is preserved inviolate without interference by the House of Commons. The right of Members of Parliament to freedom of speech is preserved intact because the courts will refuse to entertain an action which questions it.

When Denning ended: 'I would, therefore, answer the question; "Yes, the House of Commons would be acting contrary to the 1770 Act," ' he must have sorely tried the patience of his more senior brother-judges. As concerned as they to uphold the power of the state, where he perceived a threat to it from any source, he saw in this case no danger to the state but only an attempt by members of parliament to exercise repressive influence on the common people. He looked, as always, to the courts to preserve the proper balance between the interests.

The dissent in re the Parliamentary Privilege Act is no more surprising than that in Rahimtoola, taking into account the views that Denning expressly made clear in his judicial and extra-judicial utterances. Indeed, it had become possible for Denning-watchers to anticipate the line he would take on many issues, though not the paths he would follow to reach his desired conclusion.

'To go from the Court of Appeal,' Tom wrote in The Family Story, 'is rather like going into retirement.' Yet he did not feel in the least like retiring. He was only 58. 'As active as ever. No shrunk shank. No childish treble.'[1] He took on, as he described it, a new role: no longer only a judge, but also a legislator; though, by convention, he would not speak or vote on matters involving party politics. He did not speak at all in the Legislative Chamber for several months.

He started his maiden speech at 4.00 pm on 27 November 1957, when the Lords were considering a report on Administrative Tribunals, a subject on which he had many times commented, judicially and in his lectures.

My Lords, it has been my lot as a Judge to review the decisions of many tribunals, and may I say how welcome it is that this important Report should be accepted by all Parties in the State, because it contains and reaffirms a constitutional principle of the first importance – namely, that these tribunals are not part of the administrative machinery of government under the control of Departments; they are part of the judicial system of the land under the rule of law.

Giving examples from his experience, Denning stressed the importance of allowing an appeal from a tribunal to the courts on any point of law. He ended by paying tribute to the laymen who, for a great part, make up tribunals: 'Do not think that it is necessary to replace all of them by lawyers. A good layman on a tribunal is better than a bad lawyer – and there are not enough good lawyers to go around.'

He was always nervous before he spoke. 'The other peers were among the most accomplished and able men of the time. You are not supposed to read your speech: but you can use notes. You must prepare beforehand what you are to say – otherwise you will muff it. I always prepared carefully. I did research. I made notes. I tried always to introduce some little story or incident – so as to give colour to my arguments. But when I got up to speak, I put my notes aside. I did not look at them. I trusted to my memory.'[1] His maiden speech lasted a little under twenty minutes.

Harold Macmillan had replaced Anthony Eden as Prime Minister in January 1957. Years of austerity behind them, the British were enjoying a period when the Prime Minister would soon tell them: 'Most of our people have never had it so good.' In the Fifties, the young had stepped out of the shadow of their elders; a distinct youth culture was emerging, with different clothes, different music, different ways of spending their leisure. Full employment and good wages put money in the pockets of teenagers and businesses began to cater specially for their needs. To a large extent the new culture crossed the old class barriers. Not only was there a more relaxed attitude to marriage and divorce but, among large sections of the population, there was a generally more permissive attitude. In September 1957 the Committee on Homosexual Offences and Prostitution, chaired by Sir John Wolfenden, Vice Chancellor of Reading University, proposed that homosexual acts in private between consenting men over the age of 21 should cease to be a criminal offence. In the debate on Homosexual Offences and Prostitution, on 4 December 1957, Denning spoke again:

> The principles, as I understand them, under which the judges originally made this full offence a criminal offence . . . are these: first, the essential feature of a criminal offence is that it is wrongful, morally reprehensible, so that in the minds of right-thinking people it is disapproved of; secondly, it should be harmful – that is to say, it should strike at the safety or the well-being of the society at large; and thirdly, it should be fit to be punished . . .
>
> It is said that adultery and fornication are not criminal offences, so why should homosexuality be? The law answers that natural sin is different from unnatural vice. Natural sin is deplorable, but unnatural vice is worse . . .

After reference to cases of bestiality, incest, sadism, and to sterilisation, abortion and suicide – 'all within our calender of crimes', Denning came to what was, for him, the nub of the matter: 'they strike at the continuance and the integrity of the human race and that is why they are put in a different category from adultery or fornication.' Denning had no doubt that homosexuality was wrongful. The Bible called it 'an abomination', and 'it was an offence not to be named among Christians.' But its harmfulness, he thought, might 'vary infinitely in gradation.' He recommended that the law should continue to condemn 'this evil for the evil it is', but that judges should be 'discreet in their punishment of it.' As in so many things, Tom was content to leave to the judges the balance between justice and mercy. By the judges he meant himself. Combining in his person an unusual mix of benevolence and severity, of intolerance and paternalism, of austerity and great warmth, Tom was satisfied that in each case along that infinity of gradation, he would know what to do.

Though Tom was troubled by the permissiveness that he saw as a threat to stable home-life and intolerant of some of its manifestations, he had no difficulty in relating to young people; he warmed to them and their interests and enthusiasms and, in return, they gave him their admiration and affection. A visit by Lord Denning to Cumberland Lodge or to a student society attracted a full house. It was not only that they enjoyed his formal speech, with its peppering of well-loved anecdotes and quotations, but that, afterwards, he would sit or stand and talk with them, apparently regardless of time, listening – really listening – to their ideas, their hopes for the future and their problems. What is more, they could count on his remembering them, perhaps several years later, when their paths crossed again.

Before he reached the House of Lords, Denning had little experience of Revenue work. He had no difficulty in coming to grips with the complex legislation and the appeal in *Escoigne Properties* v. *IRC* in November 1957 was memorable for Denning's analysis of the method that should be applied in statutory interpretation. Mindful of the scorn that had been poured by Lord Simonds on his words in *Seaford Court Estates*, Denning put his view carefully:

A statute is not passed in a vacuum, but in a framework of circumstances, so as to give a remedy for a known state of affairs. To arrive at its true meaning you should know the circumstances with reference to which the words were used; and what was the object, appearing from those circumstances, which Parliament had in view ... But how are the courts to know what were the circumstances to which the words were used? and what was the object which Parliament had in view? ... In this country we do not refer to the legislative history of an enactment ... We do not look at the explanatory memoranda which preface the Bills before Parliament ... We do not have recourse to the pages of Hansard. All that the courts can do is to take judicial notice of the previous state of the law and of other matters generally known to well-informed people. Thus one of the best ways, I find, of understanding a statute is to take some specific instances which, by common consent, are intended to be covered by it ... I often cannot understand it by simply reading through it. But when an instance is given it becomes plain. I can say at once: 'Yes, that is the sort of thing Parliament intended to cover.'

The following month, Denning sat in the Court of Appeal, to hear, with Hodson and Morris, an important appeal on the validity of conditions in planning permissions. His approach to planning was to prevent any abuse of power by ministers or officials and to hold a balance between public and private rights. He generally required the countryside to be preserved but permitted development in towns and refused to allow ministers and officials to place unnecessary obstacles in its way. This case concerned a tripartite agreement between Pyx Granite, a quarrying company, the Malvern Conservators and the Malvern Council, in which the company gave up quarrying rights on a certain area of land and the Conservators agreed that the company's rights to quarry other land should be undisturbed. Subsequently, the Ministry refused the company permission to quarry in parts of the agreed area and imposed conditions for quarrying in other parts; the company sought declarations to the effect that the Minister's exercise of his powers was invalid. Though the Minister denied that the court had jurisdiction to grant the declarations, the judge found in favour of the company. On appeal the Minister repeated his claim that the court had no authority to grant declarations since the Town and Country Planning Act 1947 provided that the Minister's decision was final. This was not a response calculated to arouse Lord Denning's sympathy.

The three members of the Court of Appeal were not in agreement about the remedies available: Hodson dissented from one arm of the judgment and Morris from another. 'I take it to be settled law,' Denning said, 'that the jurisdiction of the High Court to grant a declaration is not to be taken away except by clear words.' He went on to provide a definition, that would be often quoted, of the circumstances in which conditions can be attached to planning permission:

Although the planning authorities are given very wide powers to impose 'such conditions as they think fit,' nevertheless the law says that these conditions, to be valid, must fairly and reasonably relate to the permitted development. The planning authority are not at liberty to use their powers for an ulterior object, however desirable that object may seem to them to be in the public interest.

When the case reached the Lords, in May 1959, the decision of the Court of Appeal was overturned on the grounds that, in the particular circumstances, planning permission was not required by Pyx Granite and it was not, therefore, necessary to consider whether the conditions the Minister had sought to impose were valid. On this occasion Simonds endorsed Denning's view that the jurisdiction of the court to grant a declaration was 'not by any means to be whittled down.'

Early in 1958 Tom began to plan the journey he proposed to make in the long vacation. He was invited to speak at a legal conference in celebration of the tenth anniversary of the new State of Israel; he was also asked to visit Poland for a legal meeting in Warsaw. He and Joan wanted Robert to come with them but Robert was still in Libya. In February 1958 he wrote to tell Joan that the 'biscuits and cakes & nuts & things' she had sent him had been used for tea in the mess. 'Daddy seems very clever,' he said, 'at fixing up jaunts. Warsaw sounds very interesting.' There was a good chance that Robert would get leave to go with them, since his National Service would be over in time to go up to Oxford in the autumn. The difficulty was Warsaw – there was a problem about a serving officer going behind the Iron Curtain. Meantime Tom took a last opportunity to tempt his son into the law, sending him two books, *Learning the Law* and *The Machinery of Justice in England*. 'I can see where the fascinating [sic] lies but it does not arouse any interest at all,' Robert wrote. 'Science, however, does.' Thereafter Tom accepted gracefully that his son's chosen field of work was different from his own.

The summer progressed and, three weeks before the journey was due to start, Robert had still not obtained leave. Urgent letters passed between Cuckfield and Libya. Robert even began to think he might need some 'judicious help' from Reg. At length, on Thursday 7 August, Tom and Joan travelled overland to Marseilles, where they sailed on an Israeli ship, picking up Robert in Naples, and reaching Haifa on 12 August. As guests of the Israeli government, they were taken to the King David Hotel in Jerusalem, where their bedroom window looked out upon the no-man's-land between Israel and Jordan and the wall of the Old City beyond. They were shown the country's irrigation schemes, the orange groves, the kibbutz settlements and the new campus being built to replace university buildings that were now on the Jordanian side of divided Jerusalem. Visiting the Hulu Valley, Joan saw crops growing where her first husband had cleared the swamps. They crossed the border for one night to visit the Old City and Bethlehem.

It was very hot during their stay and Tom suffered more than Joan from the heat. Though Robert swam, Tom and Joan were put off by the sticky, black oil polluting the beach. Nor did they try to bathe with Robert in the Dead Sea, its water so full of salts that no one could sink. As they sailed from Haifa they passed the oil storage tanks, whose foundations had been reinforced by Joan's first husband. At Venice, where John Stuart joined them, Joan would have liked to spend time exploring the city and its museums, but the men wanted more action. They hired a car and drove through the Dolomites to Bolzano and Cortona. At Turin John flew home and the rest of the family returned to Venice, where news reached them that Hazel Fox had given birth, on 28 August, to a second son. From Venice they went by train to Vienna, with time for only a brief look round and a light meal before taking another train for Warsaw. The reality of life behind the Iron Curtain soon dawned upon them. Their passports were brusquely taken away when they reached the Czechoslovak border. They settled down for the night and, next morning, asked for the restaurant car indicated in the railway time-table. They found that no food or drink were to be bought on the train. At midday the train stopped but there was a heavy wire fence between the train and the platform. At the Polish border there was another halt but no-one was allowed off the train. The family were hungry and felt helpless without their British passports; they asked the attendant whether he would buy them some food but he said he was not permitted to take money from passengers. Finally he gave them some hard plums and stale bread, though he still refused to take any money. They were relieved to reach Warsaw and get off the train, secretly slipping some Polish money into the attendant's hand.

At the hotel Tom gave their names: Lord and Lady Denning. A clerk told them the booking was in the names of Mr and Mrs Denning and they were taken to the special floor reserved for foreign guests which, they discovered, was electronically bugged. The Polish lawyers were welcoming but cautious. While Tom attended the conference, Joan, closely followed, wandered to the University, and tried to talk to the students in French. The atmosphere so depressed them that, though they had booked to return home by sea from Gdansk, they decided to travel by air. It was their first flight and they were a little nervous but, as the 'plane took off, they felt a surge of relief and a profound sense of gratitude to live in a free country.

On their return, Robert went up to Oxford – to Magdalen, Tom's own college – and Tom and Joan resumed their usual round of activities: a visit to a Parish Council in Huntingdonshire; the opening of a new ward in the Cheshire home at Bromley; attendance at the service in Westminster Abbey to mark the start of the new legal term. Joan also had the joy of seeing her new grandson.

In September 1958, while he was on holiday in Switzerland, Tom heard that Hubert Parker, with whom, a year earlier, he had discussed his own chances of becoming either Lord Chief Justice or Master of the Rolls, had been appointed to the former office, on the resignation of Lord Goddard. Since Parker was a year younger than Denning, and Raymond Evershed, the Master of the Rolls, was also a few months Tom's junior, the likelihood of Tom now obtaining either office seemed diminished. Though he was of a cheerful and optimistic disposition, he felt momentarily disheartened. It had been generally expected that the Attorney-General would get the appointment but, after an attack on Manningham-Buller in *The Times*, Tom thought he might himself have 'a vague chance'. Recalling the event in 1992, he commented: 'Of course, at that time Gavin Simonds would be about and when they were taking soundings I'm quite sure they would say "Denning's not sound enough." Also Hubert Parker had been Treasury Junior and he'd know the government side. I am afraid when it's an important appointment they think "he knows the government side".'

Tom was disappointed. He knew already that he did not find the work of a law lord as enjoyable as that in the Court of Appeal. Rarely did he hear about the problems of ordinary men and women that so much interested him. The parties to cases at the elevated level of the House of Lords were usually large companies, trustees, or the Inland Revenue. The judgment of their Lordships was always reserved and sometimes delivered in one speech, as in the matter of the Parliamentary Privilege Act, a practice of which Tom did not approve. In his own speeches, he usually tried, however technical the legal question involved, to reduce it to human terms and language that was readily understood. In a matter relating to rates and the meaning of the terms 'industrial hereditament', Denning began simply: 'My

Lords, the question whether premises are a "workshop" depends, to my mind, on the nature of the work that is carried out therein.' (*Hudson's Bay Co.* v. *Thompson*). While in *Barclays Bank Ltd* v. *Inland Revenue Commissioners* where, Lord Simonds told the court, 'this appeal once more demands your Lordships' consideration of section 55 and section 58 of the Finance Act 1940', Denning said: 'My Lords, Tom Shipside died on December 15 1955. The question is whether, during the last five years before his death, he "had the control of" a company called T. Shipside Ltd: for the amount of estate duty depends on it.'

Not only did Denning find the work less interesting but also, in a five-man House of Lords, he felt, there was less chance of his view of a matter being adopted. Nor was there much purpose in dissenting: a dissentient view in the Court of Appeal might have some influence on deliberations in the Lords but a decision in the Lords was final. Above all, Denning still chafed under the doctrine of *stare decisis*. He believed it to be the ultimate folly that the Lords, the final appeal court, should hold themselves bound by their own earlier decisions. On 21 May 1959, delivering the Romanes lecture in the Sheldonian Theatre, at Oxford, Tom put forward the proposal that the House of Lords should not be bound by a precedent that was clearly wrong:

This land of ours, this England, has been spoken of by the poet as the land where –

A man may speak the thing he will;
A land of settled government,
A land of just and old renown.
Where Freedom broadens slowly down
From precedent to precedent.

Some lawyers take pride in those words of Lord Tennyson, 'from precedent to precedent.' They think he gives the impress of a noble mind to the doctrine of *stare decisis* which, according to their interpretation, means: 'Stand by your decisions and the decisions of your predecessors, however wrong they are and whatever injustice they inflict.' But I take leave to point out that, so interpreted, the doctrine of precedent does nothing to *broaden* the basis of freedom, rather to *narrow* it. If lawyers hold to their precedents too closely, forgetful of the fundamental principles of truth and justice which they should serve, they may find the whole edifice come tumbling down about them . . . The common law will cease to grow. Like a coral reef it will become a structure of fossils.

It was not until 1966 that a more progressive Chancellor and a House of Lords from which Simonds had retired took the step that Denning had long advocated. Holding those views in 1959, Tom could not have been an easy colleague for the conservative lords of his day. Hard as he found it to be a minority of one, they were made uneasy – and sometimes alarmed – by Denning pronouncements, judicial and extra-judicial.

16

Ambassador at Large

In 1958 there were two bodies working in the sphere of comparative law: the Society of Comparative Legislation, of which Tom was Chairman, and the Grotius Society, founded by lawyers in the Foreign Office. Six years earlier Tom had told the annual general meeting of the SCL that one centre was needed for all those interested in the subject: an institution that would become a source of information on foreign laws for British business and industry and a source of information on British law and practice for lawyers overseas. In 1958 it was finally agreed to merge the SCL and the Grotius Society.

The British Institute of International and Comparative Law was incorporated in November 1958 and, at a meeting held on 16 December 1958, Tom was elected Chairman of the Council 'until the first annual general meeting.' He remained Chairman for the next 28 years, retiring in March 1986 after playing a key role in the Institute's administration and finance. As with the Cheshire Trust, so with the British Institute, Tom's diplomatic skills were as valuable as his firm grasp of affairs and his ability to obtain finance for his pet projects. With the help of Lord Nathan, Tom obtained from the Isaac Wolfson Foundation a grant of £60,000, which gave the Institute an encouraging start. Later, he was introduced to businessmen Barnett Shine and Charles Clore, who also became generous benefactors.

In November 1958 Tom and Joan made a quick journey to New York for the centennial celebrations of the Columbia Law School. They spent Christmas at home with their family, before setting off again, this time for India, under the auspices of the British Council. From Delhi, they went by car to Dehra Dun, to visit Leonard Cheshire's first home in India. It was Tom's first experience of Asia. On the 200-mile journey he was astonished by the noise, the milling crowds and the strong smells of spicy food in the air. During the night Joan was roused by the sound of Tom having a nightmare induced by the unusual scenes he had witnessed. The following morning they saw another aspect of India that moved them to compassion: disabled young residents at the Home, abandoned to die in the streets and surviving only because they were rescued by its staff. Returning to Delhi was to move back into the world to which they were more accustomed. Tom was the principal speaker at an International Congress of Jurists. During the course of the discussions he was struck by the thought that his view of the rule of law, based on its development in England over hundreds of years, required some revision. 'When I came to this Congress,' he told a plenary session on 9 January 1959, 'I thought of the rule of law as being essentially concerned with protection of the individual from arbitrary power.' After listening to the concerns of speakers from emergent Asian and African nations, about such basic needs as efficient and uncorrupt government, a democratic legislature and an independent judiciary, he realised that the rule of law was wider than he thought: it placed on governments a positive duty 'to act for the welfare of their people.'

Four years after the first of Tom's many honorary doctorates of law was presented at Ottawa, a second was awarded, on 17 June 1959, at Glasgow. Dressed in an academic gown of scarlet cloth, faced with Venetian red silk, and academic hood to match, Denning was presented to Glasgow University's Chancellor, Lord Boyd Orr, by David Maxwell Walker, the Regius Professor of Law. In his customary recital of the distinguished recipient's achievements, Professor Walker summarised Denning's career:

The career of Alfred Thompson Denning has been distinguished both on the academic and on the professional side of the law . . . he was Eldon Law Scholar at Oxford, edited *Smith's Leading Cases* and Bullen and Leake's *Precedents of Pleadings* . . . he is now an Honorary Fellow of Magdalen, President of Birkbeck College and Chairman of the Council of the recently formed British Institute of International and Comparative Law . . . his published lectures, such as *Freedom Under the Law*, have won wide acclamation . . . he has delivered many outstanding judgments, constantly showing concern for substantial justice, and impatience with the law's delays and with outmoded or purely technical rules which might defeat justice between man and man. He is a self-confessed iconoclast ... who once criticised those 'timorous souls', his brethren of the Court of Appeal, for their subservience to precedent, who has called for a 'new equity' to free the law from the shackles of antiquated principles and doubtful precedents, and has shown himself determined to make law an effective instrument of justice in society.

Gracefully, Professor Walker referred also to the problems raised by some of Denning's judgments, continuing:

Sometimes, however, for one who is an Honorary Member of the Society of Public Teachers of Law, he has by his independence of thought and bold re-interpretation of precedents, caused distress to the ordinary members of that body, who have to justify such heresies to their students.

For some time, Tom had been alive to the urgent necessity to educate African students to take over the administration of justice when their states became independent. In *Nyali Ltd* v. *Attorney General*, a case relating to a pontoon bridge in Kenya, he recognised that the common law could not be applied in foreign lands without considerable qualification: 'Just as with an English Oak, so with the English common law. You cannot transplant it to the African continent and expect it to retain the tough character which it has in England. It will flourish indeed, but it needs careful handling.' A bewildering patchwork of Islamic, Roman-Dutch, English and customary tribal law complicated the systems of most territories. At the end of December 1959 Denning chaired a conference on the future of law in Africa. In his opening address he suggested that the Judicial Committee of the Privy Council should be broadened to include experts in customary law; that the Committee should not always sit in London but, as the judges of England went on circuit, so the Committee, reinforced by African members, should hold sessions in the African capitals. The conference bore fruit: in the summer of 1960 Denning was offered and accepted the chairmanship of a Committee on Legal Education for Students in Africa.

In June 1960 he flew out to inaugurate the Sierra Leone and Gambia Appeal Court in Freetown. The Dennings were met at the airport by a large delegation and taken to Government House, where they were to stay. As Tom had been asked to bring his robes, they had economised on other baggage and found themselves unprepared for the formality with which they were entertained. Unperturbed by his lack of evening clothes, Tom outshone the company at the ball in their honour, resplendent in his court dress, complete with ruffles and knee breeches. Though Joan could not match the formal gown and tiara of her hostess, she charmed the gathering in her, then fashionable, three-quarter-length dress.

In August they were back in Africa again, going first to Lagos and all the regions of Nigeria and moving on, in September, to Uganda, Kenya, Tanganyika and Zanzibar. In each country Tom held discussions with judges, law officers and practitioners and visited courts of every kind. He became increasingly troubled that the African countries were approaching independence with so few trained lawyers to take over from the British.

On their return to England, the work of Tom's Committee – which included his old friend Arthur Grattan Bellew – began in earnest. By January 1961 the Committee reported to the Lord Chancellor urging the need to train Africans to take their proper part in the administration of justice. 'I am glad to say,' Tom commented in *The Family Story*, 'that our recommendations were for the most part accepted.'

The unanimous decision of the Lords, including Denning, in *DPP* v. *Smith*, attracted considerable criticism. The case was one of murder. In March 1960, John Smith was driving a Ford Prefect through Woolwich with a man named Artus. In the boot and back of the car they had sacks of scaffolding clips that they had just stolen. While the car was stopped by a policeman on traffic duty, a police constable, Leslie Meehan, who was on friendly terms with Smith, came up to speak to him and caught sight of what was in the car. Meehan told Smith that when the traffic was able to move forward he should pull into the side of the road. Smith started to do so, with Meehan walking beside him, then suddenly accelerated. Meehan began to run, grasping the side of the car and shouting to the officer on traffic duty to call the police station. Smith started to zig-zag and, eventually, Meehan was thrown off the car and fell under a bubble car coming in the opposite direction. He died from his injuries.

Smith drove off and, with Artus, disposed of the sacks before returning to the place where Meehan had fallen. A police constable gave evidence at his trial that Smith asked 'Is he dead? I knew the man. I wouldn't do that for the world. I only wanted to shake him off.' Smith himself said that he was 'scared' and 'frightened'. The defence claimed that Smith had no intention to harm the constable but the prosecution's case was that intention to cause grievous bodily harm ought to be inferred from Smith's conduct.

At the Old Bailey, on 7 April 1960, Smith was convicted of the murder of Meehan. He appealed on the ground that the trial judge had misdirected the jury on the effect of a rule that a person is presumed to intend the natural and probable consequences of his acts. The Court of Criminal Appeal, on 8 May, substituted a verdict of manslaughter for the verdict of murder. At the time, this was the difference between life and death: hanging was still the mandatory penalty for murder. The Crown appealed to the House of Lords and a strong court was assembled. Lord Kilmuir, the Lord Chancellor, presided and both Lord Goddard, the previous Lord Chief Justice, and Lord Parker, his successor, took part. The other members of the tribunal were Tucker and Denning. Smith's counsel argued that though there is a presumption that a man intends the natural and probable consequences of his acts, the trial judge had misdirected the jury in telling them that the presumption *must* be accepted. He referred the Lords to Denning's 1945 article on Presumptions and Burdens in the *Law Quarterly Review*. The reference was no more successful with their Lordships than the rest of his argument. The conviction of murder was restored, which meant that, unless he was reprieved, Smith would hang.

In general, no act is considered a crime unless it was committed with a guilty mind (*mens rea*). Academics and practising lawyers criticised the *Smith* decision, which seemed to change the meaning of *mens rea* in murder and accept that it was enough for the Crown to prove a reasonable man would have contemplated that serious bodily harm would result from his actions, rather than that the accused man would have contemplated it. An objective test appeared to have been substituted for a subjective one. In the words of the trial judge: 'If in doing what he did, he must as a reasonable man have contemplated that serious harm was likely to occur, then he was guilty of murder.' Though Smith was reprieved, the attack did not abate. Tom himself tried to answer the criticism in January 1961, when he returned to Israel to give a lecture at the Hebrew University of Jerusalem on 'Responsibility Before the Law'.

First he gave the facts of the *Smith* case, as they were given above. That, he said is how they were described in the headnotes of the law reports and that is how they were stated by the academics who had criticised the decision. 'Now if the facts had been as there stated,' he continued, 'I should have thought the jury would have found Smith not guilty of murder but guilty of manslaughter only . . .' Referring to the words of an academic, he continued:

> The Professor says: 'Smith zig-zagged to shake him off and eventually succeeded.' The facts, as I understood them, were that the zig-zag did not succeed in shaking him off. The policeman had too firm a grip for that. He was stretched across the bonnet and banging on the window to tell Smith to stop. So what did Smith do? He drove his car right up close to the approaching traffic so that the policeman's body was struck up against the oncoming cars. Each of the drivers of those cars gave evidence. No one of them spoke of any zig-zagging at the time he was hitting them. They spoke of the car coming at them and swerving towards them. The policeman's body was struck against one car after another . . .

Denning suggested that the criticism of the Lords' decision was because the facts had not been sufficiently understood. 'Murder,' he said, 'is unlawful killing with malice aforethought express or applied. But malice aforethought need only be an instant before. And malice is held to exist if a man has an intent to kill or to do grievous bodily harm.' On the facts he had recited there was no doubt in Denning's mind that Smith had such intention. And, he said 'intent' is very different from 'desire': 'A man may be guilty of murder even though he has no desire to kill or inflict bodily harm.'

At the end of a lengthy and detailed consideration of cases, Denning concluded:

Whence comes, then, all this criticism from some of the most respected figures in the academic world? It cannot all be entirely beside the mark, I agree. May it perhaps be that in stressing the test of the reasonable man, that is, the responsible man, the House did not sufficiently point out that it was only a test – a criterion – to help find the intention of the accused man himself: and that ultimately the question is: Did he intend to cause death or grievous bodily harm . . .? It is still, as before, the essential element of which the jury must be satisfied before they convict of murder.

Whether or not the critics read Tom's speech, they remained unsatisfied. In order to restore the position unequivocally to what it had been before *DPP* v. *Smith*, a section was included in the Criminal Justice Act 1967.

In 1959 John Stuart had married Veronica Toas in Harrogate. Only Robert, who had been best man, was now unmarried and much of the time he was away. Fair Close began to seem just a little empty, when none of the family was at home.

In 1960 Marjorie told Tom that The Lawn, the Regency house opposite The Hermitage where, in their youth, the Devenish family had lived, might be up for sale. During the war the Bank of England had bought the house in order to evacuate staff. Later it had become an officers' mess and was still occupied by the army. On a visit to Whitchurch, Tom and Joan were invited to drinks in the mess and, sitting on the terrace, facing the lovely stretch of the River Test, thought how pleasant it would be to live there. The idea of a return to his birthplace appealed to Tom. Though his home had been in Cuckfield for many years, still he felt a Hampshire man; he had chosen to become Lord Denning of Whitchurch and, though the family connection with the area went back only to his father, Tom's roots, he felt, were in the place.

There was much to consider. The house was in very poor condition and a great deal of work would have to be done before it could again be habitable as a private home. What was more, a return to Whitchurch to live at The Lawn would be very different from living above the draper's shop in Newbury Street or even – as Tom had done for brief periods – living with his parents at The Hermitage. His home would be the house where he and his friends at the National School had never been allowed, as children, to set foot.

Above all there was the question of whether Tom and Joan wanted to give up their home of many years. They loved Fair Close, but were finding it increasingly difficult to get help in the house. They were far from the village while, at The Lawn, they would be almost opposite the church and within an easy walk of the shops and – important as they were growing older – the doctor. They decided, after much deliberation, to take the plunge.

Tom found that the Bank of England was prepared to sell, subject to the tail-end of a lease to the War Department, for £7,000. There was still the question of when the War Department might be prepared to give possession and how much all the work would cost. Anthony Moir introduced W. T. Bishop, a chartered surveyor and senior partner of the firm Drivers Jonas, who started negotiations for dilapidations with the War Department. An estimate was obtained from Hilliers of the cost of restoring the gardens and grounds.

It was decided that the purchase should be made by Joan and Anthony Moir, as trustees of a settlement that had been long established for Robert, and that Tom should take a tenancy at a rack rent. At completion, with the deeds the purchaser received a much-mended, nearly hundred-year-old copy, held together with transparent tape, of the Particulars and Conditions of Sale of 'a Freehold Family Residence standing in delightful Grounds and Land, upward of Five Acres, known as "The Lawn", Whitchurch. Which will be sold by Auction on Wednesday, October 14th 1868 at One o'clock precisely.' Tom clearly recollected the Devenishes from his childhood, but here, in his hands, he held particulars of the sale of the house 30 years before he was born:

> This very delightful Property stands close to the Church and to the entrance of Lord Portsmouth's Park, is less than a mile from the Railway Station, and within two hours journey of London, presenting to a City Gentleman and others the opportunity of securing a Retreat of an unusually eligible character, with Hunting, Shooting and Fishing in its immediate vicinity.

Much of the description held good, though the occupation of the house as a Bank of England hostel and an officers' mess had severely damaged large parts of the structure and the gardens were sadly overrun. It was 18 July 1961 when Colonel Purcell wrote from the Regimental Pay Office of the Royal Engineers that the army would be out on 1 August. Tom instructed an architect to prepare plans for the demolition of part of the structure and the rehabilitation of the rest. Planning what to do with the house you have just bought is the delightful prelude to the inevitable series of delays and small catastrophes that will spoil the doing of it. Tom and Joan spent a number of pleasant weekends at The Portsmouth Arms at Hurstbourne Priors, wandering about the house and grounds of The Lawn, visualising the way they would restore the worn, but still beautiful small estate.

Tom began to add to the land owned by Robert's settlement. At Joan's suggestion they acquired the meadow on the opposite bank of the river to enhance and protect the view from all the principal rooms of the house. They would have liked to buy the cricket field, on their side of the river, from the St Cross Hospice, its owners for hundreds of years but, as St Cross were not prepared to sell, Tom took a lease of the land with the pavilion on it.

The old granary in Parsonage Meadows had become so dilapidated that the Planning Committee had agreed that it might be pulled down. Instead, Tom determined to restore it. Though he was far from ready to move to The Lawn, he began to play a part in Whitchurch affairs, if not as 'Lord of the Manor' – a role reserved for the occupant of The Park – then as a considerable local figure. John Clarke, the local solicitor and chairman of the Whitchurch Chamber of Trade, asked Tom's help. After reading about the Civic Trust experiment in Norwich, the Chamber thought that 'something similar' could be done in Whitchurch and that £500 would enable them to instruct an architect to draw up conservation plans; Tom was invited to become President and Chairman and to co-ordinate the interested parties. The idea of conservation greatly attracted him but he thought he might not be able to do much 'until I get to Whitchurch to live which may not be for a few months yet' (an optimistic estimate!).

Meantime he had to decide what to do in Cuckfield. He and Joan considered many ideas, including seeking planning permission to build on the field adjacent to their home, and letting Fair Close furnished. In the end, Fair Close was sold but Tom retained about 15 acres of land he had, over the years, added to his original purchase: a field and a plantation of trees.

In March 1960, Denning sat seven days in a strong House of Lords, with Simonds, Reid, Radcliffe and Morris, to hear an appeal involving conflict of laws and a debt expressed in foreign currency. In the voluntary liquidation of United Railways of Havana and Regla Warehouses Ltd a proof of debt was lodged, in June 1954, by a trust company and rejected by the liquidators. The questions at issue were whether any proof of debt should be admitted and, if so, for what amount.

The circumstances in which the claim arose were exceedingly complicated, arising out of a transaction in 1921 when the railway company had raised $6 million from the trust company in the United States to buy railway equipment. 'This was, in effect,' said Denning, in his speech, reducing it to more comprehensible terms, 'a hire-purchase transaction. The railway company was rather like a man who wants to buy a motor-car but has not the means to pay for it.' After examining the course of the transactions that followed, including the sale of the railway to the State of Cuba, where it was situated, Denning concluded that 'the railway company was at all material times under an obligation to pay the rentals to the trust company in full in dollars in the United States of America, together with interest at 6 per cent from the time they became due.'

Since the trust company was suing in the English courts – and 'if there is one thing clear in our law, it is that the claim must be made in sterling and the judgment given in sterling' – the question was at what date should the rate of exchange be taken? Should it be the date when the rentals fell due, or the date of the winding-up? It was settled law dating from a time when sterling was a stable currency, that the conversion rate should be that applying at the date when a debt fell due. But, Denning said, the question was whether the rule should still apply in days when sterling had lost the value it once had, when 'the pound has been devalued; and there has been much inflation.' He recognised the injustice likely to be produced to a creditor, but 'I am afraid that if he chooses to sue in our courts instead of his own, he must put up with the consequences.'

This would not be Denning's last word on the subject. His keen grasp of social and financial realities brought him to appreciate, ahead of many of his contemporaries, that the needs of the state would be better served by a modern attitude to currency than by too-great devotion to outworn rules from the past. Fourteen years after the *Havana* case, when he was back in the Court of Appeal, Denning had the opportunity to rule again on judgment in a foreign currency.

> A German company comes to an English court [he said in *Schorsch Meier GmbH* v. *Hennin*] and asks for judgment – not in English pounds sterling, but, if you please, in German Deutschmarks. The judge offered a sterling judgment. But the German company said 'No. Sterling is no good to us. It has gone down much in value. If we accepted it, we would lose one-third of the debt' . . . It has always been accepted that an English court can only give judgment in sterling . . . It was a stable currency which had no equal. Things are different now. Sterling floats in the wind . . . This change compels us to think again about our rules . . . It was . . . essential that the judgment should be for a sum of money in sterling for otherwise it could not be enforced . . . Seeing that the reasons no longer exist, we are at liberty to discard the rule itself . . . The time has now come when we should say that when the currency of a contract is a foreign currency . . . the English courts have power to give judgment in that foreign currency . . .

Denning led the Court of Appeal in overruling the House of Lords judgment in *Havana* – in which he had himself taken part.

When another case involving foreign currency reached the Lords, Wilberforce observed that the Denning-led Court of Appeal, in *Schorsch*, had been guilty of 'some distortion of the judicial process.' Just the same, the Lords recognised that in the financial climate of the 1970s judgment must be given in the currency of contract: in *Miliangos* v. *Geo Frank* they followed Denning's lead.

Tom let no chance slip past him to chip away at the edifice of precedent or outworn principle. Four months later he attacked a very sacred cow indeed. In legal terms, the *Midland Silicones* case raised the question of privity of contract and in practical terms exposed an apparent gap in commercial law. A drum of chemicals, worth nearly

£600, was sold by an American company to an English company, Midland Silicones Ltd, under a contract that provided the ownership would pass to Midland Silicones while the goods were on board ship. The seller consigned the drum by carrier under a bill of lading which contained terms having the effect of limiting the carrier's liability to less than £200, unless some higher value was declared. The seller gave no such declaration and, so far as the carrier knew, the goods were worth no more than the limitation figure. The carrier contracted with a firm of stevedores, Scruttons Ltd, to discharge their vessels in the Port of London and it was a term of the contract that the stevedores would have 'such protection as is afforded by the terms, conditions and exceptions' of the bill of lading. When the drum was damaged by the negligence of Scruttons, Midland Silicones sued the stevedores for its full value.

Diplock J, the trial judge, a unanimous Court of Appeal and four law lords – Simonds, Reid, Keith and Morris – rejected the stevedores' claim to shelter under the exemption clause in the bill of lading restricting the carrier's liability. Denning stood stubbornly and splendidly alone. While still in the Court of Appeal he had, on several occasions, suggested that there should be an exception to the rule that a person who is not a party to a contract cannot take advantage of the stipulations and conditions that it contains: when the contract is made for the benefit of a third party, he thought, it should be enforceable for the third party's benefit. This so-called 'fundamental' rule, Denning now pointed out, giving chapter and verse, was a discovery of the nineteenth century. At that time, the owner of the goods could not, in any case, have sued the stevedores, since the duty of care arose only out of contract and not as an independent tort of negligence. The owner would have been forced to look for recompense, to the carriers, whose liability would have been limited to £200. Though he knew that he would be a lone voice, Denning said:

> My Lords, I have dealt with the case at some length because it is the first case ever recorded in our English books where the owner of goods has sued a stevedore for negligence. If the owner can, by so doing, escape the exceptions in the contract of carriage and the limitations in the Hague Rules, it will expose a serious gap in our

commercial law ... no longer need you worry about the limitation to £100 or £200 a package. You can recover the value of the most precious package without disclosing its nature or value beforehand. You have only to sue the servants of the carrier for negligence and you can get round all the exceptions and limitations that have hitherto been devised ... But when you find that the carrying company has in the long run to pay for the damage, you see at once that you have turned the flank of the Hague Rules (for carriage by sea) and the Warsaw Convention (for carriage by air) ... For myself, I would not allow this gap to be driven in our commercial law. I would not give the 'fundamental principle' of the nineteenth century a free rein. It should not have unbridled scope to defeat the intentions of business men.

Midland Silicones Ltd perfectly illustrates the gap between Denning's approach and Simonds's. Simonds was no less aware than Denning of the commercial realities involved but, having read Denning's judgment before he delivered the first speech on 6 December, he said:

To me heterodoxy or some might say heresy, is not the more attractive because it is dignified by the name of reform ... The law is developed by the application of old principles to new circumstances. Therein lies its genius. Its reform by the abrogation of those principles is the task not of the courts of law but of Parliament.

It was not too difficult to shrug off Simonds's criticism on the grounds that his approach to law was exceptionally conservative and rigid. Similar objections to Denning's unorthodoxy, later to be voiced by Lord Reid and a younger generation of more liberal law lords, would be more difficult to ignore. At all events, the words of Lord Simonds remained in Denning's mind for many years. 'I, too, was ambitious,' he wrote in *The Family Story*, after telling of Thomas Cromwell, a Master of the Rolls beheaded in the time of Henry VIII, 'I, too, was accused of heresy – and verbally beheaded – by Lord Simonds. You can read it in *Midland Silicones Ltd* v. *Scruttons Ltd* [1962] AC 446.'

LORD DENNING

The years from 1957 to 1962 were years of personal happiness for
Tom and years of service; they were not years in which he had any
sense of fulfilment in his judicial role. He forged links with lawyers in
many parts of the world and was a good ambassador for England in
whichever country he visited. He undertook important work for the
Commonwealth countries, particularly Africa. He played a valuable
part in all aspects of every organisation with which he was associated;
never just a figurehead, he steered committees, introduced fresh
ideas, raised money, kept a careful eye on how it was spent and,
above all, gave generously of his time and his benevolence to those
intended to benefit from the organisation's activities.

At home, he took pleasure from Joan and the extending family. He
loved to entertain and Joan kept open house. It was no surprise to
them to hear from Robert that he was sending some 'passing'
undergraduates to Sunday lunch; all who came were thrown together
with children, grandchildren and visiting dignitaries, certain of the
warmest of welcomes and a hearty meal, with fruit and vegetables
freshly picked from the garden.

It was hardly surprising, remembering his years of struggle, that
Tom was careful with money. He watched over his personal tax
affairs. He took pleasure from the thought that, by his own
endeavours, he would leave Robert in a comfortable position. It was
not money for its own sake that interested him, but the security that
it brings. Nor, though he cared deeply about it, was land an end in
itself. Tom wanted to conserve, to leave a place better than he found
it. Not interested in art, he looked for beauty in the English
countryside. He liked to think the Whitchurch cricket team – that
same team for which his brothers once turned out – would play in his
paddock; to know that the restored granary, mounted on limestone
toadstools, would become a Whitchurch landmark.

Since the judicial day was short, Tom had time to speak in debate in
the Lords, severity tempered always with humanity. On Tuesday 9
June 1959, he moved an amendment to the Street Offences Bill to
delete the words 'common prostitute' and replace them with 'any
person'. A month later in a debate on the Legitimacy Bill, Denning,
who abhorred adultery, sought to ensure that all children were
legitimate whose parents were married, no matter whether a child
was born before the marriage or whether it was born at a time when

270

one of the parents was married to someone else. Though Christian marriage remained Tom's ideal, his sympathetic understanding of the needs of others kept him from censorious and carping attitudes.

But in the House, he was not content. In 1962, the opportunity of which he had dreamed occurred. Lord Evershed was finding the work of Master of the Rolls too heavy. There was speculation about his successor. 'Then, at lunch one day in the Lords, the Lord Chancellor, Lord Kilmuir (when the others had left the table) said to me: "I hear that you would like to be Master of the Rolls yourself. Is that so?" ' Tom had not mentioned this to anyone since he had spoken, before going to the Lords, with Hubert Parker, but he needed no time to consider before saying that he would like the job.

That year saw many changes in the world in which Tom had spent his professional life. Lord Merriman, who had introduced Tom to the chambers in Brick Court but had never forgiven him for his report on divorce proceedings, died at the age of 81. So, too, did Hubert Wallington, who was made a High Court Judge with Tom in 1944 but remained in the Divorce Division until his retirement. Sir Jocelyn Simon – Jack Simon, who once had a seat in the Brick Court chambers – became President of the Probate, Divorce and Admiralty Division. Lord Radcliffe – Cyril Radcliffe, who had taken the All Souls' Fellowship for which Tom competed – was created a Viscount. Lord Evershed was made a Lord of Appeal in Ordinary and, on the same day, Lord Denning took over as Master of the Rolls.

To say that judges are not supposed to be party politicians is not the same as to suppose that there are no politics amongst the judiciary. At the highest level the interaction between personalities is still of great account. Would Tom have left the Lords if Simonds had retired earlier or if he had seen an opportunity to be the most senior law lord in the near future? Possibly not. Once the decision was taken there was to be no turning back. Years later, when the Lords had given themselves leave to depart from precedent – though the Court of Appeal was still bound – and when a more progressive Lord Chancellor held the reins, Tom was invited to return. He refused. Only the offer of an hereditary peerage might have persuaded him, he told the author in jest, and that was never made.

On 19 April 1962 Alfred Thompson Denning assumed the mantle

and dignity of Master of the Rolls. Few outside the law may have known of the office when Lord Denning became its ninety-first recorded holder; when he retired 20 years later it was as if the title had always been associated with his name.

PART THREE

1962–1982

17

Master of the Rolls

On 23 March 1962, John Hewitt, the Secretary for Appointments, wrote to Tom from Admiralty House: 'I am desired by the Prime Minister to inform you that the Queen has been pleased to approve you be appointed Master of the Rolls. This appointment will take effect from 19 April 1962.' After a telephone call from an equerry, there followed a formal invitation from Buckingham Palace:

> I am desired by The Queen to invite you and Lady Denning to stay at Windsor Castle on Wednesday, the 4th April, for the night, arriving between 6 and 7 pm.
> Dinner jackets will be worn at dinner and you will be at liberty to leave at your convenience any time after breakfast on Thursday, the 5th April.

Anxious about her dress, Joan decided to have one made for the occasion; since short evening dresses were fashionable, she chose three-quarter length. She drove the car from Cuckfield to Windsor, where she and Tom were met at the entrance by an equerry and a footman; their car was taken away and their cases unpacked for them. They soon discovered that the equerry's assurance that there would be an informal dinner – 'just Her Majesty's Household' – had given less than the full picture: both the Archbishop of Canterbury and the Prime Minister were among the guests. 'Alas,' Tom recalled, 'all the other ladies had long dresses, including the Queen ... Of course, they all assured Joan – the Queen and everybody – that it was all right, but she was embarrassed at not having a long dress ... So we dined – they had all the gold plate out.' Over coffee, Harold Macmillan 'quite mastered the whole situation' and 'did all the talking.' The Dennings stayed overnight in a room that was, Tom remembered, 'terribly uncomfortable' and left the next day. The visit was an interesting rather than an enjoyable experience.

Tom's own self-confidence in this august society is a measure of the distance he had travelled since his first hesitant steps into the world beyond Whitchurch. There can be few offices more clearly part of the Establishment than Master of the Rolls; but Denning, a member now of the select group having authority within society, was more willing than most to break ranks in pursuit of his personal ideal of justice, rooted in morality. Up to this stage in his career, his ideal had very much accorded with opinion in the country. He entered upon his new office with a reputation for common-sense and support of the 'little man'. That alone would not have persuaded the Lord Chancellor to offer him the Rolls. Lord Kilmuir regarded Denning's as a safe pair of hands: in his speech to the Mansfield Law Club in January 1957, Kilmuir approved the view of justice Denning expressed in *Freedom Under the Law* and *The Changing Law*. Denning's reputation for scholarship was undoubted; his respect for tradition, if not always for precedent, was unchallenged; his approach to commercial law was pragmatic and business-like.

There have been Masters of the Rolls since the thirteenth century, and possibly before that. The first man known to have held the office, from 1286 to 1292, was John de Langton, chief clerk (or keeper of the rolls of parchment on which the records were written) in the Chancery of England. The Chancery was the office of the Chancellor, a man who wielded immense power as royal chaplain, the king's secretary in secular matters and keeper of the Royal Seal, which had replaced the King's signature on most documents. All the secretarial work of the royal household was conducted through his office and, by the thirteenth century, he was also employed on judicial work. As the number and variety of petitions to the King became greater, the Chancellor and justices were authorised to deal with all but the most important. Petitions began to be addressed directly to the Chancellor; in the course of time, his deputy, the Master of the Rolls, was also called upon to conduct judicial business.

Over the centuries the office of Master of the Rolls was very rewarding financially. It was always in the preferment of the King and, in 1377, Edward III assigned to the Keeper of the Rolls and his successors a valuable property known as the House for Converted

Jews. Where the Public Record Office now stands, the Master had his mansion and chapel and his own court, besides owning houses in the streets around Chancery Lane. In 1837, by Act of Parliament, the property reverted to the Crown in return for £7,000 a year free of tax (which was, as Denning said in *The Family Story*, a fortune in those days). At the time Denning was appointed to the office, the salary, £9,000 a year, subject to tax, was no longer a vast sum.

As the Master's judicial role increased, he had long ceased to be responsible for the records but, in 1838, by the Public Record Office Act, their custody was restored to him. In 1962 Denning found that he was not only Master of the Rolls but Chairman of the Advisory Council on Public Records and Chairman of the Royal Commission on Historical Manuscripts. The Advisory Committee met quarterly to deal with such matters as the release of departmental records under the 30 years rule. The Royal Commission was concerned with the preservation of private records, a subject in which Tom took a great interest; after his retirement he gave his own papers to the Hampshire Record Office. As Master of the Rolls he had also, by statute, to keep 'a fatherly eye on the Rolls of Solicitors. He is a Jack-of-all-trades and Master of *One*' he wrote, nearly 20 years later, in *The Family Story*. Whatever other duties he might perform, primarily the Master's work would be to preside over the Court of Appeal.

In 1962 the Master of the Rolls was still expected to buy the black satin robes heavily embroidered with gold, for use on ceremonial occasions. Thus attired, over knee-breeches and black tights, lace edging the jabot at his throat and emerging, white, from beneath the cuffs of his dark jacket, his long wig upon his head, Tom was sworn in by the Lord Chancellor on 19 April. The ceremony over, he took possession of his new room – more splendid by far than the one he had occupied in the House of Lords – in the centre of the Law Courts corridor occupied by the judges of the Court of Appeal.

Only two remained of those who had been his colleagues when he left there in 1957 – Sellers and Ormerod. Some had become law lords, Pearce being elevated on the day Tom returned. The Lords Justices of Appeal over whom Denning would preside were, in 1962, Willmer, Harman, Upjohn, Donovan, Danckwerts, Pearson, Arthian Davies, Diplock and Charles Russell, who was appointed to replace Pearce.

No manual existed to tell Tom how to do his job. No words of wisdom from the Lord Chancellor or the outgoing Master of the Rolls set his feet upon the path that he should follow; and, if advice had been forthcoming, almost certainly it would have been ignored. Tom admired some of his predecessors, in particular Sir George Jessel, 'the first Jew – after their emancipation in 1841 – to become an English judge. A judge, too, after my own style.'[1] He had personal experience of both Lord Greene and Lord Evershed but he intended to follow neither of them in his presidency of the Court of Appeal.

He meant to make his office a source of greater power and influence than it had been before. The Lord Chief Justice had always chosen the cases to be tried in his own court; until Denning, the Master of the Rolls had never done so. Denning's decision to select his appeals was to give his office previously untapped authority. It would enable him, time and again, to imprint his view of public policy upon the law.

The announcement of his appointment attracted a large postbag from England and abroad. Lady Evershed, the wife of his predecessor wrote: 'I think we both feel sad to be going, but Raymond knows that he has done it long enough and that it is time for a change. You will find his clerk John King quite wonderful.' Though the Privy Council would miss him, the Bar welcomed his return to the Law Courts. '*Ave atque vale,*' wrote Sir Dingle Foot. 'We shall miss you a great deal in the Privy Council.' 'It is indeed good to know,' said Michael Zander, a solicitor who would become Professor of Law at the London School of Economics, 'that you will again . . . be at the very heart of the development of the English Law.' H. W. R. Wade, Professor of English Law at Oxford, wrote:

I feel that you will be moving back to the real centre of gravity of the law, where your creative powers can be of the greatest service. I have a presentiment that your escape from the House of Lords . . . will be a great event in the legal history of our time. The odds against enlightened decisions have now shortened once more . . .

For the moment, Wade added, he regretted that Tom was not to be part of the House of Lords in the forthcoming appeal in *Ridge* v. *Baldwin*, an important case on administrative law, in which the professor had been pinning his hopes on a Denning judgment. On 13

April, Tom responded to Wade's letter that the decision had been, for him, whether to remain where he was so often in a minority or return to the Court of Appeal where so many more cases were decided.

In the House of Lords Denning had little administrative support. 'There was one clerk for all of us Law Lords.'[1] Now, in the Court of Appeal, with several hundred cases to be heard each year, he found the system little better manned. Each Lord Justice had his own clerk, all seated together in one room along the judges' corridor, which doubled as the office for appeals. Each day one or two of the clerks were deputed to accept and file the papers brought to their room by solicitors' clerks, lodging appeals. Tom's clerk, John King, presided over the business, from a small room, next but one to the Master of the Rolls's. As Lady Evershed had predicted, Tom found him helpful and efficient, with the work of the Court of Appeal office at his fingertips.

Arriving in his room some hour and a half before the courts were due to sit, Denning, attended by his clerk and secretary, dealt with the administration of the Court of Appeal. He was content to leave to King much of the day-to-day business of the office but, in matters of policy was, from the first, firmly in command. There were then four Courts of Appeal, the Master of the Rolls presiding over one, the most senior Lords Justices presiding over the other three; the remaining Lords Justices were rotated, at intervals of roughly a month, between the courts. The rota was prepared by King and submitted to the Master. Substantially the system that Denning found in 1962 was still in place on his retirement, 20 years later. He had laid down certain ground rules. Denning required that each court trying an appeal from the Chancery Division must contain at least one Lord Justice expert in that field; and so with commercial appeals, or appeals on planning or family law; newly appointed Lords Justices should always sit, for a spell in the Master's Court. He also made it clear that cases of administrative law, cases of constitutional interest and cases involving the statutory interpretation of new Acts of Parliament were to come to his court – to No. 3 Court, in the centre of the Appeal Court judges' corridor.

To take for the first time, a Master of the Rolls's-eye view of No. 3 Court is to experience a surge of power and authority. From a platform, several feet above the body of the court, he looks down, first upon the bench where sit the Associate and shorthand writers, then down again to the five rows of benches, often packed, for members of the Bar, solicitors, those concerned with the appeal and the public. Opposite him are the glass doors leading to the public parts of the Law Courts; through them and through the windows between them, from time to time, faces peer and people either enter or go away. High above these doors – above the level of the Master, too – is the public gallery, and above that the domed ceiling, with its squares of white between oak framing and its four chandeliers that only faintly supplement the dim light from a dirty skylight and from gothic windows, atop oak-panelled walls, lined with books.

If the design of the court can arouse a sense of power in the judges, from the well of the court, looking up instead of down, it provokes – and was, no doubt, intended to provoke – a sense of awe in the face of the majesty and dignity of the law. From two doors in the Appeal Court Judges' Corridor, enter the Master of the Rolls and two colleagues, directly on to the platform, raised high above the watchers' heads. Everyone stands and bows as the three judges reach their places at the long, highly polished wooden bench-desk, each standing before his capacious high-backed armchair. Together the Master of the Rolls and the Lord Justice to either side of him, all in their wigs and robes (though the gold-trimmed robes and full-bottomed wigs are not for every day), return the bow, before seating themselves in their red leather chairs, which look imposing rather than comfortable. Behind them, green velvet curtains on either side of the door through which they have come make a backdrop to the impressive sight. High above the judges' dais and the carved oak canopy that overhangs it, the Royal Coat of Arms is starkly outlined against white paint, a symbol of the majesty from which the power of the judges derives. On the wall to the judges' right, the large round face of the clock, in its oak case, marks the time. Invariably the court will sit from 10.30 am until some convenient moment for the lunch adjournment, and again, in the afternoon up till 4.30 pm.

When court rose Tom's working day was far from over. Work on reserved judgments, work on his speeches and his various extra-judicial interests, correspondence, appointments filled the hours before his evening engagements. The leisurely life in the Lords was replaced by a very much more demanding schedule. For years Tom had commuted to work from Cuckfield, met at the station in the evenings by Joan, who often left their dinner in the oven. When they attended formal evening engagements, they were accustomed to leaving early to catch the last train and had sometimes to run down the platform, in order not to miss it, with Joan holding up the skirt of a long frock. Now that he was Master of the Rolls Tom's workload was much heavier and his list of evening engagements greatly increased. As Master, he could no longer expect to leave a dinner those few minutes early that were vital to reaching home that night. A driver and car might have solved the problem but each day would have been very long and, though he had remarkable energy, Tom was 63, the age at which his predecessor had given up the job.

They decided to take a flat in Lincoln's Inn, and live there during the week. A sizeable apartment at 11 Old Square became vacant and the Inn planned to divide it into two. The Dennings would have three rooms and a small kitchen. There were 62 stairs and no lift, but they were both in good health and did not let the climb worry them. They spent the week in London, returning to Cuckfield for the weekend. There were occasional hiccups – like the Friday night they arrived at Fair Close, after dining at Fulham Palace, and, as neither had a key, had to break in through the kitchen window – but, on the whole, their new mode of life went smoothly.

They were becoming anxious about progress at The Lawn. The plans had been agreed and some demolition work carried out, but it seemed that nothing had been done to start the restoration. There was some speculation, locally, about Tom's intentions and a kind of blight had fallen upon nearby property. No buyers could be found for houses opposite, also vacated by the Bank of England. The work was clearly not going to advance at any acceptable rate without someone on the spot to supervise the builders. Marjorie's husband, John Haynes, living opposite at The Hermitage, undertook to do the job. Tom was able to relax and get on with his work though, to their travels between London and Cuckfield, he and Joan added frequent visits to Whitchurch to inspect progress.

Joan's daughter, Pauline Simond, had gone back to work at the YWCA after Katherine's birth in 1951 and later started to conduct a course for drama teachers at the Royal Academy of Music. Early in 1962, when Sir Thomas Armstrong, the principal of the Academy, announced his intention of closing the drama department the following February, a group of teachers decided to make it into a separate college. Pauline consulted Tom, who sent them to see Anthony Moir. Moir's advice to the teachers was much as Professor Cheshire's had been to his son: they must have trustees who would inspire public confidence. Pauline asked Tom to chair the trustees and he agreed, 'giving generously of his time.'[39]

Pauline's husband Derick, working in the BBC, approached Richard Dimbleby. The latter was already suffering from cancer but was happy to lend his name to the enterprise and to attend a number of the meetings at which plans were laid for the new college. Amongst others, Peter Sellers and Ralph Richardson joined the group. 'Tom was immensely supportive and presided over lovely avuncular meetings. He was a super chairman. No time was wasted.'[39] Pavlova's old house on Hampstead Heath, which had been in use as a trade-union hospital, was for sale at £46,000; Moir persuaded Lloyds Bank to give the group an advance but a more permanent source of finance was needed. At a cocktail party Joan explained the problem to a Queen's Bench Master, Jack Jacob, who pointed out to her a wealthy business man who might help. Joan introduced herself to Barnett Shine, who did, indeed, generously support the new college and also, later, another of Tom's projects.

Tom derived much personal satisfaction from his various activities outside the courts. His name had been given to societies in many parts of the world and he took more than a casual interest in the work they all did. When the Chairman of one Denning Law Society wrote, on 18 December 1962, to send Tom the Society's news, he replied: 'I hear on all sides very warm praise for your great progress in the University College of Dar-es-Salaam. It is an example to the rest of Africa and we all send our best congratulations on your efforts.' Small wonder that Tom enjoyed such popularity among students and that so many chose him for their president.

As an ambassador his reputation seemed secure. As the practical, hardworking chairman of various institutions he was greatly valued. As a judge, too, despite misgivings in some quarters, he was highly regarded; and expectations were raised as he entered office. His passionate belief that judges should not wait for statutory reform of the law but must themselves do what is necessary to achieve justice in the instant case was to imprint its stamp on the Court of Appeal.

Denning had always sided with the 'intention seekers', whether he was interpreting a statute, a contract or a will. A month after his return to the Court of Appeal, he heard an appeal from a Chancery Judge concerning a pair of wills that failed, in legal terms, to express their makers' intentions. Dr Rowland and his wife decided to sail to the South Seas in their own small boat. They each made wills leaving everything to each other, but providing, in the event of the other's death 'preceding or coinciding with my death', for their property to go to their own relatives. The vessel disappeared and, some days later, one body and some wreckage were found. To suppose that the couple had drowned together and that the property of each would pass to his or her chosen beneficiaries was to reckon without an established rule of law: when a couple die in circumstances where it is not possible to say that their deaths coincided, on the instant, it is presumed that the elder died first. Since the doctor was the elder, he was presumed to have pre-deceased his wife, who inherited just long enough to pass the property to *her* relatives. Clearly this was not what the Rowlands had intended and Denning determined to make a stand for common sense. The other judges were both Chancery men and would not go with him. 'You always knew when he was dissenting,' recalled Mavis Hill, the law reporter. 'They used to go outside and then come back again and then he used to look like a stubborn schoolboy. His face got a little pink. He used to be rather emphatic in his delivery . . . He was a bit combative, you know.'[46] In *Re Rowland* he said:

> I have myself known a judge to say: 'I believe this to be contrary to the true intention of the testator but nevertheless it is the result of the words he has used.' When a judge goes so far as to say that, the chances are he has misconstrued the will. For in point of principle the whole object of construing a will is to find out the testator's intentions, so as to see that his property is disposed of in the way he wished. True it is that you must discover his intention from the words he used: but you must put upon his words the meaning which they bore to him . . . What you should do is place yourself as far as possible in his position, taking note of the facts and circumstances known to him at the time: and then say what he meant by his words.

Denning's words were as heretical to those who, in the Chancery Division, had spent years construing wills and trusts, as his speech in *Midland Silicones* had been to Simonds. In a nutshell, Russell's conclusion encapsulates the view against which Denning would fight for the remainder of his judicial career. Applying the strict interpretation, Russell said:

> The testator's language does not fit the facts of the case, so far as they are known. To hold otherwise would not, in my judgment, be to construe the will at all: it would be the result of inserting in the will a phrase which the testator never used ... There is no jurisdiction in this Court to achieve a sensible result by such means.

There would always be some friction between Denning and his Chancery colleagues. The problem for other judges of coping with Denning's quicksilver mind, may have been best described by Russell, in his 1969 presidential address to Birmingham University's Holdsworth Club, under the guise of Lords Justices Toad, Frog and Slug. After reading each other's reserved judgments:

> Frog observes in Toad what he considers to be gross heresy and amends his draft in a manner calculated to expose it as such, hoping that thus he will bring Toad to his senses. Undeterred, Toad fortifies his draft by analogy with other branches of the law. Frog is drawn unwillingly into this new field, and by postponing his first gin and catching the last train to West Sussex, works hard at it for his third draft. Toad LJ – who lives in London and never touches gin – produces an amendment digging into ancient authorities.

Less than a month after *re Rowland*, the same court heard another appeal, where Russell's sympathies were engaged by the appellant's case, though, still adhering strictly to the law, he found himself unable to give way to them. A builder in a small way of business had purchased for £2000 a three-quarter acre plot in the village of Wraysbury, with planning permission for five bungalows to be built upon it. The usual searches and enquiries cast no doubt upon the title or the validity of the planning permission. Only when the builder started to clear the ground, did a local man remind the parish clerk that, by ancient usage, recited in a private Act of 1799, the inhabitants of Wraysbury were entitled to hold an annual fair or wake on the Friday of Whitsun week, on land including the builder's small plot. No such fair had been held in living memory, nor was there any likelihood of one being held, but four Wraysbury men demanded that any building on the site be prohibited. Unanimously the Court of Appeal decided the builder must be restrained from doing anything that would prevent a fair being held on the site. 'When in those circumstances,' said Russell, 'the [builder] finds himself restrained from the use of his land for the purpose for which he paid the particular purchase price, at the suit of four inhabitants whose leading purpose and motive is to prevent the building which the competent authority has approved . . . he has my unqualified sympathy . . . If I could find a way to decide in his favour I should be happy to do so. Alas, I cannot.' (*Wyld* v. *Silver*)

In most cases the plight of a blameless individual roused Tom's compassion and it might have been expected that his sympathy would also have been with the small builder. If it was, he did not express it in his judgment. The interest in this case for Tom was not the individual but the preservation of ancient rights. The fair had its origin, he said, 'in the vigil which used to be held on the eve of a festival in the church. The fair was a gathering of buyers and sellers. The wake was the merry-making which went with it.' Commenting upon the builder's plea that he had bought the land in ignorance of the rights of the inhabitants, Denning said 'So be it. It is one of the risks that he must take.' In some circumstances another interest overcame Tom's concern for the individual: above all came the safety of the state and the maintenance of law and order; but high on Denning's list of priorities was the preservation of a traditional way of life. Denning's often conflicting interests would be seen at work in this way, over the next 20 years.

In July there was an appeal on an aspect of contempt that had not previously been considered by the court. The Restrictive Practices Court had recently decided that an agreement made between a trade union and the Newspaper Proprietors' Association was against public policy. In the course of the hearing they received evidence

from Mr Greenlees, a member of the union, which was contrary to
the case being argued by the union. Soon after the conclusion of the
hearing, Greenlees complained, he was relieved of his appointment as
a branch delegate and branch treasurer. The Restrictive Practices
Court declined to commit ten men, alleged to be responsible, for
contempt of court, as they could find no precedent for committal
where conduct 'adverse to a witness' had taken place after the
conclusion of proceedings. The Attorney-General, Reginald
Manningham-Buller, appealed to the Court of Appeal (*AG* v.
Butterworth). Here was conduct likely to interfere with the administration of justice. If no authority could be found for dealing with it,
Denning said, 'the sooner we make one the better . . . How can we
expect a witness to give his evidence freely and frankly, as he ought to
do, if he is liable, as soon as the case is over, to be punished for it by
those who dislike the evidence he has given?'

The case lingered in Tom's memory for another reason than his
interest in 'keeping the streams of justice clear and pure':[23] it was the
last in which Manningham-Buller would appear as Attorney-
General. The short period since Tom watched Harold Macmillan
hold centre stage at Windsor had not been a happy one for the Prime
Minister or his government. Throughout the 1950s, the economy had
been growing, if slowly and not too steadily, but by the end of the
decade the growth came to a halt. The Government tried various
methods to stimulate the economy, including a pay pause which was
unpopular and unsuccessful. By the summer of 1962 Macmillan was
seriously concerned and, on 12 July, replaced his Chancellor of the
Exchequer. The following night, Friday 13th, as his biographer
Alistair Horne described it: 'mayhem took place'. Among the
casualties in Macmillan's cabinet on the 'Night of Long Knives' was
the Lord Chancellor, Lord Kilmuir – the man who had invited Tom
to become Master of the Rolls. Tom little expected, when he was
sworn in by Kilmuir on 19 April that he would himself swear in a new
Lord Chancellor – Reginald Manningham-Buller (who took the title
Lord Dilhorne) – barely three months later, on Tuesday 17 July 1962.

The economic condition of the country remained perilous, the
Cold War between the communists and the West was threatening and
spy fever gathered force. One security scandal followed another and
rumours began to circulate about security at the Admiralty. In this

climate the Soblen case reached the court of the Master of the Rolls in August 1962 (*R*. v. *Governor of Brixton Prison ex parte Soblen*). Dr Soblen was a doctor of medicine who had practised in Lithuania, the country of his birth, until he went to America in 1941. Twenty years later he was charged there with conspiring in 1944 and 1945 to give defence information to the Russians. He was convicted and sentenced to life imprisonment. While out on bail, pending appeal, he escaped to Israel, where he was refused entry and was put aboard an aircraft for the United States. Shortly before the plane was due in London, for a short stop, Soblen gravely wounded himself with a knife. In order to save his life he was taken to hospital but it was intended, when he was sufficiently recovered, to return him to New York. Before that could happen Soblen challenged the validity of the notice refusing him leave to enter the United Kingdom and applied for a writ of *habeas corpus*, saying that he wanted to go to Czechoslovakia. The government was in a quandary. The Americans wanted Soblen back and the British wanted to send him but his offence was not extraditable. The Home Secretary therefore made a deportation order and ordered Soblen's detention in Brixton Prison, until it was carried out. Soblen appealed, claiming that his detention was illegal.

On this issued Denning saw no need to challenge the Minister: though every alien is free, as soon as he lawfully sets foot in Britain, he said, 'the Crown is entitled at any time to send him home to his own country, if in its opinion his presence here is not conducive to the public good.' *Soblen* was the first of a number of cases where Denning revealed his reluctance to extend to aliens the same protection he vigorously afforded citizens.

The trial and conviction, in October 1962, of William Vassall, an Admiralty clerk, for handing secret documents to the KGB, was momentarily eclipsed by events in Cuba, where the United States and the Soviets hovered on the brink of nuclear war. That danger passed, the press returned its attention to the spies. Articles were published which reflected gravely on ministers, naval officers and civil servants in the Admiralty. A special tribunal, chaired by Lord Radcliffe, was appointed to investigate the allegations. In the course of their inquiries, the tribunal called a journalist, Brendan Mulholland of the *Daily Mail*, to give evidence and asked him to disclose the sources of information contained in articles he had written. He declined to do so. Radcliffe certified that Mulholland had refused to answer questions that were necessary and relevant to the inquiry. The Attorney-General, John Hobson, moved in the High Court for Mulholland's committal; Mulholland's claim of privilege to keep his sources secret was rejected and he was sentenced to six months' imprisonment. In similar circumstances, a second journalist, Reginald Foster of the *Daily Sketch*, was sentenced to three months' imprisonment. Both appealed. The Master of the Rolls decided that the cases should be heard together in his court and, on 12 February 1963, the appeals came before him, sitting with Donovan and Danckwerts.

It was rare, amongst the judiciary, to find a man patently at ease with the press. Even those who had been politicians before taking judicial appointments assumed reticence with their judicial robes. Denning had no such reservations. He was happy to use the media to put across his ideas and recognised that their failings were balanced by their power to influence reforms. In speeches to the Guild of British Newspaper Editors and the Religious Weekly Press, while still a law lord, he had emphasised the leading part played by the press in the formation of public opinion and its responsibilities as a bastion of freedom.

Though Denning was fundamentally opposed to any class of citizen claiming a privilege to keep information from the court he was inclined, where public policy was not at issue, to protect a journalist's source; but in *Mulholland* and *Foster* he took a serious view of the refusal to reveal sources. There were two questions to be answered, he said. First, was it necessary for the journalists to answer the Tribunal's question about their sources, in order for proper investigation to be made? Second, 'have the journalists a privilege in point of law to refuse to answer?' He concluded that the answer to the first question was yes and to the second no. Unanimously the Court dismissed the appeals of the two journalists (*Attorney-General* v. *Mulholland*). Against this background it was inevitable that the next whiff of scandal attending the Government would be blown by the press into a full-scale crisis.

18

Profumo

The crisis was not long in coming. There lived in a mews flat in Marylebone a fashionable osteopath, Stephen Ward, who was also a talented painter, a lover of low life and of high society. On 14 March 1963 the trial was to start of Edgecombe, a West Indian marijuana-pusher, accused of firing shots from an automatic pistol outside Ward's flat. The principal prosecution witness was a young call-girl, Christine Keeler, who was in the flat with her friend Mandy Rice-Davies at the time of the shooting. Edgecombe was Keeler's lover; for this and other reasons she was reluctant to give evidence and when the trial opened it was found that she had disappeared. It did not take long for the newspapers to find her in Spain and, on 28 March, they brought her back to England and took her to Scotland Yard.

It was the type of sleazy, police-court story found, usually, only in the pages of the more lurid newspapers. But this story had an added ingredient. For some time rumour had linked the name of Christine Keeler with that of John Profumo, the Secretary of State for War. As this story unfolded it would fascinate the nation, bring closer the fall of the Government, and lead to Tom's most extraordinary best-seller, entitled *Lord Denning's Report*.

When, in April 1963 Tom opened the new law courts at Plymouth, where once he had been Recorder, staying with Joan in the house on Plymouth Hoe that was given to the City by Lady Astor, once its Member of Parliament, he little imagined that the name of her son would shortly be on every gossip's lips.

John Profumo met Christine Keeler in July 1961, when he was staying with his wife, the actress Valerie Hobson, at Lord Astor's estate, Cliveden. After dinner the party walked down to the swimming-pool, where they found Stephen Ward, who rented a cottage on the estate, with some friends, including Christine Keeler. Profumo started an affair with Keeler, meeting her at times in Ward's flat. It might have been no-one's business but their own, if it had not been for another of Ward's friends, Captain Yevgeny Ivanov, who was also at the pool that hot summer's night. Ivanov was the Naval Attaché at the Soviet Embassy in London; he was also engaged in gathering intelligence. A discreet word from the security services to the Cabinet Secretary, who passed on the warning to Profumo, decided Profumo to end the affair. It was all over by the end of 1961, bar the consequences.

On 28 January 1963 the Attorney-General was told that a girl was preparing to sell to a Sunday newspaper the story of her relationships with a number of men, including Profumo; the newspaper was in possession of a letter written to her, starting 'Darling', and ending 'Love, J'. Quite independently a story reached Macmillan's private secretary a little later, suggesting there appeared to be a security matter, involving the Secretary of State for War. To both of them, and to the Chief Whip, Profumo protested the innocence of his relationship with Keeler. He told them that, since he, Astor and Ward, had become aware of Keeler's proposal to publish, they had done their best to dissuade her. It had been proposed to re-imburse her for the loss of the fee for her story and to give her the means to go abroad for a time, *after* the Edgecombe trial, but this plan had fallen through when it seemed that Keeler wanted £5000, though her fee from the *Sunday Pictorial* would have been only £1000. As for the letter, Profumo explained, he commonly used the word 'darling' because, being married to an actress, he had become accustomed to the term and it had no significance.

Whether or not Profumo's explanation was accepted, his stated intention to bring an action for defamation and to prosecute Keeler for extortion persuaded them that the damage could be contained. It was a vain hope. Keeler's disappearance before, not after, the Edgecombe trial, started fresh rumours that Profumo was involved. There were, in any case, too many people who knew the story and, for the opposition party, the opportunity was too good to miss.

On 21 March, when the Commons were debating the imprisonment of the two journalists, George Wigg, a Labour Member with a particular interest in security matters, referred to speculation about a minister and invited the Government to deny it. The following morning Profumo told the House, as he had everyone else, that 'there was no impropriety whatsoever' in his acquaintance with Miss Keeler and that he would issue writs for libel and slander if 'scandalous allegations' were made outside the House.

The opposition pressed the Prime Minister. Its Leader, Harold Wilson, sent Macmillan a memorandum about the lives of Ward and his set and a letter from Ward alleging that Profumo's statement to the House had not been the truth. At the end of May, just before the parliamentary recess, Macmillan asked the Lord Chancellor to investigate the matter. Two weeks later Dilhorne sent a memorandum to the Prime Minister informing him that there was no ground for supposing any breach of security occurred and that no further inquiry seemed necessary.

By the time the Lord Chancellor reported the scandal had escalated. Ward had been arrested and charged with brothel-keeping and procuring. Another West Indian lover of Christine Keeler, 'Lucky' Gordon, had been tried at the Old Bailey for attacking her in a street brawl. The *News of the World* had begun to publish Keeler's story in instalments. Keeler herself was telling people that Ward had asked her to find out when the Americans intended to give Germany the atomic bomb. John Profumo had admitted lying to the Commons and tendered his resignation.

When Parliament re-convened on 17 June, the storm broke. Though the country was awash with rumours of sexual scandal, Harold Wilson concentrated his attack on Macmillan's neglect of the security risk. Macmillan embarked on a damage limitation exercise. That day, he asked Denning to undertake an inquiry with these terms of reference:

> To examine, in the light of the circumstances leading to the resignation of the former Secretary of State for War, Mr J. D. Profumo, the operation of the Security Service and the adequacy of their co-operation with the Police in matters of security, to investigate any information or material which may come to his attention in this connection and to consider evidence there may be for believing that national security has been, or may be, endangered and to report thereon.

On the following day, Tom replied: 'It is a great responsibility with which you have entrusted me – and I feel very apprehensive of my ability to carry it out. All I can say is that I will do my best very faithfully to perform the task.'[23]

This was a surprising commission. It was not at all unusual for a government to defuse a difficult situation by the appointment of a tribunal or committee of inquiry under the chairmanship of a judge. What was unusual about this appointment was the absence of a committee: with only a small ancillary staff, Denning alone was to take the evidence, to sift it and report.

From 24 June 1963, when he started, to 16 September 1963, when he signed his report, nothing was allowed to interfere with the inquiry. Secluded from the eyes of public and of press, some 160 witnesses gave evidence to him in Treasury Chambers. Since all Downing Street connects, ministers could come and go with only his small staff knowing whom Denning saw. To encourage witnesses to speak freely, he promised them anonymity and omitted from his report the usual list of those who gave evidence; 'but they covered a wide range: The Prime Minister, eight Cabinet Ministers, four other Ministers, as well as three Law Officers, five Members of the House of Lords, 15 members of the House of Commons, several Civil Servants, including the official Head of the Civil Service, the Secretary of the Cabinet . . .'[55] and so on. One of them, Mandy Rice-Davies, later described Tom as 'quite the nicest judge' she had ever met.

It has to be asked why Macmillan chose Denning for the job. The Profumo episode was painful to the Prime Minister. Out of touch, by his own admission, and out of sympathy with the mode of life of those who had collectively damaged his administration, he was principally concerned to obtain a clean bill of health with regard to security. He could have been in little doubt that the Profumo affair had never, in fact, been a danger to security; it was the perception of danger that had to be addressed. In so far as any judge was known outside the limited circles of the law, Denning was that judge. He enjoyed a reputation for striving after justice: it seemed likely that a Denning report would be acceptable to the public. But there was always the danger that Denning might find that the operation of the security service and its co-operation with the police were not adequate; that the Profumo affair could have become a source of danger to security and, in that event, that the security services could not satisfactorily have dealt with matters.

Macmillan's path had seldom crossed Denning's. He had little personal knowledge of the Master of the Rolls. The law officers could have told him Denning's reputation for unorthodoxy; his tough stance towards authority, when defending a citizen's right; his more compliant approach to government where security matters were at issue. But security was not the only aspect of this inquiry: rumours concerned the improprieties of ministers and the choice of Denning was surprising. Recognised by all who knew him to be a man of Christian conviction and strong morality, Denning had less experience even than Macmillan of the world into which he was being asked to delve. If Jowitt, in 1946, thought Denning would find it uncongenial to chair a committee inquiring into divorce procedures, how much less appealing would it have seemed to investigate tales of licence and debauchery and scandal in high places. Yet Denning found it unexpectedly fascinating. Meeting Mavis Hill, in the Strand, in a break from taking evidence, he told her that he was hearing the most remarkable things – terrible stories – though he could not tell her what they were. 'He was really rather like a schoolboy with a secret.'[46] At a party in the garden of the Public Record Office, he waved a black briefcase, saying: 'All the secrets are in this.'[56]

Macmillan, clearly, was not confident of the outcome. In his diary, on 7 July 1963, he noted that, if things went badly with the Denning report, he would have no alternative to resignation; and on 16 August, after giving evidence to Denning for half an hour, he wrote that he feared there would be trouble for two ministers.

The cost of work on The Lawn and the problems of dividing his limited leisure between three places had persuaded Tom to put Fair Close on the market. Every year, on the anniversary of Mary's death he returned to Cuckfield to visit her grave. At The Lawn, he and Joan had planned to make a separate cottage from the billiard room and staff bedrooms over it. They had pressed the builder to get this part of the work finished, so that they could live there until the house was ready.

Tom was at work on the report when the time came to move from Fair Close; it was Robert who helped Joan decide what to do with the accumulation of a quarter of a century and two marriages. The Lawn was nowhere near ready: they stored the furniture in the house and put just enough in the cottage and communicating bedrooms over the stables to make them habitable. Tom's library – once the drawing-room of The Lawn – was the first room to be finished and Joan put his *Law Reports* in order on the shelves. At weekends, when Tom was in Whitchurch, the greatest care had to be taken of any papers he brought with him. Wherever he went, it seemed, the press or television were waiting to take pictures.

Excitement increased as it became known the report was near completion. One Sunday in September, when typescripts of all the sections were at the house, the Dennings found cameras waiting at the church as they arrived for early morning service and reporters calling at The Lawn for news, when they got home. They persuaded all to go away until three o'clock, when Tom promised them an interview. Then, on a long trestle table, they sorted out the script and put it in order, carefully covering everything before the media men returned.

On Monday morning, with the report in his briefcase, Tom found that the station-master had reserved a carriage for him as there were reporters on the train. On 16 September 1963, less than three months after he started work, Denning reported to the Prime Minister. Where the facts were beyond controversy, he said, he would state them as objectively as he could, 'irrespective of the consequences to individuals', but when the facts were at issue, he would remember 'the cardinal principle of justice – that no man is to be condemned on suspicion.' It was with great relief that Macmillan noted in his diary that the rumours against two ministers had been dismissed as unfounded. The style of the report, he thought, owed something to a 'penny dreadful'.

In the first part Denning set out the circumstances leading to Profumo's resignation. Introducing the people involved, he started with Stephen Ward, before giving brief sketches of Eugene Ivanov, Christine Keeler, Mr Profumo and Lord Astor. Probably uncon-sciously, Tom revealed in these headings his attitude to the dramatis personae: thoughout the report he used courtesy titles in writing of some of the parties, while others were invariably called only by name.

Wherever he could, Denning put in a good word for most of them: Astor had done valuable work for hospitals; Profumo had a fine war record; even Christine Keeler was not to be judged too harshly because of her youth. Only Stephen Ward – who had killed himself with a drug overdose taken overnight, while the judge was in the course of summing up at the end of his trial – was 'utterly immoral', catering for those of his friends who had perverted tastes. Denning had interviewed Ward at the start of the inquiry and again, at Ward's request, a few days before the suicide. Though the jury found Ward not guilty of procuring, Denning had no doubt that Ward 'picked up pretty girls of the age of 16 or 17' and 'procured them to be mistresses of his influential friends.' It may be the fact that Ward was the son of a clergyman that made his behaviour the more blameworthy in Denning's eyes.

Turning to the role of the security service and the responsibility of all those concerned, he decided that none of the governmental services was to blame. Yet blame there was. 'We are,' Denning said, addressing himself more to the damage he perceived to public life than to any breach of security, 'I suggest rightly, so anxious that neither the police nor the Security Service should pry into private lives, that there is no machinery for reporting the moral misbehaviour of Ministers . . . when a Minister is guilty of moral misbehaviour and it gives rise to scandalous rumour, it is for him and his colleagues to deal with the rumour, as best they can. It is their responsibility and no one else's.' Though Profumo was asked by colleagues about his conduct, Denning suggested 'Parliament may wish to consider further' – whether they should have asked themselves, not whether Profumo *in fact* committed adultery, but whether his conduct was 'such as to lead ordinary people *reasonably to believe* that he had committed adultery.' (This proposition would be strongly criticised by lawyers in the Tory Party.) Denning concluded that it was the responsibility of the Prime Minister and his colleagues to deal with this situation, 'and they did not succeed in doing so.'

Finally Denning set out – respecting the anonymity he had promised, even though the names had been published in journals abroad – the various rumours arising directly and indirectly from the Profumo affair. In no case, he concluded, was there 'any evidence for believing that national security had been or might be endangered.' The latter conclusion was not to pass unchallenged.

So far as the public at large was concerned, the Denning Report gave Macmillan the clearance, as regards security, that he sought – though at the price of being blamed for his own deception by Profumo. It did not satisfy those with a specialist interest in the subject. The journalist Chapman Pincher thought Denning was repeatedly misled by witnesses, particularly the chief of MI5. Nor did it satisfy the opposition. In the Commons debate, on 16 December 1963, on Security and the Denning Report, Harold Wilson questioned 'the qualified exoneration' of the security services for their failure to go to the Prime Minister about the security aspect of the Profumo – Keeler relationship. In the same debate, George Wigg said:

> If any Hon. Member thinks that the Denning Report contains the truth, the whole truth and nothing but the truth, I beg him to think again . . . I will now tell the House what happened when I went to see Lord Denning. I was sitting on these benches on 27th June when I was handed a letter. It had come by hand from Lord Denning who asked me if possible to see him that afternoon . . . when I opened the letter I was a little surprised, because I thought I remembered the terms of reference had something to do with events leading to the resignation of Mr Profumo and with security. But in his letter to me Lord Denning said:

> 'As I expect you know, I have been entrusted by the Prime Minister with the task of inquiring into reports which are circulating which affect the honour and integrity of public life in this country.'

> I suggest that Lord Denning was never asked to do anything of the kind.

By some Lord Denning's Report was said to be a whitewash – a charge he pre-empted in his introductory remarks. It would have been wholly out of character for him to whitewash anything that he believed had endangered the security of the state. It may be that wool was pulled over his eyes – the one thing that now seems certain about security in 1963 is that *nothing* was certain. But once Denning was satisfied that there had been no risk to security, it was totally in character, when he believed 'the honour and integrity of public life' was affected, for him to put the best possible gloss on matters in his report. In the report there are passages of gossip that are scarcely relevant to an examination of the adequacy of the security service. Those passages, almost certainly, contributed to making the Denning Report into a popular best-seller; but their inclusion was out of line with Denning's usual style. In *Due Process of the Law*, Tom said that some of the evidence he heard was 'so disgusting – even to my sophisticated mind – that I sent the lady shorthand-writer out and had no note of it taken.' Perhaps his first brush with this, to him, astonishing world, which for three months occupied all his waking hours, was simply too much for a man who was essentially naive and innocent. Or perhaps, Denning's object in writing as he did was to lay rumour and speculation finally to rest. In the Denning Report the public could read, once and for all – though names were not named – stories the press had touched upon for months. Titillating they might be, but hardly cause for national alarm.

Before the report was published, Tom and Joan went to stay with their old friend John Morris – Lord Morris of Borth-y-Gest – at his home in North Wales. Far from the glare of publicity, they saw the pictures of a queue stretching well into Drury Lane from HM Stationery Office in Kingsway, when the report went on sale at half-an-hour past midnight on Thursday 26 September 1963. That day's *Times* reported that 4,000 copies, at a price of 7s 6d, were sold by 1.30 am; demand was so great that the Stationery Office printed 90,000 copies, instead of the 30,000 planned. If it was Tom's intention, in publishing the lurid details of the Profumo affair, to satisfy the public thirst for information and bring the matter to an end, he was largely successful. His report was later described by the then Warden of All Souls as 'surely the raciest and most readable Blue Book ever published.'[57] In 1966 the Royal Commission on Tribunals and Inquiries, under the chairmanship of Lord Justice Salmon (later Lord Salmon) said:

> Lord Denning's report was generally accepted by the public. But this was only because of Lord Denning's rare qualities and high reputation. Even so, the public acceptance of the report may be regarded as a brilliant exception to what would normally occur when an inquiry is carried out under such conditions.

Writing 20 years later, Tom called the Profumo Inquiry his most important case. It was, he said 'an inquiry to find out the truth.'[52] It will probably never be known how close to the truth he came. From time to time the subject surfaces again, as when, in 1992, after the fall of the USSR, the Soviet spy Yevgeny Ivanov claimed in his memoirs more success in espionage than Denning had credited to him. Whether or not the Denning Report contained the whole truth, Macmillan was grateful to Tom. On 28 July 1982 he wrote:

> I feel impelled to write to you now that your long and distinguished career as a judge is coming to an end.
>
> My reasons are twofold. First, I owe you a great debt of gratitude for the kindness which you did to me nearly twenty years ago at a very difficult and delicate time in my life as Prime Minister. I never shall forget the trouble you took, the goodness of heart which you showed and the understanding which you displayed . . .
>
> Secondly, I have always been interested in the law and made some attempt to study it at one time. It seems to me that there were two different streams in English law which sometimes meant that on the whole their waters did not mix.
>
> The first has become much more prevalent since the vast mass of legislation which has been passed in the last one hundred and fifty years tends to base itself on a somewhat pedantic or at any rate a very close interpretation of the words of an Act of Parliament. The second which goes back to the great periods of the 17th and 18th century tends to base itself more upon commonsense, equity (in the non-technical sense), fairplay and justice. Of these the greatest proponents were perhaps Lord Mansfield and Lord Camden. To them will be added the name of Lord Denning.

At a very difficult and delicate time in Tom's life, Harold Macmillan's generous words brought him comfort.

The Denning Report was an extraordinary response in exceptional circumstances. Before it, Tom was probably the best-known judge outside the precincts of the courts; after 1963 he was a national figure. He was delighted to get back to the Law Courts. Though he tackled all his work with remarkably youthful enthusiasm, it was as Master of the Rolls that he found true fulfilment. In 20 years of office, appeals would pass through his court in most, if not all, branches of civil law; they would provide an illuminated picture of the events and preoccupations of a generation.

19

A Portia Man

After Christmas 1963, Tom and Joan went on official visits to India and Pakistan. The tour was strenuous: most mornings they were on the move by 6.00 am and nearly every evening there was a dinner with speeches. In India they visited Delhi, Madras and Calcutta; called on President Jawaharlal Nehru; laid a wreath on the memorial to Ghandi; and saw the Taj Mahal, though not by moonlight. In Pakistan they stayed in Lahore and drove through the Khyber Pass, a place that conjured up memories of an Imperial past, to the Afghan frontier, where Tom took the salute from the border guards. They visited the eastern sector of the country, soon to become the independent state of Bangladesh. Wherever he spoke, the Master of the Rolls drew admiring audiences and Tom made friends.

On their return, they found The Lawn nearly ready for occupation. While they were away, the family had moved them from the cottage into the spare bedroom of the main house. Much had been done by the builders with no-one there to watch them: it was months before Joan discovered that the sink had not been connected to an outlet pipe and that all the water draining from it had soaked into the foundations of the house, beneath the kitchen floor.

Beyond Tom's library, the annexe was self-contained; a place where the children and grandchildren could visit undisturbed – and undisturbing. Together the family restored the gardens at The Lawn. As, once, they had excavated stone slabs from the golf course and taken them back to build the terrace at Fair Close, so now they used discarded stones from the old gateway at Lincoln's Inn. For many years there were large gatherings at weekends, even when Tom and Joan were on their travels.

In the new term Denning was sitting with Harman and the newly appointed Lord Justice Salmon, of whose sense of justice Tom strongly approved, when the first of a series of cases in which the Crown claimed the privilege to withhold a document reached the Court of Appeal. Merricks and Clark had been, at one time, the two chief officers of the Metropolitan Police in Peckham. Early in 1957 there had been unease about the activities of street bookmakers in the area and, without telling Merricks anything about it, Scotland Yard appointed an Inspector Fleming to investigate. On receipt of Fleming's report, Merricks and Clark were summarily transferred and when Clark protested that this would cast reflection upon their integrity he was told that it was just too bad. Two years later, Fleming was found guilty of misconduct in an entirely different matter. When Scotland Yard refused to reconsider the cases of Merricks and Clark, the two men brought an action alleging that the disciplinary machinery, that should have ensured them a fair hearing, had been by-passed by Sir John Nott-Bower and the two other commissioners involved in 1957. Damages for libel were claimed in respect of a minute sent by the then Assistant Commissioner to Nott-Bower, shortly before the transfer. The defendants applied to strike out the claim on the ground that it was frivolous and vexatious and disclosed no reasonable cause of action. They produced a certificate from the Home Secretary claiming Crown privilege for documents, including the minute to Nott-Bower.

The court was unanimous in holding that Merricks and Clark had an arguable case. 'It is a well-known principle of our law,' said the Master of the Rolls, 'that any powers conferred by statute or regulation on an executive or administrative authority must be exercised in good faith for the purpose for which they are granted. They must not be misused or abused by being applied to an ulterior purpose.' Turning to the Home Secretary's certificate, Denning was up against the power of precedent. During the Second World War, at a time of national crisis, Lord Simon had set out, in *Duncan* v. *Cammell Laird*, the classes of document for which the Crown could claim privilege in litigation. The catch-all formula 'where the practice of keeping a class of documents secret is necessary for the proper functioning of the public service' had proved very useful to ministers; they tended to prefer it when claiming privilege, as had the Home Secretary in *Merricks*. Denning, strongly supported by Salmon, challenged precedent.

'The practice seems to have grown up,' he said, 'of giving a certificate in common form using those words. All that a secretary of state has to do is to put in the words, as if pronouncing a spell, and this makes all documents taboo . . . I must say that, if that state of affairs were to be accepted, it would indeed be deplorable.' Salmon was prepared to go even further than Denning in distinguishing *Duncan*'s case and it was unanimously held that the certificate in this case afforded no grounds for striking out the claim of libel. The court had thrown down a strong challenge to precedent.

Two months later, when a second claim of Crown privilege came before the same court, Denning developed the theme (*Grosvenor Hotel (No. 2)*). 'The actual decision in *Duncan*'s case cannot be questioned,' he said, paying lip-service to precedent before he attacked it by referring to the law in Scotland and in Commonwealth countries, where the Court had power to override objections from the Crown. He continued: 'In view of these developments, I think it is open to the House, and I believe to us, to reconsider the matter . . .' (This, at a time when the House of Lords still regarded itself as bound by its own precedent!) 'After all, it is the judges who are the guardians of justice in this land: and if they are to fulfil their trust, they must be able to call upon the Minister to put forward his reasons so as to see if they outweigh the interests of justice.'

Before the appeal in *Conway* v. *Rimmer*, brought to Denning's Court three years later, in June 1967, another case involving Crown privilege, a momentous change had taken place: the House of Lords had issued a statement that it would in future depart from one of its previous decisions when it appeared right to do so. Denning recognised that the opportunity had now arrived for an authoritative ruling on Crown privilege but, on this occasion, he had a differently constituted court, who were not prepared to disregard *Duncan*'s case. In one of his greatest dissents, Denning laid the ground for reform.

Conway v. *Rimmer*, like *Merricks*, was a case concerning the police. In December 1964, a young probationer in the Cheshire Constabulary lost an electric torch worth 15s 3d. He found a torch, which he said was his, in the locker of another probationer, Michael Conway. The matter was investigated by Superintendant Rimmer and Conway insisted the torch was his. In the course of the investigation Conway was told that his probationary reports were not good and he was urged to resign. He refused. He was charged with larceny and, at the end of the prosecution's case, in which Rimmer gave evidence, the jury stopped the trial and brought in a not guilty verdict. Shortly afterwards Rimmer dismissed Conway as a probationer; Conway then sued Rimmer for malicious prosecution. When discovery of documents was sought, the existence of five documents was disclosed and both Conway and Rimmer asked for discovery. It was refused on the ground of Crown privilege. Again, as in *Merricks*, the Home Secretary relied on Simon's words in *Duncan*'s case.

This time, Denning was alone in seeking to overrule them. 'I ventured to dissent,' he said in *The Discipline of Law*. 'Conway had no means. He could not appeal to the House of Lords unless he got legal aid. In order to get legal aid, it is helpful to have a dissenting judgment in your favour.' Repeating his words in the *Grosvenor Hotel* case, he continued:

> The objection of a Minister, even though taken in proper form, should not be conclusive. If the court should be of the opinion that the objection is not taken in good faith, or that there are no reasonable grounds for thinking that the production of documents would be injurious to the public interest, the court can override the objection and order production. It can, if it thinks fit, call for the documents and inspect them itself so as to see whether there are reasonable grounds for withholding them . . .

Denning referred to 'the classic judgment' of the Privy Council in *Robinson* v. *State of South Australia (No. 2)*, which was not followed by the Lords in *Duncan*'s case. He emphasised that, being free to choose, the courts of the Commonwealth had unanimously chosen to follow *Robinson*, not *Duncan*.

In the Lords, *Conway* v. *Rimmer* became the leading case on Crown privilege. Reid, Morris of Borth-y-Gest, Hodson, Pearce and Upjohn unanimously overruled the ruling of Lord Simon in *Duncan*'s case.

The words of Tom's friend, John Morris, must have been bittersweet to him:

My Lords, it seems to me that [the *Duncan*] decision was binding upon the Court of Appeal in the present case. Your Lordships have, however, a freedom which was not possessed by the Court of Appeal. Though precedent is an indispensable foundation upon which to decide what is the law, there may be times when a departure from precedent is in the interests of justice and the proper development of the law.

At a time when a less conservative House of Lords was moving closer to Denning's views on many legal questions he embarked on a crusade – doomed to failure – to win for the Court of Appeal the freedom that the House of Lords, at last, had awarded themselves.

Though it was the cases with a public aspect that caught the public eye, much of Denning's judicial work remained of a private nature. Aspects of the personal injury litigation that occupied much of the courts' time concerned him. He would have preferred to avoid altogether the dispute over 'fault'; it was wrong, he thought, that two people might suffer from virtually the same disability but the one who could prove someone responsible for his injury would receive damages, while the other had to make do with nothing. Knowing that the introduction of 'no fault' insurance was beyond the power of judicial law-making, Denning concentrated on a reform within his reach: the standardisation of damages. Part of the difficulty in achieving uniformity was a jury's lack of knowledge of awards in previous cases. Denning concluded that trial by jury should be restricted. At the end of 1964 the opportunity was afforded to him, by the appeal in *Ward* v. *James*, to lay down guidelines for the exercise of the court's discretion to order trial by jury in civil cases. He convened a Court of Appeal of five judges and reserved judgment until 25 January 1965, when he said:

Let it not be supposed that this court is in any way opposed to trial by jury. It has been the bulwark of our liberties too long for any of us to seek to alter it. Whenever a man is on trial for serious crime, or when in a civil case a man's honour or integrity is at stake, or when one or other party must be deliberately lying, then trial by jury has no equal . . .

But, when it came to awards of damages, so important was the question of a standard, that 'the judge ought not, in a personal injury case, to order trial by jury save in exceptional circumstances. Even when the issue of liability is one fit to be tried by a jury, nevertheless he might think it fit to order that the damages be assessed by a judge alone.'

In 1964 Tom's contributions to English prose writing were recognised by the English Association, who elected him their President. In July, following in the footsteps of men such as Arthur Bryant, Osbert Sitwell, G. M. Trevelyan and Kenneth Clark, he delivered his presidential address.

> You may wonder why I have chosen the title 'Gems in Ermine'. It is because I wish to speak to you of judges and of judgments. The judges wear the fur of the ermine as a mark of their calling. They give their judgments by word of mouth. These judgments have been taken down and recorded in our law books for over 700 years. There are to be found there 'full many a gem of purest ray serene.' When great issues have been at stake the judgments are marked by eloquence, wisdom and authority. They have laid the foundations of freedom in our land.

Tom was determined that his own judgments would rank among these gems in ermine and was conscious of the importance to him of law reporting. He took a keen interest in the proofs always submitted to a judge before inclusion of his judgment in the *Law Reports*: apart from the acknowledged tidying-up, 'he made many suggestions about the headnote.'[15] He might mark them with comments – reminiscent of his school-teaching days – such as 'a very good short summary' or 'with so many out of 10 – usually 9 if I remember correctly.'[34]

In the long vacation Tom and Joan went again to the meetings of the American and Canadian Bar Associations, this time by air. Joan was particularly looking forward to the visit, because her son was working in New York. On the first day of the conference security was tight as the opening speech was to be made by Richard Nixon, the President of the United States. Tom compared the size of the audience with the nearly empty room to which he had made his speech in Philadelphia, nine years earlier and wondered whether, on this occasion, the delegates would stay to hear him speak. He need not have worried: this time his reputation preceded him and he addressed a crowded hall. From New York the Dennings went to Vancouver Island to visit Tom's niece, then spent a few days in Banff, before travelling on to Montreal. There they were engulfed in a generous wave of hospitality: the Canadian Bar Association had taken Tom to their hearts and remained, ever after, among his most devoted friends.

They were home at the end of September and spent the first weekend of October 1964 at Cumberland Lodge with students from Lincoln's Inn. Their lives at the time, had either of them the leisure to consider it, were a strange mixture of the humdrum and the highly ceremonious. For Joan, the contrast was more pronounced: running two homes with very little help, seeing her grandchildren whenever she had time, were the hidden backdrop to the moments of pomp and splendour. At the State Opening of Parliament each year, as wife of the Master of the Rolls, Joan was assured of a seat, without depending on a ballot as most peeresses had to do.

The Chamber of the Lords was a colourful sight: the peers in their red robes, peeresses in full-length evening dress, with long gloves and tiaras, the diplomatic corps in court dress, all awaiting the arrival of the Queen. Tom, in his ceremonial dress sat on the woolsack at the foot of the throne. The absence of a back to his seat during the long wait was compensated by his excellent view. Always he liked to share with his family the good things that came his way; he was usually able to obtain one or two tickets to stand in the Royal Gallery and, over the years, most of the family – and many friends – shared his pleasure at the State Opening.

The re-opening of the Law Courts, after the long vacation, brought another moment of pageantry. In their full-bottomed wigs and robes, judges and Queen's Counsel, wearing knee-breeches, black stockings and buckled shoes, gathered in Westminster Abbey, as the bells pealed for a special service. After it, preceded by his mace-bearer and an officer carrying the tasselled and embroidered purse of the Great Seal, and followed by his train-bearers, the Lord Chancellor led the procession from the east end of the Abbey, through the street to the House of Lords. Behind him walked the

Lord Chief Justice in scarlet and ermine, the Master of the Rolls, the President of the Probate Divorce and Admiralty Division and the Lords Justices of the Court of Appeal, all in black and gold. After them went the judges of the High Court, the silks and a few junior members of the Bar. In the Long Gallery of the Lords they were entertained to the Lord Chancellor's breakfast – more of a drinks party than a breakfast – before the procession made its way, most resorting to motor vehicles, to the Central Hall of the Law Courts in the Strand. There they changed into workaday attire, less heavy wigs and plain linen bands to replace the lace jabots; Tom's gold-encrusted gown replaced by a simple black one, he took his seat in No. 3 Court and another legal year began.

The third of the autumnal ceremonies – Lord Mayor's Day – always took place on a Saturday in November. It was a wonderful treat for children and the Dennings usually had a family party. They watched the passing of the Lord Mayor's procession, with its many colourful floats and marching bands, from the balcony over the main entrance of the Law Courts. Then, while the outgoing and incoming Mayors were greeted in the Court of the Lord Chief Justice, Joan sat her guests, in readiness, on either side of the bench in No. 3 Court. Very soon, the Mayor and other dignitaries crowded into the Master of the Rolls's court and he made a speech of welcome, before taking the family back for lunch in the Lincoln's Inn flat.

Away from the glare of publicity and the pomp of ceremony there were many tasks that fell to the Master of the Rolls. For centuries courts kept their own records until, in the nineteenth century, all legal records – and, later, departmental records as well – were gathered together, under control of the Master of the Rolls, in the Public Record Office, built on the site of the old Rolls Estate in Chancery Lane. By 1877 'it became apparent that the Public Record Office was being cluttered up with useless documents'[58] and the Master of the Rolls was authorised to make rules for getting rid of valueless papers. In 1952 responsibility for public records was transferred to the Lord Chancellor. At the same time there was a change in emphasis: instead of asking which documents could be destroyed, the question became which ought to be kept. Still the volume of paper increased. By 1963 the legal records in High Court civil cases alone occupied some four miles of shelving in the Public

Record Office; original wills took up half as much again. A new look at records was clearly required and, on 4 January 1963, the Lord Chancellor asked the Master of the Rolls to chair a committee on legal records. Twice the Committee's terms of reference were extended, until its brief included 'nearly all the legal records of the realm.'[56] It was a formidable task and a 'finicky' one.[56] The Committee included officials of the Record Office, a High Court Judge, Sir Denys Buckley, and Master A. S. Diamond of the Queen's Bench Division. Before work began, Denning saw the young barrister from the Lord Chancellor's Department seconded to act as secretary, Thomas Legg, gave him a broad outline of how he saw the job, then left Legg to get on with arranging the details.

Though meetings were 'friendly and agreeable',[56] there was a certain difference of approach between lawyers and non-lawyers over who should hold what records, and why. None disputed the courtesy with which Denning conducted the meetings, but some believed that, where there was an issue between lawyers and other professions, the Chairman put more weight on the opinions of the lawyers. Their suspicion was correct: in his work, his lectures and his writing Tom never hid his view that the legal profession was entirely special and though he did not say it in so many words, superior to all others.

Pauline Simond described her step-father's conduct of meetings of the drama school as 'avuncular'. In the more formal setting of the committee on legal records, Tom was exactly the same. Lord Denning was 'like a friendly uncle', Legg, who had become Permanent Secretary in the Lord Chancellor's Department, recalled in 1990, 'he presided over meetings in the same way – gave just the right amount of steer and left the experts to say their bits. He struck just the right balance.' Legg enjoyed the job and it was with some regret that he left the Committee before its work was finished. In the general election of October 1964 the Labour Government obtained a majority; Harold Wilson became Prime Minister and Gerald Gardiner was made Lord Chancellor. In 1965 Tom Legg was appointed Lord Gardiner's private secretary. His place as secretary to the Committee was taken by one of its members, E. W. Denham, an official of the Public Record Office, who edited the first part and wrote the second part of the report. Over a long weekend, Tom re-wrote it in his own style. He did not change the substance: 'There were some ambiguities which disappeared under his treatment . . . It just gave a bit of flexibility if things turned out unworkable.'[56]

On 16 May 1966 the Master of the Rolls addressed his report to the new Lord Chancellor, a man who had been his contemporary in his last year at Magdalen College. 'If our proposals are implemented,' he wrote, 'the Public Record Office alone will be relieved of two hundred tons of records (occupying 15,000 feet of shelving) . . . The effect in other offices where legal records are stored is not easily calculated, but it is safe to forecast that many times this quantity of records will be similarly released.'

Tom Denning was not interested in politics, though he had great diplomatic skills. In *The Closing Chapter*, he wrote: 'I have never been a member of a political party. I have never voted in a parliamentary election.' In his lack of interest, he followed his parents. He had no recollection of his father or his mother speaking about politics or showing any interest in elections. He was, Joan told the *Daily Express* in June 1972 'entirely unpolitical . . . interested in a broad outlook no matter what party is in power.' Indeed, he went beyond pure uninterest; he took care to distance himself from any political association: 'I have refused invitations to any meeting, fete or dance sponsored by a political party. I regard this of the first importance so that all should know that I am independent of any political party whatsoever.'[59] His relations with Lords Chancellor were determined by personal and judicial attitudes, rather than by politics; they were not always easy. Though Tom had never put a foot wrong as he climbed the ladder of the Bar, once appointed to the Bench, he made clear that he was his own man. Except where security and the maintenance of law and order were issues, Denning could not be depended upon to toe the established line. Jowitt, who led Tom at the Bar and knew him, probably, as well as any Chancellor, wrote to tell him that judges should not publish books; Simonds – a lawyer rather than a politician – regarded much of Denning's judicial work as heretical; Kilmuir thought highly of Tom's book *The Road to Justice* but believed that a judge should not be too much in the public eye.

Lord Gardiner was the son of a prosperous shipping director; he was educated at Harrow, and was an officer in the Coldstream

Guards before going up to Oxford. At the time he showed more interest in acting than the law and was reputed to have gone to the Bar on the principle that it would be easier to try the stage as an unsuccessful barrister than the other way about. In the Fifties and early Sixties, he was a highly successful Queen's Counsel who defended Lawrence's *Lady Chatterley's Lover* against prosecution for obscenity. He was known for his sponsorship of left-wing and humanitarian causes: a supporter of reform of the law on homosexuality and abortion, as well as the abolition of hanging. Gardiner and Denning were very different men but shared a desire for law reform. The one great difference between them was over capital punishment and, in the end, Tom came to recognise that his own position had been wrong. Where other Chancellors were disturbed by Denning's high profile, Gardiner seemed untroubled. The two men, each in his way an old-fashioned Victorian liberal, regarded one another with 'mutual respect'.[60]

Denning had always expressed concern at aspects of trade unionism and recognised that a man's freedom to earn his living would sometimes have to be defended against his union; but until 1964 he had never pronounced judicially on a trade dispute case. The position over industrial action was not straightforward. There was no positive legal right to strike: an employee's withdrawal of his labour was a breach of his contract of employment. A union official organising any form of action would commit the tort of inducing breach of contract, unless he came within the immunity given by the Trade Disputes Act 1906 for actions in 'contemplation' or 'furtherance' of a trade dispute.

In 1963, while Denning was engaged in the Profumo Inquiry, the courts had to deal with the threat to call a strike at the British Overseas Airway Corporation, unless the Corporation dismissed an employee who had resigned his union membership. *Rookes* v. *Barnard*, in which Denning took no part, reached the House of Lords in January 1964 and the effect of their decision was virtually to render useless the protection given by the 1906 Act. The government introduced legislation to restore the position but, before it could come into effect, Denning moved to counter the Lords' decision.

At the time, the Union of Watermen, Lightermen, Tugmen and Bargemen organised most of the watermen in the area of the Port of

London. Disappointed in its attempts to reach an agreement with Bowker & King where most employees belonged to the TGWU, the union tried to bring pressure on the company by blacking J. T. Stratford & Son, another company controlled by Bowker & King's Chairman, Mr Jack Stratford, where all the employees were members of the Watermen's union. Denning declined to find the union officials had done anything wrong, other than this: 'In order to get recognition for their union, they have induced or threatened to induce the lightermen to break their contracts of employment.' With Pearson dissenting, he and Salmon found that the officials had acted in contemplation of a trade dispute and were protected from the company's action by the 1906 Act. The House of Lords disagreed. Holding that the union had not proved there was a trade dispute, they allowed the company's appeal.

If Denning had not been anxious to reassert the protection for the organisers of a strike, seemingly lost because of *Rookes* v. *Barnard*, it is difficult to believe that he would have found for union officials bringing pressure to bear on a company with which they had no dispute. His upbringing and his instincts predisposed him to favour organisations that improved the lot of the working man, but he abhorred any group's power to intimidate and threaten. Subsequent events on the industrial scene affected Denning's view of union activities, as, indeed, they began to polarise attitudes in much of the country. *Stratford* v. *Lindley* presented the mirror image of cases like *Duport Steel* at the end of the 1970s, when Denning would become the bugbear of the unions.

During the 1950s Britain's economy had achieved a level where people talked of 'the affluent society'. The next decade saw deepening economic problems. Though wages and prices increased, productivity lagged behind that of other industrial countries and successive governments were forced to resort to income policies and wage restraints. There was considerable industrial unrest but the return of a Labour government, in 1964, raised hopes, that were not fulfilled, of better labour relations. Less than two years later, in May 1966, the Wilson Government was forced to declare a State of Emergency when the seamen went on strike over the number of hours to be worked before they were paid overtime. In July it imposed a freeze on pay and dividends because of the economic crisis and in October, strikes reduced the car industry to chaos. Looking at the industrial scene and at student demonstrations and 'sit-ins' which seemed to have more to do with politics than education, many people asked whether Britain was becoming ungovernable.

Never troubled by political consideration, always confident that he knew what was right for the country, Denning struck a balance in his union cases between the rights and duties of conflicting parties. If, in one decision, he stated a principle too widely, he backtracked in another to meet new circumstances. The right to strike, the right to protest and demonstrate were to be protected while they were lawfully exercised but not when they endangered the good order of the state.

In January 1968 he started to dismantle the barriers to success when companies claimed that unions had induced the breach of a commercial contract. The Transport and General Workers' Union formed a branch in Torquay to organise hotel workers and wrote to the managing director of the Torbay Hotel, insisting on a meeting 'in order to avoid serious consequences.' The reply was that no useful purpose would be served by a meeting in view of the hotel's negotiations with another union, whereupon members of the TGWU working at the hotel withdrew their labour and picketed the hotel. The tanker drivers, who delivered oil to the hotel and were members of the union, were instructed not to cross the picket lines and, within a few days, the hotel had run out of fuel. After an inaccurate report in a local newspaper that the manager of the Imperial Hotel had said the Hotel Association was determined to stamp out the intervention of the TGWU, pickets were posted at that hotel also and its oil suppliers, Esso Petroleum, were warned to stop deliveries. Having managed to obtain supplies at a much higher price, the owner of the Imperial, Torquay Hotel Co. Ltd, sought an undertaking from the union to withdraw blacking instructions; as they did not get it, they issued a writ against the union, its general secretary, Frank Cousins, and other officials, seeking damages for wrongful procurement of breach of contract and interference with trade or contractual relations. The trial judge, Stamp J, granted an interlocutory injunction restraining the union and some of its officials from interfering with contracts to supply the hotel with oil and from picketing at the Imperial. The union's appeal reached the Court of Appeal in

November 1968. Sitting with Russell and Winn, Denning allowed the appeal of the union itself, but dismissed the appeals of the officials. Though he agreed there was a trade dispute with the Torbay Hotel, he found none with the Imperial. In acting as they did, he said, the officials 'were not furthering a trade dispute, but their own fury.'

Though they agreed that the appeal should be dismissed, neither Russell nor Winn was prepared to go so far as Denning, who suggested that interference with a contract which fell short of causing a breach could also be wrongful. Just the same, the scene was set for the extension, by the judiciary as a whole, of the liability of union officials for causing breaches of commercial contracts, while preserving their right to induce breaches of contracts of employment.

'It is not that Lord Denning is excessively liberal,' wrote the *Sunday Mirror*, on 16 October 1966. 'It is merely that he always seems to decide a case the way you or I would.' Examples were legion. Denning disliked the time-honoured construction put upon the words 'child or children' in wills, so as to exclude any but the legitimate child of a mother's body, and other constructions that would keep an illegitimate or adopted child from benefit under a Trust. In *Jebb* he returned to the method he used in *Rowland*: 'In construing this will, we have to look at it as the testator did, sitting in his armchair, with all the circumstances known to him at the time. Then we have to ask ourselves: "What did he intend?" We ought not to answer this question by reference to any technical rules of law . . .'

His heretical approach roused a torrent of criticism amongst Chancery lawyers and academics. Dr John Morris wrote an article in the *Law Quarterly Review* headed 'Palm Tree Justice in the Court of Appeal', claiming that the Court seemed to have 'usurped the function of the legislature' and reduced the construction of wills 'to the level of guesswork.' The quip was heard that, instead of eminent lawyers of the past, the upholders of Denning's coat-of-arms might better have been two monkeys.

When *Sydall* v. *Castings Ltd* came up, the following year, Denning again challenged the established rules of construction – this time of a group life assurance scheme – on behalf of an illegitimate child. The case is memorable for Lord Justice Russell's claim to follow Portia in his refusal to 'wrest once the law' to his authority. In *The Discipline of Law* Denning had the last word. Reminding his readers of the way in which Portia, in *The Merchant of Venice*, achieved justice, he claimed, triumphant, that he, too, was 'a Portia man'.

For the 750th anniversary of Magna Carta, in June 1965, Tom wrote an article in *The Times*. It was history, Denning-style, appealing to those with little knowledge of the subject.

> Seven centuries and a half ago, in the month of June 1215, the meadow of Runnymede looked much as it does today. The season was early and the commoners of Egham had cut their hay. To this meadow came the King and the Barons. Their parleys culminated in the greatest constitutional document of all time. It is commonly called Magna Carta, or the Great Charter.

1965 was a good year for Tom and for his brother Norman, who was appointed Deputy Chief of Defence Staff (Intelligence). At the Encaenia at Oxford, on 23 June 1965, Tom was made an Honorary Doctor of Civil Law, together with the Prime Minister, Harold Wilson, and the law lord, Patrick Devlin. After delivering in Latin his speech presenting Denning to the Chancellor, A. N. Bryan Brown of Worcester College translated:

> Some have complained that our judicial system does not always produce justice, but we mostly agree with Cicero that law is the foundation of freedom and the fount of equity; and this view is confirmed by the services of Lord Denning.

With all his honours, it was a proud moment for Tom, when the Chancellor of his own university addressed him thus:

> Distinguished lawyer, you have constantly presided over important cases with the greatest wisdom and judgment; with my authority and that of the University as a whole, I admit you to the degree of Doctor of Civil Law *honoris causa*.

Three years into his period as Master of the Rolls, Tom Denning was already regarded by lawyers as a phenomenon. Even those who observed his idiosyncratic style of judgment with suspicion, mostly recognised and admired his flashes of genius. There was a certain amount of speculation about Tom's extraordinary appeal to young lawyers and to those outside the law. In 1983, writing a Foreword to a book published after Tom's retirement,[49] Lord Devlin gave his answer: 'The secret of Lord Denning's attraction – for the professions as well as for the general public – is, I think, the belief that he opens the door to the law above the law.' No better explanation can be found of the admiration and affection with which Tom was surrounded in his early years as Master of the Rolls.

20

The Streams of English Justice

After a busy summer, with guests most weekends at The Lawn, Tom and Joan flew to South America on 14 August 1965, on a month's tour sponsored by the British Council. They were to visit Brazil, Uruguay, Argentina, Chile and Peru, before flying north to Mexico City, Washington and Winnipeg. Everywhere Tom had speaking engagements and in Buenos Aires Joan, too, was to talk, at the British Club. When she asked her audience what they would like her to talk about, the response was immediate: they wanted to know what the Master of the Rolls does.

Meeting judges, lawyers and their wives, Tom and Joan were splendid ambassadors for England and its legal system. Their mixture of dignity and informality, their obvious fascination with the laws and customs of the lands they visited and their interest in the sights they were shown, always endeared them to their hosts. From Rio de Janeiro they were taken to see Brasilia, still in the first stages of construction; in Argentina they stayed a night on the vast *estancia* of one of the country's major cattle ranchers; on the spectacular flight over the Andes from Cordoba to Chile, the pilot invited them onto the flight deck for a better view. Though the journey was strenuous, the people they were meeting and the sights they were seeing were exciting, invigorating and new.

In the next decade a large part of all Tom's vacations would be spent in overseas travel. On 6 January 1966 the Dennings flew to Malta, where Tom had engagements to speak to legal and lay audiences. At Easter they went further afield, by way of San Francisco and Fiji to New Zealand for the law conference at Dunedin. They arrived on Good Friday and were taken to Taupo, the volcanic centre of the North Island, to spend the holiday. Then they crossed to the South Island for the conference, where Tom so impressed an Australian visitor that he was invited to speak at the Australian Law Society Conference the following summer.

Their journey to New Zealand had an improbable sequel. While they were in Dunedin, the Dennings heard that people present with them at a lunch party in Taupo on Easter Sunday had been taken ill. They were shocked to learn that, though most had recovered, their hostess and her neighbour's young son had died from arsenic poisoning. There was a police investigation and samples of hair taken from Tom and Joan, after their return to England, were thought to have traces of arsenic. Only some time later did they discover the story behind the deaths. Their hostess had planned to commit suicide by putting poison in her own food at the party – she had, indeed, made a previous attempt of this kind. Unexpected help from her neighbours in preparing the lunch party had caused food to become mixed in a way that she had not anticipated and arsenic had contaminated some of the salads.

In 1965 matters came to a head in a long-running dispute between women horse-trainers and the Jockey Club, when the Club allowed a Belgian woman trainer to enter and run horses at Ascot, while maintaining that it was their policy 'not to allow women trainers in this country.' Mrs Florence Nagle, the daughter of Sir George Watson, founder of Maypole Dairies (now part of Allied Suppliers), was one of the first women to hold a driving licence; she had owned racehorses since 1922 and bred them since the early 1930s. She had consistently applied for and been refused a trainer's licence. She had both the determination and the money to challenge the Jockey Club in the courts. She applied for an order against the Club and was refused by the judge.

In February 1966 the matter came before Denning, sitting with Danckwerts and Salmon. Unanimously they allowed Mrs Nagle's appeal. Not only did Denning reiterate in *Nagle* v. *Fielden* some of his old themes on the right to work but also, before it became a major issue, he commented on the illegality of sex discrimination. Twenty years later, when Tom was in retirement, Mrs Nagle wrote to him. On 31 January 1986 he replied:

I am simply delighted to have your letter – your case against the Jockey Club is a leading case in the law – it is often cited by lawyers and in the Text Books. I was very pleased to have the opportunity of hearing it.

So you are 91 – and still going well . . .

I am 87 – with eyesight and hearing failing – but still keeping on in the House of Lords . . .

It was the salute of one English eccentric to another.

Strong as was Denning's conviction that 'the judges are the guardians of justice in this land,' he recognised that the courts could interfere with a ministerial decision only if the minister had gone outside the powers given to him by the statute under which they were exercised. In July 1966, sitting with Diplock and Russell, the Master of the Rolls considered an exercise of power by the Minister of Agriculture Fisheries and Food. Since 1933 dairy farmers had been compelled to sell their milk to the Milk Marketing Board at prices that were fixed periodically and which differed within the eleven regions of England and Wales. The Board bore the cost of distribution from the farm gate, so that the regions furthest from the large centres of population were paid less from the fixed total sum available than those close to the ultimate consumers of the milk. In 1964 the farmers in the south-east complained that the differential in their favour should be increased because it was set when fares were lower. The Board refused to increase the price paid in the south-east and the farmers asked the Minister to exercise his discretion to refer their complaint to the statutory committee of investigation. The Minister refused. The farmers obtained an order of *mandamus* commanding the Minister to consider their request, without taking into account irrelevant considerations. On the Minister's appeal, Diplock and Russell decided that the court was not justified in ordering the Minister to reconsider the complaint. Denning did not agree. After examining the facts, he said:

It is plain to me that by these provisions Parliament has provided machinery by which complaints of farmers can be investigated by a committee which is independent of the board and by which those complaints, if justified, can be remedied . . . This case raises the important question: How far can the Minister reject the complaint out of hand? . . . I can well see that he may quite properly reject some of the complaints without more ado. They may be frivolous or wrong-headed: or they may be repetitive of old complaints already disposed of. But there are others which he cannot properly reject. In my opinion every genuine complaint which is worthy of investigation by the committee of investigation should be referred to that committee. The Minister is not at liberty to refuse it on grounds which are arbitrary or capricious . . .

(*Padfield* v. *Minister of Agriculture*)

On this occasion, the Lords, with Morris dissenting, agreed with Denning.

After being 'verbally beheaded' by Simonds over his dissenting judgment in *Midland Silicones*, Tom had not given up the fight against the doctrine of privity of contract. He continued to believe that a third party with a sufficient interest in a contract should be allowed to rely upon it. Diplomatically he used other arguments than those which the Lords had rejected but, in 1966, when *Beswick* v. *Beswick* reached the Court of Appeal, once again he directly challenged the Lords. The facts, as he gave them, were these:

Old Peter Beswick was a coal merchant in Eccles, Lancashire. He had no business premises. All he had was a lorry, scales and weights. He used to take the lorry to the yard of the National Coal Board, where he bagged coal and took it round to his customers in the neighbourhood. His nephew, John Joseph Beswick, helped him in the business.

In March 1962, old Peter Beswick and his wife were both over 70 . . . The nephew was anxious to get hold of the business before the old man died. So they went to a solicitor, Mr Ashcroft, who drew up an agreement for them. The business was to be transferred to the nephew: old Peter Beswick was to be employed in it as a consultant for the rest of his life at £6 10s a week. After his death the nephew was to pay the widow an annuity of £5 per week, which was to come out of the business.

After the old man's death, in November 1963, the nephew paid the widow the first £5 and then refused to pay any more. She sued the nephew, both as administratrix of her husband's estate and in a personal capacity. Her action was dismissed by the judge on the ground that she had no right to enforce a contract to which she was not privy. 'If the decision . . . truly represents the law of England,' said the Master of the Rolls, at the appeal, 'it would be deplorable.' He repeated his earlier arguments about the interest of the third party being sufficient to justify her enforcement of the contract in her personal capacity, and added a new one relying on a section of the Law of Property Act 1925. Though the House of Lords upheld the decision of the Court of Appeal to order the nephew to pay the widow, as administratrix of her husband's estate, they did not agree with Denning's view that she was also entitled to an order in her personal capacity. The third-party citadel was beyond the reach of the Master of the Rolls.

Fundamental to the notion of a fair trial, Denning believed, was the independence of the Bar. Relying on this proposition, he vigorously repulsed an attempt, in June 1966, to make barristers, like all other professional men, liable for negligence. The case of *Rondel* v. *Worsley* was in every way extraordinary and not one likely, at any event, to attract the court's sympathy. Mr Worsley was a barrister and Mr Rondel was a client he had defended, seven years earlier, on a dock brief. The facts of Rondel's trial and conviction were as astonishing as his decision to seek damages from his barrister for professional negligence. In April 1959 Rondel, who was employed as a rent collector by Peter Rachman, a notorious slum landlord, went to a house where a dance was taking place. After a row with a man at the door, Rondel, by his own admission, so severely damaged the doorkeeper's hand that nine stitches had to be put in it, and also bit off the lobe of the man's right ear. At the Old Bailey Rondel pleaded not guilty and asked for legal aid. He was told that he could not have legal aid but, if he had £2 4s 6d, he could have the services of any barrister in court, on a dock brief. Rondel picked Michael Worsley, a barrister of four years standing. After an adjournment to enable him to take instructions, Worsley cross-examined witnesses and addressed the court on Rondel's behalf. The jury found Rondel guilty and he was sentenced to 18 months' imprisonment. Rondel complained about his barrister to the Court of Criminal Appeal but his appeal was unsuccessful and he served his sentence. After his release, he was soon in trouble again and, in September 1960, was sentenced to another three years. In February 1965 he issued a writ against Mr Worsley, writing out his own statement of claim. His allegations were, in essence, that Worsley had not cross-examined sufficiently and had not called the witnesses Rondel wanted. He was serving another sentence of 18 months – for stealing – when he wrote out a second statement of claim, which was later described by a judge in chambers as 'well-nigh unintelligible'.

In May 1965 Master Lawrence, in chambers, ordered that the statement of claim be struck out and the action dismissed. Rondel appealed to a judge in chambers, Browne J, who realised that the matter raised a point of general public interest: whether an action for negligence can be brought against a barrister for the conduct of a case in court. The judge adjourned the case into open court and asked the Official Solicitor to appoint counsel to bring to the court's attention all the authorities on the subject. When the hearing of the appeal was ready, Browne was not available and the case was heard by Mr Justice Lawton. After a comprehensive analysis of the authorities and the arguments, Lawton concluded that, for reasons of public policy, an advocate could not be sued for negligence in the conduct of his client's case in court. The judge stressed that the immunity was due to an advocate rather than a barrister, arising from the part which an advocate plays in the administration of justice, not from membership of an Inn of Court. The plaintiff, still in prison, obtained leave to appeal and, at that stage, got help from a solicitor, Michael Zander, who was interested in the point of law and drew up a new statement of claim.

The question of whether a barrister could be sued for professional negligence was one the Master of the Rolls intended for his own court. He heard it with Danckwerts and Salmon. Denning's influence on the development of the law of negligence in the second half of the century was immense. In general, he seemed to work from the assumption that, where there was an injury, there must be a remedy; his sympathy was usually with the person injured. Claims of professional negligence affected Tom differently. He always insisted that negligence should not be found too easily against a professional man, who might well be covered by insurance, but whose reputation was at risk. In this case, where the defendant belonged to his own profession, his sympathy was doubly engaged.

THE STREAMS OF ENGLISH JUSTICE

Unanimously the court upheld Lawton's decision that the immunity of an advocate for his conduct of a case in court was based on public policy. Salmon dissented when Denning and Danckwerts went on to extend a barrister's immunity to advisory work and to settling documents having no connection with court work. Barristers, unlike any other professional men, were to be protected from suit for every aspect of their work; not just because public policy demanded it as regards their court work, but because a barrister should be able to 'settle a prospectus or a tax-avoidance scheme' without being subject to the thought: 'if I should make a mistake and the client is made liable, he may sue me for a million pounds.' No other advocate was to be accorded such immunity. Special pleading for their own profession must have prompted Denning and Danckwerts expressly to enlarge its immunities and, at the same time, to negate the possibility that other advocates deserved protection in the name of public interest. Their decision was upheld when the case reached the House of Lords; but in 1978, in *Saif Ali* v. *Sidney Mitchell*, different law lords by a majority confined the immunity of barristers to the actual conduct of a case in court and some pre-trial work, thus re-stating the law as, in *Rondel*, it was thought to be by Lawton and Salmon. By a majority – which included Lord Salmon, as he had then become – it was also decided that the same immunity attaches to a solicitor acting as an advocate.

Though Tom had little time to attend debates in the House of Lords, there were some subjects on which he wanted a voice. In the summer of 1967 there was great concern about attempts to suborn jurors in cases of highly organised crime, such as bank robbery. The Lord Chancellor proposed that majority verdicts should be accepted, and Denning opposed the change in the debate on 6 June. Fifteen years later he still felt there was no room for complacency though, in *What Next in the Law?*, he admitted that majority verdicts of ten to two had proved very successful.

The Australian Law Society Conference of 1967 was to take place at Adelaide and Tom planned to spend the week there, then visit Sydney, Perth, Melbourne, Brisbane, Alice Springs and Tasmania. Altogether he would be out of England for five weeks. He and Joan left England on 8 July. The Conference went well and the Dennings flew on to Sydney. There, Tom was to speak at a students' dinner at the University. At a previous dinner, he heard, there had been slow hand-clapping for a boring speaker, and his hosts were hoping there would be no trouble on this occasion. After the meal, the first speaker was treated to the slow hand-clap; then it was Tom's turn. He stood up and bread rolls were thrown about the room. It was a challenge. Tom told the students they were giving a welcome fit for the Master of the Rolls. He caught their attention and he held it. He spoke for three-quarters of an hour and, at the end, received a standing ovation. Students crowded his table for his signature on their menu-cards. The crush became so great that the top of the trestle-table began to slip gradually backwards, the guest of honour with it. For another hour Tom signed his name and talked to the students. Again he demonstrated his mastery of an audience and, after his visit, the University started a Denning Law Society in his honour.

On their way home, there was a four-hour evening stop at Delhi. Never liking to waste time, the Dennings decided to give a dinner for members of the Indian judiciary and Bar who had welcomed them during their visit in 1963–4. They took off, at midnight, for England, arriving home in the second week in August, to enjoy the rest of the summer vacation at The Lawn. The family had expanded: Joan now had eight grandchildren and the annexe was regularly in use. During the year Robert, who had taken a three-year appointment at the University of Illinois, became engaged to Elizabeth Chilton, a friend from his Oxford days; they were married on 30 December 1967, in the Chapel at Magdalen College, with John Stuart as best man and John's twins as bridesmaids.

In 1967 Tom had made a brief visit, on his own, to Montreal, to add an honorary doctorate from McGill University to his collection. During the Whitsun recess the following year, he returned to Canada with Joan. They left England for Vancouver on 28 May 1968, to visit Tom's niece and her family in Victoria. Then they were taken by car on another spectacular journey through the Rocky Mountains to Calgary, where Tom addressed a dinner for the Bar.

These journeys abroad brought Tom and Joan many friends who, in the summer-time, often visited England. The Dennings were always pleased to return the hospitality they had received and summer months at The Lawn saw a succession of weekend guests.

On one occasion in 1968 there were friends from Canada, New Zealand and Australia staying for the weekend, and the High Commissioner for India with his family coming for lunch. Tom basked in company and delighted to add any members of the family or English friends who happened to be about. Some – Reginald Dilhorne and Gavin Simonds among them – came with their wives to fish in Tom's beautiful stretch of river. Whatever tension there might be between Denning and Simonds over legal issues, their relationship outside the courts was cordial.

There were times when official duties overran weekends and, with Joan, Tom travelled about the country: to a celebration of the Magna Carta Trust, when he walked to a civic service through the streets of St. Albans, holding in his hand part of the original charter; to a meeting of the Birmingham Law Society; to a conference of the Magistrates' Association on the Isle of Wight and to Exeter for the Bracton Memorial celebrations (in honour of the 13th-century judge who established the concept of precedent in English Law). There were other times when Tom's working week was punctuated by the semi-official social round: receptions at the Inns of Court, the Royal Garden Party and the Lord Mayor's Dinner for the Judges. Whatever he did and wherever he went Tom enjoyed himself and spread enjoyment to those around him. On Call Night at Lincoln's Inn he made a point of talking with newly called barristers and their families; he did the same at the Law Society with young solicitors he had just admitted to the Rolls. So popular did he become with the young that, ten years after his retirement, it was not unusual for a newly qualified solicitor to have a photo taken in front of the portrait of Lord Denning on the Law Society's staircase.

If Lord Denning invoked public policy in 1966 to exempt barristers from liability for negligence, in the next few years he called upon it to make others liable: the Home Office, when Borstal boys escaped and caused damage to a yacht in Poole Harbour; a local authority which issued a clear certificate to a developer that failed to show a registered land charge, resulting in the developer's being able to take the property free of the charge; and Bognor Regis UDC for its surveyor's failure to notice, when he made his inspection, that a house was being built without proper foundations. Alongside Denning's willingness to consider the decisions of ministers, statutory bodies or domestic tribunals, was his liberal view of *locus standi*, or standing to sue. English law always took a restrictive approach to the question of who has the right, as a person aggrieved, to seek a remedy in the courts: by and large, standing was limited to people suffering particular loss of money or property rights, over and above any damage to the public in general. In his fight against the abuse of power, Denning was prepared to open the door more widely. His concern was always that wrong-doing should not pass unchallenged for lack of someone both able and willing to bring a matter before the court. His recognition that Miss Maurice might have an interest in protecting the amenities of Battersea Park (*Maurice* v. *LCC*); and that the Peachey Property Company, as a ratepayer, was entitled to challenge the rating valuation list, even though their own valuation would not be affected by the decision (*R.* v. *Paddington Valuation Office*) was only a foretaste of the cases where he would allow a private citizen to challenge the Attorney-General or the Commissioner of the Metropolitan Police for their failure to act in matters of public importance.

Tom was often attracted by maverick personalities and Raymond Blackburn, who had been a Member of Parliament and retained an interest in matters of public concern, was a welcome litigant in his court. Nearly always, Tom thought, Blackburn's intervention 'proved most useful'.[24] The first time Blackburn came before Denning was on 24 January 1968. In his judgment, Denning gave the facts:

> In 1966, Mr Blackburn was concerned about the way in which the big London clubs were being run. He went to see a representative of the Commissioner of the Police of the Metropolis and told him that illegal gaming was taking place in virtually all London casinos. He was given to understand, he says, that action would be taken. But nothing appeared to be done.

> There was, in fact, a policy decision that no proceedings would be taken unless there were complaints or the clubs became haunts of criminals.

> No prosecutions were instituted in the Metropolis against these clubs. That is what Mr Blackburn complains of. He says that the

policy decision was erroneous and that it was the duty of the commissioner to prosecute.

R. v. Commissioner of Police ex parte Blackburn

With this view Denning agreed. Since the Commissioner had undertaken to take the necessary steps, the question of whether Blackburn had a sufficient interest to protect was left open. In the last paragraph of his judgment, Denning used the words 'the day of reckoning is at hand.' The High Court journalists presented him with a cartoon showing an unfortunate sandwich-board man, whose board bore those words, being knocked about by thugs, outside a gambling club, protesting 'Dear Friend, I repeat – I am not Lord Denning.' Twelve years later, in *The Discipline of Law*, Denning gave the sequel: 'The Home Secretary (Mr James Callaghan) invited me to see him to discuss the reform of the law.' Whether or not Blackburn had *locus standi*, Denning's intervention ensured that the Commissioner's promised steps were to be taken.

On 26 February, Blackburn was back with a complaint about the Rt Hon. Quintin Hogg, QC, MP. Son of a Lord Chancellor and himself a minister in the previous Conservative Government, Hogg had returned to the Bar when the Labour Government was elected. Blackburn's complaint concerned an article Hogg had written for *Punch*, vigorously criticising the decision of the Court of Appeal in the gaming case: it was, said Blackburn, contempt of court. Denning sat with Salmon and Edmund Davies to hear the first case in which the Court of Appeal had to consider an allegation of contempt of itself. He said:

Let me say at once that we will never use this jurisdiction as a means to uphold our own dignity. That must rest on surer foundations. Nor will we use it to suppress those who speak against us. We do not fear criticism, nor do we resent it. For there is something far more important at stake. It is no less than freedom of speech itself.

It is the right of every man, in Parliament or out of it, in the press or over the broadcast, to make fair comment, even outspoken comment, on matters of public interest. . . . We must rely on our conduct itself to be its own vindication.

Replying to Hogg's suggestion that, for the judges, 'silence is always an option', Denning commented: 'Silence is not an option when things are ill done.'

> So it comes to this: Mr Quintin Hogg has criticised the court, but in so doing he is exercising his undoubted right. The article contains an error, no doubt, but errors do not make it a contempt of court. We must uphold his right to the uttermost.

Quintin Hogg, who would shortly become Lord Chancellor, wrote that day to thank Tom for his 'magnanimous attitude' and to apologise 'abjectly' for any offence or embarrassment caused.

In the series of cases where Denning spearheaded reform of the machinery for controlling administrative power, he stressed that impartiality and fairness must guide decisions; and that the same remedies should be available when these rules were broken, regardless of whether the decision could be called judicial or administrative. It might be argued before him that the decision to exclude a would-be immigrant, or the decision to refuse a licence to a gaming club were administrative decisions, not subject to the rules of natural justice, but Lord Denning's view was to the contrary: immigrants 'have no right to come in, but they have a right to be heard', the Gaming Board 'have a duty to act fairly' and must let an applicant know 'what their impressions are', so that he has the opportunity to satisfy them.

None of this meant that Denning was always on the side of the challenger. It was the streams of English justice that 'must be kept clear and pure', a subject on which he would write eloquently in *The Due Process of Law*. When it came to the applicants themselves, there were some classes with whom Lord Denning had less sympathy than others. These were people who had either behaved badly, or, it seemed to Denning, were likely to do so. He followed his instincts. As he wrote in *The Changing Law*, 'The English distrust abstract philosophy as much as they distrust formal logic . . . The English approach is empirical.' In 1968, when the Home Secretary refused, without a hearing, to extend the stay of students from the United States who belonged to a group calling themselves scientologists, Lord Denning upheld his action. A fair hearing could only be claimed, he said, when the applicant had some right, some interest or some legitimate expectation.

After a family Christmas at Whitchurch, on 28 December 1968 Tom and Joan left for India again, on a two-week official visit with the Attorney-General, Elwyn Jones, and Sir John Widgery, who was to become Lord Chief Justice. Everywhere they were entertained by Indian judges and members of the Bar; everywhere Tom's speeches were acclaimed. He still worked hard to make his words fresh and striking, to attract and hold the attention of his audience. He introduced new material and up-to-date commentary; but, in essence, wherever he went, he repeated the themes that he had made his own. He was accustomed now to the sights and sounds of an Indian street and much of what he saw was familiar to him. This time they saw the Taj Mahal by moonlight and wondered again at its beauty. The rides on elephants, high in the hills overlooking Jaipur, and the visit to the holy city of Benares were new and marvellous experiences. When the time came to leave for home, Sir John Widgery later told his friends, Tom was still making speeches, surrounded by crowds of eager young people.[61]

The number of requests for Tom's patronage grew as steadily as the demands upon his time. In 1969 he and Joan became Founder members of the British Museum Society; he was re-elected Honorary President of the Law Students' Society of the University of Canterbury in New Zealand; elected Vice-President of the Supreme Court Sports Association and of the Society of Genealogists; and Patron of the Whitchurch Branch of the British Legion. He declined to become a Vice-President of the Homeless Children's Aid and Adoption Society, on the grounds that he never liked 'to take part in anything unless I can really do something to help.'

That year Denning was invited to arbitrate in a dispute between the growers of sugar-cane in Fiji and the Australian owners of the sugar-refining mills. Since the Lord Chancellor had no objection to Tom's accepting, provided he did not take a fee and carried out the work in the long vacation, Tom and Joan left England at the end of July.

There are 840 Fijian islands, of which 100 are inhabited. Siwa, the capital and chief port, is in the south of the largest island, Viti Levo; the sugar-growing area is in the north. In the centre of the island is a wonderful range of mountains covered with thick tropical vegetation on the wetter, southern side and dry grassland on the north. The islands have palm-fringed beaches, coral reefs and, in the winter months, when the Dennings were there, a warm and pleasant climate. Tom and Joan stayed in the northern region, at the Mocambo Hotel, some seven miles from Lautoka, where the arbitration was held. To emphasise his neutrality, Tom decided to have no contact with government officials but, for lunch each day, the Governor put at their disposal a bungalow at Lautoka, with panoramic views of the distant mountains beyond the sugar plantations. There, for much of the time, Joan painted or explored the islands, enjoying what she described as the best holiday of her life. Tom, meantime, with his co-arbitrator, Robert McNeill, a former President of the Institute of Chartered Accountants, took evidence from the sugar-growers, mostly the Indian descendants of labourers who migrated to Fiji to work on the plantations and mostly smallholders, farming perhaps ten acres apiece.

Since 1961 arrangements between growers and mill-owners were governed by a contract that was due to end on 31 March 1970. The Australian mill-owners had done well from it; the growers were unable to understand its complicated price formula and believed that all the risks were theirs. They demanded a better deal; the response of the mill-owners was to threaten to pull out of Fiji if their profitability was not to be maintained. At the start of the arbitration, there was criticism of Denning from both sides. Then, as the *Pacific Islands Monthly* reported in October 1969: 'Lord Denning poured oil on troubled waters. He charmed everyone with his smile and made exactly the right remarks when a difficulty arose.' Under a new formula, Denning proposed a guaranteed price to the growers, and a right for them to have the accounts of the mill-owners inspected by an accountant. 'If I have erred at all,' he said, 'I think it will be because I have been too favourable to the growers.' The millers, he thought, had for long enjoyed the better part of the bargain: in his award he tried to restore the balance. 'The great public companies of today owe a duty, not only to their shareholders to make a profit, but to the people amongst whom they live and work, to do their best for them.' A fine example of Tom's paternalism, and not, in 1969, a generally accepted sentiment.

The award was largely overtaken by events. After Fiji became an independent member of the Commonwealth in 1970, sugar was nationalised and the industry went through a difficult period, before signing a marketing agreement with the European Economic Community. Tom's handling of the arbitration prompted an invitation from the Foreign and Commonwealth Office to report on the banana industry in Jamaica. He agreed to do so in the Easter vacation of the following year.

21

Justice and Policy

During September, Tom interrupted the sugar arbitration to fly to San Francisco, where he had a long-standing invitation to address the State Bar. The gift given to him by his hosts remained one of his proudest souvenirs, occupying an honoured place on the mantelpiece in his library. It was a framed, illuminated quotation from Francis Bacon, with an inset brass plaque, inscribed:

> Presented to the Right Honourable Alfred Thompson Denning, Master of the Rolls, who brought lustre to the proceedings of the Annual Meeting of the State Bar of California in San Francisco, California, USA in September 1969 and who rekindled our deep pride and gratitude as inheritors of the precious rights of Englishmen.

The Dennings' travels for 1969 were not yet over. Later in the year, Tom was asked by the Lord Chancellor to stand in for Lord Morris who was prevented by a bereavement from attending a judicial conference in New York. At 24 hours' notice, Tom and Joan flew to New York for a three-day visit and were given an enthusiastic welcome.

In the 1950s and early 1960s many people, sued for failure to pay hire-purchase instalments on grossly defective motor vehicles, found themselves bound by agreements in standard form exempting the hire-purchase company from every conceivable liability. It was accepted law that some breaches of contract were so serious that they entitled the other party to treat the contract as at an end. Denning built upon this to counteract the injustice of unreasonable exemption

330

clauses, developing the doctrine of fundamental breach. In *Karsales (Harrow) Ltd* v. *Wallis* he said:

> [I]t is now settled that exemption clauses of this kind, no matter how widely they are expressed, only avail the party when he is carrying out his contract in its essential respects. He is not allowed to use them as a cover for misconduct or indifference or to enable him to turn a blind eye to his obligations . . .

After the Hire Purchase Acts of 1964 and 1965 brought under control some of the worst abuses, the need for such a doctrine was largely eliminated. In March 1966, in the *Suisse Atlantique* case (not one of Denning's), the House of Lords made clear their view that the control of contractual terms was a matter for parliament, not the judiciary. Denning remained convinced that there was work for his doctrine and waited to re-establish it.

In October 1969, the case of *Harbutt's Plasticine* v. *Wayne Tank and Pump* came before the court of Denning, Widgery and Cross. Their unanimous decision to hold the suppliers of plastic pipe liable for the destruction by fire of Harbutt's mill at Bathampton, despite an exemption clause in the contract, was much criticised and was reversed by the Lords. Undeterred, Denning continued to rely upon the doctrine of fundamental breach until it was finally struck down by the House of Lords in 1980.

Before that, in 1974, a case reached the Court of Appeal that would be often quoted as an example of his style and as one of his most adventurous judgments in the law of contract. First he gave the story:

> Broadchalke is one of the most pleasing villages in England. Old Herbert Bundy, the defendant, was a farmer there. His home was at Yew Tree Farm. It went back for 300 years. His family had been there for generations. It was his only asset. But he did a very foolish thing. He mortgaged it to the bank . . . Not to borrow money for himself, but for the sake of his son. Now the bank have come down on him . . . They want to get him out.
>
> (*Lloyds Bank* v. *Bundy*)

There could be no doubt where Denning's sympathies lay. Nor

would there have been any difficulty, on the facts, in rejecting the Bank's claim, as the other two members of the court did, solely under the traditional heading of undue influence. Denning used the opportunity to develop a broader doctrine of inequality of bargaining power, which, he thought, embraced all such cases as undue influence, undue pressure and unconscionable transactions with heirs.

> By virtue of it, the English law gives relief to one who, without independent advice, enters into a contract on terms which are very unfair or transfers property for a consideration which is grossly inadequate, when his bargaining power is grievously impaired by reason of his own needs or desires, or by his own ignorance or infirmity, coupled with undue influences or pressures brought to bear on him by or for the benefit of the other.

Though the concept was much criticised, some thought it no more than a tidying of categories and, while Denning confined his attention to cases where there was inequality of bargaining power, there was not too much concern. When, in 1978, he tried to overcome the exemption clauses in a purely commercial contract, the Lords stipulated that such clauses must be strictly construed (*Photo Production* v. *Securicor Transport*), and the doctrine of fundamental breach was finally overthrown.

Lord Denning's idiosyncratic way of moulding the law to do justice in a particular case benefited countless litigants who found favour with him. (In July 1966, Kenneth Diplock sent round to Tom a letter written to Diplock and Russell, saying 'judges who disagree with the MR are always wrong.') Just a few classes of applicant – convicted criminals, people Denning thought lacking in integrity, those whose beliefs he thought dangerous or whose morals offended him – received less impartial treatment. With a delicate touch he would alter the scope of the rules of natural justice, back-track from a previous decision or bend the legal rules to ensure that justice fitted the needs that he saw in the instant case.

In March 1970 two French nationals claimed natural justice, complaining of the Gaming Board's refusal to give them a 'certificate of consent', to apply for a gaming licence. After a three-day hearing Denning read his judgment on 23 March:

Crockford's is one of the most famous gaming clubs in London. It has premises of distinction at 16 Carlton House Terrace, which it holds from the Crown Estate Commissioners. It seeks a certificate to enable it to apply for a gaming licence. The Gaming Board have refused their consent. So Crockford's is faced with extinction. It applied to this court to quash the decision of the Gaming Board. It says that it did not act in accordance with the rules of natural justice.

(*R. v. Gaming Board*)

Then Denning turned to the history of the matter; the profitability of gaming clubs which had found a way to get round the Gaming Acts of 1960 and 1963; the arrival in England of the two Frenchmen, whose names were Gilbet Benaim and Youssef Khaida and who 'had run gaming clubs in Algiers and in Paris'; the circumstances in which the two had come to run Crockford's; the conviction of Crockford's for illegal gaming devices; the passing by parliament of the Gaming Act 1968; the prohibition of gaming at any premises without a licence; and the establishment of the Gaming Board, without whose 'certificate of consent' no establishment could apply for a licence.

By this point it was possible for observers of Denning judgments to recognise that his sympathies were not with the applicants. He outlined the deliberations of the Board – which he called 'a responsible body' – and the steps it had taken before reaching its conclusion and proceeded to consider whether the Board was bound by the rules of natural justice. The task of the Board, he said, was 'to see if the applicants are fit to run a gaming club.' They were under a duty to act fairly. They must give applicants the opportunity to satisfy them, but had no need to 'quote chapter and verse' as though they were dismissing a man from office or depriving him of his property.

Seeing the evils that have led to this legislation, the board can and should investigate the credentials of those who make application to them. They can and should receive information from the police in this country or abroad who know something of them. They can, and should, receive information from any other reliable source . . . I do not think they need tell the applicant the source of their information, if that would put their informant in peril or otherwise be contrary to the public interest.

Turning to the requirement that a tribunal should give reasons – on which he always insisted where a man's livelihood or property were at risk – Denning thought there was no need for the Gaming Board to do so. 'After all, the only thing that they have to give is their *opinion* as to the capability and diligence of the applicant.'

Despite Denning's determination to remedy the wrongful deprivation of a man's livelihood, he was more conservative in his assessment of damages for it than for personal injuries. On 15 July 1970 he presided over an appeal from Sir Denys Buckley, in the case of *Edwards* v. *SOGAT*. It was admitted that the union had withdrawn Edwards's membership in grossly unfair circumstances (though eventually he was restored to membership): the only issue, at trial and on appeal, was the amount of damages. Buckley awarded Edwards £7791, his financial loss to the date of the trial and future loss of earnings calculated on the formula used to assess loss of future earnings in a personal injury case. Supported by Sachs and Megaw, Denning reduced the award to £3500 in all. 'There is a great difference,' he said, 'between permanent incapacity due to personal injury (which cannot be overcome) and loss of membership . . . (which can be overcome by learning another skill or by being reinstated and so forth).'

Those who unreservedly admired Denning and those who tempered admiration with criticism of his increased disregard for precedent and his populist approach to the law, were united in respect for Denning's handling of the litigant in person. Unable to rely upon any of the rules by which the Bar presented their cases, most judges dreaded the appearance of a litigant acting for himself. Lord Denning had no such apprehensions. Every Monday morning he heard the cases of litigants in person. Courteously, helpfully, he took them through their paces. Whether or not they were successful in their suits, most left with the conviction that they could not have had a fairer hearing.

Denning controlled his court with the same confidence that conquered the most unruly audience. He had no need to rely upon such mechanisms as contempt of court: his sense of what was appropriate and his personal dignity took him safely through the most awkward of moments. In *The Due Process of Law* he told the story of Miss Stone, a frequent appellant in Denning's court, who 'picked up one of Butterworth's "Workmen's Compensation Cases" and threw it at us ... She had hoped we would commit her for contempt of court – just to draw more attention to herself. As we took no notice, she went towards the door. She left saying: "I congratulate your Lordships on your coolness under fire." ' The law reporter Alan Bray also described the occasion, as he saw it from his place, two rows behind Miss Stone:

> She threw the book so as to pass directly between Lord Denning, in the centre, and Lord Justice Diplock on his left. Lord Justice Diplock with a smile, ducked his head. Lord Justice Harman slowly raised his eye-glass as if to see what was happening. Lord Denning did not blink an eyelid but remained perfectly calm. 'Madam, you must leave the court' [he said].[15]

Denning's confidence and the certainty of his touch increased with his years on the bench. In 1975, when Stephen Balogh, the son of a professor of economics, had served 14 days of a six-month sentence for planning to introduce laughing-gas into a courtroom, Denning said:

> Insults are best treated with disdain – save when they are gross and scandalous. Refusal to answer with admonishment – save when it is vital to know the answer. But disruption of the court or threats to witnesses or to jurors should be visited with immediate arrest. Then a remand in custody and, if it can be arranged, representation by counsel. If it comes to a sentence, let it be such as the offence deserves.

In Balogh's case, Denning thought 14 days 'enough to purge his contempt, if contempt it was.' Denning relied upon contempt only when it was necessary to uphold justice, as in the *Mullholland* case and the case of the Welsh students (*Morris* v. *Crown Office*). On Wednesday 4 February 1970, Mr Justice Lawton was trying a libel case in the High Court, when his court was invaded by a group of students from Aberystwyth University, shouting slogans, singing songs and scattering pamphlets. The hearing could not continue until the students were removed. When the judge returned, three of them were brought before him and sentenced to three months' imprisonment for contempt of court. After the court rose, 19 others were brought before Lawton, who asked each whether he or she would apologise. Eight did so and each was fined £50 and bound over to keep the peace. Eleven said that, as a matter of principle, they would not apologise: each was sentenced to three months' imprisonment.

As a matter of urgency, Denning arranged to start their appeals on the following Monday with Salmon and Arthian Davies, who spoke Welsh. The appeal lasted two days; on the Wednesday morning the judges discussed it and, in the afternoon, gave judgment. After giving the background to the power of a High Court Judge to commit instantly to prison for criminal contempt, Denning proceeded to discuss the sentences:

> I do not think they were excessive, at the time they were given and in the circumstances then existing. Here was a deliberate interference with the course of justice in a case that was no concern of theirs. It was necessary for the judge to show – and to show to all students everywhere – that this kind of thing cannot be tolerated. Let students demonstrate, if they please, for the causes in which they believe. Let them make their protests as they will. But they must do it by lawful means and not by unlawful. If they strike at the course of justice in this land – and I speak both for England and Wales – they strike at the roots of society itself, and they bring down that which protects them.

These were salutary words at a time when student protest and student sit-ins had become disruptive, not only in the United Kingdom but throughout the western world. Having spoken them, Denning went on to consider what should be done. Having shown the students that they were wrong, the court decided, they 'should permit them to go back to their studies, to their parents and continue the good course which they have so wrongly disturbed.'

The reaction from Wales was entire satisfaction. From England,

Tom received a couple of anonymous and abusive postcards which, like others that arrived from time to time, he treated with amusement. He had a happy facility to see the brighter side of most experiences. He had also a streak of arrogance that lifted him above the pinpricks that upset lesser mortals.

Tom was not happy with the brief to conciliate between the Fyffes Group and the Jamaica Banana Board over the supply of bananas to the United Kingdom. He thought the task of conciliation 'most unsatisfactory – almost impossible' and would have preferred an arbitration. He spent a week, at the start of the vacation, trying, with little success, to bring the two sides into a more conciliatory frame of mind. He was unusually despondent – and more than a little tired – when he left for his promised journey to Jamaica, which had to be combined with a short visit to Dalhousie, in New Brunswick, where he was to receive an honorary degree. Tom and Joan arrived in the Caribbean via Newfoundland, Nova Scotia, New Brunswick and Toronto, Ontario. They were relieved, after such a long and circuitous journey, to find themselves in a hotel set in lovely grounds, that seemed more like an old colonial house. The next morning they were taken on a little train, to see where the bananas were grown, cut, sorted, packed and stored for export. The problem for Jamaica, they learned, was the loss of market to the growers in Ecuador who produced a larger banana.

As Tom learned about the trade, which depended largely on cheap labour, he found its problems difficult to solve: badly-needed modernisation would inevitably bring unemployment to people for whom no alternative work was available. The banana report was the least rewarding of the many tasks he had undertaken, though he was heartened, in March 1971, when both Fyffes and the Jamaica Banana Board told him that his work had contributed to their reaching an agreement.

Over the years Tom and Joan kept in touch with Delmar Banner and his wife, the sculptor Josephina de Vasconcellos, who lived in Ambleside. In April 1970, on Delmar's fortieth wedding anniversary, he wrote to Tom, enclosing photos of the holiday home for boys that the Banners were planning in Westmoreland. Tom promised 'to see what we can do to help.' He did what he was expert in doing, becoming a trustee of the charity Outpost Emmaus, advising Josephina on fund-raising, adding his name to a letter here and having a word in an ear there. Tom remained involved when Outpost Emmaus planned a second project for the disabled, Combined Action Now, and in 1980, when the old trawler *Harriet*, beached off the Cumbrian coast, was converted into a holiday home for the disabled, Tom was still lending a hand. In the year of his retirement, Josephina's bust of Tom would be placed in the Judges' Gallery of the Law Courts at Winchester.

In July 1970, Denning considered the application of natural justice in a new context. The Board of Trade had appointed inspectors to investigate the affairs of Pergamon Press, a company run by Robert Maxwell. Claiming that the investigation should be conducted as though it were a judicial inquiry in a court of law, the directors sought the right to cross-examine witnesses. The inspectors replied that theirs was not a tribunal that had to reach a determination or decision, but only an investigation, which was not bound by the rules of natural justice.

> It is true, of course [said Lord Denning] that the inspectors are not a court of law . . . They only investigate and report . . . They do not even decide whether there is a prima facie case. But this should not lead us to minimise the significance of their task. They have to make a report which may have wide repercussions. They may, if they think fit, make findings of fact which are very damaging to those whom they name . . . they may ruin reputations or careers. The report may lead to judicial proceedings. It may expose persons to criminal prosecutions or to civil actions. It may bring about the winding-up of the company.

Inspectors, he concluded, can obtain information 'in any way they think best', but before they condemn or criticise a man, they must give him a fair opportunity for correcting or contradicting what is said against him. A fair hearing was to be the basis of proceedings at Board of Trade inquiries, as much as at any other tribunal; beyond that Denning was not prepared to go.

In the summer vacation the Dennings drove to Wales to stay five days with John Morris, then on to St. Davids, where John and Veronica Stuart had taken a holiday bungalow. At the start of the next term, Denning's comments on public policy with regard to legal representation before a domestic tribunal, were to bring him an unusual reward from Toronto University. Because it had not kept its accounts correctly, Enderby Town Football Club had been censured by the County Football Association and wanted to be represented by solicitors and counsel when it appealed to the FA. The Football Association had a rule that any person summoned 'must attend personally and not be legally represented.' The Club applied for – and was refused – an injunction restraining the FA from hearing its appeal unless it was permitted to be legally represented. Denning considered that the important issue was that a domestic tribunal should not, by its rules, fetter its own discretion to permit legal representation in a suitable case. Considering whether the court had power to go beyond the words of the rule and consider its validity, he referred to cases – many of them his – in which 'the judges have decided, avowedly or not, according to what is best for the public good.' He continued:

> I know that over 300 years ago Hobart CJ said: 'Public policy is an unruly horse.' It has often been repeated since. So unruly is the horse, it is said . . . that no judge should ever try to mount it lest it run away with him. I disagree. With a good man in the saddle, the unruly horse can be kept in control. It can jump over obstacles. It can leap the fences put up by fictions and come down on the side of justice.

In the end Denning concluded that the court should not insist that the Club must be legally represented before the FA. The Club was 'at liberty' to raise any points of law before the courts: 'If it chooses not to bring them before the courts, but prefers to put them before a lay tribunal, it must put up with the implications of that tribunal and must abide by its ruling that there be no legal representation.'

For his birthday, the following January, a card arrived from the students of Toronto University, carrying a cartoon of a judge jumping his horse across a wall, labelled 'Obstruction to Justice', the horse's tail festooned with a streamer bearing the words 'Public Policy'. Though his feet are not in the stirrups, and his wig and spectacles are flying through the air, there is no suggestion that this judge will be unseated.

Committed to the protection of the right of workers to strike and of union officials to organise action, Tom nevertheless, in common with much of the nation, regarded the industrial scene with alarm. 'It is all very well to strike,' he said in *The Road to Justice*, 'but I know of no law which gives any man or any group of men the right to strike at the community at large.' That, increasingly, was the method used in industrial disputes – official and unofficial – and people were tired of it. In June 1970 the country returned a Conservative Government, under Edward Heath, committed to the control of union power. Within a year, the Industrial Relations Act 1971 was on the statute book, introducing a code of conduct for industrial disputes and regulating relations between workers and unions. Central to the legislation was registration: only registered unions would benefit from provisions in the Act, replacing the protection of the Trade Disputes Acts for organisers of industrial action. The legislation was bitterly opposed by the Labour Party and the unions.

Parliament hoped that the new machinery would curb unofficial 'wildcat' strikes and make unions accept responsibility for the actions of their shop stewards. Those injured by any of the statutory 'unfair industrial practices' would be able to complain to the new National Industrial Relations Court, which could command workers and their unions temporarily to refrain from industrial action or to take a ballot of members. While the parties were at a hearing, it was hoped, the NIRC would be able to encourage a settlement of their differences.

The Act was passed on 5 August 1971, but the part conferring important rights on workers, with regard to membership of trade unions, had not been brought into effect when the case of *Hill* v. *C.A. Parsons Ltd* reached the Court of Appeal in October. Mr Hill was a chartered engineer, who had worked for Parsons for 35 year and was two years' short of retirement age. It was important for him to serve the final two years when his salary would be increased, since his pension depended upon his average salary for his last three years. Until 1968 none of the professional engineers had joined a union, though other employees belonged to one or other of two unions, which were engaged in a membership battle, causing frequent interruptions of work. The professional staff were disturbed by these disputes and in 1968 joined a union of professional engineers that was not affiliated to the TUC. In March 1970 one of the two disputing unions, DATA, determined to compel all employees to join them, called their members out on strike and threatened to black the company's products. Two months later, the company capitulated to the financial pressure and signed an agreement, including a clause that, after a period of 12 months, they would operate a closed shop with DATA. A year later, in May 1971, Parsons warned the professional engineers that it was now a condition of their employment that they must belong to DATA, unless they had belonged to another TUC-affiliated union before the company entered into the agreement with DATA in May 1970. Neither Hill, nor the other 37 professional engineers agreed to join DATA and, on 30 July 1971, the company reluctantly gave them one month's notice, to take effect on Tuesday 31 August 'unless prior to this date you have taken steps to comply with the condition of your contract of employment regarding DATA membership.' On 13 August 1971 – as a test case for all the professional engineers – Hill claimed damages for breach of contract and conspiracy; he sought an injunction restraining the company from implementing the notice before trial and from purporting to import new conditions into his contract of employment. The Chancery Judge, Brightman J, refused an injunction, believing himself to have no power to grant it, but the company agreed to hold its hand, pending an appeal.

It was established law that an injunction would not be granted to compel an employer to keep a man in his employ. Even if the employer was in breach of contract by giving less than the proper period of notice, the employee could only look to the court for damages, not an order for re-instatement. Lord Justice Stamp, a Chancery man, thought Brightman had reached the right conclusion. What assurance could there be that DATA would hold its hand, even if the company was forced to keep the men in its employ until trial? Stamp was in a minority. Denning and Sachs found ways to allow the appeal and make the order, though their paths to the decision were different. Both regarded one month's notice as unreasonable for a man who had worked for the company in a professional capacity for 35 years. A period of six months would, they thought, have been more appropriate. At common law, if he was dismissed with only a month's notice, Hill's damages would be limited to the amount he would have earned in the remainder of the six months; but if he could be kept in employment until Part II of the Industrial Relations Act came into effect – which, taking into account the law's delays, it certainly would if he were kept in employment until trial – the picture would be entirely different. Hill could, if dismissed, become entitled to re-instatement or to compensation amounting to considerably more, in his case, than six months' salary.

Denning had little sympathy for the company, caught between the hammer and the anvil:

> In these circumstances, it is of the utmost importance to Mr Hill and the other 37 that the notices given to them should not be held to terminate their employment. Damages would not be at all an adequate remedy. If ever there was a case where an injunction should be granted against the employers, this is the case. It is quite plain that the employers have done wrong. I know that the employers have been under pressure from a powerful trade union. That may explain their conduct, but it does not excuse it. They have purported to terminate Mr Hill's employment by a notice which is too short by far. They seek to take advantage of their own wrong by asserting that his services were terminated by their own 'say-so' at the date selected by them – to the grave prejudice of Mr Hill. They cannot be allowed to break the law in this way. It is, to my mind, a clear case for an injunction.

By May of 1972, when *Secretary of State for Employment* v. *ASLEF*, reached the Court of Appeal, where Denning was sitting with Buckley and Roskill, the Industrial Relations Act was up and running. Three railway unions, ASLEF, the NUR and TSSA, had pressed for increases in pay and, refusing offers from the Railways Board, instructed their members to work strictly to rule and refuse to work overtime, or on rest days or Sundays, from 17 April. Their intention – which succeeded brilliantly – was totally to disrupt the working of the railway system, without in any way breaching their members' contracts of employment. It was exactly the kind of damage the Act had been designed to counter. The Employment Secretary invoked the emergency provisions to seek a 'cooling-off' period for negotiations and, on 19 April, the National Industrial Relations Court, presided over by Sir John Donaldson, ordered a period of 14 days from the time that normal railway service was resumed. When the period ended the dispute remained unresolved and the unions resumed their work to rule. Invoking other sections of the Act, the Employment Secretary returned to the NIRC, seeking an order for a ballot of union members to establish whether they genuinely wished to take part in this industrial action. On 13 May, the NIRC ordered the taking of a ballot and the union appealed.

It was the first appeal in a wholly new branch of employment law and was allocated to the court of the Master of the Rolls on short notice. The hearing lasted five days. Counsel left the Court in little doubt that their decision would be of the utmost importance in determining the relations between government and the unions. In his judgment, Denning returned first to an old theme: 'If Parliament gives great powers to a Minister, these courts must allow them to him; but at the same time we will be vigilant to see that he exercises them in accordance with the law.' Considering whether the Employment Secretary had done so, Lord Denning acknowledged that he 'did not get all the facts of his application quite right', before going on to consider whether the conditions precedent to the grant of an order for a ballot had been fulfilled. First, there must be a threat to the national economy, which Denning was sure there had been:

> . . . the railway services have been, and will be, utterly dislocated; hundreds of commuters have been, and will be, put to misery, discomfort and loss; goods services have been, and will be, gravely disrupted and may break down altogether; supplies to power stations and coke ovens will soon be much reduced.

Turning to the second requisite, that it must appear to the Secretary of State that 'irregular action short of a strike' was about to begin, Denning considered the course of conduct which the men were required to take. He agreed 'that a man is not bound positively to do more for his employers than his contract requires . . . But what he must not do is wilfully to obstruct the employer as he goes about his business.' On the evidence, Denning found there was ample ground for the Employment Secretary to believe that 'irregular industrial action short of a strike' was likely to begin.

The third prerequisite to an order for a ballot had to be the Secretary of State's doubt that the workers really wanted to take part in the industrial action. As he had done many times before, Denning considered the meaning of the words 'If it appears to the Secretary of State' and concluded that when the Minister 'honestly takes a view of the facts or the law which could reasonably be entertained, then his decision is not to be set aside simply because thereafter someone thinks his view was wrong.'

'Of course,' he continued, 'it is to be remembered here that we are concerned with a grave threat to the national economy. The steps that are proposed do not imperil the liberty, livelihood or property of any man.' There was no question, in such circumstances, but that Denning would uphold the Government. He had first to dispose of his own words, in *Padfield* that a minister must give reasons and, if he gives none, the court may infer that he had no good reasons: 'Whilst I would apply that proposition completely, in most cases, and particularly in cases which affect life, liberty or property, I do not think that it applies in all cases.'

Buckley and Roskill found their own ways to dismiss the appeal. The ballot was held and confirmed the belief of the union leaders that their members supported the industrial action. The pay claim was settled and the railways returned to their normal state; but the *ASLEF* case left a legacy of suspicion of Lord Denning's judgments in the employment field amongst union members and Labour Party supporters, though the Court of Appeal, unlike the National Industrial Relations Court, largely escaped public identification with Conservative party policy.

The dispute about the 'container revolution' provided the decisive test for the new legislation. For many years registered dockers had enjoyed unmatched job security, giving them the power to command high wages. With the growth of technology, it became possible to ship goods in containers, which could be loaded, at less cost, by workers outside the dock area. Determined to protect their jobs, dockers at Liverpool and Hull started to black transport companies that employed cheaper labour to load containers at depots just outside the docks. After 28 February 1972, when the TGWU de-registered, the union became liable to complaints from the companies that they were engaging in an 'unfair industrial practice'. Heatons

and two other firms blacked by the dockers complained to the
NIRC. During the hearings, Donaldson gave a clear explanation of
the role of the NIRC and a conciliatory account of the facts. At first,
the TGWU ignored the Court, though it advised its branches to
comply with the Court's orders, but after the imposition of fines, the
union changed its policy and was represented in court, claiming that
it was not responsible for the actions of shop stewards. On 12 May
the NIRC refused to accept this plea or to review its orders. Denning
heard the union's appeal, with Buckley and Roskill. Clearly he was
seeking a way to defuse the issue; in finding it, he was thought to put
a nail in the Act's coffin. He decided, contrary to the NIRC, that 'the
shop stewards did not profess to be acting on behalf of the union; nor
did the union hold them out as having authority.' If the union were
registered, he said, the shop stewards would be guilty of unfair
industrial practices but the union would not. 'Why then should the
union be mulcted in heavy fines and large compensation, simply
because it was not registered? If the legislature had intended that an
unregistered union should be so penalised, it should have said so in
terms . . .' On 13 June, the Court of Appeal set aside the orders of
the NIRC and the fines.

Three days later, flashpoint was reached in the case of dockers
picketing an East London container depot (*Churchman* v. *Joint
Shop Stewards' Committee*). After the NIRC's order to stop
picketing was ignored, three shop stewards were warned that, unless
they gave some explanation of their conduct by 2.00 pm on Friday 16
June, the Court would have no alternative but to commit them to
prison. In *The Due Process of Law*, Tom described the situation:

Now everyone knew that the dockers would take no notice of the
Court. They would continue to disobey. They would continue
their picketing. They would not appear before the Industrial
Court to give an explanation. They would not apply to the Court
of Appeal. The warrants would issue. They would go to prison.
They would be martyrs. The trade union movement would call a
general strike which would paralyse the country.

The committal brought every docker out on strike. After a leading
counsel told Denning he had points to make against the Order but

could not get instructions from the three shop stewards, it was arranged that, on behalf of the dockers, the Official Solicitor would ask the Court of Appeal to quash the order of the NIRC. When the appeal came on, Lord Denning, believing that 'the weapon of imprisonment should never be used ... in the case of industrial disputes'[24] took notice of the Official Solicitor's request and said:

> It seems to me that the evidence before the Industrial Court was quite insufficient to prove ... a breach of the court's order.
>
> ... It may be that in some circumstances the court may be entitled, on sufficient information being brought to it, to act on its own initiative in sending a contemner to prison. But ... it seems to me that all the safeguards required by the High Court must still be satisfied.

The Court of Appeal set aside the orders of committal, somewhat to the chagrin of the three dockers involved.

22

The Watershed

Tom was never insensitive to opinion but, as he wrote of Coke and Mansfield, 'your reformer must be sensitive to criticism but not so as to discourage him too much. Else nothing will be done.'[66] Lord Denning intended to get things done in the way he thought best. His reputation as the defender of the 'little man' required some qualification: where the security of the state was concerned, where disorder threatened or economic and social well-being were at risk, the individual took second place. Even these exceptions were added to at times.

Denning was by no means opposed to the right to demonstrate or protest, provided it was done peacefully; he pointed out, in a dissenting judgment, that the right to demonstrate was an important aspect of freedom of speech. (*Hubbard* v. *Pitt*) Though sympathetic to the need for housing, he had no patience with squatters. 'If homelessness was once admitted as a defence to trespass, no one's house would be safe.' (*Southwark LBC* v. *Williams*) Wrongdoers, however desperate might seem their plight, did not attract Tom's compassion. Nor was he sympathetic to the complaint of parents, whose children attended a Roman Catholic junior school, that their local authority confined their choice of secondary education to Roman Catholic schools. (*Cumings* v. *Birkenhead Corporation*) On numerous occasions, judicial and extra-judicial, he made plain his view of the responsibilities of women: their first duty was to look after their husbands, homes and children. Denning could be ruthless in decision, where he believed there remained a possibility of salvaging a marriage: he reversed a trial judge's decision to give the custody of two small children to their mother, thinking that there was no chance of reconciliation if the wife had the girls. (*Re L(infants)*) In that case his own strong paternal feelings must have got the better of his usual concern for the welfare of children: where the breakdown of a marriage was inevitable his aim was usually to bring about an end with the least possible damage to the children. Where a blood test of a child was sought in order to prove that adultery took place ten years earlier, Denning commented 'these adults should fight their own battles without bringing the infant into it.' (*M(D)* v. *M(S)*)

The love of 'a good woman' was, for Tom, the greatest of blessings. Yet he was surprisingly liberal in his recognition that a stable relationship can exist outside marriage and led the movement to treat co-habiting couples as though they were married. Alone of the court in *Sydall* v. *Castings Ltd*, he would have recognised the right of an illegitimate child to benefit from a group life assurance scheme, of which her father had been a member. The company 'should not be compelled, against their will, to shut out this little girl simply because she is illegitimate.' Though he and Joan upheld the moral principles of an earlier age, it was to their home in Cuckfield that a young member of Tom's family came from hospital, after the birth of an illegitimate child.

Compassion and understanding were central to Tom's faith. His out-of-character – and much-criticised – judgment in *Ward* v. *Bradford Corporation* was provoked by his belief that a teacher should set the young a good example. A female student was expelled from Bradford Teachers' Training College for allowing a man to live in her room contrary to regulations. The decision was taken by the Board of Governors, in circumstances that would, in most cases, have earned Lord Denning's censure. In this case, they did not. He found the girl's conduct so outrageous that he did not think she had been unfairly treated. He said:

> She had broken the rules most flagrantly. She had invited a man to her room and lived there with him for weeks on end. I say nothing about her morals. She claims they are her own affair. So be it. If she had wanted to live with this man, she could have gone into lodgings in the town and no one would have worried, except perhaps her parents.

(As it happened, the landladies of the town were so indignant at his remarks, Tom told the Nottingham MGC in September 1977, that one of them wrote to say 'she would not allow it. And that it was a libel on the landladies to suggest that they would.')

The cases of *Re L* and of Miss Ward are reconcilable with the body of Denning's judicial work in the light of his fundamental beliefs. The welfare of the nation could be maintained, he thought, only by the upbringing of its children in a stable background where, within the family and at school – and, preferably, also in church – they would learn the values that Tom, himself, acquired in his youth. A decent man with a strong sense of justice, striving to do his best for his country and his religion, Denning's judgments in personal matters always reflected his personal view of the world. It was paradoxical that, as he grew older, the admiration felt for him by so many of the young was balanced by an increasing dissociation from his beliefs.

In 1971 Denning embroiled himself in one of his most serious clashes with the House of Lords over the question of exemplary damages for libel. Until 1964 it was settled law that, when the conduct of a defendant was particularly blameworthy, a jury could award, over and above compensation for the damage suffered by the plaintiff, an additional sum by way of exemplary, or punitive, damages. In *Rookes* v. *Barnard* Lord Devlin limited to three categories the cases in which exemplary damages could be awarded. Several years later, in February 1971 Denning sat for nine days with Salmon and Phillimore, to hear the appeal of an author and publisher against a jury's award of £40,000, including £25,000 exemplary damages for a libel contained in a book entitled *The Destruction of Convoy PQ17*. In the introduction to his judgment, Denning gave the facts of the war-time disaster with typical force and immediacy:

Early in July 1942 a large convoy of 35 merchant ships – it had the code number PQ17 – was sailing in the Arctic seas laden with materials of war for Russia. They were between North Cape and Spitzbergen, near the ice fields. At that time of the year there was no nightfall. It was light all the time. The convoy was approaching the most dangerous part of the voyage. The German battle fleet had come up swiftly and secretly. It was lying in wait in Alten fiord, just by North Cape. It consisted of the most powerful warship afloat – the *Tirpitz* – with the cruisers *Hipper* and *Scheer*, and six destroyers. Nearby, at Banak, was an airbase whence the German aircraft could make sorties of 400 miles to bomb the convoy. Under the sea there were German submarines watching through their periscopes for a chance to strike.

(*Broome* v. *Cassell*)

The trial judge was Sir Frederick Lawton. (This had been the trial interrupted by the demonstration of the Welsh students.) In his summing-up, Lawton read to the jury the relevant passages from Devlin's speech – 'if I start paraphrasing it I might get what Lord Devlin said wrong and that would not do anybody any good' – and instructed them that the plaintiff, Commander Broome, had to show his case came within Devlin's definition in order to win exemplary damages. So certain were the jury that Broome had done so – the writer David Irving and Cassells, the publishers, had disregarded clear warnings of the gravity of the defamation – that they added £25,000 exemplary damages to a compensatory award of £15,000.

The convoy, said Lord Denning, on appeal, was in good hands. It was guarded by the Royal Navy. 'The close escort was under the command of Commander Broome, RN, in the destroyer *Keppel*.' In support was a cruiser covering force under Rear-Admiral Hamilton; behind that, the Home Fleet under Admiral Tovey. Then he outlined the events of 4 July 1942 when, following instructions, Broome had told the convoy to scatter:

The convoy scattered to the four winds. Without protection, they were attacked by the enemy from the air and from beneath the sea. Many were sunk. Out of the 35 only 11 reached Russian ports: 153 merchant sailors were lost and vast quantities of war material went to the bottom. It was a tragedy. A severe blow to the allied forces.

Commander Broome, Denning continued, was not blamed by his superiors or his brother officers. He was 'kept in sea-going commands and finished the war in command of the battleship *Ramillies*.' Turning to the libel, which singled Broome out for blame in a book purporting to give 'an authentic account' of the disaster, Denning said:

Many persons afterwards wrote about the disaster. The official historian of the war wrote about it. He did not condemn Commander Broome. Nor did Mr Winston Churchill. The condemnation was made 20 years later by an author who knew nothing about the war, because he was a small boy at the time . . . It is plain that Mr Irving was warned from most responsible quarters that his book contained libels on Commander Broome, and yet he determined to go on with it. In order to make it a success, he was ready to risk libel actions. In the apt French phrase he was looking for a *success de scandale*.

Though they had been told by Irving that his usual publishers were alarmed at the libel possibilities, Cassells agreed to publish the book. They hesitated for a time, after a warning from Broome, but decided to go ahead and distributed 60 proof copies. On 5 March 1968 Broome issued a writ for libel and on 21 May delivered a Statement of Claim. In their defence Irving and his publishers pleaded justification and fair comment. Cassells made up their mind to publish though the action was pending and, on 7 August 1968, brought out a hard-back edition. 'That conduct speaks for itself,' Denning commented. 'I have no doubt that the jury thought that the conduct of the defendants in publishing the hard-back edition was absolutely outrageous.'

Since all three judges of the Court of Appeal agreed that the conduct fell into one of Devlin's categories, the appeal of Irving and his publisher could have been dismissed without controversy. But Denning thought Devlin's three categories were too limiting and invited counsel to agree that the Court should depart from the ruling in *Rookes* v. *Barnard*. Though the Court of Appeal had followed Devlin's new doctrine, he commented, it had not been accepted in the Commonwealth. Indeed, it had been repudiated in Australia, Canada, New Zealand and the United States. 'This wholesale condemnation,' he concluded, 'fortifies us, I think, in examining this new doctrine for ourselves and I make so bold as to say that it should not be followed any longer in this country.'

Here was a flagrant challenge to the supremacy of the Lords. For the inevitable appeal, a panel of seven law lords was chosen and, not surprisingly, roundly rebuked Denning for his departure from precedent. As regards the libel itself, the law lords unanimously agreed with the Court of Appeal that it fell within Devlin's second category. There was a consensus that the award was over-generous but, by a majority of four to three, it was decided to uphold the jury's assessment. Denning's deliberate challenge to the Lords was a costly exercise for both parties and achieved nothing.

Since few cases went to the Lords, the decision of the Court of Appeal was usually final. Denning could often have achieved the result he thought just by distinguishing the case from earlier decisions, with a slight blurring of the edges. But that was not Tom's way: he always preferred the direct route to changes he thought right, regardless of consequences. In March 1971 the other members of the court, in an agency case, decided that – even though he had never had the money – the vendor must reimburse the purchaser for the deposit held by his bankrupt estate agent. (*Burt* v. *Claude Cousins*) Tom thought that wrong. Six months later, sitting with two other Lord Justices, Denning heard a similar story. (*Barrington* v. *Lee*) This time the others agreed that the vendor should not have to pay the money but, in order to reach that conclusion, they distinguished the facts of the two cases. Denning found that 'too tame a course for my liking.' He preferred 'to straighten out the law here and now' and declined to follow the earlier decision of his own court.

The appeal in *Hussey* v. *Palmer*, heard with Phillimore and Cairns on 22 June 1972, perfectly illustrates the difficulties posed by some of his decisions. Mrs Hussey's claim, which should have been for money lent, was dismissed, because her representatives had taken the wrong form of action. In his eagerness to give Mrs Hussey the redress that 'justice and good conscience' required, Denning's line of reason changed a long-established principle of law. Cairns, the third member of the court, would have preferred to give Mrs Hussey the opportunity to amend her claim and have a re-trial.

Dedicated to the pursuit of justice, Tom was prepared to sacrifice certainty. Though he clung with great obstinacy to a view until convinced that he was wrong, he cheerfully – and regardless of the consequences – admitted any change of heart. He was the only judge known to have reversed his own judgment after giving it: in 1965 he recalled a court to deliver a new judgment in *Varty* v. *BSA*, which swung the decision by changing the majority.

✣

In 1972, shortly after becoming a Lord of Appeal in Ordinary, Cyril Salmon, as Treasurer of Middle Temple, welcomed Tom as an honorary bencher. It was only the second time, said Salmon, that 'anyone who has committed the youthful indiscretion of being called to the bar by another Inn has been elected an honorary bencher of this one.' He recalled the 'eight happy years' when he was lucky enough often to sit with Tom in the Court of Appeal. 'It was an exhilarating experience because of the marvellous speed with which you assimilated facts and the equal speed with which you grasped the relevant points of law and all their implications.' Denning had been, Salmon said, 'the greatest liberating influence in the law of our time.'

At home, Tom's life was serene. He saw more of his son after Robert's appointment as Fellow and Tutor in Inorganic Chemistry at Magdalen in 1968, though he would never see him as much as he would have liked. He relished the weekend visits of Joan's children and their families, finding the company of young people as congenial as the visits to his home for fishing weekends of friends and colleagues from all his spheres of activity. He maintained his loyalty to the wider Denning family. Always fond of his sister Marjorie, after her husband's death in 1970 Tom took care that 'within an hour of arriving from London'[62] every Friday evening, he crossed the road to see her at The Hermitage. Meetings with Reg and Norman were a source of pleasure. He was enormously proud of their achievements. Norman's appointment as Secretary of the Defence Press and Broadcasting Committee since 1967 seemed to Tom a fitting crown to a fine career. 'Descent by blood counts a good deal,' Tom wrote in *The Family Story*, and for every one of his parents' descendants he felt a warm concern. His nieces and nephews were as welcome at The Lawn as, once, they had been at Fair Close; he rejoiced at their successes and was grieved by their sorrows. His family feeling extended even more widely, to embrace the descendants of his Denning and Thompson grandparents. It was of real interest to him to hear from any cousin and to revive childhood memories.

Though he retained his youthful enthusiasm and energy – and had developed an impish streak – Tom could no more escape the signs of age than his more sober brethren. His hair, always thin, was little more than a wispy circlet to the back of his head; from time to time he found himself prey to a giddy spell and carried Horlicks tablets in case he felt faint; he no longer walked with quite the springy stride of earlier years. His eyes were still good: woe betide any litigant so unwise as to hope Lord Denning would miss a comma in a document! Though he heard what he wanted to hear, he realised that his hearing was not so acute as once it had been. Still, for a man in his seventies he showed exemplary vigour. He loved his work and believed there was still much for him to do. At an age past that at which many men would have retired, Tom no more thought of giving up or returning to the House of Lords than he would have thought of giving up breathing.

He was supremely conscious of his position, and never reluctant to use his influence for the benefit of his family and friends, and of Whitchurch in general. He still retained the simple personal tastes of his boyhood and never forgot the financial straits of his early days. He was careful with money and quite free from extravagance. He cared deeply for land and, as soon as he could, had bought property, first at Cuckfield, then in Whitchurch. He made reasonable, rented accommodation available for the elderly and for young married couples but could be high-handed in dealing with neighbouring owners or local authorities. Practical and decisive, he was ready to seek planning permissions and improvement grants when it suited him but opposed the proposal to build a new vicarage and rooms for the elderly on the field that he rented from the Hospital of St. Cross. When he entered into correspondence – sometimes acrimonious – with neighbouring landowners or people having rights over his, he drafted and redrafted his letters with the care he had once taken over his Opinions. He kept open house for local fetes or parties but became upset if people trespassed on his land.

On official visits abroad, Tom expected comfortable arrangements to be made for himself and Joan; when he travelled on holiday, in the United Kingdom or elsewhere, he would not have thought of seeking preferential treatment, though almost certainly, if he had asked, it would have been given. He took the greatest pleasure from 'dressing-up' for the various roles he played; the official robes, the tricorne hat, the caps and gowns in which he received his honorary degrees all delighted him; but, at home, he had little interest in clothes. He liked the food that he had always liked, cooked as he had always liked it cooked; meat with vegetables from his own garden, apple pie and custard; bread and butter pudding. He rarely drank anything stronger than lemonade. At dinners in the Guildhall or at the Inns of Court, his tastes were now well-known and a bottle of mineral water was left beside his place. He took a little glass of port for the toasts.

Lord Denning had become a figure larger than life. Everyone in the law had a 'Denning Story'; those who could, did a 'Denning imitation'. It gave Tom as much amusement to come upon someone 'doing Denning' as it gave those who were doing it. As his reputation grew, so did Tom's tendency to live up to it. The Hampshire burr became, perhaps, just a little more pronounced. The familiar twinkle in his eye as he lifted his bowler hat and crossed Chancery Lane to greet someone who scarcely dared to hope himself recognised by the Master of the Rolls, shone a little brighter. His known interests and partialities persuaded lawyers, from time to time, that their clients' case would receive a sympathetic hearing in Lord Denning's court: his clerk became accustomed, when the papers were filed, to the suggestion that 'this would be one for the Master of the Rolls.'

One of Tom's vacation tasks was to deal with his own financial affairs. His affairs were closely bound up with his son's. The Trust that Tom had established for Robert in 1952 was wound up in October 1966, when the entire fund was appointed to Robert, but Tom continued to take an active interest in the investments it had made. The Lawn – a substantial part of that investment – belonged to his son and Tom was careful to pay a full rent for it. The other property Tom had purchased in and around Whitchurch, including fishing rights on the River Test, was all in his son's name.

Tom's intense love for his only child made him, at times, a little too eager to smooth Robert's path. Though Tom never actively intervened to assist his son's career, Robert never felt sure, until he obtained his appointment at the University of Illinois, in 1964, that being the son of someone so famous had not indirectly contributed to his own success.[32] Much as Tom wanted to give his son the financial security so lacking in his own youth, he was proud of Robert's independence. In September 1970, when he prepared a summary of dealings with Robert's property, he noted that Robert 'earned his own living ever since he went to the USA.'[29] The warmth between them is clear from the letter of 16 September 1970 that accompanied the copy of the summary he sent to Robert still signed with the words 'Lots of love from Daddy'.

Preparing notes of his dealings on behalf of Robert – there is more than one in the Hampshire Record Office – was a source of satisfaction to Tom. Other financial matters were often a cause of irritation. The renewal of the lease of the flat at 11 Old Square came up for consideration in the summer of 1968. Tom had thought the rent of £375 a year fixed in 1963 was high; he was not at all happy with the increase of nearly 100 per cent proposed by the Honourable Society of Lincoln's Inn.

Rent, at the time, was more than usually hedged about with restrictions. The Rent Officer proposed a rent of £565 per annum and the matter was referred for hearing to the Rent Assessment Committee. Putting on his old mantle of the advocate, the Master of the Rolls sent them a memorandum.

Before our tenancy, there was one large flat on the second floor, which was occupied by Lord Pethwick-Lawrence. On his death the Inn converted it into two separate flats and we took one of them. But the conversion was very difficult and leaves our flat much inferior to many smaller ones, which are 'purpose-built'.

In particular the kitchen is a narrow slit, partitioned off from a former bedroom. It is so confined that it is most inconvenient and uncomfortable to work in. It is ill-ventilated and steams up quickly, getting unbearably hot. There is no provision for food storage. It can only accommodate a little refrigerator. It is far too small for the size of the flat, so that it is not possible to entertain more than one or two guests at the same time. Similarly with the bathroom.

Tom went on to describe the defects of the bathroom, the absence of heating, the smells coming from the drainage and from the old chimneys which 'seem to collect dead pigeons', and the staircase which had been 'dingy, draughty and dirty for years.' He continued: 'The 62 steps are, of course, a great hindrance to comfortable living. Lady Denning has to struggle up and down several times a day with her shopping and often we have bags and baggage to carry up . . .'

He added his coup de grace:

I suppose that my personal point is irrelevant – but if the rent is increased to the figure suggested by the Inn, I would not be able to afford it, and I would have to commute between London and my home in the country – and be unable to fulfil many of the evening engagements which attend to my office.

In the event, the interaction of the statutes governing rent increases caused the Inn to offer Tom, on 31 July 1968, a three-year lease at £401 for the first year, £536 for the second and £562 for the last year which, they hoped, he would not think 'an unfair way of dealing with the problem.' He was to stay in the flat for the remainder of his tenure of office.

As a consequence of his return to the Court of Appeal at the age his predecessor left it, Denning was sitting, in his seventies, with men who were considerably his junior. Most of those who sat with Tom regarded him with, sometimes exasperated, affection. Some complained that, because he seldom took the longer cases, he lacked sympathy with their need for time out of court to write their judgments: Denning thought it essential for the courts to be fully manned between the hours of 10.30 and 4.30, or the work of the Court of Appeal could never be done. Some judges, with dismay, found occasions when they thought they had agreed a decision after the Court rose at 4.30, only to find, the next morning, that Denning seemed to have changed his mind overnight and was starting to give a completely different judgment. It was sometimes difficult to know whether they agreed with him or not: he always gave the first judgment and, at times, it was not too clear which line he would take and 'often he would switch right at the very end, which made it rather difficult.'[63]

Sitting as the second judge became awkward: 'You could not communicate with No. 3 across him, so were not sure what to say.'[61] As time passed, the others found a way to deal with the difficulty and a newly appointed Lord Justice was advised to 'prepare a judgment in the sense you wanted and agreed, in case he turned round and did the other thing.'[64] This line of criticism surprised Tom. He was unaware that he ever changed tack without further discussion. He was more prepared for the suggestion that all the interesting work came to him, since he considered it a function of his office to hear the cases of public importance. With few exceptions, Chancery lawyers found it difficult to come to terms with Denning's idiosyncratic style, fearing it damaged the law by causing uncertainty. Those who understood how to manage Tom were able to save him from his worst excesses: on one occasion Lawton and Templeman persuaded him to delete from a judgment the phrase: 'When the yeoman of England are outraged . . .' All agreed that Tom ran a happy court, showing benign tolerance and never seeking to put pressure on those who disagreed with him.

The most endearing thing was the humour with which Denning met defeat. Lord Donaldson, his successor as Master of the Rolls, recalled a case in which they sat together: 'When it was over he said: "Well John, we're allowing the appeal, aren't we?" I said, "No, Tom, we are not." "Fine," said Tom. Then he turned to the other judge and said: "We're allowing the appeal, aren't we?" "No, Tom, we are not." "Right," said Tom, with a big beaming smile and no rancour whatever, "You two will have to dissent." '

For the public, the Court of Appeal and Lord Denning were synonymous. Newspaper reports of cases were headed 'Lord Denning says . . .' or 'Lord Denning decides . . .' and, to an extent never before known, the law was becoming personalised. Successive Lords Chancellor were concerned but there was nothing they could do: Denning was appointed a judge before there was a retirement age and had begun to say that he practised every Christian virtue except resignation. This might not have mattered if Tom had not started to betray an increasing tendency to challenge the Lords and, on occasion, even to challenge the supremacy of parliament.

The case of Pickin and the British Railways Board was a perfect example of the English eccentric as a litigant. British Railways's title to much of its land came from the old, private Acts of Parliament, authorising 19th-century railway promoters to acquire land, compulsorily if necessary. Many contained provisions that if the proposed railway was discontinued, the land would revert to owners of the adjoining land. Some time after nationalisation, this right of reversion was removed by the British Railways Act 1968, passed at a time when many lines were being closed, as uneconomic.

Mr Pickin was a railway enthusiast and wanted the Clevedon–Yatton line kept open. On 20 October 1969 he purchased for 10s an adjoining owner's interest in a few feet of land – whatever that interest may have been – and tried unsuccessfully to prevent BR from taking up the railway lines. On 23 October he laid claim to half the old railway land adjoining his few feet, seeming to allege that BR had fraudulently concealed certain matters from Parliament in order to procure the passing of the 1968 Act. Some paragraphs of his pleadings were struck out, as being frivolous, vexatious and an abuse of the process of law, but the Court of Appeal, on 3 October 1972, unanimously allowed his appeal. Denning gave his opinion that 'it is the function of the court to see that the procedure of Parliament itself is not abused and that undue advantage is not taken of it.'

The Law Lords were appalled. If the order of the Court of Appeal had stood, the judiciary would have been on a collision course with parliament. BR's appeal reached the House in October 1973 and, after hearing argument for seven days, the Lords reserved judgment until 30 January 1974. 'The idea that a court is entitled to disregard a provision in an Act of Parliament on any ground,' said Lord Reid, 'must seem strange and startling to anyone with any knowledge of the history and law of our constitution . . .' 'The remedy for a Parliamentary wrong, if one has been committed,' added Lord Wilberforce, 'must be sought from Parliament, and cannot be gained from the courts.' Lord Simon of Glaisdale, who had been a Member of Parliament and Attorney-General, summed up the constitutional position:

> The system by which, in this country those liable to be affected by general political decisions have some control over the decision-making is parliamentary democracy. Its peculiar feature in consti-tutional law is the sovereignty of Parliament . . . the courts in this country have no power to declare enacted law to be invalid.

Tom was at a watershed. His great gifts as a judge were still seen; but creeping into his work, was a mischievous disregard for the consequences of judgments that trespassed in the field of politics and others that left the law uncertain. His campaigns became more urgent: to secure for the Court of Appeal the freedom from precedent that the Lords had awarded themselves; to update the law to meet current commercial and social needs; to remind a generation brought up in the Welfare State that they have duties as well as rights. There was still much for Denning to achieve, but increasingly, by his admirers as well as by his critics, the thought was voiced that the Master of the Rolls was going on too long.

23

No Retiring Age

Though Denning thought it right to punish the writer and publisher in *Broome* v. *Cassell* with exemplary damages, he usually opposed, on grounds of public policy, awards that were greatly in excess of what was required to compensate a victim or would place potentially enormous burdens upon wrongdoers.

The Lords' endorsement, in *Hedley Byrne*, of his own views on negligent misstatement, had opened up the possibility of liability for purely economic loss. Denning believed that some economic loss should be recoverable, but was appalled at the consequences that would follow any wide extension of the classes to whom a duty of care is owed.

In April 1972 Martin & Co., a firm of contractors, appealed from an order to pay damages for metal spoiled and profits on work that should have been processed during the whole of the time that a steel manufacturer's furnace was out of use because Martins had damaged an electricity cable while digging up the road. Martins did not deny their negligence, but contested liability to pay for more than the loss of value of the metal in the furnace at the time of the accident.

Denning repeated the arguments he had used in an earlier case. The cutting of the electricity supply, he said, was

> a hazard we all run. It may be due to a short circuit, to a flash of lightning, to a tree falling on the wires, to an accidental cutting of the cable, or even to the negligence of someone or other . . . Such a hazard is regarded by most people as a thing they must put up with – without seeking compensation from anyone . . . They try to make up the economic loss by doing more work the next day.
>
> (*Spartan Steel* v. *Martin & Co.*)

The difficulty in doing so, for Spartan Steel, would have been considerable, since theirs was a 24-hour working day and Edmund-Davies would have dismissed Martin's appeal. Denning and Lawton thought that Spartan Steel could recover only the loss of material in the furnace plus loss of profit on that material.

Denning was also concerned at vast awards of damages in personal injury cases, where the victim was unlikely to benefit from them. In *Lim Poh Choo* he made an attempt to deal with this problem, which most lawyers believed could only be resolved by Parliament. In 1973, following a minor operation, Lim, who was a senior psychiatric registrar, suffered irreparable brain damage, due to the negligence of hospital staff. She was 36 years old, had no dependants, and there was no hope that she would ever be anything but a helpless invalid, unaware of what was happening to her. She was flown to Penang, where she was looked after by her mother and servants. When her mother could no longer care for her, she would probably be returned to England and placed in an institution near to her married sister's home. In an action started on her behalf by her mother, the judge followed the principles on which awards for personal injuries were based, to reach the unprecedented sum of £250,000. The appeal of the Health Authority responsible for the hospital came before Denning, sitting with Lawton and Browne. Denning dissented when the other two found no grounds for overturning the award.

He found the award 'staggering'. He believed that the victim must 'be kept in as much comfort and tended with as much care as compassion for her so rightly demands', but saw that she would be unlikely to derive benefit from much of the sum awarded. She would, in all probability, be nursed by the national health service that had now to pay the award. He foresaw that 'if these sums get too large, we are in danger of injuring the body politic.' He thought it just to reduce the award to some £137,000, administer it through the Court of Protection and treat it as an interim payment if it should prove inadequate. To do this, Denning had to overcome the rule that such awards must be a lump sum, and, with 'some ingenuity', he thought, this could be done.

Lord Scarman, delivering the speech when the appeal reached the House, found Denning's hope that the sum could be regarded as an interim award, attractive and ingenious, but accepted that 'so radical a reform' could be made only by parliament.

Denning was always anxious that a wrong should not escape the eye of the court because there was no one competent to complain about it. He particularly disliked the idea that the Attorney-General could refuse to take action in matters of public interest that were left entirely to his discretion. On 16 January 1973 the Court of Appeal was asked by a member of the public to prevent the Independent Broadcasting Authority from televising, that evening, a film about the American producer, Andy Warhol, which journalists had described as offensive and indecent. After the Attorney-General had refused to act, Ross McWhirter sought an injunction without his agreement. Denning adjourned the court until 5 pm, to enable the IBA to be represented at the hearing.

The question was whether McWhirter had the right to bring the action without the involvement of the Attorney-General – though everyone knew that if he waited for the Attorney-General's leave, it would be too late to stop the broadcast. Denning had no doubt that the Court had power to grant an injunction at McWhirter's suit, if that were the only way of seeing the IBA's statutory duty was fulfilled. Lawton agreed that an injunction should be granted, until the matter could be more fully debated. Cairns thought it 'very much against the public interest that this programme should be broadcast,' but took the traditional view that a private individual is not to be allowed to enforce a matter of public interest. As often happened, the matter was resolved in the Court of Appeal but the question of whether a member of the public could enforce matters left by parliament in the hands of the Attorney-General came up again in 1977, in a highly charged political case.

When John King ceased to clerk the Master of the Rolls in 1971, Ross Chesney took over until he became ill in 1974. Temporarily, Tom turned for help to Peter Post, the clerk to Lord Justice Buckley. Post had an affection for the Master of the Rolls. In 1967, when he was clerk to Lord Justice Salmon, he had mentioned to Salmon that his wife was unwell. A week later he met Tom, coming out of court after a heavy day, seeming deep in thought. He was surprised and touched when Tom 'looked up, smiled and said "How's your wife, Peter?" '[65] Post's loyalty and his 'amazement' at Tom's 'kind thoughts, his grasp of the apparently insignificant and his incredible "human touch" ' outlasted Tom's life on the bench: with a short break, when Chesney was able to return to the courts, Peter clerked the Master of the Rolls until Tom's retirement, and soon after took on the work connected with Tom's property and other matters.

At 4.30 on a Friday most judges and their clerks hurried away; Peter Post was almost alone on Friday 14 January 1977 when solicitors for Mr Gouriet asked for a court the following morning to hear an urgent appeal from the refusal of a judge in chambers to grant an injunction against the Union of Post Office Workers. It was later suggested that the Court for this highly political case was carefully chosen: the reality was more haphazard. Another clerk volunteered that 'his judge' – Fred Lawton – was still there, if he was needed and it was found that Ormrod was also willing to sit on the Saturday. When Tom looked in, to say goodnight, Post told him about the case and, when Tom said he would preside, offered to meet him at the station with the car. The Saturday morning did not start well: when Tom's train arrived at 10.10, Peter discovered he had locked his car with the keys inside it, and the Master of the Rolls, refusing the offer of a taxi, hurried over the bridge, arriving a few minutes late for the 10.30 hearing.

On Thursday 13 January, the court was told, Tom Jackson, the union's General Secretary, in a gesture against apartheid, had said on the nine o'clock television news that his union would stop handling all mail to South Africa for a week, starting from midnight on Sunday. When it was suggested by the interviewer that this would be unlawful, Jackson replied that the law had never been tested in the courts. The following day, Gouriet asked the Attorney-General for his consent to bring an action to stop this proposed breach of law and, when the Attorney declined to become involved, Gouriet issued a writ in his own name. His request for an injunction was refused by the judge, who held he was powerless to act without the Attorney's consent. 'Are the courts to stand idly by?' asked Denning. 'Is the Attorney-General the final arbiter as to whether the law should be enforced or not?' The Court of Appeal granted an interim injunction until Tuesday 18 January, gave Gouriet leave to add as a party the Post Office Engineering Union – which had also announced its intention to disrupt links with South Africa – and included it in the terms of the injunction. Finally, the Attorney-General was also made a defendant.

On 18 January, the Attorney-General contested the court's right to review the exercise of his discretion; Gouriet conceded this point but claimed that, if the Attorney would not act to prevent the law being broken, a citizen was entitled to do so. Judgment was reserved until 27 January. Denning alone retained a lingering belief that the court must have power to review the Attorney-General's decision and to grant a permanent injunction without the Attorney's consent to the proceedings. Since the Union had obeyed the interim injunction the questions that went on appeal to the House of Lords were academic. For all practical purposes, the intervention of the Court of Appeal had averted the breach of law.

The point was not lost on activists who would have preferred the union to defy the court. The newspaper *Socialist Worker* discovered that Joan had 450 shares in Plessey, a company trading with South Africa, and used the information to attack the judges: 'These three wealthy bigots, who have never been elected by anyone, have assumed the right to dictate to elected union executives, and even the elected government.'

With the danger of interference with communication safely past, the Lords affirmed that the exclusive right of the Attorney-General to represent the public interest was constitutional, though two of them observed that a firm statement from him that the Union's proposed action would be illegal might have saved a lot of trouble. Commenting on the case, the *Law Quarterly Review* said that if the Attorney-General would not act to keep his political allies from breaking the law, it could not be satisfactory to put him in exclusive charge of law enforcement. Typically, Tom noted in *The Discipline of Law* that his disappointment was not so great as might be supposed: 'If the case had been brought – not by Mr Gouriet – but by a firm which communicated daily by telephone, telex or mail to South Africa, such a firm would have *locus standi* because of its private right.'

Tom had always thought financial matters should be settled, once and for all, at the time of a divorce and the Matrimonial Proceedings and Property Act 1970 at last provided a statutory framework for making adjustments. His words in *Wachtel* v. *Wachtel*, on 8 February 1973, became for a time tablets of stone in matrimonial proceedings.

The Divorce Reform Act 1969 made 'the irretrievable breakdown of the marriage' the only ground for divorce but the question of conduct was still bandied about in the courts because it was relevant to financial adjustments. The trial judge in *Wachtel*, Roger Ormrod, reminded the parties that it was 'no longer appropriate, if indeed it ever was, to talk about an "innocent" or a "guilty" wife' in the context of financial settlement, save, perhaps, where misconduct was 'obvious and gross'. Denning took up Ormrod's theme:

> Parliament has decreed: 'If the marriage has broken down irretrievably, let there be a divorce.' It carries no stigma, but only sympathy. It is a misfortune which befalls both. No longer is one guilty and the other innocent. No longer are there long contested divorce suits. Nearly every case goes uncontested. The parties come to an agreement, if they can, on the things that mean so much to them. They divide up the furniture. They arrange the custody of the children, the financial provision for the wife, and the future of the matrimonial home. If they cannot agree, the matters are referred to a judge in chambers . . .
>
> It has been suggested that there should be a 'discount' or 'reduction' in what the wife is to receive because of her supposed misconduct, guilt or blame (whatever word is used). We cannot accept this argument . . . There will no doubt be a residue of cases where the conduct of the parties is in the judge's words . . . 'both obvious and gross,' so much so that to order one party to support another whose conduct falls into this category is repugnant to anyone's sense of justice . . . But, short of cases falling into this category, the court should not reduce its order for financial provision merely because of what was formerly regarded as guilt or blame. To do so would be to impose a fine for supposed misbehaviour in the course of an unhappy married life.

How, then, were the family assets to be divided? What provision should a husband make for a wife? Over the years Denning had made various attempts to attribute a share in family assets to a partner who lacked legal entitlement but had contributed to their acquisition by work or by paying for other expenses of the family. The 1970 Act enabled the Court to order the transference of assets from husband to wife or vice versa and the *Wachtel* case gave Denning the opportunity to explain how it would work. It was, he said, 'one of the most important we ever had. It was argued before Lords Justices Phillimore, Roskill and me. The argument took three days: but we took over two months to prepare the judgment . . . We each played our part. We discussed it point by point. Each of us wrote a portion of the judgment.'[23] They concluded that there was 'much good sense' in taking one-third as a starting point for the wife's share of family assets. Their reasons make fascinating reading:

> When a marriage breaks up there will thenceforward be two households instead of one. The husband will have to go out to work all day and must get some woman to look after the house – either a wife, if he remarries, or a housekeeper, if he does not. He will also have to provide maintenance for the children. The wife will not usually have so much expense. She may go out to work herself, but she will not usually employ a housekeeper. She will do most of the housework herself, perhaps with some help. Or she may remarry, in which case her new husband will provide for her.

Though the idea of many divorced husbands being able to afford a housekeeper was out of touch with reality, in other ways the judgment was full of common sense. It stressed that the proposal for division of assets was not a rule; that courts should not order the payment to the wife of a lump sum 'unless the husband has capital assets out of which to pay it – without crippling his earning power;' that the most important question will usually be what is to happen to the matrimonial home. *Wachtel* gave Denning the opportunity to bring together the strands of his efforts over the years to make a just division of assets between husband and wife, however slender those assets might be.

In 1973, Sir Thomas Skyrme, the Secretary to Tom's Committee on Procedure in Matrimonial Causes who had become President of the Commonwealth Magistrates' Association, invited the Master of the Rolls to address the Association's Conference, to be held in Nairobi that August. Since Tom would go abroad only if Joan was invited, Skyrme had to obtain finance from two different sources to pay their expenses. The effort was worth it: Tom was 'always good value'.[33] Some visiting speakers might deliver their talks and leave straight away but Tom always stayed, joining the discussions, both formal and informal, a magnetic attraction to delegates from all countries.

After so many years of speech-making, Tom had developed a fund of favourite themes and stories. He still worked hard to please and, to some extent, tailored his words to the occasion, but he never modified them to suit a particular audience. He was unaware that a favourite tale might give offence and his listeners responded exactly as he expected. The peroration of his story about Lord Mansfield and the slave – 'let the black go free!' – might cause embarrassment to some white listeners in a predominantly black audience but neither that audience nor Tom himself were disturbed.

In Nairobi he talked about the state of law in Africa since independence. The role of the law, he said, was 'to keep the balance between the power of the State on the one hand and the freedom of the individual on the other hand.' He drew attention to 'the great responsibility' which fell upon the judges when there was a revolution such as those in east and west Africa, since last he was there. It was the judges who had to decide whether the revolution had succeeded, in which case the imposed new constitution became the law of the country; or whether it was not completely successful, in which case the old constitution continued to govern. He spoke about the conflicts that may arise between the power of the executive and freedom of the individual: about preventive detention; about the return to India and Pakistan of illegal immigrants into Britain – 'that law was said to be contrary to the liberty of an individual. But it had been passed by Parliament. The Judges were bound to enforce it.' He ended with his definition of justice: 'The nearest we can get to defining justice is to say that it is what the right-minded members of the community – those who have the right spirit within them – believe to be fair.'

Moving a vote of thanks, S. K. Sachdeva, the Chairman of the Kenya Magistrates' Association, said 'that in all the countries of the Commonwealth where the system of common law has held roots, Lord Denning's judgments are studied, discussed, criticised, admired and praised continuously by the judiciary as well as the members of the Bar and, of course, he is a hero to all law students.'

When the Conference ended, Tom went to Dar-es-Salaam, where he saw that the Denning Law School, founded before independence, had become the University Law School. The members of the Denning Law Society, which had kept his name, presented Tom with a magnificent ebony walking stick, which he delighted to show to visitors at Whitchurch. There followed a visit to Lake Victoria, flying low over the reserve, in the private plane of the Tanzanian game warden, to give Tom and Joan a wonderful view of the wild life. At the lake, they spent the night in primitive conditions, warned to shut the wire door to their verandah, whenever they left their hut. Since Tom's excellent memory was fallible when it came to matters that did not interest him, Joan found a male baboon stalking round their verandah, while his mate shook the wire grille on their bedroom window. Back in Dar-es-Salaam they met the President of Tanzania, Julius Nyerere, before returning to Nairobi for the flight home with other members of the conference.

On 1 January 1973, when the European Communities Act 1972 came into force, the United Kingdom became a member of the European Economic Community and the Treaty of Rome, which had established the EEC, was made part of English law. It was not until March 1974 that Denning had to consider its effect, in an interlocutory appeal, *Application des Gaz* v. *Falks Veritas*. Judgment was reserved and, the following month, a second case came to appeal, concerning the use of the word 'champagne' on drinks, other than wine produced in the Champagne district of France.

From the start, Denning appreciated the impact of the Treaty on English law. When it came to matters with a European element, he said, 'the Treaty is like an incoming tide. It flows into the estuaries and up the rivers. It cannot be held back.' In *Bulmer* v. *Bollinger* he set about making it a useful tool, rather than an impediment to his method of judgment. He was greatly desirous of the freedom enjoyed by the judges of the European Court of Justice to give due weight to considerations of policy and economics and to take decisions unhampered by precedent. He was less keen that English courts should too often refer questions to Luxembourg, though at the end of 1979, he told the Law Society: 'We are in Europe to stay. Use the great influence of the past to help Europe forward as a whole in the future.'

With the same selectivity that he increasingly applied to statute and precedent, Tom drew upon the Treaty and the European Convention on Human Rights when they served his purpose and disregarded them when they became inconvenient. Romantically attached to England's past and to the white, Anglo-Saxon, Protestant backbone of her people he found unpalatable some consequences of the right to freedom of movement within the EEC, bringing into the country immigrants whose presence he regarded as inimical to the general welfare. He upheld a local authority's refusal to house an Italian family on the ground that, by leaving Italy without having arranged accommodation in England, they had deliberately made themselves homeless. (*De Falco* v. *Crawley BC*)

The thalidomide case was, for Tom, an early proof of the value of the European Court of Human Rights. Pregnant women who had taken the drug thalidomide had given birth to deformed children and, after many years, Distillers, the distributors of the drug, had agreed to settle their actions for damages. Five parents refused to accept the terms and an application was made to have their children represented by the Official Solicitor so that settlement could go ahead. *The Sunday Times* launched a campaign against Distillers and, on 12 October 1972, the Attorney-General issued a writ against the paper, claiming an injunction to prevent their publishing an article. The case reached the Court of Appeal in January 1973 and Denning took the view that, on such a matter, the law authorised the paper to make fair comment – the public interest in having the case discussed out-weighed any prejudice that might be occasioned to Distillers. The Lords did not agree with him but, when *The Sunday Times* took the case to the European Court of Human Rights, the paper's right to give information on the subject was upheld.

At first Tom could see no reason for the Convention to be incorporated by statute into English law. By the end of 1979, he had changed his mind. Without the authority of statute, he said, some judges were not strong enough to protect the fundamental freedoms. The thrust of Tom's speeches was the same as it had been for a quarter of a century but he had become less diplomatic in his phrasing and in the choice of audience for his remarks.

With the return to government of Labour in 1974, Elwyn Jones became Lord Chancellor. The Trade Union and Labour Relations

Act 1974 swiftly repealed the Industrial Relations Act and gave to the unions greater immunity from action than they had ever enjoyed. Denning addressed himself to the problems rising from 'secondary picketing' of companies not involved in a trade dispute. When officials of SOGAT instructed their members at the *Daily Express* not to handle increased output during a strike at the *Daily Mirror*, he refused to accept that the SOGAT action was in furtherance of the *Mirror* dispute. (*Express Newspapers* v. *Keys*) In *Associated Newspapers* v. *Wade* he said: 'Some acts are so remote from the trade dispute that they cannot properly be said to be "in furtherance" of it.' He held the NUJ's actions illegal when, to advance its dispute with provincial newspaper proprietors, it called out its members at the Press Association and, when Press Association members continued to provide copy to national newspapers, demanded that its members in those newspapers black copy. (*Express Newspapers* v. *McShane*)

New issues occupied the public: immigration and its containment on the one hand and, on the other, the creation of good race relations within the state. When appeals on immigration and deportation matters reached his court, Denning tended to interpret the relevant legislation restrictively and was less likely than usual to question the exercise of executive discretion. He decided that international law did not require the admission of Ugandan Asians, British protected persons, expelled by the government of Idi Amin (*R.* v. *Secretary of State ex parte Thakrar*); and he refused to accept that the right to marry given under the European convention entitled an Asian illegal immigrant, awaiting deportation, to be freed in order to enter an arranged marriage, which would secure for him the right to remain (*ex parte Bhajan Singh*). He confirmed the deportation order on an illegal immigrant, who had managed to work in the UK and evade capture for three years (*ex parte Azam*). There were also occasions when he showed sympathy with a would-be immigrant. He thought it wrong that lengthy procedures required to be carried out in India should prevent a wife and family joining the husband, who was legally in England (*ex parte Phansopkar*); and refused to allow the Home Secretary to rely upon a technicality to prevent a student's appeal to remain. (*Mehta* v. *Home Secretary*)

Construing the Race Relations Acts, Denning adopted his usual approach to legislation and gave effect to the policy behind them. He even went further than parliament intended, at the time, when he held that private clubs must not discriminate against black applicants (and was reversed by the Lords). After the Commission for Racial Equality challenged the court's right to review judicially its terms of reference for an inquiry, he began to regard it with more suspicion. (*R. v. CRE ex parte Hillingdon LBC*)

Changing social perceptions, with which Tom was fully in agreement, also gave birth to legislation intended to outlaw forms of discrimination against women and to secure for them equal pay for equal work. Though Tom still believed that it was the woman's place to bring up the family and the man's to provide for her, he interpreted this legislation liberally.

The clash of political ideologies, so clearly seen in labour relations in the Seventies, was evident also in other branches of law, notably housing. Balancing the rights and duties of parties, as he saw them, Denning frequently reached decisions that were said to be political, though they depended more upon his ethical values. When Manchester's newly elected council reversed its predecessors's policy of selling council houses, Denning was prepared to ignore, in 1976, the long-accepted rules for the formation of a contract to sell property, in order to permit a tenant to buy his council house. (*Gibson* v. *Manchester CC*)

Early in 1974, the case of *Asher* v. *Secretary of State for Environment* reached his court. In September 1972 the councillors of Clay Cross in Derbyshire had resolved to ignore the Housing Finance Act 1972, which required them to make progressive increases in council house rents, while also bringing into operation rent rebate and allowance schemes. They claimed that they were morally obliged to refuse since they had been elected on a pledge not to raise rents. The Environment Secretary declared the Council in default and instructed the district auditor to hold an extraordinary audit of their Housing Account. The councillors were surcharged and appealed. 'To my mind,' said Denning, 'their plain obligation, moral as well as legal, was to carry out the duties imposed on them by law.'

In April 1974 Tom became a member of the Drapers Company, and on 15 May was made a Freeman of the City of London. As soon as the summer term ended, the Dennings set out on their travels, starting in South Africa, where Tom gave a series of lectures at Cape

Town University and continuing, by way of Mauritius to Melbourne. At Monash University, Tom spoke to 2000 students, while another 2000 watched on closed-circuit television. Despite airport strikes they were able to keep appointments in Hobart and Sydney, attending a performance of *La Bohème* at the opera house, before leaving for Japan. By now, both Tom and Joan were seasoned travellers, but they found Japan a new and fascinating experience, starting with the landing on a water-logged runway after a typhoon over Tokyo. They attended a tea-making ceremony, marvelled at the delicacy of the china and the courtesy of their hosts, visited shrines, temples and the Imperial Palace of Kyoto. During their visit to the court of the Chief Justice in Tokyo, Joan had what was her first attack of angina – though she did not recognise it as such – and, characteristically, managed to keep it from Tom for fear that he would worry. Going home, they visited Tom's niece in Vancouver, before Tom fulfilled speaking engagements in Edmonton – where, for the first time they saw the Northern Lights – and Winnipeg.

During the next term Tom, as President of Queen Elizabeth College, Greenwich, founded in the reign of the first monarch of that name, was host to her successor, Queen Elizabeth II, at the celebrations held on 19 November 1974, to mark the grant of confirmatory Letters Patent. A lunch was planned by the Drapers Company to precede the event but wives were not invited. Eventually as a concession to Tom, Joan and the wife of the guild's Master were both allowed to attend.

In 1975, travel filled Tom's vacations. At Easter he spoke in Ghana; in May he addressed the International Union of Judges in Belgium. Tom and Joan had both enjoyed the conference in Nairobi in 1973 and the Commonwealth Magistrates were so delighted with Tom's contribution that they invited him to become their Honorary Life Vice-President. In that capacity he went to their Conference of August 1975 in Kuala Lumpur, which was also attended by Lord Elwyn-Jones. The contrast between the cordial welcome given to the Lord Chancellor and the enthusiastic greeting for Tom – who arrived separately – was pronounced. It seemed to Skyrme that most of the lawyers in Malaysia and all of the law students had turned out at the airport to meet Lord Denning. On the last day of the conference, Saturday 16 August, Denning thanked the Association for electing him their first Honorary Life Vice-President. 'I suppose,' he added, with a joke that appeared more often in his speeches, 'that, as with the office of Master of the Rolls, there is no retiring age.'

During the week he had spent in Kuala Lumpur, Tom told his audience, he was filled with a sense of pride in 'our Commonwealth, which encompasses the world, which crosses the continents, from Australia to Zambia, from Guyana to Sierra Leone, from Trinidad to Scotland; all peoples – of all colours and of all religions – all . . . equal before the law. That is the justice we seek to achieve: that everyone whatever his colour, race or religion, is equal before the law.' He talked about the Notting Hill riots of 1958 and the heavy sentences imposed on white youths for attacking coloured youngsters; he spoke with hope of the ending of discrimination in England on the grounds of race, religion or sex. Urging the delegates to retain their common language of the law, he said:

> Our fathers have in the process of centuries provided this realm of England, its colonies, its dependencies and, I may add, its Commonwealth with a speech malleable and pliant as Greek, dignified as Latin, masculine yet free of teutonic guttural, capable of being as precise as French, dulcet as Italian, sonorous as Spanish and of capturing all those excellences to its service.

It was not hypocrisy that prompted the judge who interpreted immigration rules restrictively to speak with genuine enthusiasm of the Commonwealth and the ideal of equality. Tom was a mass of contradictions but his views were honest. His prejudices and predilections were those he had grown-up with – typical of the England of his youth. Only very rarely did they interfere with his sense of justice. They never stopped him, on an individual basis, from reaching across racial and religious barriers: if Tom liked someone, their colour, nationality or religion was no bar to friendship.

24

The Judge on the Clapham Omnibus

It seemed that everyone who met Tom – and many who had not – turned to him for help. (He even had a request for advice on the amendment of birth certificates from a trans-sexual.) Usually he sent their letters, under cover of his own, to those who could deal with the problem. Sometimes he had, politely but firmly, to decline assistance: to students who hoped for his opinion of their course work he said 'no', often suggesting that they ring his secretary for a time when he could see them. Young people came to his room and sat, nervously, on the edges of their chairs. Five minutes later they left, 'relaxed, happy, enchanted and enriched.'[65]

Just after Christmas the Dennings went to India again for a series of lectures, feeling a pang of regret to be away from home when their family – 21 in all – saw in the New Year of 1976 together at The Lawn. Later that year they attended their third meeting of the American Bar, in Dallas, where the temperature was over 100°F by the time they had breakfasted. The gift of the American lawyers – a week's holiday at Cape Cod, after the conference – gave them a welcome opportunity to relax after a hectic schedule. The vacation, to Joan's mind, ranked second to Fiji only because it was shorter.

Many of their journeys were, by now, return visits. Hong Kong, where Tom spoke to university students in April 1977, was a first. It was also, as things turned out, the last of their tours for some time. That summer they were busy at home. On 3 July Reg and Eileen Denning celebrated their Golden Wedding. On 6 July, to mark the naming of the University College of Buckingham's new Denning Law Library, Leslie Scarman held a reception in the Bencher's Room of Lincoln's Inn, praising Tom as 'one of the few geniuses of the

English common law.' Tom and Joan were also much involved in celebrations of the Queen's Silver Jubilee. They attended the ceremony at Westminster Hall, the thanksgiving service in St. Paul's and a party on board the royal yacht *Britannia*. Tom was prominent in the Whitchurch festivities and his portrait appeared on one of the ubiquitous souvenirs: a plate picturing the Queen surrounded by her law officers.

Throughout the summer, Joan had spasms of intense pain in her chest, such as she had first experienced in Japan, without yet appreciating that this was angina. During the vacation, they stayed a week in Kent, where John Ward was painting Tom's portrait for Birkbeck College. On 27 August, Tom was due to unveil a plaque at the University College of Buckingham and planned to spend the previous night at the home of John and Veronica Stuart in Beaconsfield. He and Joan had a quick lunch with Reg and Eileen before leaving Kent. It was intended that Tom should navigate on the drive to Beaconsfield but, on the congested roads around Windsor and Slough, he found difficulty and both of them were tired when they finally arrived at the Stuarts, late in the afternoon. To make matters worse, it was clear that the car had a flat tyre. John tried to jack it up to change the tyre, but found the car so old and rusty that the jack simply broke the jacking point on which it was fixed. 'Can we get it on the insurance?' asked Tom, before the realisation that Joan would not be able to drive him to Buckingham drove other matters from his mind. It was not usual for the Dennings to be despondent, but on this occasion they were. It seemed to Tom that he had better cancel his visit to Buckingham. John pointed out that, if the College wanted Tom to speak, they would certainly send a car; and so it was arranged. The Dennings spent the day at Buckingham, while John had the puncture mended, and later Joan drove home. On the Monday her pain recurred and the doctor not only diagnosed angina, but also found that she had duodenal ulcers. Rest was prescribed to be essential.

The time had come to slow down the pace at which they had been living. Without Joan's constant smoothing of his path, Tom would find it more difficult to continue the style of life to which he had become accustomed in the past 15 years but, though he recognised that foreign travel would have to be limited, if not eliminated, he determined to continue in office. All his life there had been people ready to come to his help: now a lady messenger kept the flat in Old Court clean for him and, during the week, if he had no engagements, he took most of his meals in Lincoln's Inn. During 1978 Tom refused invitations from Canada and India, explaining that Joan was unwell and 'I like to be with her at home as much as I can.' It was not until the summer of 1978 that Joan was again able to join Tom's life outside Whitchurch. By that time Tom was beginning to suffer from arthritis in his hip, though it never prevented him from accepting an invitation to speak.

Tom still had the power to confound his critics – and there were many at the time he passed his seventy-sixth birthday – by his fresh and original approach to pressing problems, one of which was how to prevent a defendant from moving assets out of the jurisdiction prior to a judgment against him. On 22 May 1975 Denning, sitting with Browne and Geoffrey Lane, heard an appeal against the refusal of Donaldson to prohibit Greek charterers from moving funds held in a London bank outside the jurisdiction. (*Nippon Yusen Kaisha* v. *Karageorgis*) The Greeks owed hire on a charter-party to Japanese ship-owners and these monies were their only resources.

The argument that a thing had not been done before had never appealed to Denning. Recognising the commercial sense of restraining the debtor from putting his only assets out of reach of his creditor, the Court of Appeal unanimously agreed that there was no reason why the court should not grant an injunction in these circumstances. Four weeks later they heard the appeal that was to give its name to the new procedure: *Mareva* v. *International Bulk Carriers*. Again charterers who had money in a London bank defaulted; again the court granted an injunction. This new development was highly regarded by the commercial community but could not yet be considered established.

In March 1977, sitting six days with Orr in the Divisional Court, Denning heard argument from both sides in *Rasu Maritima Pertambangan*, another charter-party case, where the only connection with England was cargo worth US $12 million, lying in the docks in Liverpool awaiting shipment. Counsel for Pertambangan, Michael Mustill, argued that law reform should be left to parliament. It was not a submission likely to find favour with Denning, who regarded this, at any rate, as 'a field of law reform in which the judges can proceed step by step. They can try out a new procedure and see how it works. That is better than long drawn out discussions elsewhere.' Though on the merits, the court decided that this was not a case for an injunction, they made it clear that *Mareva* injunctions would be available where appropriate.

Lawyers, as well as the business community, approved this development. Lord Diplock thought Denning was 'quite wrong, but the thing was so good that he personally would resist every attempt to get the matter to the Lords until it was firmly established.'[64] When the case of *The Siskina* reached the House in 1977, the broad principle of *Mareva* was left in place. In *Prince Abdul Rahman* v. *Abu-Taha*, Denning proposed an enlargement of the new procedure, stating that a Mareva injunction could be granted against a man based in England, if it seemed likely that he would abscond or move assets out of the jurisdiction.

Parliament, as often it had done, caught up with Denning in the Supreme Court Act 1981, giving the court power to restrain an individual from dealing with his assets, when it appears 'just and convenient' to do so, regardless of his domicile or residence. How Denning would have sought to build upon this principle of his old age cannot be surmised, since his time as Master of the Rolls was running out. One of his last judgments, in *Chief Constable of Kent* v. *Verdon-Roe*, suggests he might have gone too far.

Apart from the development of *Mareva*, Denning's charter-party cases were not among his more successful. His determination to stop charterers claiming that hire money had not been paid on the due date, in order to re-hire their vessels at an increased price, ran counter to the law's insistence on the strict letter of the charter-party. In *The Laconia*, *The Mihailos Xilas* and *The Chikuma* the Court of Appeal was reversed by the Lords, who feared that commercial confidence would be undermined by uncertainty as to the law. Yet, of *The Chikuma* at least, Professor Atiyah would write that the Lords' decision seemed 'an outrage to commonsense, and must run totally counter to all reasonable business expectations.'[49]

Denning's other shipping cases were similarly received in the Lords. They ranged from the unjustifiable decision in *The Koningin Juliana*, to *The Maratha Envoy*, where, in 1976, Denning proposed a simple, practical and modern solution to the question of when a ship has 'arrived', though the Lords were not prepared to uphold it.

The solid body of Denning's judicial work was still carried out with the ability and flair that characterised his early years. He never lost the 'remarkable capacity to seize the essence of a case'[67] and came quickly to grips with the most complicated legislation. When he heard his first VAT appeal he was in his seventies and 'within half an hour'[67] had achieved an overall view of how it all worked, the interaction of one section with another. When it came to public law, he seemd to move from one controversy to another. Complaints that Denning pursued his own idea of public policy, regardless of the intention of parliament were countered by those who thought he spoke for England. There was, for instance, the dispute over the proposed increase of £6 in the fee for a television licence.

Mr Congreve, like some 24,000 other licence holders, had applied for a new licence before his old expired, in order to beat the date of the rise. When he refused to pay the additional £6 demanded by the Home Office and his licence was revoked, he sought a declaration that the Home Secretary's action was unlawful. During the argument in the Court of Appeal, Roger Parker, counsel for the Crown, warned that 'If the court interferes in this case it would not be long before the powers of the court would be called in question.' To call in question the independence of the judges was certain to anger Denning. In his judgment, he commented: 'We trust that this was not said seriously but only as a piece of advocate's licence.' The Court's declaration that the Home Office notice of revocation was unlawful was widely acclaimed and, on 5 December, Bernard Levin wrote in *The Times*: 'Blow the loud trumpets of victory for US over THEM in the TV Licence War.' Subsequently, Parker apologised to the court and, in the House of Commons, on 9 December, the Home Secretary, Roy Jenkins, acknowledged that it was unthinkable for any Home Secretary to question the vital independence of the judiciary.

The *Gouriet* case of January 1977, with its political overtones, was followed, six months later, by *Grunwick*. The employment protection legislation introduced by the Labour Government had provided machinery for unions to claim bargaining rights from an employer and, if they were refused, to apply to the new Advisory Conciliation and Arbitration Service (ACAS) to investigate and make recommendations. By the time the case of the Grunwick Processing Laboratories reached the Court of Appeal in July 1977, it was widely known from media reports that ACAS had been unable to ascertain the views of Grunwick's workforce, since the company had refused to cooperate with them. The ACAS recommendation for recognition was therefore based almost entirely on a ballot of ex-workers, dismissed while on strike, before ACAS had become involved. ACAS urged a liberal interpretation of the statute but Denning replied that 'liberal' could be used in two ways. 'Not only in construing powers, but also in construing safeguards.' Since the act required the opinion of the workers to be ascertained which it had not, the recommendation of ACAS was void. As he had interpreted the employment legislation of the Conservative Government in a way that accorded with his own view of public policy, so he treated the Labour Government's replacement.

In April 1977 Tom made himself the centre of another controversy, when he said in debate in the House of Lords that a year or two after the Profumo Inquiry he had agreed to the destruction of the only copy of the evidence. 'He's torn up history' was the headline in the *Evening News* of 21 April, which reported the angry reaction of MPs and demanded that Lord Denning justify his action. Two days later the Prime Minister, James Callaghan told the Commons that Lord Denning at one time suggested that the records be destroyed; instead, a copy was kept in the Cabinet Office, though it was agreed that the records should not be handed over as public records.

By the late 1970s Denning's battle against 'the strict constructionists' was largely won. The Renton Committee on 'The Preparation of Legislation' had endorsed Denning's purposive approach and it was more commonly used by the judiciary. Even the Lords agreed with Denning's decision to read words into an Act to prevent 'as glaring an example of discrimination against a woman on the ground of her sex as there could possibly be. (*Nothman* v *Barnet Council*) Controversy seemed not to deter Tom's student admirers. In 1977 the Holdsworth Club of the University of Birmingham elected Tom its President for the third time, an unusual honour but, for the members, Denning was 'the outstanding personality of his generation.'[68] For the Club's Jubilee Presidential Address in 1978, Lord

Denning spoke on 'Restraining the Misuse of Power'. Into a familiar theme he wove more recent cases: *Gouriet*, *Laker Airways*, the thalidomide tragedy and the story of Dr Wallersteiner and his multiplicity of puppet trusts and companies; his own cases, as always, provided his audience with a commentary upon the events of their time.

At home, Tom's life remained serene. Each Saturday, after he moved to Micheldever in 1972, Norman called on Tom at Whitchurch; once a week Tom spoke with Reg on the telephone. A small shadow disturbed the family harmony as Marjorie became frail and entered a nursing home: who was to take over The Hermitage? It was eventually agreed that Tom would pay off the mortgage and assume responsibility for Majorie's maintenance. In April 1978 Tom placed The Hermitage in trust for his grandsons and let it.

The birth of his first grandson, Mark, on 7 April 1974, was the supremely fulfilling moment of his later years. Robert and Robert's sons – the second boy, Paul, was born on 13 January 1977 – occupied a special place in Tom's heart. As he had wanted to smooth Robert's path, now he was anxious to provide for his grandchildren. On 24 May 1978 the publishing director of Butterworths wrote to ask Tom whether he would be sympathetic to the publication of a collection of his judgments and extra-judicial writings, linked by short passages of commentary. Tom built upon the idea to write *The Discipline of Law* in the long vacation. He spent his advance royalties of £6000 on work to The Hermitage and transferred the copyright to Robert and Elizabeth, as trustees of the settlement, on the day the book was published, 23 January 1979, his 80th birthday.

Tom was delighted with the reception given in the boardroom of Butterworths and deeply moved by birthday tributes from all over the world. It normally took several weeks to complete the procedure for the election of an Honorary Bencher of Gray's Inn but, on 17 January, the Treasurer, Leonard Caplan, suggested that Tom should be made an Honorary Master of the Bench in time to make a birthday present of it. The secret was closely kept until the morning of Tom's birthday, when Leonard gave him the news in Chancery Lane. With Tom, emotion was never far from the surface: he flung his arms around Leonard and, 'with tears in his eyes', said how happy he was.[69] From the solicitors of England and Wales Tom received a copy of *Paradisi in Sole*, beautifully bound in green, its spine embossed in gold, inscribed 'with respect, affection and esteem'. Whatever criticisms of Denning there may have been, an all-party greeting from the House of Commons expressed 'its gratitude for his outstanding contribution to the humane development of law and the administration of justice in Great Britain.'

The Bar Theatrical Society produced a celebratory programme for their long-time President, in which he took part. On 16 February the Western Circuit gave a dinner and, on 21 February, he was fêted in Lincoln's Inn. Amidst laughter, the Treasurer, David Renton, said that, in the Court of Appeal, Tom's motto *'fiat justitia, ruat coelum'* was translated 'Let Justice be done though the Lords overrule us.' Tom had become, as the BBC announced on his birthday, a legend in his own lifetime. Every newspaper had its comment: 'The Judge on the Clapham Omnibus', proclaimed *The Observer* and 'Maverick Man of the Law', the *Sunday Telegraph*.

The Discipline of Law, an entertaining account of some of Tom's judicial campaigns, was an immediate success. On Wednesday 24 January, when Tom signed copies in the Butterworth bookshop, the queue stretched into Chancery Lane. Many lawyers were amused by the choice of title – though, in his preface, Tom explained that he used the word 'discipline' in its less familiar sense of instruction imparted to disciples or scholars. In an affectionate review, Scarman reminded the student that 'Vintage Denning, whatever the year, is stimulating, heady stuff' but law reform, in the world's common law jurisdictions, had become legislative, rather than judicial. Pleased as he was by the reception of his book, Tom was less than happy about the tax to be paid on the gift of the copyright to the settlement; and about the consequences of other arrangements that, mindful of his advancing years, he was making to transfer to the settlement those assets still in his own name.

It would have been better for Tom and the law if he had resigned on his 80th birthday. His intellect and memory were unimpaired; he could still produce a closely reasoned argument in clear and simple terms; but the quick perception of what was apposite that distinguished his early years could no longer be trusted. He was, perhaps, an old man in a hurry; or an Old Testament prophet, convinced of his righteousness and determined, while he could, to guide the footsteps of his people. He knew his hearing had declined and had a strategem to deal with this. When he was not sure that he had heard correctly, he would repeat what he thought counsel had said; if he got it wrong, counsel would tell him again and he would repeat that also. Once he had it right, he was sure to remember it.

His schedule was still punishing. In a typical week, 5 March 1979, he lunched at Scotland Yard on Monday; presented prizes on Tuesday at the Polytechnic of Central London; lectured at Birkbeck College on Wednesday; and was the guest of honour at the Annual Dinner of Legal Aid Chairmen on Thursday. All this in addition to court work that was found tiring by many a younger man, meetings before and after court, and a weekend visit to The Lawn by BBC Bristol. However tight his timetable, Tom always found a few minutes to see schoolchildren or students visiting the courts. To what other judge would a young man from Ilford have sent the request to brighten his girlfriend's birthday by signing the enclosed card and inscribing it: 'I hope you have a pleasant and happy Birthday. Good luck for your future exams'? What other judge would have done so?

The variety of Tom's engagements, in the course of 1979, was astonishing. There were dinners at the Inns of Court and at the Law Society; at the Mansion House, Guildhall and the Royal Academy of Arts; the State Opening of Parliament; retirement parties, memorial services, luncheons, visits to schools, universities, the Police College, Wimbledon and a hundred and one other places. There was the Annual Service of the Lawyers' Christian Fellowship in Temple Church on 9 July, followed by a reception, when Tom spoke on 'The Influence of Religion on Law'. Perhaps the occasion on which he felt the greatest pride was the Grand Night at Middle Temple, on 10 May, which he attended in white tie, wearing his decorations, with his brothers Reg and Norman, who had devoted their lives to the service of their country.

In April 1979, with a general election pending, Tom went to receive a doctorate in Ottawa. There he said that the 'greatest threat to the rule of law today is posed by big trade unions.' The remark became a serious election issue and the Lord Chancellor wrote to Tom, on 23 April, to remonstrate. It nevertheless reflected the view of a large part of the electorate and, a month later, the Conservatives were returned, committed to a policy of monetary restraint and control of the unions.

Tom had rarely missed a day of work through ill health but in the summer of 1979 his hip and leg began to trouble him seriously. Walking home with Joan, one day, Tom limped so badly that Joan was afraid they would not make it. In bed, the pain eased and Tom insisted upon going to work the next day. By the time he reached the courts he was in such pain that he could not mount the stairs. Joan was called and four men carried Tom – no light weight – on a chair, down the steps of the Judge's Entrance and into an official car. A bed was found at the Nuffield Hospital and there Tom remained for ten days, visited each morning by his secretary, Miss Burgin, and twice a day by Peter Post.

Because his leg had shortened from arthritis, one of Tom's shoes was built up an inch and a half and he had to learn to walk again. A bed was moved into the sitting room at The Lawn and, when he was there, Tom got into the habit of a rest after lunch. He found he could still manage to mow the lawn by resting his weight on the handles of the machine, and he still swam in the river when the water was not too cold, but his movements were slow and he needed help on stairs that lacked a hand-rail. He chafed against the new restrictions on his physical activity. It was probably a relief to both him and Joan that he was writing his second book in the Long Vacation.

Tom was anxious to minimise the incidence of tax on the books he wrote that year and in the following long vacation, *The Due Process of Law* and *The Family Story*. 'It means there will be very little left for the grandchildren,' he wrote to his solicitor on 5 April 1981, 'whereas it was the whole object of the trust to provide for them.' His solicitor's account was, itself, a source of surprise: like most old people, he thought everything had become very expensive.

Making the money for the grandchildren was important for Tom; he also derived immense satisfaction from packing and despatching copies of his books to his nearest and dearest. The death, in December 1979, of his younger brother Norman, from a heart attack induced by a tetanus injection, had been a great blow. The reactions of his remaining brother and sister to his work were particularly gratifying. Half an hour after Reg found his copy of *Due Process* on his breakfast table, on 18 February 1980, he wrote: 'I am touched that you should, yourself, have packed it.' He was 'more than touched' by Tom's inscription, on the first page, of the words with which the brothers still ended their letters to one another: Ever your loving brother. *The Family Story* was welcomed by Reg; Marjorie wrote from Winchester Clinic, on 19 May 1981, 'You describe Mother and Father so perfectly ... You are like them both. I feel you have Father's lovely genial manners.' The affection between the brothers was manifest in their exchange of letters when Tom sent Reg a cheque – promptly returned – as his contribution to all that Reg had done for the family.

Though in general (for other judges) he approved the recommendation to reticence, Tom had become a considerable media personality, giving interviews to newspapers, appearing on Person to Person with David Dimbleby in July 1979, and other programmes. As the castaway in Roy Plomley's Desert Island Discs in May 1980, he 'chose simple tunes such as please simple folk'[1]: 'the very English "Greensleeves" '; 'Colonel Bogey', which was played as he entrained in 1918; 'To be a Pilgrim', reminding him of his much loved *Pilgrim's Progress*; 'Mine eyes have seen the glory of the coming of the Lord', which was used at Norman's memorial service; 'Roses are blooming in Picardy', which again recalled the First World War; 'The King and I' sung by Valerie Hobson, from a show to which he and Joan had taken the family; 'The Judge's Song' of Gilbert and Sullivan; and 'Land of Hope and Glory', 'which reflects the very spirit of England.'[1] For his book he chose Palgrave's *Golden Treasury* and for his desert island luxury, hot tea with fresh milk, bread and butter and rice pudding – surely, the simplest of luxuries.

The promise to deliver the Dimbleby Lecture on 20 November 1980 was an altogether more serious undertaking, giving Tom the opportunity to comment publicly on justice and the law to a television audience of millions. He intended to propose that judges should have the power to review legislation. The BBC made careful preparations for the lecture, to be televised before an invited audience at the Royal Society of Arts. Edward Mirzoeff, the Senior Producer of General Features, discussed Tom's drafts with him asking 'if the judges are to have the power to review legislation, will there not be a much greater risk of political appointments to the Bench?'

Tom was hot under the television lights and very nervous. Responding to Mirzoeff's question, he told his audience that if ever some future Prime Minister 'should seek to pack the Bench with judges of his own extreme political colour', they need have no fear. 'Every judge on his appointment discards all politics and all prejudices . . . The judges of England have always in the past – and always will – be vigilant in guarding our freedoms. Someone must be trusted. Let it be the judges.'

Tom's postbag after each appearance was heavy and mostly appreciative but after he was interviewed on Radio 4's *With Great Pleasure*, one correspondent wrote that he found difficulty in reconciling Tom's views on air with the reports of his judgment in the *Harman* case. He believed, he said, that Denning's justification of secrecy for civil service files failed to protect the principles of freedom and truth for which Denning's brothers had died in the First World War. The observation must have been painful but Tom replied with his usual courtesy, though he could not forbear to add that he had received 'many nice letters' from people who had enjoyed the programme, 'quite different from yours.'

The *Harman* judgment appeared, indeed, to be out of character. It might have been expected that Denning's interests and those of Miss Harman in the protection of the individual from inhuman and degrading punishment would have coincided. Harriet Harman was the legal officer of the National Council for Civil Liberties, who had acted as solicitor for Michael Williams, suing the Home Office in relation to his treatment in an experimental prison 'control unit'. For some time the NCCL had sought information on this unit and, in the course of the proceedings the Home Office disclosed documents, including six for which it had tried to claim public interest immunity. Amongst those present when they were read out in court during the hearing was a journalist, David Leigh. Several days later Miss Harman allowed Leigh to see the documents for an article, appearing in the *Guardian*, on 8 April 1980, which quoted from them. The Home Office commenced proceedings against Miss Harman for contempt of court in supplying to the newspaper copies of documents that had been disclosed to her only for the purposes of the action. The questions to be decided, said the judge, were whether the reading out of the documents in court had destroyed the implied undertaking to use them only for the purposes of the action and, if not, whether her action constituted a breach of the undertaking. He concluded that she was in contempt of court, but had acted in good faith, and he imposed no penalty. The question was one of considerable interest to the press and was widely followed. *The Times* declared Miss Harman's offence was 'extremely trivial'. There was discussion in the Lords and an amendment was put down to the Contempt of Court Bill then going through the House. The Harman appeal against the finding that she was in contempt was eagerly awaited.

On 28 January 1981 it reached the Court of Appeal, where Denning sat with Templeman and Dunn. When a document is read out in court, Miss Harman argued, it loses its confidentiality and can be disclosed to reporters, to assist them in reporting or commenting upon the proceedings. If a shorthand writer had taken down the words, a transcript would have been available for all the world to read. Denning regarded Miss Harman's conduct as reprehensible. The documents had been disclosed to her, he said, as solicitor for Williams, in an action funded by legal aid, but her disclosure to the *Guardian* had been made in her capacity as solicitor for the NCCL, which had waged a lengthy battle to obtain evidence of what had taken place in the experimental unit. Only his belief that she had behaved badly could explain Denning's conclusion, so much at odds with his usual views:

> When Ministers and high civil servants are forming important governmental policy, their discussions and their memoranda are, and should be, treated as highly confidential. No court should order the disclosure of these confidential documents to outsiders, even in the interests of justice, except under the most stringent safeguards against abuse. The danger of disclosure is that critics – of one political colour or another – will seize on the confidential information so as to seek changes in government policy, or to condemn it . . .

The comments on Denning's judgment were scathing. On 19 February the *New Law Journal* wrote tartly: 'Lord Denning's claim to stand like some judicial Horatio against every manifestation of the abuse of power has, in our view, been growing distinctly tarnished of late.'

When the *McShane* appeal reached the House of Lords, shortly after the election that returned the Conservatives to office, the law lords disapproved Denning's construction of the employment legislation but invited parliament to change the law. Again Denning moved judicially before the legislation could do so. A month after the Lords delivered their speeches, *Duport Steels* v. *Sirs* was heard in the Court of Appeal. The public sector British Steel Corporation was refusing to meet the pay demands of their unions. The Government regarded the outcome of the dispute as an important test of its pay policy and the unions were disappointed that their action at BSC was not having the effect they expected because the private sector was still working. To put more pressure on the Government, the unions called out their men in the private sector. Duport Steel, which had no dispute with its unions, applied for an interlocutory injunction and was refused by the trial judge on Friday 25 January 1980, on the grounds of trade dispute immunity.

Since the beginning of term, Fred Lawton had been sitting with Lord Denning and had, that day, jokingly told Peter Post that he was disappointed not to have heard even one case of public importance. That evening Post delivered to Lawton's home the papers in *Duport Steels*, inquiring of the judge whether he was now doing better. The appeal, heard on the Saturday morning, was so high profile, with media interest centred on Denning's judgment, that no-one – certainly not the Lords when it reached the House – seemed to notice that Lawton and Ackner also delivered carefully reasoned arguments in favour of granting the injunction.

Following their decision 500 steel workers came down to King's Cross and marched to the Law Courts, shouting 'Denning out!' Post hurried into court, where he tried, in whispers, to tell Denning, who was still sitting with Lawton and Ackner, that the men were demanding to see him. Tom said: 'Oh, have them all come up,' but Lawton suggested it would be better for the clerk to deal with them himself. Three representatives were taken by Peter Post into 'a little cubby hole' off the main hall and told that Lord Denning would like to hear their representations. As they spoke the tension eased and they 'finished up talking about the difference between Newcastle United and Sunderland'[65] before the three men emerged to face the photographers and lead the steel workers back to Kings's Cross.

The launch party for *The Due Process of the Law* took place on 7

February and two days later Tom went to sign books in Oxford. He was met by flying pickets of steel workers, determined to make his hour there as difficult as possible, but who stayed to cheer and shake his hand. He could not so easily win over the Lords. His findings brought down upon his head their wrath. He should, they insisted, have followed the *McShane* decision: parliament had not intended judges to act as back-seat drivers in industrial disputes. Tom was hurt but unrepentant. He managed to insert into his judgment in *R. v. Sheffield Crown Court ex parte Brownlow* a last word on the subject of *McShane*, saying that the four Law Lords who found against him were wrong – 'Yet, as they had the last word, no-one can gainsay it.' Most people thought that matters could not long continue in this way but no-one knew how to resolve them.

25

What Next in the Law

On 18 February 1980 Joan reached her 80th birthday. She celebrated in the way she liked best – a family lunch party at The White Hart. She had given up the hope of Tom's retiring at 80 but watched anxiously as his commitments took their toll. While making a speech at a meeting in Cumberland Lodge one Friday evening, after a day in court, Tom dried up. Speaking without notes, he forgot the details of a case. With charm and dignity he overcame the lapse, saying that he was too tired to remember and had better stop talking. It was another sign that the strain was taking its toll.

Mishaps that might have been brushed aside when they were young, now upset both Tom and Joan. A break-in at their flat and the loss of objects that had sentimental value – a clock that had come to Joan from her grandfather, a 21st birthday gift, a brooch given to her by Tom and Tom's gold cufflinks, studs and waistcoat buttons – was disturbing.

Tom's first and second books were, in effect, devoted to the struggle of the Court of Appeal to modernise the law and the determination of the Lords to oppose it. Enjoyable as they found the books, most lawyers did not see things quite like that. Some, indeed, thought that it was not reactionary law lords who now endangered judicial law-making but the indiscipline of Denning, who disobeyed the rules. Early in 1981 a number of academics published *Justice, Lord Denning and the Constitution*; their theme that Denning's way of exercising judicial power was unconstitutional.

In November 1981, an issue was heard in the Court of Appeal, on which everyone living in or around the capital took sides, the Fair Fares Case. Labour had control of the Greater London Council (GLC) and fulfilled its electoral promise to reduce fares on London Transport's buses and trains. To recoup the loss of 25 per cent of its revenue, the GLC planned to raise a supplementary rate on the London boroughs; Bromley Council, claiming that the GLC was acting outside the powers given to it by statute, sought a judicial review. Unanimously the Court of Appeal – and, later, the House of Lords – upheld Bromley's application. But the press concentrated on Denning's remarks that a manifesto should not be 'taken as gospel'.

During this time Tom addressed students at University College, London, who welcomed him warmly. Outside the building others made plain their disapproval of his remarks, throwing flour at Tom, as he emerged. As if to show that Tom's public had not forsaken him, on his 83rd birthday some students brought him a cake, with a Dinky bus and 'Is this fair?' written on top of it. They took off the bus and Tom and Peter Post shared the cake with them. Only when the last crumb had gone, was it noticed that the bus had now only three wheels – someone had eaten the fourth.

The perception that Denning was now being regularly overruled by the Lords was again belied by their upholding his decision, in *British Steel* v. *Granada*, to order the television company to reveal who had given them secret British Steel papers. This out-of-character decision, which seems to have been provoked by Denning's view that Granada had not behaved properly, lost him the support of the media, whose enthusiasm for his pursuit of justice became somewhat muted after his *Granada* decision made investigative journalism more difficult. His subsequent spirited (and dissenting) support of press freedom came too late to bring the press wholly back behind him. The belief that 'Denning must go' was now widespread.

When Tom spoke to the judiciary at the Lord Mayor's dinner on Thursday 9 July 1981, he drew upon the themes he had used many times before. Familiarity, perhaps, made him choose his words less carefully; the freer tongue of old age did not help. At all events, there was dismay amongst many of those present as Lord Denning spoke of a recent trial by jury in Bristol of 12 'coloured people' charged with riot; and of what he called 'an abuse of the right of challenge.' The subject was to prove his downfall. In the long vacation Tom worked on another book. He decided, he said in the preface, 'to reach forth to the reform of the law in the several branches where it is most in need of reform', and 'deliberately' made it controversial. In one section he repeated the story of the Bristol riot, claiming that the peremptory challenge had been used at the trial to obtain a sympathetic jury. After proposing reforms of the jury system, he wrote:

> It grew up in the ages when the English were a homogenous race . . . They shared the same standards of conduct, the same code of morals, and the same religious beliefs. Above all they adhered uniformly to the rule of law . . . The English are no longer a homogenous race. They are white and black, coloured and brown. They no longer share the same standards of conduct. Some of them come from countries where bribery and graft are accepted as an integral part of life: and where stealing is a virtue so long as you are not found out. They no longer share the same code of morals. They no longer share the same religious beliefs. They no longer share the same respect for law.

With virtually every member of the population qualified to sit as a juror, Denning said, the chances were heavily loaded against jurors being the 'sensible and responsible members of the community.' During the next term, the book was typed by Vi Legg, Tom's Whitchurch secretary. At Christmas, after reading the typescript, Joan suggested that Tom think again about the section on jury reform, which might upset some people. Tom brushed this idea aside and the script went, as originally written, to the publishers.

Denning had concluded that the old jury system was no longer suitable to a multi-racial society and made no bones about saying so, but he was not alone in feeling concern. Awareness of the issue was heightened amongst lawyers and the public by the trial, at the Old Bailey, of 15 black youths charged with rioting in South London, where a physically handicapped white youth had been killed. A few weeks before Tom's book went to the reviewers, Justinian, in *The Financial Times* of 19 April had referred to the relief that verdicts of guilty were at least recorded 'where the evidence was compelling' and went on to call for a thorough review of the value of the jury in contemporary society. That week, coincidentally, the Society of Black Lawyers called upon the Bar Council to protect black barristers by a public statement that, in recent trials, they had done nothing wrong in challenging potential jurors.

In earlier days, Tom usually communicated his views without giving offence (though in 1966 he had to be coerced into making alterations to his foreword for a book written by Desmond Neligan, a former legal adviser to the Colonial Office, because it was thought that countries of the Commonwealth might read into Tom's words some slight on their parliaments). In his later years there had been a change in his approach to controversial subjects. Impatience, carelessness, a failure to appreciate – or even care -- how his words would strike other people replaced the restraint that characterised his early speeches and writing. The measured passion was lost: in its place was wilful provocation.

The early reviews of *What Next in the Law* gave attention to Denning's call for reform of the jury system, not all of them referring to the racial aspect. The *Daily Express*, on 17 May, thought it would be apparent 'to the great majority of law-abiding citizens' that his diagnosis was 'sound and his remedies sensible enough.' The book contained, in addition to the section on trial by jury, practical proposals on legal aid, on personal injuries, on libel and the right to privacy – enlivened by Tom's skilfully interwoven fund of legal stories. It was published on Thursday 20 May 1982. By the weekend it was known that the Society of Black Lawyers took exception to the passages dealing with the capacity of black or coloured people for jury service and that solicitors had written to Denning on behalf of black jurors in the Bristol riot trial.

On Saturday 22 May there was an article in *The Times*, which said that the Society of Black Lawyers would be calling on the Lord Chancellor to ask Lord Denning 'politely but firmly' to retire. The full implications of his position were gradually dawning on Tom though he had not as yet, perhaps, fully accepted where they led. In an interview for the BBC, later that day, Ludovic Kennedy put it to Tom that the passage about black jurors showed he was racist and gave Tom the chance to withdraw. Though Tom would fiercely deny the imputation, he stuck by his words. As a result, when faced with the threat of libel proceedings from the Bristol jurors, he had to tell the BBC that the programme might itself be defamatory and it was not broadcast. In the evening, David Leigh, the writer of the article in the *Harman* case, told Tom on the telephone that black jurors intended to sue. Tom declined to comment and, after a sleepless night and an eight o'clock attendance at church, read in *The Observer* Leigh's detailed account of what had happened in Bristol and forthright rebuttal of Denning's allegations. Tom began to realise that the letter from a Bristol barrister, on which he had based his remarks, was factually incorrect. He had not yet seen the letter from solicitors Birnberg & Co. – sent to him care of Butterworths – about the jurors.

Joan tried to comfort him but Tom knew it was unthinkable that the office of Master of the Rolls should be tarnished by the issue against him of a writ for libel. Bitterly he regretted that he had not taken steps to check the letter from Bristol. He must have looked back with a pang to the launch party – a bare three days ago – when he had quoted from Tennyson's *The Brook*: 'For men may come and men may go, But I go on forever.' Only the visit to The Lawn that Sunday of Robert, Elizabeth and his grandchildren, brought him some relief, though he was too busy talking over his position with his son to pay much attention to the boys.

On Monday, under the heading '*A Judgment Too Far*', *The Times* asked whether it was in the interests of the public or of the reputation of justice that Denning should furnish commentary and opinion, outside the courts, on his own work and 'on areas of the law of which he has less experience.' It was not only Tom's remarks about the jurors that offended, but his disclosure in the book that he had changed his mind about the *Granada* case. 'What reliance can be placed on precedent, on the certainty of the law,' asked the leader writer, 'when it can be challenged by the judges themselves outside the court rooms?'

As soon as he reached his room, Tom asked Max Williams, president-elect of the Law Society, to slip over to see him. They discussed the implications of Birnberg's letter of 21 May, which asked for an apology, the removal of the offending passages and damages for injury to feelings and reputation. That morning, Tom sent by hand to the Lord Chancellor his resignation. He had it in mind, for some time, he said, to retire at the end of the summer term but, in view of the circumstances, he offered to go at once. Hailsham replied 'sympathetically'[59] that he should go at the end of the summer term. Later this date was changed to 29 September, the last day of the summer vacation.

On Tom's behalf, Williams briefed Andrew Leggatt, Chairman of the Bar Council, and a libel specialist, David Eady. In the course of the week's negotiations with Gareth Pearce of Birnberg & Co. Tom was shown the transcript of the Bristol trial and learned that the challenges had been used there at the invitation of the judge, to secure a representative jury. The mistake of basing his comment on incorrect facts was one that Tom would have condemned in other lawyers. It was yet another sign that he had held on to office too long.

Tom's remarks were condemned on almost every hand and there was no doubt about the relief now that his departure was assured: but there was compassion for the man who had been greatly loved and admired. Rudy Narayan, Secretary of the Society of Black Lawyers, who had called for Tom's retirement after the Mansion House speech, wrote on 26 May to *The Times*: 'A great judge has erred greatly in the intellectual loneliness of advanced years; while his remarks should be rejected and rebutted he is, yet, in a personal way, entitled to draw on that reservoir of community regard which he has in many quarters and to seek understanding, if not forgiveness.'

The jurors, too, were restrained in their demands once assured of Denning's resignation, seeking no more than the vindication of their reputations. Tom wrote to each of them a personal letter of apology. After court, on Friday 28 May, a press statement announced Tom's resignation and, on Tuesday 1 June, an agreed apology was made public. In it, Tom deeply regretted having given offence, 'especially among any of the racial or religious peoples who have long formed part of our community.' People from Commonwealth countries, he said, were as suitable for jury service as any other citizens. 'The idea of "second class" citizens in this country would be as abhorrent to me as to anyone else.'

Supportive as ever, Joan told a *Daily Mirror* reporter that Tom was very distressed and realised he had made a mistake. 'He has done more for the black people in this country,' she said 'than any other judge.' Privately, like other members of the family, though sad at the manner of his going, she felt relief. Tom had gone on too long: the strain had become too great. He should have made the decision to retire at 80: in the end events made it for him.

On the whole the press were kind to Tom. *Private Eye* published a cartoon of two barristers reading the headline 'Denning to Retire', one saying to the other: 'I expect the House of Lords will overrule his decision.' 'The ordinary people of this country have lost a spokesman,' wrote Fenton Bressler in the *Daily Mail*. Denning was, according to a Special Correspondent in *The Times* of 29 May, 'a brilliant lawyer and undoubtedly one of the great judges of the century.' *The Daily Telegraph* said it had had its differences with Lord Denning, but he was 'a very great man'. When the *Guardian* commented that those who loved him and those who resented him could unite in 'wishing the departing Master of the Rolls the longest and happiest of retirements', one correspondent, irked by the London Transport fares decision, wrote that in his personal fantasy of Denning's retirement Tom would spend his declining years 'trapped at a bus-stop every night in outer Ealing, without the money to pay for a taxi, in the stimulating company of blacks, gays, trade unionists and women.'

Tom tried to act as though he had intended, all along, to leave at the end of the summer term, but few believed it. The book was re-issued without the offending passages and did well in the bookshops. The fund of goodwill towards him was responsible for the attempt to make Tom's last term as close as possible to what it would have been if, indeed, he had chosen to go because he was too old. Since he was not to retire immediately, the work of No. 3 Court had to go on. Controversial to the end, Lord Denning attracted the headlines on 29 July, when the Court of Appeal unanimously upheld a judge's decision that the headmaster of a private school had not discriminated on racial grounds in refusing to admit a Sikh boy, who insisted upon wearing his turban.

Away from the court, in that last term, Tom remained busy. 'But behind it – to me – was the distress caused by the book.'[59] On 5 July, the Speaker of the House of Commons gave a party for 30 people in Speaker's House in honour of Tom's retirement. In *The Closing Chapter*, Tom described the evening: 'The long table sparkled with silver. The chandeliers shone with softening light. The ladies' dresses glittered with diamonds and jewels. On the walls the portraits of previous Speakers looked down . . .' Tom sat between the Speaker and the Prime Minister, Mrs Thatcher; also present were the Archbishop of Canterbury, the Lord Chancellor, the Chancellor of the Exchequer, the Lord Chief Justice and the Home Secretary. Tom was delighted that, in proposing his health, the Speaker, George Thomas, paid 'a special tribute to my wife, "the lovely lady by his side", without whom I could do nothing. It gave us the greatest pleasure.'

On 8 July Joan brought home a catalogue from Goodes and she and Tom chose a carriage clock for Max Williams and a pair of decanters for Andrew Leggatt. In the evening they both went to Carey Street, where Tom dined with the Law Society and Joan with 'the Law Society ladies'. Tom had always enjoyed an excellent relationship with the Law Society, guiding it with only the lightest hand on the reins. When called upon to give advice or consider a decision of the Disciplinary Committee, he exercised his authority with sympathy and understanding. Only recently he had expedited the restoration to the Rolls of a dying man, whose name had been struck off.

As a farewell gift, the Law Society gave Tom a pair of gold cufflinks. On 26 July he performed his last official function as Master of the Rolls, presiding at the Admission Ceremony in the Law Society's Hall. His themes were those on which he had spoken for more than 30 years but his audience received them with the same rapt delight. He ended with a quotation of which he was particularly fond:

> Four things a man must learn to do
> If he would make his record true,
> To think without confusion clearly,
> To act from honest motives purely,
> To love his fellow man sincerely
> And trust in God and Heaven securely.

After the usual period of speculation, the announcement was made in July that John Donaldson would be the new Master of the Rolls. When Tom found that Donaldson intended to reorganise his room and did not want many of the familiar things that he cherished, he proposed to take them with him. A valuation was made and Tom was able to buy the vast desk that had belonged to Lord Jessel, six mahogany chairs with the words 'C. O. Rolls' carved into their backs and, on their legs, the royal insignia of William IV; a portrait of Sir Nicholas Bacon, father of Francis; and two heavy, beautifully bound volumes from the Rolls Chapel – a Bible and a Book of Common Prayer. For his part, Donaldson was about to inherit a number of appeals that Tom had put aside to hear himself.

The last day of term, Friday 30 July was not quite Tom's last day. He had still to prepare and deliver four judgments reserved for the start of the new term. Photographers surrounded Denning as he walked from his flat to the Courts. In his own court, as he had done many times before, he paid tribute to a man retiring that day: this time it was Lord Justice Ormrod, who had helped to shape the modern system of divorce. Then, dressed still in his old robes Lord Denning went to the court of the Lord Chief Justice. Some 300 lawyers were crowded into the court, spilling out, with clerks and ushers and members of the public, into the gallery and the corridor outside. Only the Lord Chancellor, who presided, wore his ceremonial robes. From the jury box, Joan listened to the tributes paid to Tom. 'We shall miss you,' Hailsham told him, '. . . come and see us often. Whenever lawyers are gathered together they will always rejoice to see you in their midst.' The Attorney-General, Michael Havers, recalled his days as Tom's marshal on assize at Leeds; and Ashe Lincoln, who had served in the navy with Tom's brother Norman, remarked on 'the humane consideration that one always received from members of that family.' There were speeches from other members of the Bar and from Max Williams, for the Law Society.

Tom was deeply moved as he made his farewell speech. He covered his emotion with one of his repertoire of jokes: the one about the Lord Chancellor who told Queen Victoria that her judges were deeply sensible of their own many shortcomings, only to be corrected by Lord Justice Bowen's 'That ought to be amended . . . we are deeply sensible of one another's shortcomings.'

Tom, who inherited from his father his 'lovely, genial manners' and never failed to commend work 'well done' or acknowledge a service, thanked those with whom he had worked and on whose services he had depended. The Bar, solicitors, the law reporters – Mavis Hill and Alan Bray – shorthand writers and ushers, all were remembered. 'I have been privileged,' Tom said, 'to have the best of clerks – John King, Ross Chesney and now Peter Post.' The measure of Tom's achievement, in human terms, was the extent to which those who had served him believed the privilege was theirs.

Many presentations were made to Tom on his retirement from one or another of his offices. On 30 July he made a presentation of his own. A Parsee member of Lincoln's Inn, delighted with a case decided in the Court of Appeal, sent from Bombay a symbolic gift. Tom read her letter:

> Here are seven elephants drawing a dainty silver carriage. The square piece on the rear of the carriage has the single word 'Justice' inscribed on it. All the elephants are engaged in the task of pulling the carriage of Justice along the narrow white path, the straight and narrow road.
>   The great white elephant has no tusks for he does not need tusks to do his work in Nature. This elephant's mind and thought force power is so highly developed in Nature that he can do the work of spreading Justice and maintaining the Divine Law and Order among all souls . . . This elephant represents you, Lord Denning, as the greatest force for truth and Justice tempered with mercy, alive today.

After a lighter touch (his own parody of Lewis Carroll) Tom ended: 'I wish I could say, as a great man did once, "I have fought a good fight; I finished my course; I have kept the faith." ' Looking back on the quotations that indicated Tom's aspirations, in his letter to his brother Jack, at the outbreak of the First World War, it seems that, for the most part, he kept the faith.

That Saturday, at the invitation of Plymouth's Lord Mayor, Tom and Joan went to stay a few days at the lovely house on Plymouth Hoe, given to the city by Lady Astor. The war with Argentina over the Falkland Isles had come to an end and, during their stay, they had the pleasure of cheering home two of the frigates – 'one with a hole right through her hull by an Exocet. Fortunately above the water line.'[59]

They spent the rest of August and September at The Lawn, with Tom working on his reserved judgments, Joan preparing an exhibition of her paintings for October, and teams of television people from the BBC, Granada and TVS preparing documentary programmes on Tom's life and work. Joan entertained the players in the usual cricket match between Whitchurch and Lincoln's Inn – Tom was President of both and presented the shield to the winners. They also relaxed with the family: Robert ran Tom and Joan over to see Reg and Eileen in Kent. (Marjorie died earlier in the year.) They took great pleasure in the marriage of Joan's first grandchild, Katherine Simond; they drove across to the Isle of Wight with Robert and his family, with Tom pointing out the places he had known at Fawley, as they crossed on the ferry.

In the last week of the vacation Tom delivered his reserved judgments. On 29 September, dressed in his old black robes and tattered wig, he sat for the last time as Master of the Rolls. Fittingly, perhaps, the case concerned exemption clauses (*Mitchell* v. *Finney Lock Seeds*) and Denning dissented. After judgment was given, leave was sought to appeal to the House of Lords. The last words Tom spoke in court were: 'No, we do not give leave to appeal.' In *The Closing Chapter* he described what happened next:

> I walked out along the corridor to my room. I took off my robes and put on my ordinary clothes. I said goodbye to my clerk and secretary who had served me well. I left the building. I had entered it first 60 years before as a pupil. I have never been in it since.

PART FOUR

1982–1992

26

The Last Years

When Lord Denning walked down the steps of the Law Courts for the last time his place in legal history was set: nothing he would say or do in his remaining years could change it. The extraordinary public impact of his personality makes that place difficult to assess. Unlike most judges, his memorial will be more than the body of doctrine found in his judgments. The influence of his speeches, reproduced in his books, was immense; but if he is remembered for them alone, it will be as a prophet, as a wise man rather than a judge. If he is remembered for the contentious public cases at the end of his career it will not be as a judge, but as a maker of policy.

Acute awareness of the snobbery of Bar and Bench, when he joined the legal profession, must have been a spur to his native ambition. Through drive, intelligence and sheer hard work he rose to occupy one of the highest offices in the land; somewhere along the road he lost his youthful diffidence and saw himself as one who speaks for England – a solid core of English men and women always agreed with him. The shy boy became a superb performer. He loved to be the centre of an admiring crowd. He delighted in doing something superlatively well, deriving almost sensual pleasure from solving a difficult problem and giving judgment. Confident, authoritative, Tom left uncertainty behind him. Only his delight in stressing his achievements – not at all necessary when they were so evident – betrayed a lingering need for reassurance. Clinging to office was also, perhaps, a sign that the early years had left their mark.

To many of his colleagues Tom remained an outsider. He was a much more complex character than his public persona suggested. Few could dislike a man so friendly, courteous and considerate; many condemned him as a publicist and some believed he had done damage to the law. There was much affection for Tom though he made no close friends. He was warm and caring but, apart from his family, he did not seek intimacy.

Denning never accepted that religion, morality and law had become severed. 'Without religion there can be no morality,' he told the Lawyers' Christian Fellowship in 1977, 'and without morality there can be no law.' Though his talks were embroidered with jokes and stories, he never lost sight of his object – to instruct his audience about the law, abuse of power, the vital importance of an independent judiciary and about the morality in which law should be rooted. To people all over the world, Tom imparted his belief that English justice, founded in the Christian religion, was fundamental to English liberty.

Even when they did not share his background and beliefs, those who met him were usually captivated by his air of benevolence, his unassuming manner, his humour, charm and, above all, by his own keen interest in *them*. Time and again, people remarked on his ability to pick up a conversation, years after it took place; to cross a room to greet, as an old friend, someone he met but once, and that long ago. As a speaker he could be spell-binding but it was in personal encounter that he was at his best.

Only posterity will be certain whether Denning stands – as he would like – beside Lord Mansfield, the great 18th-century judicial law-maker. In many ways the two men are comparable. Each found the law in a straitjacket and sought to free it from pedantry, technicalities and narrow-mindedness. Each spoke eloquently of justice and equity. Each liked to generalise the principles of the law and to state them for the guidance of the future. Each left the law less rigid than he found it.

As a judicial law-maker, Denning worked under constraints unknown to his predecessor. Statute, in Mansfield's day, scarcely intruded: it was judges who made the law. By the time Denning went on the Bench it was generally accepted that reform was a matter for parliament. Most judges knew, as well as he, the desirable end to a case but, if the law led firmly in another direction, they were content to hope that parliament would change it. For Denning that was not enough. When the case cried out for new law Denning dared to make it.

There were areas – particularly contract and tort – where legislation had only lightly encroached. There, working within his much-loved common law, Denning was particularly effective. His fertile, ingenious mind, his immense learning enabled him to develop principles and bring about new directions in the law. Not only what he achieved, but what he stimulated others to achieve will ensure his place in legal history. In administrative law Denning's influence was also immense. He was not alone in recognising the dangers in the new powers of ministers and burgeoning authorities but he was more ready than most to find ways to control them.

Despite misgivings about his methods among sections of the judiciary, Denning was well regarded. Lord Diplock once observed that Denning was the only post-war judge 'who may have been touched with genius',[61] Lord Scarman called him 'one of the few geniuses of the English common law.'[71] Expectations were high in 1962 when Denning returned to the Court of Appeal.

Paradoxically, it may be that by the time Tom became Master of the Rolls, his most productive period was reaching its end. Three years later the Lords' decision that there were cases where it was right for them to go against precedent put in their hands such judicial law-making as they were prepared to sanction. Denning was still creative, still produced flashes of genius, but, as time passed, his statements of principle became less influential as he made wider pronouncements than were necessary for the case in hand and fought to gain for the Court of Appeal the freedom the Lords had awarded themselves. Many litigants were grateful for his ability and his sense of justice; one at least recalled that Denning's understanding of complex interest calculations saved his company from a costly defeat. Others complained that he added to the uncertainty of law – and the expense. Though he still sought to bring the law into line with the needs of the time, as he saw them, in his later years he was out of sympathy with the changed social structure of the country.

The words with which Denning started *The Discipline of Law* encapsulate his attitude: 'If we never do anything which has not been done before, we shall never get anywhere. The law will stand still whilst the rest of the world goes on: and that will be bad for both.' Denning had the vision, the ability and the learning to ensure that his desire to do something and get somewhere were often the source of badly needed advances in the law. Writing in the first issue of the University of Buckingham's *Denning Law Journal*, Tom expected to be remembered for *Candler* v. *Crane, Christmas*; the *Northumberland* case and *Barnard* v. *Dock Labour Board*.

Denning's long reign came to an end in a mixture of bitter sweetness. The brilliantly creative law-maker, who should have been remembered for *High Trees*, his development of the law of negligence, defence of the individual and judgments deserving a place in English literature, might be remembered for prejudice, a refusal to follow precedent and conflict with the Lords. The regard in which Tom had been held – and the knowledge that only rarely had prejudice impinged on Denning's judicial work – ensured that his achievements were fully recognised. Only one legal honour was missing from those heaped upon Tom in the course of his long career and afterwards. He was never the guest of honour, as were Lord Reid and J. P. Benjamin, the author of the classic book on *Sale*, at a celebratory dinner of the combined Bench and Bar; in every other way his colleagues did him proud.

Though Lord Denning's place in legal history was set, the verdict on Tom, the man, remained open. Tom had courage, integrity, humanity and a rare ability to give pleasure to others. There were also, beneath his friendly approach and apparent simplicity, streaks of arrogance and pride. He had fun acting the *enfant terrible*. About the time of his 80th birthday he became mischievous. As he passed into old age, unaccustomed vanity obscured his sense of judgment and led him into damaging utterances.

Even at 83, it was hard for Tom to give up the work he loved. He had no intention of settling into leisurely retirement. He planned another book to continue his life where *The Family Story* left it and bring up to date his comments on the law. Invitations to speak continued to arrive. On 2 October he started the new electric wheel of the restored silk mill, almost opposite his home, on the other side of the river. On 17 October, wearing morning dress instead of his accustomed robes, he read the lesson at the special service for judges, magistrates and lawyers of the county in Winchester Cathedral. He spoke at a luncheon to mark the 30th year of Agatha Christie's play, *The Mousetrap*; gave the address at the legal service in Norwich Cathedral; and presented the Plain English awards at the Waldorf Hotel.

On 2 November, he and Joan were entertained to dinner in the Inner Temple by 36 of the judges who had sat with him in the Court of Appeal. They were warmly welcomed by Kenneth Diplock, at that time the senior law lord. Tom's own speech did not, he thought, go down so well as when he spoke spontaneously. Perhaps the occasion was too emotional for him. He was delighted with the sequel. There were calls for Joan to speak and, with her off-the-cuff true story, she stole the show:

> I have never made an after-dinner speech in my life. Tom does all the speaking. But once he did show me a judgment he was going to give. I told him I thought he was coming out the wrong way. He said 'Oh, do you?' and wrote a judgment the other way. The other two judges did not agree but afterwards the Lords overruled them. So he won in the Lords.[59]

For Tom, the spirit of Christmas was not to be found in Bethlehem or in any building or place, but 'in the hearts of man and wife: and in a home made by them together for their family.'[59] That Christmas Day, he and Joan went to the Stuarts, at Beaconsfield; the rest of the family came to The Lawn, either on Christmas Eve or Boxing Day.

It soon became clear that, in retirement, Tom would be no less controversial than he had been as Master of the Rolls. In February there was a strike in the water industry. Patrick Evershed, a cousin of Tom's predecessor, telephoned Tom to say that the people of his street had been without water for two days. Could they, he asked, repair the pipes themselves or employ contractors to do the job and, if so, could they charge the cost to the water authority. Tom spent two hours looking up his books – 'I knew a good deal of the problem already. So it took me less time than it might do others'[59] – before advising that water authorities were under a statutory duty to provide a supply of water; if they did not repair the pipes, householders could do the job themselves or employ contractors and charge the cost to the authority. This advice was published in the newspapers and Tom was blithely unconcerned by the criticism of his intervention: it may indeed have given him a new lease of life.

His hip was becoming troublesome and this time Mr Sweetnam, who had looked after him in the Nuffield Clinic, advised a hip replacement. The operation was done in March 1983 and Tom made a remarkable recovery. A little later, while going up the steps from his library to the dining room, he fell and twisted his knee. For six weeks he lay on the bed in the sitting room and the family thought he would not survive. At last, Joan's nursing 'got him back on his feet',[40] but there was concern at how he would manage the stairs. When Reg recommended to Tom the lift-seat that had been installed in his own home, Tom had one fixed to the staircase at The Lawn, much to the delight of the children in the family.

As soon as he was able Tom returned to his interests and activities. He now had more time to spend in the chamber of the House of Lords and enjoyed speaking in debates that interested him. In the next five years, he supported a Bill to amend the Abortion Act; spoke in favour of administration for companies in difficulties and, when abortion was under consideration, endorsed extra safeguards for the unborn child. With few exceptions, he opposed Sunday trading, and he was against the legalisation of euthanasia and mercy-killing, believing that hard cases should be dealt with by the refusal of the Director of Public Prosecutions to prosecute. He joined in debates on the co-ownership of the matrimonial home, equal pay and the accountability of the security services. On 14 July 1987 he returned to the subject of jury challenge, saying that the peremptory challenge was out of date and must go. Always he prefaced his views with experiences drawn from his own cases, earning, on 15 December 1982, after references to *Williams & Glyn's Bank* v. *Boland*, a rebuke from the Lord Chancellor:

> There is . . . something droll about the fact that the judge of first instance should be making his maiden speech [as Lord Templeman] and the Master of the Rolls who reversed him should be saying 'How right I was.' I am not sure how desirable it is, I must say to the noble and learned Lord, Lord Denning, for those who have pronounced in a judicial capacity to say 'How right I was' in a legislative capacity.

With his speeches, television and radio programmes and articles, Tom made sure his views were still before the public. Reviewing on radio *The Law Lords* by Alan Paterson, he summed up, as he saw them, 30 years in the law: In the 1950s, under the influence of Lord Simonds, the law was static; under Lord Reid it became moderately progressive; and 'nowadays' some of the Lords 'are for progress rather than standing still.' For his part, Tom said, he would always strive to do justice, regarding certainty as often 'a will-o-the-wisp'.

In a cameo television appearance in Channel 4's *Book Choice*, Tom reviewed David Pannick's *Judges*, tongue in cheek. 'This book is very entertaining,' he began, proceeding to outline the author's proposed reforms and gently poke fun at them. For himself, he declared, he would keep the judges exactly as they were: 'the best in the world.'

The Last Chapter was published in 1983 and, a year later, he brought out *Landmarks in the Law*. In a section on 'Martyrdom', he responded obliquely to the accusations that he was anti-union. Starting with the treatment of the Tolpuddle Martyrs, which he described as 'a blot on our social history', he went, by way of the 1906 Act and the General Strike, to cases heard after his retirement. In the 19th century, he concluded, trade unions were persecuted and oppressed; in the 20th 'they exploited their immunity beyond measure.' They should be put on probation 'for they have more useful things to do for their members. But if they should flout the law, they will find that their end will be at hand.' There remained in Tom's style something of the 19th-century preacher.

He could still take a surprisingly liberal view. In a section on 'Blasphemous Libel' Tom discussed the case of the newspaper for homosexuals, *Gay News*, that had been charged with publishing an obscene poem and illustration 'vilifying Christ in his life and in his crucifixion.' The majority of the Lords upheld a finding that *Gay News* was guilty on the grounds that the publication shocked and horrified, whatever the publishers may have intended. Tom, unexpectedly, was doubtful of the Lords' finding. Still concerned to make his readers think, he put the argument for the publisher and, telling them that *The Times* had called for a change in the law, asked 'What do you think?' When he asked that question in his books, he had always prepared the ground for the reply he wanted.

Tom's last book, *Leaves from my Library*, was published in 1986, subtitled 'An English Anthology'. It was a collection of his favourite pieces of prose, each with his introduction. That year, when the Bill to amend the European Communities Act was passing through the

Lords, Denning argued passionately against the erosion of parliamentary sovereignty. Once it was clear that the argument was lost,
his lifelong pragmatism persuaded him to make the best of what could
not be changed. 'Let us give the Single European Act our whole-
hearted support,' he wrote in *The Salisbury Review* of April 1987.
Returning to his simile of the incoming tide, he suggested that the
ship *European Union* was in difficulties and that the 'good boat'
United Kingdom should be sent out to help her. His style had become
a bare reminder of the ringing cadences of the Fifties.

Talking and writing were not enough for Tom: he liked to have a
campaign going. His interest in footpaths was aroused when he
bought the tenanted Oak Tree Farm at St Mary Bourne, where there
was no other means of access. A new subject began to occupy his
attention, when he opened hostilities with Hampshire County
Council over the future of the disused church school where he had
started his education. A delightful picture in *The Sunday Times* of 25
September 1988 showed him, surrounded by small children, in
another disused village school, at Upton Grey. The media still gave
extensive cover to his activities, and his various brushes with
authority, over the next years, made good copy. The stories attracted
attention from people with similar problems in different parts of the
country. The library in Whitchurch began to double as an office,
when Lord Denning took up their causes, as well as his own.

Delighted to find that the former Master of the Rolls might be
available to give legal advice, people began to consult him about other
difficulties. Tom always found it hard to resist a plea for help and
sometimes went further than was wise. 'If you have already paid the
rates,' he wrote to one correspondent. 'I do not see that you can be
made to pay more simply because of a change of Government
Regulations, so resist the demand.'[70] Perhaps the most astonishing of
his post-retirement legal activities was his keeping a kind of 'watching
brief' in 1990 and 1991 on behalf of a group in Lancashire taking
action against the implementation of planning permission by a
developer.

With so much to occupy his attention, it might have been hoped
that Tom would refrain from the commentary upon current affairs
that had provoked so much criticism in his last years as Master of the
Rolls. The fact that he did not was to have serious consequences on

two occasions. During 1988 three people were charged at Winchester with conspiracy to murder the Home Secretary, Tom King. They all exercised the right to remain silent. As the trial drew to a close, King in reply to a question in the House of Commons on 20 October, announced that the Government intended to change the law on the right to silence. That evening the Minister talked on television about the need for reform and Tom was also seen, on Channel 4, speaking in favour of the change. The Winchester Three were found guilty and sentenced to 25 years' imprisonment. On appeal, they were released by the Court of Appeal because the jury might have been influenced by the television programmes. Tom was angered by references to himself in the judgment; on 30 April 1990 he wrote a letter to *The Times*, complaining that, in effect, he had been condemned, unheard, for contempt of court. Justice, he said, the words certain to cause anger, had been done at Winchester by the judge and 'a Hampshire jury' but not by three judges in the Court of Appeal.

On 12 June 1984, Tom and Joan, with all the Denning family had celebrated Reg's 90th birthday at his home in Kent. For Tom's 90th birthday, Middle Temple gave him a dinner. Happy to be again surrounded by lawyers, he made a long speech, full of quotations. At the end, pointing to himself, he said '90 – not out.' Then, pointing to Joan, he added: '89 – not out.'

Though they were not out, both Tom and Joan were frail. Tom had experienced occasional giddy spells for some years. Falling to the ground as he got out of a train at Waterloo was an altogether more disagreeable experience. He was advised that he must no longer travel to London, unless he was taken by car. To give up attendance at the Lords was a hardship but Tom found a new way to entertain himself: the written question, to be followed, when an answer came from the House, by supplementaries. He also added to his list of campaigns the preservation of Greenham Common as common land, after its vacation by the military.

Tom felt both proud and protective of his increasingly frail, remaining brother. Reg's death, at the age of 95, on 23 May 1990, was a blow. It left him 'desolate', he wrote for *The Daily Telegraph*, two days later. 'If I were to name his qualities, I would put above all his courage. His courage when severely wounded; his courage against all odds.' Tom was not well enough to go up to London for the memorial service, on 26 July, where there was a reading from that favourite of the Dennings, *The Pilgrim's Progress*.

That summer he was interviewed by A. N. Wilson for an article in the *Spectator*. With his agreement the conversation was taped in the library and over lunch. Tom was within his own doors and expansively at ease. The talk ranged widely, with Tom speaking unguardedly, as now he usually did. There was discussion of the cases of the Birmingham Six and Guildford Four, Irish people convicted of terrorist activity who had continued, through long years of imprisonment, to protest their innocence. (The Guildford Four had been recently released after fresh evidence proved there had been a miscarriage of justice.)

After Wilson left, Tom wondered if he had been wise to comment on those cases. He wrote to Wilson, asking to see 'beforehand anything you propose to publish ... especially as some of what I said was not for publication, just chatting to you.' In reply, Wilson assured Tom that there was no need to fear he would be quoted out of context. Having been told that Tom's concern centred on the Irish cases, Wilson wrote that, though it was not usual for the *Spectator* to provide a transcript of interviews, he was sending the relevant three pages. After reading the three pages, Tom confirmed that they could be published. He had not been sent a fourth page, where, later in the interview, he spoke again of the Irish cases, in a discussion on hanging. The words on that page were further to injure Denning's reputation.

When the *Spectator* for the week ending 18 August 1990 was published, its front cover gave an indication of the line it would take. Against a painted flower border, with a church spire in the background, was a representation of Denning, smiling benevolently and walking with the aid of a stick in the form of a gallows. Beneath it was the title: 'Hanging on'.

The article began well, with Wilson's tribute to 'the old Denning magic', still very much alive. As Tom read on, his worst fears were realised. After Tom's reported comment that the death penalty should have been retained for 'murder most foul', Wilson asked whether, if the Guildford Four had been hanged, the wrong men would not have been killed, and Tom replied: 'No. They'd probably have hanged the right men. Not proved against them, that's all.'

Further on, in a discussion about Europe, Tom persisted that the United Kingdom's European Commissioner, Leon Brittan, was 'a German Jew telling us what to do with our English Law.' Quite apart from the fact that the description was not accurate – Brittan was a Jew born in England of Lithuanian parents – it was offensive and caused dismay.

Tom's comments on the Guildford Four were made at a time when the issue of miscarriage of justice, in connection with the Irish cases was highly controversial. There was an outcry in the press. The real shock of Denning's remarks, for Andrew Brown in the *Independent*, was their coming 'from a man whose whole reputation stemmed from favouring justice over the law and the individual over the state.' *The Times* thought it a mistake to take a very old man seriously. They thanked his lordship for letting them glimpse his opinions – 'The rest of the country can now discuss judicial prejudice with a freer hand.'

Tom felt angry and betrayed. He was indignant at the publication of remarks he considered off the record. He must have been humiliated to have his prejudices thus exposed. The only good to come from the whole affair, he thought, was Robert's coming home for two days to help him. In a sense, it was a replay of the events leading to Tom's resignation and he understood that he would have to apologise to the Guildford Four, who were threatening legal action.

Tom was the product of his age and upbringing. His likes and dislikes, prejudices and predilections were founded in his childhood. Alongside deep patriotism was an antipathy to foreigners; hand-in-hand with his profound attachment to the Established Church went a suspicion of different forms of religion. When it came to meeting people, Tom was not anti-black, anti-Irish, anti-Catholic or anti-Jew: he took everyone on their personal merits and demerits. In the abstract, when he thought about groups, he remained wedded to the stereotypes accepted – and acceptable – amongst all classes, when he was a boy. Whatever may have been his prejudices, he was unstinting in the help he gave to any group that asked it.

For Tom a 'true-born Englishman' was a person born and raised in England – 'and his family, for generations.' In principle he conceded that a second generation immigrant could be English, but his heart was not in it. It was harder, too, for a non-Anglican to belong. Readily and happily he accepted the alternative label 'British'. None

413

of which is to say that Tom did not treat individual outsiders with the greatest courtesy and consideration, if he regarded them, in other ways, as worthy. Strangely for a man who was usually thoughtful and kind in personal relations, he simply did not realise how offensive some of his remarks could be.

Tom's observations might not have landed him in trouble, had they been worded with sensitivity; but by the time Tom reached his eighties, he was no longer subject to restraint and self-examination. Years of adulation had reinforced his belief in his own judgment and given him a sense of invulnerability. Constant repetition of themes lessened the care that he gave to expressing them. Though he could, at times, be persuaded that he was wrong, he became stubbornly attached to his own ideas and there were few who could gainsay him. Devoted to Reg, as he was, Tom did not usually take his advice on matters outside the family. In any case, Reg seems to have regarded his younger brother as virtually infallible. Joan must have realised that Tom was losing his humility and sense of what was fitting. She had urged him to resign, though he did not take her advice, and after his retirement would have liked him to take a less public profile.

At the time of his retirement, the fund of goodwill towards Tom saved him from the consequences of his folly. The same still held true in 1990. The Guildford Four were content with an apology and admirers made allowances for him, on account of his age. Tom took his mind off the humiliation by fighting. Against all advice, he determined to win from Wilson and the *Spectator* an apology for the breach of his copyright in the words on the tape. It was a small victory for him when the Christmas issue published a letter from Wilson, apologising for his oversight in omitting the damaging fourth page and regretting the distress suffered by Lord and Lady Denning.

At this stage Tom might have retired into the obscurity of old age but to do so would have gone totally against the grain of his character. Independence was very important to both the Dennings: as much as they could, they liked to do things for themselves. Increasingly, they suffered the effects of being very old; each worried when the other was unwell; more than ever they depended upon help from others. Still, with great gallantry, each contrived to carry out a self-appointed role: Tom's to remain of use to the community; Joan's to look after Tom.

Their families rallied about them. Local people helped in various ways. Peter Post came regularly to deal with Tom's business affairs. A young part-time secretary sat in the annexe to Tom's library, typing and filing his correspondence with the House of Lords, councils, groups in dispute over footpaths, byways, common land and schools. There was still a large post from admirers from many parts of the globe. At his desk, the centre of all activity, sat Tom, with telephone and hearing aid. Ten years after his retirement, editors still regarded him as a valuable source of material. Answering the telephone himself, Tom was willing to give an instant view on many news items and on all the subjects that he had made peculiarly his own.

Over the years he seemed to have persuaded himself that he retired only because his hearing was going. He missed the company that he had always enjoyed. Though he tired easily, visitors gave him great pleasure, and despite her own fatigue Joan welcomed them with her old hospitality. The visits of their grandchildren were a particular source of delight. Tom was proud that Mark showed the cricketing skill of the Harveys.

From all around the world, on 23 January 1992, Tom's 93rd birthday, there were good wishes. Tom and Joan themselves no longer hoped for 'many happy returns': the struggle to maintain a dignified independence had become difficult and neither ever felt truly well. During the year, Tom fell more often and Joan suffered a severe heart attack. The Denning legend remained powerful. In September 1992, a television quiz on etiquette, *Ps and Qs*, asked a player to respond correctly to a caller who identified himself as the Master of the Rolls. The reply came immediately: 'Hello, Lord Denning.' To such an extent had Denning's name become associated with the office.

Though dimmed, Tom's charm was very much in evidence. Stubborn, opinionated, obstinate and selfish, he was also warm, considerate, generous of heart, courageous. While life continued he would keep some of his youthful eagerness to see tomorrow.

On 19 October Joan suffered another massive heart attack and was taken to hospital in Winchester. It was some comfort to Tom that he and all the family – Pauline, Hazel, John and Robert – were with her when she died on Friday 23 October. The communion service was held in her room and Joan, herself, had said 'Amen'.

At first, Tom was devastated. The mainstay of his life was gone and he hoped that he would not be long in joining her. After the funeral, his remarkable resilience gave him the courage to go on, for as long as he must, keeping as far as possible to his old routine. He determined to reply in his own hand to the hundreds of letters of condolence. After much thought, he wrote out and had photocopied a letter which could be sent – with added 'top and tail' – to everyone who had written to him:

All Saints' Day
1992

Dear

Thank you for your letter of sympathy.

The funeral service for Joan was lovely. It was all arranged by her children, both the words and the music. The sun shone all the day long on the autumn leaves. The church bells rang. The organ played. The choir sang. In thanksgiving for her life and work.

Her daughter Pauline calls to mind the words of Henry Vaughan about 1660 AD:

They are all gone into the world of light
And I alone sit lingering here
Their very memory is fair and bright
And my sad thoughts doth clear

But if I can carry on, I must do so for a while, as she would have me do, until I have finished my work as she has finished hers.

Yours in gratitude,

A few days later, on Remembrance Sunday, Lord Denning read out in church the names of all those Whitchurch men who had given their lives in the First World War. He paused a moment after each name, remembering each familiar youthful face, particularly those of his brothers Jack and Gordon. Beneath the memorial in the church lay Tom's wreath of poppies, with a card bearing his quotation from the letter written by Jack on the night before his death on the Somme, in September 1916: 'You may rest assured that should I get pipped I shall have done my duty.' Like his brothers, Tom Denning always did his duty. Sadly, but with faith undiminished, he advanced towards his 94th birthday. Not yet out.

References

Quotations are from Lord Denning's taped conversations with the author, unless otherwise indicated.

To keep references to a minimum, quotations from the same source, wherever they may appear in the book, are given the same number. Unless otherwise indicated, letters and papers are in the Denning Archive at the Hampshire Record Office, Winchester (202 M86).

There is a separate table of cases.

1 *The Family Story* by Lord Denning. 1981. Butterworths.
2 Mr R. F. Weeks's memoir. Whitchurch Historical Society.
3 Lt.-General Sir Reginald Denning in interview with author.
4 *Andover Grammar School 1569 to 1951* by Stella M. Longstaff M.A.
5 Jack Denning's letters.
6 Tom Denning's letters.
7 *The Amazing Discovery of Magdalen College 1915–1919* by R. W. Windram. Magdalen College Archives.
8 *Oxford 1914* by J. Brett Longstaff. Magdalen College Archives.
9 Battels Ledger. Magdalen College Archives (AO/57/1).
10 Departmental Records of the Ministry of Defence.
11 Gordon Denning's letters.
12 *Hampshire Chronicle* 23.11.18.
13 Letter in Magdalen College Archives.
14 Letter to author.
15 Letter from Mr Alan Bray to author.
16 Mary Denning's letters.
17 Clara Denning's letters.
18 Student Admission File B1 D in Lincoln's Inn Library.
19 Students Admissions Committee Minutes 1921–9. Page 29. Lincoln's Inn Library (A2 a 11/3).

20 Letter from J. Darlington dated 5.12.80.
21 His Honour B. Gillis QC in interview with author.
22 Sir Frederick Lawton in interview with author.
23 *The Due Process of Law* by Lord Denning. 1980. Butterworths.
24 *The Discipline of Law* by Lord Denning. 1979. Butterworths.
25 *The Dictionary of National Biography*.
26 Mary Denning's diaries.
27 Letters of congratulations on engagement of Tom and Mary.
28 Records in Middle Temple Library.
29 Family and legal papers.
30 Letters of congratulation on taking silk.
31 *Freedom Under the Law* by Lord Denning. 1949. Stevens.
32 Dr Robert Denning in interview with author.
33 Sir Thomas Skyrme in interview with author.
34 Letter from Miss C. Ellis QC to author.
35 Letters of congratulation on becoming a judge.
36 Lord Simon of Glaisdale in interview with author.
37 *Hampshire Chronicle* 12.1.45.
38 Lady Denning in interview with author.
39 Mrs Pauline Simond in interview with author.
40 Mr John Stuart in interview with author.
41 Joan Stuart's letters to Tom Denning.
42 Letters of congratulation on going to King's Bench.
43 Sir Max Williams in interview with author.
44 Speeches.
45 *Ultramares Corporation* v. *Touche* (1931) 174 N.E. 441.
46 Miss Mavis Hill in interview with author.
47 Lord Cheshire in interview with author.
48 Mrs Margot Gibb in interview with author.
49 *Lord Denning: The Judge and the Law* ed. by Jowell & McAuslan. 1984. Sweet & Maxwell.
50 *The Road to Justice* by Lord Denning. 1955. Stevens.
51 Letter from Principal of Witwatersrand University, dated 12.11.54.
52 *Landmarks in the Law* by Lord Denning. 1984. Butterworths.
53 Lady Fox in interview with author.
54 Robert Denning's letters.
55 *Lord Denning's Report* 1963 HMSO.

56 Mr E. W. Denham in interview with author.
57 *Controversial Essays* by John Sparrow. 1966.
58 Report of the Committee on Legal Records. 1966. HMSO.
59 *The Closing Chapter* by Lord Denning. 1983. Butterworths.
60 Sir T. Legg in interview with author.
61 Lord Roskill in interview with author.
62 Note from Mrs Betty Beach to author.
63 Sir Denys Buckley in interview with author.
64 Lord Donaldson in interview with author.
65 Mr Peter Post in interview with author.
66 *What Next in the Law* by Lord Denning. 1982. Butterworths.
67 Lord Woolf in interview with author.
68 Letter from Mr R. W. Hodgin to author.
69 Note from Mr Leonard Caplan QC to author.
70 Letters from members of the public on legal problems and Lord Denning's replies.
71 *Guardian Gazette* 27.7.77.

Pre-decimal Coinage

Decimal currency came into use in 1971. Before that time prices were given in £–s–d (Pounds, shillings and pence). There were twenty shillings in a pound; twelve pence in a shilling. In 1971 15 shillings was equivalent to 75p; 2d was less than 1p.

These equivalents do not give a true picture of, say, 6s 8d at any particular time prior to 1971. Its value was what it would buy *at that time*. For that reason the book does not give equivalents where £–s–d are mentioned. The Easter bonnet sold by Charles Denning for 6½d in the early years of the century might now cost £16 and though Lord Denning lived comfortably on £3000 a year in 1938, a man would need many times that amount to live in the same style today.

Table of Cases

Whitchurch,
Hants.

Dear Jack,
                                    Sunday Evening
        As Father did not write to Reg last week he is
writing this week, & he has told me to write to you.
You see I am obeying the command. Well, I hope you
are well & prosperous.

        Norman has got a new flannel suit
with long trousers, 10 pockets, button hole,
a plus hole for (his) watch chain to pass
through. They are the same colour as my
old ones. He wore them to-day for the 1st time & after
I had told him about pulling the trousers up when
he sat down, in church he forgot to do so when he
was kneeling but when he was sitting down, he
get kept gradually pulling them up till the "permanent
turn-ups" reached his knee. He also has a straw hat.

        A week ago yesterday This (now) young gentleman fell
into the river at Roe's; it appears he was endeavouring to
get a ball out of the river with Madge bending over him
(real soft) when Madge slipped & put her hand on Norman
and — great was the fall & splash thereof. He did not get
the ball whilst he was in there. He looked like a
scarecrow after a thunderstorm.

        I have tried, but poorly, to show the
difference in his appearance on the two
instances of his daily life. They look like

In the summer of 1914, Tom wrote to his eldest brother, Jack.

Dear Reg

I have only done the above to amuse you. There is
so little to write about. It is a fresh fad of mine,
not fad but only a fancy, an idea to interest you.
The first you have seen similar ones before. It is like
the competitions in weeklies but it is my own work.
The second is in cipher. Here is the key.
It would be interesting for us to correspond in it when
we haven't much to say, as it is interesting

a	bc	def	g	hi
j	kℓ	mno	p	qr
s	tu	vwx	y	z

and dots put for letters such
as for h   o   in the
right places.
That photo of Polly did not come out.
I am enclosing the 3 you took at Roc's. Emily said it was
not what she wanted as dogs were not big enough but
I think she couldn't see them owing to bad eyesight.
She ran into a wall the other day.

Tom started a letter to his brother Reg in two kinds of cryptic writing
1915.

Index

Names have been given in the form often used in the book and any relationship to Lord Denning indicated in brackets. The letter 'D' indicates Lord Denning.

There is a separate table of cases.

sells The Lawn 264
Banner, Delmar 49, 337
Bar, D at
addressing the court 93–4
Assize work 89–90
briefless period 89
call to 84
chambers, takes own 109–10
childish interest in 36
confidence grows 101
Court of Appeal, in 94–5, 118, 133–4, 140
decision to join 70
devilling 85, 89, 106
divorce, never handled 150
difficulties in starting 78–9
early cases 89–91
foot wrong, never put 308
good manners 139
High Court, first appearance in 94
homicide case 141–2
House of Lords, in 102, 112, 115, 122, 134
middle period 100–101
practice
grows 106, 108–9, 115
off the ground 89–93
pupils, takes 111–12
red bag, given, 106–7
reputation of 121, 140
silk taken 120–21
wartime work 130–31, 133–4, 138, 139–43
see also Chancery, D's work in; fees
Bar
call-night 84
education for 78–84
Final Examination 78, 83–4
independence of 319
women at 84, 89
Bar Council 131, 392, 395
Bar Theatrical Society 230, 382
Barnard, Harry 147, 149
Battels see Magdalen, expenses
Beach, Betty (née Haynes) (niece) 54, 83, 108
Beatty, Admiral 40
Beaufort Street 79, 82, 109, 118, 149, 241
see also Mrs Cross
Beaumont, Sir John 241, 244
Beerbohm, Max 66
Zuleika Dobson 66
Belcher, Doris 139
Bell, Hilary 68
Bellew, Sir George see Garter King of Arms
Benchers, right of admittance of 75
Benjamin, J. P. 406
Bentham Club 227
best man 97, 112
Bevan, Elsie (cousin) 24, 33

Bevan, Nell (née Thompson) (aunt) 24, 32, 33
Bevan, Ted (uncle) 24
Beyfus, Gilbert 122
Bible, reading from embarrasses D 52–3
bigamy 131
Bill of Rights 246
Binyon, Lawrence 30
Birkbeck College 226, 376, 383
Birmingham Law Society 323
Birmingham Six 412
Birmingham University see Holdsworth Club
Birnberg & Co. 394–5
Bishop, R. O. (headmaster) 21–3, 24, 27, 39, 84, 149
influences D 23, 32, 36
Bishop, Mr W. 91
Bishop, W. T. 264
Blackburn, Raymond 324–5
Black Lawyers, Society of 392, 393, 395
Blackley, Canon William Lewery (Mary D's grandfather) 65
Blackley, Dr (Mary D's cousin) 104
blasphemy, Gay News case 409
Blériot, Louis 19
Book Choice see Channel 4
Booth, General 19
Borstal escapees, liability for damage of see negligence, Home Office of
Botley, D buys pony at 36–7
Bowen, Lord Justice 398
Bowra, Sir Maurice 47
Boyd Orr, Lord 258
Bracton Memorial celebrations 323
Bray, Alan 335, 398
breach of contract see contract
Bressler, Fenton 396
Brick Court 79, 82
chambers in 109–11, 114
flat in 112, 114, 117, 118
work at 85
Bridge of Harwich, Lord 210–11
Bridges, Edward 63, 230
Brightman, Mr Justice 341
Britannia (royal yacht) 376
British Broadcasting Company 131, 164, 282, 382, 383, 393, 399
see also broadcasts
British Council 257, 315
British Guild of Newspaper Editors 288
British Institute of International and Comparative Law 181, 257
British Legion 170–71, 172, 327
British Movietone News 221–3
British Museum Society 327
British Railways 358–9

INDEX